The Complete
Bogo-Indian Defense

Maxim Chetverik

The Complete Bogo-Indian Defense

Author: Maxim Chetverik

Translated from the Russian by Ilan Rubin

Typesetting by Andrei Elkov (www.elkov.ru)

Follow us on Twitter: @ilan_ruby

www.elkandruby.com

ISBN 978-5-6041769-7-9

About the author

Maxim Chetverik, born in Voronezh in 1963, is one of Russia's biggest chess opening experts. He has written books published in Russian, English, French and German on the Queen's Indian Defense, Catalan Opening, English Opening, Benoni System, Queen's Gambit Accepted, Sicilian Defense, Petroff Defense, Dutch Defense, Alekhine Defense and Albin Counter Gambit, as well as more general opening books, a book on middle-game strategy, and books on the games of Alekhine, Tal and Spassky.

He became an International Master in 2003 and is a regular tournament player to this day, as well as being a coach in his native Voronezh. His best tournament results include Budapest Open, 1st place, 1996, Open championship of Slovan Club, Bratislava, 1st place, 1998, Prague Open, 2nd equal, 2002, Kecskemet (Hungary) round robin tournament, 1st place, 2003, Stuttgart Open, 2nd place, 2009, Yaroslavl Open, 3rd place, 2015, Olomouc (Czech Republic), 2nd place, 2017, and Heraklion (Greece), 2nd place, 2019.

CONTENTS

HISTORICAL INTRODUCTION

The Bogo-Indian Defense is a relatively young opening. The first game to be found in the database is that of Mackenzie – Noa (London 1883). By an odd coincidence, Hungarian player Josef Noa also defended the honor of the black pieces in the earliest-known Queen's Indian Defense (Blackburne – Noa, Frankfurt 1887). Unfortunately, the chess content of both games was somewhat lackluster and so we are better off taking a time machine to the 20th century.

The 10th game of the Rubinstein – Bogoljubov match (Gothenburg 1920) began with the following opening moves: 1.d4 ♘f6 2.c4 e6 3.♘f3 ♝b4+ 4.♝d2 ♝xd2+ 5.♕xd2 b6 6.♘c3 ♝b7 7.g3 0-0 8.♝g2 d6 9.0-0 ♘bd7 10.♕c2 ♜e8. This was a hybrid set-up that I review in chapter 12 of my book *The Queen's Indian Defense: Main Line 4.g3 System* (published in 2018 by Elk and Ruby Publishing House) in the move order 1.d4 ♘f6 2.c4 e6 3.♘f3 b6 4.g3 ♝b7 5.♝g2 ♝b4+ 6.♝d2 ♝xd2+ 7.♕xd2. A fragment from this Rubinstein versus Bogoljubov game is included in game 2 of that same book. However, count of games in the Bogo-Indian proper in the last century should really start from the later (tournament) game Bogoljubov – Seleznev (Gothenburg 1920). It began 1.d4 ♘f6 2.♘f3 e6 3.c4 ♝b4+ 4.♝d2 ♝xd2+ 5.♘bxd2 c5 6.dxc5 ♕a5 7.g3 ♕xc5 8.♝g2 ♘c6 9.a3 ♕e7 10.0-0 0-0 11.e4 d6 12.♜e1 ♝d7 13.b4 ♜fd8 14.♕b3 ♝e8, where black's sole weakness was d6 and he had a solid position. White eventually won a long-drawn game. These Russian emigre masters Efim Bogoljubov and Alexei Seleznev were friends and most probably discussed their game after it ended.

We begin our analysis of historical games with a well-known battle won in brilliant style by the future world champion.

No. 1 A. Alekhine – E. Bogoljubov
Budapest 1921

1.d4 ♘f6 2.c4 e6 3.♘f3 ♗b4+ 4.♗d2

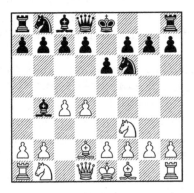

4...♗xd2+ 5.♕xd2 0-0

Bogoljubov is no longer thinking here of playing a Queen's Indian Defense – after 5...b6 apart from 6.g3 black has to contend with 6.♘c3 (game 53) with the idea of the advances e2-e4 and d4-d5.

6.♘c3 d5 7.e3

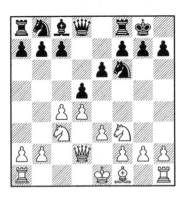

The pawn structure is mostly settled, and is the same as that seen in the orthodox Queen's Gambit. The exchange of the dark-squared bishops should in theory favor white, though one should not forget the advantageous role played by simplifications in cramped positions.

7...♘bd7

The setup 7...♕e7 and ♖f8-d8 is considered in chapter 8 (games 56 and 57).

8.♗d3

The exchange 8.cxd5 exd5 is structurally close to game 56.

8...c6 9.0-0

Alekhine believed that this standard castling enabled black to gain equal play by opening the center and hence recommended the prophylactic 9.♖d1 (which has not been tested). The continuation 9.0-0-0 ♕e7 10.e4 dxe4 11.♘xe4 c5 12.♖he1 cxd4 13.♘xd4 ♘xe4 14.♗xe4 ♘f6 15.♗c2 was met in the game A. Grigoryan – Tomov (Bansko 2010). Now 15...♕c5!? supports the completion of development after 16...b6 or an attack against the white king with a7-a6 and b7-b5.

9...dxc4 10.♗xc4

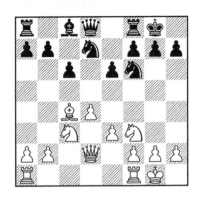

10...e5!

This break is possible due to the interim exchange with check – 11.dxe5 ♘xe5! 12.♕xd8 ♘xf3+ 13.gxf3 ♖xd8.

11.♗b3

The bishop evades the attack ♘d7-b6 and protects against e5-e4 (as black loses the pawn after ♘f3-g5 and ♗b3-c2). The sacrifice 11.♗xf7+!? is only enough to draw (as correctly pointed out by Alekhine): 11...♖xf7 (11...♚xf7 12.dxe5 ♘g4 13.♖ad1 ♕e7 14.e6+! ♚xe6 15.♕d4 ♘ge5 16.♘xe5 ♘xe5 17.f4 places the black king in danger) 12.dxe5 ♘g4 13.e6 ♖xf3! 14.exd7 ♗xd7 15.gxf3 ♘xh2! 16.♚xh2 ♕h4+.

11...♕e7?!

Thus far, Alekhine's annotations to the game are comprehensive and objective. He compares the potential of the opposing pawn groups and major pieces on the open file. Each side's potential proved to be equal in the later game Johner – Gruenfeld (Piestany 1922): 11...exd4 12.♕xd4 ♕b6 13.♕f4 ♘c5 14.♘a4 ♘xa4 15.♕xa4 ♗f5.

12.e4 exd4 13.♘xd4 ♘c5 14.♗c2 ♖d8 15.♖ad1 ♗g4 16.f3 ♘e6 17.♕f2 ♘xd4 18.♖xd4 ♗e6 19.♖fd1 b6 20.h3

"The game is practically over" (Alekhine). A premature verdict, as black is ready both to fight for the open file and cope with the enemy pawn storm. The position after 20... ♘h5 21.e5 c5 22.♖xd8+ ♖xd8 23.f4 g6 is defensible.

20...c5?! 21.♖4d2 ♖xd2 22.♕xd2 c4?

Here the pawn is vulnerable, whereas the white queen gains an excellent square in the center from where it can support the pawn bind. Alekhine suggested the best defensive approach – 22...♘e8 and f7-f6 with chances of saving the game.

23.f4 g6 24.♕d4 ♖c8 25.g4 ♗xg4 26.hxg4 ♘xg4 27.♚g2 h5 28.♘d5 ♕h4 29.♖h1 ♕d8 30.♗d1

Black resigned.

Bogoljubov began to actively promote the opening named after him, and with both colors. In the game Bogoljubov – Walter (Ostrava 1923) white introduced the move 4.♘bd2. That game wasn't of interest, however, and I prefer a slightly later example from Bogoljubov's career.

No. 2 E. Bogoljubov – W. Winter
London 1927

1.d4 ♘f6 2.♘f3 e6 3.c4 ♗b4+ 4.♘bd2

4...b6

In QID type positions the knight stands worse on d2 than on c3, hence this move will always be popular. Black is willing to grant his opponent the advantage of the bishop pair in return for comfortable development and control over e4.

5.a3

As with 4...b6 this is by far the most popular move.

5...♗xd2+ 6.♘xd2

A rare choice (captures by the queen and bishop are reviewed in chapter 6). Its rationale is clear – white decides his priority is to fight for control over e4.

6...♗b7

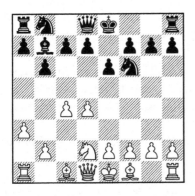

7.♕c2

Bogoljubov takes control of the e4 square, but doesn't occupy it with a pawn. Were he to opt immediately for an extended fianchetto black would be first to conduct operations in the center: 7.b4 0-0 8.♗b2 d6 9.e3 ♘bd7 10.f3 e5 11.dxe5 ♘xe5 12.♗e2?! (12.♕c2!?) 12...♘fg4! 13.fxg4 ♗xg2 14.♔f2 ♗xh1 15.♕xh1 (Gareev – Megaranto, Surakarta 2018) 15...♕h4+ 16.♔g1

♘xg4 17.♕g2 ♘e5, and the rook and pawn pair are stronger than the minor pieces.

7.f3 places a barrier in the bishop's path, at the cost of worsening white's structure. After 7...d5 8.e3 ♘bd7 9.♗e2 a5 10.b3 e5 11.dxe5 ♘xe5 12.♗b2 ♕e7 13.0-0 ♘g6 (Rindlisbacher – Erdos, Biel 2014) 14.♖f2!? it's risky for black to capture on e3, but on the whole he has nothing to worry about.

7...d6

The game Vuilleumier – Andersson (Geneva 2012) continued 7...c5 8.dxc5 bxc5 9.b4 0-0 10.♗b2 d6 11.bxc5 (the immediate 11.e3 is slightly more precise) 11...dxc5 12.e3 ♘bd7 13.♗d3 ♕c7 14.0-0 ♘e5 15.♗e2 ♘eg4 16.g3 ♖fd8. Soon the grandmaster playing black took advantage of the weakening of the long diagonal, although at this point chances were equal.

8.b4 0-0 9.♗b2 c5 10.e3 ♘bd7 11.dxc5 dxc5 12.♗d3

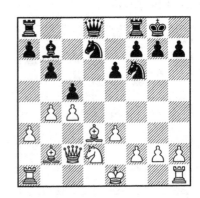

12...♕c7

Winter could have exploited the somewhat hanging position of the bishop on d3 by playing 12...cxb4

13.axb4 a5 14.bxa5 ♘c5 15.♗e2
bxa5. Black is no worse here.

**13.0-0 ♘e5 14.♘e4 ♘fg4
15.♘g3 f5!? 16.♖fe1 h5 17.♗e2 h4
18.♘f1 h3 19.gxh3**

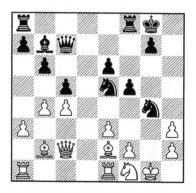

19...♕c6?

In a battle against his opponent's
energetic pawn bind white has
carefully set up his pieces and
convincingly parries the English
master's direct action. Black had to
try 19...♘f6 20.♗xe5 ♕xe5 21.f4
♕c7 22.♘d2 e5 with an unclear
position.

**20.e4! fxe4 21.b5 ♕d7 22.♗xg4
♘xg4 23.hxg4 ♖f3 24.♖e3 ♖af8
25.♖xf3 exf3 26.♖d1 ♕e7
27.♕g6**

Black resigned.

At the same time, players tried
to find alternatives to the lackluster
exchange of bishops after 4.♗d2.
In 1926 Aron Nimzowitsch first
introduced the defense 4...♕e7
into play. Its history began with an
unusual story. A game was played
at the Olympiad Palau – Kalabar
(London 1927) where the Yugoslav
player's "fingers slipped" and he

placed his king on e7, rather than his
queen!

So let's see how Alekhine
deployed Nimzowitsch's idea nine
months before he became world
champion.

No. 3 M. Vidmar – A. Alekhine
New York 1927

**1.d4 ♘f6 2.♘f3 e6 3.c4 ♗b4+
4.♗d2 ♕e7**

5.g3

"As is known, flank development
gives white perfectly solid play, but
accords him only a small initiative"
(Alekhine). Well, with today's state
of opening theory a small initiative is
rather good!

5...0-0 6.♗g2 ♗xd2+ 7.♘bxd2

"Here it made sense, given black's
intent to play d7-d6 followed by
e6-e5, to capture with the queen in
order to develop the knight on c3;
in that case: 1) white's possession
of the d5 square would have been
more effective, 2) the opening of the
d-file via d4xe5 would have been
much more favorable for white.
Obviously, black in that case would

not play e6-e5, but instead c7-c5, after the necessary preparations" (Alekhine). The author was right in his assessment of the capture by the queen, but the plan with c7-c5 that he recommended has not found any adherent.

7...d6 8.0-0 e5

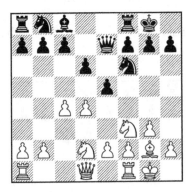

9.♕c2

Vidmar takes control of the b1-h7 diagonal, and then strengthens the d4 square via e2-e3. 9.e3 c5 10.♘b3 ♘c6 11.h3 h6 12.♖e1 ♗f5 13.a3 e4 has also been played (a change of plan: from pressurizing d4 to capturing space) 14.♘fd2 ♖fe8 15.♘b1 ♖ad8 16.♘c3 b6 17.♔h2 d5! 18.cxd5 ♘xd5 (Mirzoev – R. Ibragimov, Sort 2008). The pawn advances in the center ensured black a tiny advantage.

In the game Gruenfeld – Euwe (London 1927) the future world champion played far from the best moves in the main line: 9.e4 ♗g4 10.d5 ♕d7?! 11.♕b3 b6 12.c5! followed by a bind with c5-c6. After the obvious 10...a5 black exchanges his bishop and finds convenient squares for his other pieces. There

are a lot of games in this line, but very few in which strong players have played white.

9...♘c6 10.e3 ♗d7

Alekhine plans to bring his queen's rook to e8, in order to support the e5-e4 push. Immediately this would be a bad idea due to 11.♘g5, so 10...h6 would have been another good way to prepare e5-e4.

11.a3 ♖ae8 12.d5 ♘d8 13.b4

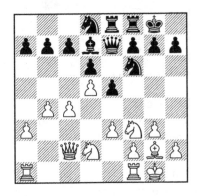

13...e4

After the d4 pawn freed up the square for the knight, this pawn push no longer looks a no-brainer. If 13...♘h5!? 14.c5 f5 15.cxd6 cxd6 it's hard for white to extract any advantage from the open files.

14.♘d4 c6

Black frees his knight from d8 and gains some chances to grab the initiative.

15.dxc6 ♘xc6 16.♖fe1 ♕e5 17.♘e2 ♗f5 18.♘c3

The knight's transfer to attack e4 prevents his enemy's threats on the kingside.

18...♖e7 19.h3 h5 20.♖ad1 ♖c8 21.♕b3 ♘d8

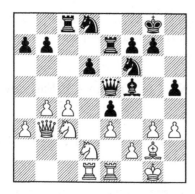

22.f4

Alekhine awarded white an exclam here. He believed that otherwise black would concentrate his forces against the c4 pawn. Interesting complications begin.

22...exf3 23.♘xf3 ♕xg3 24.♘e2 ♕g6 25.♘f4

White cannot win the pawn back because of 25.♖xd6? ♗xh3 26.♘f4 ♕g3 27.♖xd8+ ♖xd8 28.♘xh3 ♘g4.

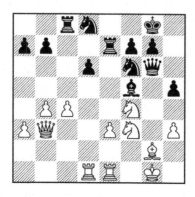

25...♕g3 26.♘e2

Now 26.♖xd6? doesn't work because of 26...♘e6! However, Vidmar nevertheless manages to re-establish a balance, as the only way for black to avoid a move repetition is by withdrawing his queen from the valuable g-file.

26...♕g6 27.♘f4 ♕h7 28.♖xd6 ♘e6 29.♘xe6 ♗xe6 30.♘g5 ♕f5 31.♘xe6 ♖xe6 32.♖d4 ♖ce8 33.♕d3

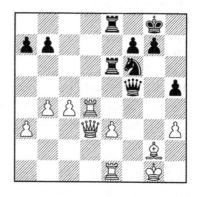

33...♘e4

After the double exchange of minor pieces black ends up with a small advantage. White has an extra pawn island, while a breeze is blowing on the kingside. Instead of the move played it was more promising to try 33...♕e5 34.e4 b6.

34.♖f1 ♕g6 35.♖d8 ♖xd8 36.♕xd8+ ♔h7 37.♕d5 ♘g3 38.♖f3 h4 39.♔h2! ♖d6

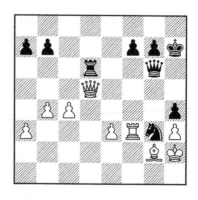

40.♕xf7

White is forced to transpose to the endgame. 40.♕xb7?? would be met by 40...♖d1 with the elegant and immediately decisive threat of 41...♖h1+!! 42.♗xh1 ♘f1+! 43.♖xf1 ♕g3 mate. Obviously, white isn't too upset at the exchange of queens, as he already enjoys a slight advantage.

40...♖d2 41.♕xg6+ ♔xg6 42.c5 ♖a2 43.e4

If 43.♖f4 Alekhine suggests 43...♔g5, while he considered the exchange of rooks with 43...♘f5 44.♔g1 ♖a1+ 45.♖f1 ♖xf1+ 46.♗xf1 ♘xe3 47.♗d3+ ♔f6 48.♔f2 ♘d5 49.♔f3 to be clearly in white's favor. He missed that after 49...♔e5 50.♔g4 ♔d4 51.♗e2 ♔c3 52.♔f5 (52.♔xh4 ♘e7) 52...♘xb4 53.axb4 ♔xb4 black is saved by the h8 square being the wrong color for white's bishop.

43...♘xe4 44.♖f4 ♘g5 45.a4 ♘e6 46.♖xh4 ♔f5 47.♖g4 g5 48.♔g3 ♘f4 49.♗xb7 ♖a3+ 50.♗f3 ♖a2

Draw agreed – a high-quality and interesting draw.

Later tries were almost entirely confined to the three variations already mentioned (4.♘d2, 4.♗d2 ♗xd2+, and 4...♕e7). The "travelling bishop" 3...♗b4+ 4.♗d2 ♗e7 has been seen rarely, especially among GMs. The famous pair Bondarevsky – Romanovsky (Leningrad 1939) switched to the orthodox defense after 5.♘c3 d5 6.♗g5 which is beyond the scope of this book.

Two important lines were disseminated later. The seventh world champion Vasily Smyslov played an important role in popularizing one of them.

No. 4 N. Krogius – V. Smyslov
Moscow 1967

1.d4 ♘f6 2.c4 e6 3.♘f3 ♗b4+ 4.♗d2 a5

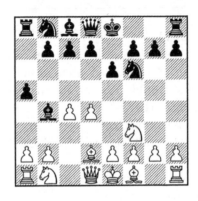

This doesn't simply defend the bishop but acts as an introduction to a plan of mobilization that had been invented earlier. It remains relevant today. Formally, 4...a5 can be called the Amsterdam Variation – Bob Wade played it in the Dutch capital back in 1961, and then David Bronstein tried it in the same city in 1964.

5.g3 d6 6.♗g2 ♘bd7 7.0-0 e5

Black has rapidly organized counterplay in the center, and he's waiting for the appropriate moment to castle. Most variations are covered in chapter 13, while here we consider the modest reply by the white central pawn.

8.e3

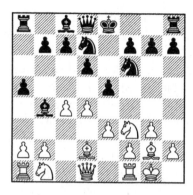

Yes, modest, but now there is no point in black exchanging pawns on d4.

8...♗xd2

LANDMINE. If 8...0-0?! 9.♗c1! and the black bishop faces an unpleasant future. In the rapid GM game Fridman – Jaracz (Warsaw 2010) black found himself a pawn down in a poor position after 9...e4?! 10.♘g5 d5 11.cxd5. He should have opted for the forcing line 9...exd4 10.exd4 d5 11.c5 b6 12.a3 ♗a6 13.axb4 ♗xf1 14.♔xf1 axb4 15.♖xa8 ♕xa8 16.cxb6 ♘xb6 – in return for the lost exchange black has picked up a pawn and hopes to hang on. As a whole, the Bogo-Indian Defense doesn't feature many landmines, but there is a minefield around the bishop on b4. Stepping on this landmine isn't fatal, but there are worse ones to come.

Note that after 8...c6 the continuation 9.♗c1 is unclear even though it gains material. In the amusing game Baryshpolets – Romanov (Voronezh 2012) the white queen liquidated both enemy rook pawns despite the menacing glares of black's rooks: 9...e4 10.♘g5 d5 11.c5 h6 12.♘h3 a4 13.a3 ♗a5 14.♕xa4 (the first feast) 14...♘f8 15.b4 (15.♘f4!?) 15...♗xh3 16.♗xh3 ♗c7 17.♕d1 h5 18.f4 exf3 19.♕xf3 h4 20.g4 ♘8h7 21.♕f5 g6 22.♕f2 ♕d7 23.♕xh4 (and the second). Black has compensation for the material – white's queenside is undeveloped and his king isn't safe. In recent years, after 8...c6 white has preferred to force the exchange of dark-squared bishops with 9.♕b3. After 9...♗xd2 10.♘fxd2 0-0 11.♘c3 I recommend Grandmaster Turov's setup – 11...♕c7, then ♖f8-d8 and ♘d7-f8 with a very solid position.

9.♕xd2 c6

Smyslov aims to create a long pawn chain. Black can settle the tense situation in the center by other means: 9...0-0 10.♘c3 ♖e8 11.♖ad1 ♕e7 12.e4 (a more precise choice would be 12.♕c2 h6 and either prevent e5-e4 with an exchange on e5 or make the brave sacrifice 13.c5!?) 12...♘b6 13.b3 ♗g4 14.h3 ♗xf3 15.♗xf3 exd4 16.♕xd4 (Ivanchuk – Bjerre, Caleta 2018) 16...a4! 17.b4 c5 18.bxc5 dxc5 19.♕d3 ♕e6 20.e5 ♘fd7 21.♗g4 ♕xe5 22.♘xa4 ♖xa4 23.♗xd7 ♘xd7 24.♕xd7 ♖xc4 25.♕xb7. In order to save his pawn white has prompted drawing simplifications.

10.♘c3 e4

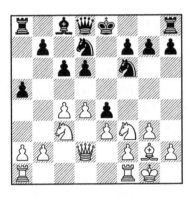

11.♘h4

White has not gained much from the opening, but what he has gained he needs to beef up. It was worth considering 11.♘g5 d5 12.cxd5 cxd5 13.♖fc1, counting on using the open file.

11...♘b6

The threat of 12...g5 forces Krogius into an exchange after which a Carlsbad structure appears. Black has no difficulties here.

12.♘xe4 ♘xe4 13.♗xe4 ♘xc4 14.♕e2 d5 15.♗d3 ♘d6 16.♕h5 ♕e7 17.♖fe1 ♗e6 18.♖ac1 g6

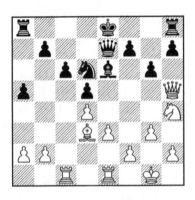

19.♕d1

The queen's expedition has concluded with an embarrassing return to base. If 19.♕h6 Smyslov

planned to continue 19...f5 20.♘xg6 ♘f7 21.♘xe7 ♘xh6 22.♘xc6 bxc6 23.♖xc6 ♔f7 with a knight for three pawns and an unclear position. If black desires, he can offer his opponent a draw via move repetition with 19...♕f8 20.♕f4 ♕e7 21.♕h6 ♕f8, and white would be advised to go along with that.

19...0-0 20.♕c2 ♖fc8 21.♘g2 ♗f5 22.♘f4 ♗xd3 23.♘xd3 ♖e8 24.♘f4 ♕f6 25.♖f1 ♖e7 26.♖ce1 ♖ae8 27.b3 ♘e4 28.f3 ♘d6 29.♘g2 ♘f5 30.♕d2 b6

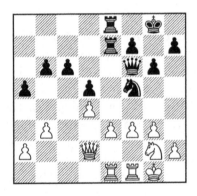

31.♕f2?!

White is not on top of this manoeuvering battle. First he made the committal pawn push f2-f3, and now he moves his queen to an awkward square. The correct continuation was 31.♕c2, targeting the pawn on c6.

31...♕g5 32.g4 ♘xe3! 33.h4 ♘xg2 34.hxg5 ♘xe1

This non-equivalent exchange has delivered black a clear advantage. The black rooks are dominant on the open files, while white's is cramped on f1. The white king is exposed, while his opponent is set to create a passer.

35.♕g3 ♖e3 36.♕f4 c5 37.♔h1 ♖e2 38.dxc5 bxc5 39.♕d6 d4 40.♕xc5 d3 41.♕d5 d2 42.♕d7 ♘xf3 43.♖xf3 d1♕+

White resigned.

The final "historical" event in the Bogo-Indian Defense happened at the end of the 1970s. In reply to 4.♗d2 the late Rigan International Master Alvis "Elvis" Vitolins introduced the move 4...c5, which until then hadn't occurred to anybody. Vitolins enjoyed mixed success with his c-pawn push, but twice used it to crush his fierce opponent from Odessa.

No. 5 V. Tukmakov – A. Vitolins
Frunze 1979

1.d4 ♘f6 2.c4 e6 3.♘f3 ♗b4+ 4.♗d2 c5 5.♗xb4 cxb4

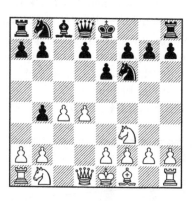

It's only at first glance that the capture away from the center appears to compromise black's position. The b4 pawn is easily defended, it cramps white and is most often exchanged for white's a-pawn. White gains a pawn advantage in an extended center, but his "extra" c-pawn is far from ideally-placed and frequently turns into a target of attack.

6.♘bd2 0-0 7.g3

After the exchange of dark-squared bishops, the move 7.e4 looks positionally unjustified. For example, 7...d6 8.♗e2 b6 9.0-0 ♗b7 10.♕c2 (e4-e5 is a step towards death) 10...♕c7 11.♖fe1 e5 12.♗d3 a5 13.a3 ♘a6 14.♘f1 ♖fe8 15.♘g3 g6 with a comfortable game for black (Cofman – Fridman, Neustadt 2018). The setup ♕d1-d3, ♘b1-d2 and e2-e4 (from game 60) is somewhat more promising, as the queen doesn't get in the way of coordinating the rooks.

7...b6 8.♗g2 ♗b7 9.0-0 d6

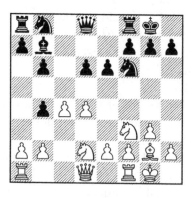

One of the many setups in which black makes quite standard moves, while white waits for the right time to play the key idea a2-a3.

10.♖c1

11.♖e1 to prepare e2-e4 was preferable.

10...♘bd7 11.♕b3 a5 12.a3 bxa3 13.♕xa3

The rook can no longer capture on a3, and Tukmakov opts for the non-standard capture by the queen. If 13.bxa3, black starts to aim at c4. Obviously, continuing a3-a4 fixes the pawn on b6, but black's pawn would remain deeper in its own territory, where it feels safer.

13...♕c7 14.♖fd1

14...e5

Black should probably have waited to play this standard break until rooks were exchanged on the central files.

15.♘b1

The knight just got in the way on d2, so it's useful to send it home.

15...♘e4

After 15...♖ad8 16.♘c3 ♕xc4 17.♕xd6 exd4 18.♖xd4 there is no sensible queen retreat that would promise black a comfortable position.

16.dxe5?! After 16.♘h4! the computer doesn't see any way for black to avoid the loss of the pawn on d6 or to gain compensation for losing it. Tukmakov overestimated the power of his queen's invasion of the enemy camp.

16...dxe5 17.♕e7 ♗c6 18.♘c3 ♖ae8

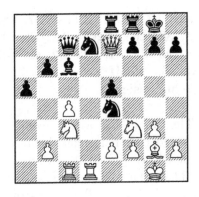

19.♘d5!?

This non-standard exchange operation creates a passed d-pawn. Vitolins immediately blocks the passer and gradually outplays his more illustrious opponent.

19...♗xd5 20.cxd5 ♕xc1 21.♕xf8+ ♔xf8 22.♖xc1 ♘dc5 23.♘e1 ♘d6 24.♗h3 e4 25.♘g2 ♖e5 26.♘e3 f5 27.♔f1 g5 28.♔e1 a4 29.♗g2 g4 30.♔d1 ♔e7 31.♔c2 ♔d7 32.♔b1

Tukmakov evacuates his king to the queenside, thereby somewhat reducing the value of his opponent's queenside pawn majority. However, he fails thus far to reanimate the unfortunate bishop.

32...h5 33.h4 ♖e8 34.♗f1 ♖a8

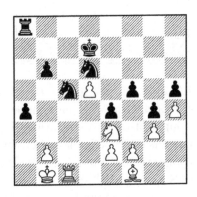

35.Nc2?!

He should have defused the threat of a4-a3 with the logical 35.Ka2. After 35...Rf8 36.Ng2 e3!? 37.Nxe3 f4 38.gxf4 Rxf4 39.Nd1 white successfully resists and has even grabbed a pawn along the way.

35...Nc4 36.Rd1?

He would have preserved modest chances of saving the day with 36.Ka2 e3 37.f3 Nb3 38.Re1.

36...e3! 37.fxe3

The clumsy position of the rook is highlighted by the continuation 37.f3 Nd2+ 38.Ka2 gxf3 39.exf3 Nxf1 40.Rxf1 e2 41.Re1 Nd3, and the passer is untouchable.

37...Re8 38.Bg2 Nxe3 39.Nxe3 Rxe3 40.d6 Ne4 41.Bxe4 fxe4

42.Rd5 Rxe2 43.Rxh5 Kxd6 44.Rg5 e3 45.Rxg4 Kd5 46.Kc1 Rh2 47.Kd1 b5 48.Rb4 Kc5 49.Re4 Rxb2 50.Rxe3 b4 51.Kc1 a3 52.h5 Rh2

White resigned.

Thanks to Vitolins's invention the Bogo-Indian Defense became a fully functioning opening. While some lines have died out, others have flourished due to new ideas. You can follow the chronology of novelties in the notes to the games in the three main parts of this book. Its theory continues to evolve today, as this solid opening remains part of the repertoire of top-level players.

Part I

System with 3.g3 ♗b4+

Introduction

1.d4 ♘f6 2.c4 e6 3.g3 ♗b4+

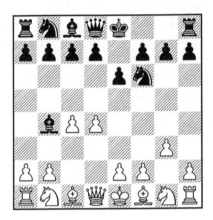

Although this check is encountered less often than 3...d5, it is quite common. If black prepared it in response to 3.♘f3, then the fianchetto won't change his mind. Most often, this opening merges into standard Bogo-Indian Defense lines, but there are also original variations that we consider here.

Interestingly, the theory of 3.♘f3 ♗b4+ first appeared in the 1920s in the West, whereas 3.g3 ♗b4+ was first tried in Soviet tournaments, and only in the late 1930s. As a rule, the Soviet masters still pushed their knights to f3 and transposed to 3.♘f3 ♗b4+ lines.

Chapter 1

4.♘d2 variation

1.d4 ♘f6 2.c4 e6 3.g3 ♗b4+ 4.♘d2

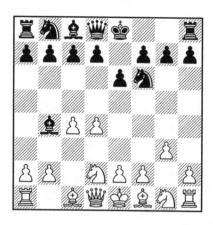

Whereas after 3.♘f3 ♗b4+ the block ♘b1-d2 is only seen half as frequently as ♗c1-d2, here the difference is six-fold. The reason is that if white hasn't played ♘g1-f3 then he usually intends e2-e4 and ♘g1-e2, but placing both knights on the modest second rank is too unambitious. Therefore, in games 6-8 we review other ideas for white.

No. 6 V. Mikhalevski – R. Janssen
Antwerp 1998

1.d4 ♘f6 2.c4 e6 3.g3 ♗b4+ 4.♘d2

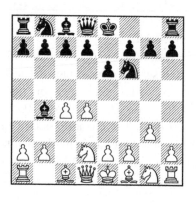

4...c5

If 4...♘e4?! the reply 5.♗g2 forces the knight to commit before black is ready. The game Kozul – Drazic (Nova Gorica 2019) continued 5...♗xd2+ 6.♗xd2 ♘xd2 7.♕xd2 0-0 8.e3 d6 9.♘e2 ♘d7 10.0-0 a5 11.♖ac1 c6 12.♖fd1 ♕e7 13.b3 ♖e8 14.♘c3 ♘f6 15.♘a4 e5?! (after the weakening of the b6 square it's not advisable to open the file) 16.dxe5 dxe5 17.♘b6 ♖a6 18.c5 ♗g4 19.f3 ♗e6 20.e4 ♕c7 21.♗f1 ♖a7 22.♗c4, and the exchange of bishops destroyed black's defenses.

If black wants to play along Catalan lines, then white's king's knight occasionally develops on h3. An example is V. Mikhalevski – Pelletier (Biel 2010): 4...d5 5.♗g2 0-0 6.♕c2 b6 7.♘h3 ♗a6 8.b3 ♘bd7 9.0-0 c5!? 10.dxc5 ♗xc5 11.♗b2 ♖c8 12.♕d1 dxc4 (12...♕e7!?) 13.♘xc4 ♕e7 14.a4 ♗b4 15.♕c2 ♖c7 16.♖fc1 ♖fc8 17.♘f4 ♘c5. Black's pieces stand on excellent squares and white needs to think about how to equalize.

5.a3

White immediately establishes the advantage of the bishop pair. In games 7 and 8 we review 5.dxc5.

5...♗xd2+ 6.♕xd2

6...cxd4

After 6...♘c6 7.dxc5 black easily wins the pawn back. At the same time, it's not so easy to neutralize white's tiny advantage. The game Aronian – Ponomariov (Wijk aan Zee 2011) continued 7...♘e4 8.♕e3 ♕a5+ 9.♗d2 ♘xd2 10.♕xd2 ♕xc5 11.♖c1 b6 12.♗g2 ♗b7 13.♘h3!? (unlike 13.♘f3 this does not block the diagonal or prevent 13...♘d4) 13...♕e7 14.0-0 0-0 15.♖fd1 ♖fd8 16.♕g5 ♖ab8 17.♖c3 ♕xg5 18.♘xg5 h6 19.♘e4 d5 20.cxd5 exd5 21.♘d2 ♘d4 22.♖d3 ♘xe2+ 23.♔f1 ♗a6

24.♘b3 ♘xg3+ 25.hxg3 ♖bc8 26.♘d4 g6 27.♗f3 ♗xd3+ 28.♖xd3. Black eventually held the endgame.

7.♘f3

If 7.♕xd4, black completes his development and breaks in the center – 7...♘c6 8.♕d3 0-0 9.♗g2 b6 10.♘f3 ♗b7 11.0-0 d5 12.cxd5 ♕xd5 13.♕xd5 ♘xd5. There is no retreat here for white's bishops.

7...♘c6

TRANSPOSITION ALERT. The continuation 7...b6 8.♗g2 ♗b7 leads via a different move order to the variation 3.♘f3 b6 4.g3 ♗b7 5.♗g2 ♗b4+ 6.♘d2 c5 7.a3 ♗xd2+ 8.♕xd2 cxd4 from the Queen's Indian Defense.

8.♘xd4

8...♘a5

From now on, black's main aim is to defuse the advantage of the two bishops. The exchange of queens after 8...♘e4 9.♘xc6 ♘xd2 10.♘xd8 ♘xc4 doesn't really address that task. White would retain a small advantage after 11.b3 ♘a5 12.♗b2 ♔xd8 13.♗xg7 ♖g8 14.♗f6+ ♔e8 15.b4

♘c4 16.e3 ♖g6 17.♗xc4 ♖xf6 18.0-0.

Grabbing the center with pawns via 8...d5 9.♗g2 e5?! is questionable due to the double attack 10.♘xc6 bxc6 11.♕g5. If instead of 9...e5 black plays 9...♕b6, the queen heads for c3, opening up the path for the bishop to e3. It makes sense to switch the move order with 8...♕b6!? 9.♘b5 d5. Now 10.♘d6+ ♔e7 doesn't cause the king any harm, but the exchange of the bishop on c8 merely helps black's development. There are almost no games in this line.

9.♕b4

In the game Baryshpolets – Matsenko (Costa Mesa 2017) the exchange of queens didn't lead to the bishops being activated: 9.♕d3 d5 10.cxd5 ♕xd5 11.♕b5+ ♕xb5 12.♘xb5 0-0 13.♗g5 ♗d7 14.♘c3 ♗c6 15.f3 ♘b3 16.♖d1 ♖fd8 17.♖xd8+ ♖xd8 18.e4 a5 19.♔f2 h6 20.♗e3 ♘d7 21.♗e2 ♘dc5 22.♖d1 ♖xd1 23.♗xd1 ♔f8. The cavalry are strengthened in outposts, and only a blunder by black ruined an almost equal position.

9...d5

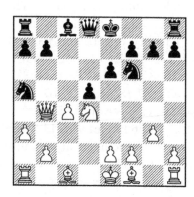

10.e4!?

A discovery by Adrian

Mikhalchishin. Seeing as the queen has held black's king in the center, opening up the game at a small price is logical. If 10.♘b5 ♘c6 the repetition suggested by the computer after 11.♕d6 ♕xd6 12.♘xd6+ ♔e7 13.♘b5 dxc4 14.♗g2 a6 15.♘c7 ♖b8 16.♗e3 ♖d8 17.♗c5+ ♔d7 18.♗b6 ♔e7 appears to be the best outcome for white.

10...♘xe4?

If 10...dxc4 we can follow Mikhalchishin's line 11.♘b5, or white can confine himself to operations in his own half of the board – 11.♗e3 a6 12.♖d1 ♗d7 13.♗g2 ♖c8 14.0-0. It's not easy to evaluate the trade-off between the initiative and the material, however 10...♘xc4!? threatens to completely liquidate the initiative. White will find it hard to play better than 11.♗xc4 dxc4 12.♘b5 ♘xe4 13.0-0 a6 14.♕xc4 axb5 15.♕xe4 ♕d5 16.♕xd5 exd5 17.♗d2 with a draw expected in an opposite-colored bishop ending even a pawn down.

11.cxd5 exd5 12.♗b5+ ♗d7 13.f3 ♘f6 14.0-0

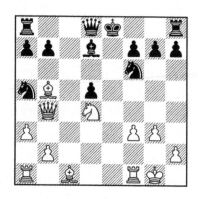

14...♗c6

White's attack runs like clockwork. 14...♝xb5 15.♖e1+ ♚d7 16.♕xb5+ ♚c8 17.♝f4 ♕b6 18.♖ac1+ ♘c6 19.♖e7 is also hopeless.

15.♝d2 ♕b6 16.♖fe1+ ♚d7 17.♖e7+♚d8 18.♕d6+♚c8 19.♝xa5 Black resigned.

No. 7 Al. Donchenko – G. Meier
Apolda 2017

1.d4 ♘f6 2.c4 e6 3.g3 ♝b4+ 4.♘d2 c5 5.dxc5

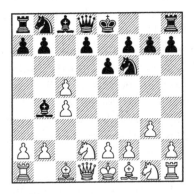

5...♝xc5

Black's pawn pair in the center may turn out to be his trump card, but the existence of the semi-open file suggests that his d-pawn will be under pressure.

6.♝g2 ♕c7

LANDMINE. After 6...♝xf2+?? 7.♚xf2 ♘g4+ 8.♚e1 ♘e3 9.♕b3 ♘xg2+ 10.♚f2 the knight won't get out alive.

Meier isn't planning to castle in the near future, which accords the game an unusual trait. 6...♕b6 lures white's knight to h3 and in the game

I. Saric – Bistric (Rijeka 2001) led to a small advantage for black: 7.♘h3 a5!? 8.0-0 a4 9.♘f4 ♝e7 10.♘d3 0-0 11.e4 d6 12.♖b1 ♘c6 13.b4 axb3 14.axb3 ♘b4 15.♘xb4 ♕xb4. In this line, the plan with b2-b4 was dubious, and the bishop should have been developed along the c1-h6 diagonal.

7.♘h3

The knight's voluntary development on h3 is intended to target black's pawn if it moves to d5. Therefore, black opts for a hedgehog-type setup.

7...h6 8.♘f4 ♘c6 9.0-0 b6 10.a3 ♝b7

11.b4 ♝e7

Undermining the pawn chain with 11...♝d4 12.♖b1 a5 fails to gain equality due to the reciprocal break 13.♘b3 ♝e5 14.c5!, and if 14...axb4 15.axb4 ♘xb4? 16.cxb6 ♕xb6 17.♝e3 ♕c7 18.♝xb7 ♕xb7 19.♘c5 black loses a piece due to a pin.

12.♝b2 d6 13.♖c1 ♘e5 14.♝xe5!?

Donchenko found a rather unusual tactical idea based on the fact that black's king is still in the center. 14.c5 bxc5 15.bxc5 ♝xg2 16.cxd6 ♕xd6 17.♘xg2 is only sufficient for equality.

14...dxe5 15.♕a4+ ♘d7

16.♘d5! exd5 17.cxd5 ♕b8

If 17...♕d8, then 18.d6 ♗xg2 19.dxe7 ♕xe7 20.♔xg2 0-0 21.♖c7 ♖ad8 22.♘e4 with an unpleasant knight pin.

18.♗h3 0-0 19.♗xd7 ♗xd5 20.♗c6 ♗xc6 21.♖xc6

With his next moves, Meier skillfully reanimates his queen's rook and gains equal chances.

21...a6 22.♖fc1 b5 23.♕b3 a5 24.♘e4 axb4 25.axb4 ♕b7 26.♕f3 ♖a7 27.♕f5 f6 28.♕e6+ ♔h8 29.♘c5 ♗xc5 30.♖1xc5

30...♕d7?!

Switching to a rook ending a pawn down is an overly elaborate way to achieve a draw. After 30...♖a1+ 31.♔g2 ♖a6 the b5 pawn remains

alive, while the passiveness of the black army isn't critical.

31.♕xd7 ♖xd7 32.♖xb5 ♖a8 33.♖bc5

After 33.♖c2 white could still torture his opponent for some time. Still, due to his nice pawn chain and active rooks black should draw.

33...♖a4 34.b5 ♖b4 35.b6 ♖b7 36.h4 ♖4xb6 37.♖xb6 ♖xb6 38.♔g2 ♖b4 39.♖a5 ♔h7 40.♔f3 h5

Draw agreed.

No. 8 H. Nakamura – P. Eljanov
Moscow 2010

1.d4 ♘f6 2.c4 e6 3.g3 ♗b4+ 4.♘d2 c5 5.dxc5 ♗xc5 6.♗g2 0-0 7.♘gf3 ♘c6 8.0-0 d5

If 8...b6 9.a3 ♗b7 10.b4 ♗e7 11.♗b2 white has the more promising chances with the pair of long-range bishops whether black plays d7-d5 or makes do with a hedgehog. If 9...a5, then 10.♘b3 ♗e7 11.♘fd4, heading for b5.

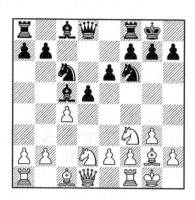

This is a critical position that occurs via various move orders, including via the Reti and Catalan openings. The conflict in the center will settle the structure in the next few moves.

9.e3

Adding the rook pawns' pushes allows black to create a bind on the queenside: 9.a3 a5 10.e3 a4!? (highlighting the clumsy position of the knight on d2) 11.♕c2 ♕e7 12.♖d1 ♖d8 13.b4 axb3 14.♘xb3 ♗d6 15.cxd5 exd5 16.a4 ♗g4 17.♕e2 ♘e4 18.♗b2 ♗b4 19.h3 ♗h5 20.♘bd4 ♘c3 21.♗xc3 ♗xc3 22.♘xc6 bxc6 23.♖ac1 (Shabalov – Popilski, Philadelphia 2018). The exchange on f3 leaves opposite-colored bishops on the board, which is why the players agreed a draw. White should probably have continued 10.♕c2 and after d5-d4 looked for an advantage in blockading play.

> **TRANSPOSITION ALERT.** The exchange 9.cxd5 exd5 leads to the Tarrasch Defense – 1.d4 d5 2.c4 e6 3.♘f3 c5 4.cxd5 exd5 5.g3 ♘f6 6.♗g2 ♘c6 7.0-0 ♗e7 8.dxc5 ♗xc5 9.♘bd2 0-0. This is a quiet blockading line with a microscopic advantage for white.

9...♕e7 10.cxd5 exd5 11.♘b3 ♗b6

12.a4

I don't know whether the players were familiar with the old games Iliesco – Najdorf (La Plata 1944) and Sosonko – Pachman (Barcelona 1975). The second continued 12.♘bd4 ♘e4 13.b3 ♗g4 14.♘xc6 bxc6 15.♕c2 c5 16.♗b2 ♕e6 17.♘d2 ♘xd2 18.♕xd2 ♖ad8 19.♖fe1 ♕h6 20.a4 a5 21.♗c3 d4 with a logical draw given the upcoming exchange of queens.

12...a6 13.♘bd4 ♗g4 14.♕b3 ♗a7

The variation 14...♗a5 15.♗d2 ♘xd4 16.exd4 ♗xf3 17.♖fe1 ♕d7 18.♗xa5 ♗xg2 19.♔xg2 would not have caused black any problems, whereas the development of the "bad" bishop on c3 now creates trouble.

15.♗d2 ♘e4 16.♗c3 ♘xc3 17.bxc3 ♖fd8

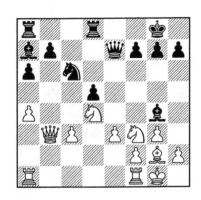

18.♘d2

The continuation 18.♘xc6 bxc6 19.♕b4 ♕e6 20.♘d4 ♗xd4 21.cxd4 leads to play against the weakness on c6, although it doesn't promise much.

18...♘a5 19.♕a2 ♕d7 20.♘2f3 ♕e7

Instead of watching over c4 it was better to occupy it with 20...♞c4 21.♞d2 ♖ac8.

21.♞e2 ♗f5 22.♞f4 ♗e4 23.♖fd1 ♕c5

Black is not forced to give up the pawn, although here 23...♞c4 is weaker than on move 20.

24.♞g5 ♗xg2 25.♔xg2 h6 26.♖xd5 ♖xd5 27.♞e4 ♕c4 28.♕xc4 ♞xc4 29.♞xd5

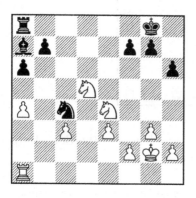

29...♖e8?!

He could have resisted better with 29...♖d8. Because of white's broken queenside pawns it would have been quite difficult to grind out a win.

30.♞ef6+ gxf6 31.♞xf6+ ♔f8 32.♞xe8 ♔xe8 33.♖b1 ♞d6 34.e4 b6?

Eljanov plays the endgame far below his ability. After 34...f6! 35.f4 b6 the break 36.e5?! is premature due to 36...fxe5 37.fxe5 ♞c4.

35.e5!

Now 35...♞c4 36.♖b4! ♞xe5 leads to the loss of the knight via a pin, and the rook unexpectedly finds the door open to get to the h6 pawn.

35...♞b7 36.♖b4 ♞c5 37.♖h4 ♔f8 38.♖xh6 ♔g7 39.♖c6 ♞xa4 40.e6

Black resigned.

In the variations considered in this chapter play is not really typical of the Bogo-Indian Defense and often leads directly to play along the lines of other openings. This is to the advantage of players with wide opening knowledge able to cause problems for weaker opponents. Given the unambitious position of the knight on d2 white is advised to continue 5.a3 (game 6).

Chapter 2

4.♗d2 variation

1.d4 ♘f6 2.c4 e6 3.g3 ♗b4+ 4.♗d2

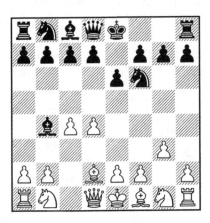

This is the line recommended by Boris Avrukh against the Bogo-Indian in his book on the Catalan (Quality Chess, 2015).

No. 9 E. Gleizerov – M. Sjoberg
Gothenburg 1997

1.d4 ♘f6 2.c4 e6 3.g3 ♗b4+ 4.♗d2

4...♗xd2+

I have not included any games where the bishop retreats to e7. In the vast majority of cases the knight develops on f3 and play reverts to Bogo-Indian Defense main lines.

5.♕xd2

If white captures with the knight he should aim to then develop that knight on f3. After 5.♘xd2 d6 6.♗g2 0-0 7.e4 e5 8.♘e2 ♗g4 the d4 pawn is under severe pressure, while the move 9.f3 restricts the bishop. A Modern Benoni structure arose in the game Maletin – Rozum (Vladivostok 2015): 5.♘xd2 d6 6.e3 0-0 7.♗g2 c5 8.♘e2 ♕c7 9.0-0 ♘c6 10.d5 exd5 11.cxd5 ♘e5 12.♘c3 ♗d7 13.f4 ♘g6 14.a4 a6 15.e4 c4 16.♔h1 b5? 17.e5! dxe5 18.d6! ♕xd6 19.axb5 ♖ad8 20.bxa6, and the advanced passer accorded white a significant advantage. However, countering the break in the center (16...♖fe8 17.a5 ♗ac8) would have ensured black a decent position.

5...c5

Avrukh suggested that the continuation 5...0-0 6.e4 d6 7.♘e2 e5 8.d5 was better for white. He would plan f2-f4, while counterplay for black on the queenside is difficult.

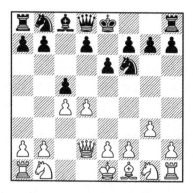

6.♗g2

TRANSPOSITION ALERT. 6.♘f3 leads via a different move order to the variation 1.d4 ♘f6 2.c4 e6 3.♘f3 ♗b4+ 4.♗d2 c5 5.g3 ♗xd2+ 6.♕xd2 with the main move being 6...♘e4, which is impossible after 6.♗g2.

6...cxd4

The game Ulibin – Rau (Vienna 2011) witnessed a complicated battle after 6...♕b6!? 7.dxc5 ♕xc5 8.♘c3 0-0 9.♖c1 ♘c6 10.♘b5 ♖b8 11.♘h3 d5 12.cxd5 ♕xb5 13.dxc6 bxc6 14.b3 ♗a6 15.♘f4 ♖fd8 16.♘d3 ♕h5. GM Ulibin had previously played the line in the analyzed game and hence his response to black winning

a pawn after 8...♕xc4 would have been interesting. It would appear that white has compensation for the material.

7.♘f3

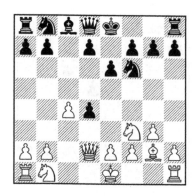

7...d5

This has also been played several times by Slovenian IM Aljosa Grosar.

8.♘xd4

Grosar is a strong player, and in agreeing three times to the strategically debatable continuation 8.cxd5 ♕xd5 9.0-0 0-0 10.♘xd4 ♕h5 11.♖c1 ♘bd7 12.♘a3, had surely weighed up the consequences. This is a typical Catalan position with two open files that is pleasant for white thanks to the contrast in the positions of the light-squared bishops.

Well, while Grosar continues to insist that he is right, Gleizerov seeks a new path, as does Serbian GM Markus. By playing 8.0-0 dxc4 9.♕xd4 ♘c6 10.♕xc4 (the exchange of queens is also decent) 10...0-0 11.♘c3 ♗d7 12.♖fd1 ♕e7 13.♘d4 ♖fc8 14.♘db5 ♘e8 15.♕f4 a6 16.♘d6 ♘xd6 17.♕xd6 ♕xd6 18.♖xd6 ♗e8 19.♖ad1 Draw (Markus – Naiditsch,

Zlatibor 2007) white used his microscopic advantage to score a half point with the initiative.

8...dxc4 9.♘a3 0-0 10.♘xc4 ♕e7 11.0-0 e5

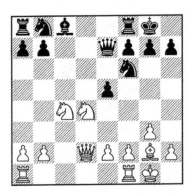

12.♘b3

This is another Catalan position that favors white. The black pawn has opened the path for his bishop, but there is no debate that white's pieces are better located. The game G. Agzamov – Barlov (Rakovica 1992) continued 12.♘b5 ♖d8 13.♕e3 ♘c6 14.♖fd1 ♗d7 15.♘bd6 ♘g4 16.♕c5 b6 17.♕a3 with the threat ♘d6-b7 and a huge advantage. Georgy Agzamov has a reputation as an excellent strategic player and should be trusted, though Gleizerov hasn't gone far wrong either.

12...♖d8

It was more precise to play 12... ♘a6, in order to meet 13.♕d6 with 13...♖e8 and preserve the status quo. Now the e-pawn has to make another, very committal move.

13.♕e3 e4 14.♖fd1 ♘c6 15.♖xd8+ ♘xd8 16.♖d1 ♗e6 17.♘d6 ♘d5

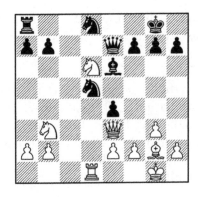

18.♕c5

Gleizerov plays along the dark squares (in "Agzamov style"). That said, Sjoberg wouldn't have gained compensation for the pawn after 18.♕xe4 ♕xd6 19.♕d3 and 20.♗xd5.

18...b6 19.♕a3 ♘c6 20.♘xe4 ♘db4?!

This apparently simple position proved too tricky for the Swedish master. After 20...♕xa3 21.bxa3 ♖ad8 there is still lots of play left in the game.

21.♘c3 ♕e8?

Black had voluntarily got tied in a knot, yet 21...♖d8 didn't lose immediately.

22.♘d4

Black resigned, and not too soon. For example: 22...♖d8 23.♕a4 ♘xd4 24.♖xd4 a5 25.a3 ♘a6 26.♖d6!, and the rook captures on b6.

No. 10 V. Laznicka – P. Jaracz
Aix les Bains 2011

1.d4 ♘f6 2.c4 e6 3.g3 ♗b4+ 4.♗d2 a5

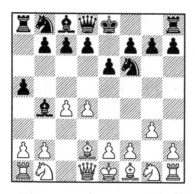

Game 4 of the historical introduction acquainted us with one of the lines where the bishop is protected by the rook's pawn. Other lines in the 3.♘f3 ♗b4+ 4.♗d2 a5 system are reviewed in chapters 12-15.

5.♗g2 d6

The continuation 5...0-0 6.e4 usually leads to variations from this game after 6...d6, but 6...d5 has also been tried. The game should follow 7.e5 ♘fd7 8.cxd5 exd5 9.♘c3 with better prospects for white thanks to his kingside pawn majority. Attacking the base of the pawn chain d4 with 9...c5 10.a3 ♗xc3 11.♗xc3 or 11.bxc3 doesn't create any real threat.

6.e4 0-0 7.♘e2 e5

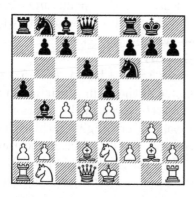

This strong pawn group is without doubt white's pride and joy. However, his pieces are less impressive and it's not easy to find an effective plan for him. He should probably be thinking about how to execute f2-f4.

8.a3

In the game Yakubboev – Gareev (St. Petersburg 2018) black skillfully operated along the dark squares and easily maintained equality: 8.0-0 exd4 9.♘xd4 ♘c6 10.♗c3 ♗g4 11.♕d2 ♘xd4 12.♕xd4 ♗c5 13.♕d3 ♘d7 14.h3 ♗e6 15.♘d2 ♘e5 16.♕e2 ♘c6 17.♔h2 ♗b4 18.♖ac1 ♖e8 19.a3 ♗xc3 20.♖xc3 a4 21.f4 f6 22.♖d1 ♕e7 23.♘f1 ♘a5.

8...♗xd2+   9.♘xd2   exd4 10.♘xd4 ♘c6 11.♘b5 ♘e5 12.0-0 c6 13.♘c3

According to Avrukh, white's position is preferable due to his spatial advantage. Laznicka needs to come up with something concrete.

13...♗e6 14.b3 ♕b6 15.♕c2 ♘fd7 16.♘e2 ♗g4 17.♖fe1 ♘c5 18.h3 ♗d7 19.♕c3 f5!?

One has the impression here that only black is trying to play. On the grounds that his pieces are better placed, Jaracz goes on the offensive.

20.exf5 ♞ed3 21.♖f1

After 21.b4 axb4 22.axb4 ♛xb4 23.♛xb4 ♞xb4 24.g4 black's pawn majority on the queenside is more tangible than white's advantage on the kingside.

21...♝xf5 22.♚h2

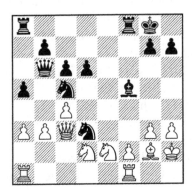

22...g5 23.♞d4

It was worth considering 23.f4!? gxf4 24.♞xf4 ♞xf4 25.♖xf4 ♝g6 26.♖af1 ♖xf4 27.♖xf4, and now white has the advantage. This is the result of the questionable g7-g5 break.

23...♝g6 24.♞2f3 h6 25.♚g1 ♖ae8 26.♞e1 ♞e5 27.♖d1 ♞e4 28.♛c1

It was more accurate to exchange the knight, as black now has a tactic.

28...♞xf2!? 29.♖xf2 ♖xf2 30.♚xf2 ♞d3+ 31.♖xd3 ♝xd3 32.♛c3 ♝g6 33.♞ef3 ♛c5 34.b4 axb4 35.axb4 ♛a7 36.g4 c5 37.bxc5 ♛xc5 38.♚g3 d5 39.♞f5

The players were probably now in time trouble, as 39.♝f1 was clearly safer. **39...♛c7+ 40.♚f2 ♝xf5 41.gxf5 ♛c5+ 42.♚g3 ♛c7+**

Draw agreed. Jaracz didn't try 42...dxc4!?, making do with repeating moves.

No. 11 Lei Tingjie – V. Gunina
Astana 2019

1.d4 ♞f6 2.c4 e6 3.g3 ♝b4+ 4.♝d2 c5

We were introduced to this idea in the historical introduction (game 5) via the move order 3.♞f3 ♝b4+ 4.♝d2 c5. With the knight in its starting position the fianchettoed bishop better supports the pushes e2-e4 and d4-d5. This game was of great sporting significance: in the world team championship the Russian and Chinese women's teams were undefeated at this point and their clash effectively determined who would win the tournament.

5.♝xb4

After 3.♞f3 ♝b4+ 4.♝d2 c5 5.g3 (chapter 9) the main continuation is 5...♛b6. However, in the position in this game, after 5.♝g2 ♛b6 black has to contend with 6.d5. Still, in the game Antic – Rozentalis (Skopje 2014) black easily maintained equality, and the game ended fairly quickly by move repetition: 6...exd5 7.cxd5 0-0 8.♘c3 d6 9.e4 ♘bd7 10.♘ge2 ♘e5 11.0-0 ♗g4 12.a3 ♗xc3 13.♗xc3 ♖fe8 14.f3 ♗d7 15.♘f4 a5 16.a4 h6 17.♖f2 c4 18.♗d4 ♕b4 19.♗c3 ♕b6. The position's closed nature nullified the advantage of the two bishops.

5...cxb4 6.♗g2

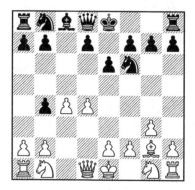

6...0-0

> **KEY TIP.** In the system with 4...c5 (whether or not the knight is on f3) the break d7-d5 doesn't fit with the arising pawn structure and although not a complete mistake is a second-rate plan.

7.e4 d6 8.♘e2 e5

Black doesn't need to rush with this natural move. After 8...♘c6 9.a3 bxa3 10.♘xa3 ♕a5+ 11.♕d2 ♕xd2+ 12.♔xd2 ♖d8 and ♘f6-e8 black is very solid. 10.♖xa3 prevents the exchange of queens, but then 10...e5 11.d5 ♘b4 is promising, with pressure on c4 to come.

9.0-0

Avrukh preferred 9.a3. GMs have taken a mixed view, alternating the pawn attack with castling. An example line would be 9...♕b6 10.♕d2!? b3 11.♕c3 ♘c6 (11...a5 12.♘d2 a4 13.c5) 12.d5 ♘a5 13.♘d2, and black still hasn't equalized given the pressure on b3.

9...♗g4

Luring pawns to the same-color squares as the g2 bishop can be carried out in various ways. Black can also try 9...♖e8 10.a3 ♕b6 11.axb4 ♕xb4 12.♕c2 (immediately protecting three pawns, but black attacks another one) 12...a5 13.b3 ♘c6 14.d5 ♘b8 – and black's strategic achievements are obvious.

10.f3 ♗e6

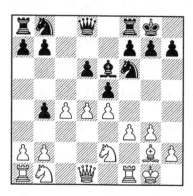

11.♕d3

The Chinese GM doesn't push her queenside pawns to avoid granting her opponent the opportunity to counterattack along the lines of Bosiosic – Farago (Austria 2011): 11.b3 a5 12.a3 ♘a6 13.axb4 axb4 14.♔h1 ♕b8 15.♘d2 b5 16.cxb5 ♕xb5 17.d5 ♗d7 18.♘c4 ♕b8 19.f4 ♗b5 20.♖c1 ♗xc4 21.♖xc4 ♘g4 22.♖f3 ♕a7 23.♕g1 ♕xg1+ 24.♔xg1 ♖ac8, after which the position is equal.

11...♕b6 12.♔h1 a5 13.♘d2 ♘a6 14.♖fd1 ♖ac8 15.♖ac1 ♖fd8 16.♘f1

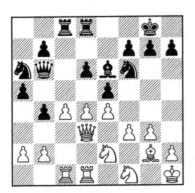

Black's prospects on the queenside look murky, while white is ready to attack on the kingside. Therefore, Gunina's next move should be criticized as creating a hook for a pawn storm.

16...h6 17.♘e3 ♗d7 18.♖d2 a4 19.♖cd1 ♕a5 20.b3 b5 21.g4

The computer recommends 21.♘c1 and ♕d3-f1 in order to prepare an exchange on e5 and demonstrate the strength of white's rooks. However, from the practical point of view we should approve of the pawn attack against the black king's defenses.

21...♘c7 22.h4 ♕a7 23.♘g3 bxc4 24.♘xc4 ♗b5

It was worth considering the multi-plan move 25...♘e6 aiming at both d4 and f4, as well as countering g4-g5.

25.g5

The continuation 25.dxe5?! dxe5 26.♕xd8+ ♖xd8 27.♖xd8+ ♔h7 28.♘xe5?! ♘e6 29.♖8d6 ♘e8 30.♖6d2 axb3 31.axb3 ♕b8 is to

black's advantage given the hanging knights along the diagonal.

25...hxg5 26.hxg5 ♘h7

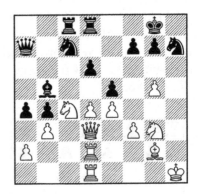

27.g6! fxg6 28.♗h3 ♖b8?

A couple of moves later it becomes clear that the rook needed to protect the queen. After 28...♖a8 29.dxe5 ♘g5 30.♗g4 axb3 31.axb3 ♘f7 the position remains equal.

29.dxe5 dxe5 30.♕e3 ♕a8?!

Finding the continuation 30...♖xd2! 31.♕xa7 ♖xd1+ 32.♔h2 ♖a8 33.♕xc7 axb3 34.axb3 ♖a2+ 35.♗g2 ♘g5 36.♕b8+ ♔h7 37.♕xb5 ♘xf3+ 38.♔h3 ♘g1+ 39.♔g4 ♖xg2 40.♘xe5 ♘e2 41.♕xe2 ♖xe2 42.♘xe2 is beyond the capability of humans, and anyway black isn't guaranteed to draw from that position.

31.♘xe5 ♘f8 32.♕c5?!

This sortie with the intermezzo 32.bxa4! ♗xa4 would effectively win, thanks to the idea of 34.♕c4+.

32...♖xd2 33.♖xd2 ♘e8?

Valentina has clearly lost her way and fails to show her usual inventiveness. If 33...♖d8 34.♖f2 ♖d1+ 35.♔h2 ♕d8 36.bxa4 ♗xa4

37.♕c4+ ♔h7 38.♕xb4 resistance was still possible.

34.♕e7   ♖b6   35.♕f7+   ♔h7 36.♖h2 ♘f6 37.♗f5+

Black resigned.

No. 12 S. Bogdanovich – K. Borsuk
Omelnik 2018

1.d4 ♘f6 2.c4 e6 3.g3 ♗b4+ 4.♗d2 ♕e7

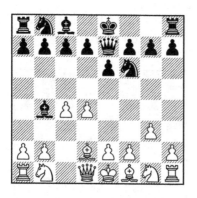

This is where we find the highest number of divergences from ♘g1-f3 setups. They usually involve developing the knight on e2 after e2-e3 or e2-e4.

5.♗g2 ♗xd2+

Very occasionally we see the move 5...e5 – somewhat akin to the Budapest Gambit. Sometimes black gains an extra pawn as compensation for white's powerful initiative: 6.dxe5 ♘g4 7.♘f3 ♘c6 8.♗xb4 ♕xb4+ 9.♘c3 (Ghaem Maghami – Hoffmann, Dresden 2010) 9...♕xb2 10.♖c1 0-0 11.0-0 ♘cxe5 12.♘xe5 ♘xe5 13.♘d5 c6 14.♘c7 ♖b8 15.♕d6. Instead of the queen's expedition into the enemy camp black has the safer 7...♘xe5 8.♘xe5

♗xd2+ 9.♕xd2 ♕xe5 10.♘c3 0-0 11.♖d1 with a minimal advantage for white.

Let's also consider the position after 5...0-0 6.♘c3 ♘c6 7.a3 ♗xc3 8.♗xc3 d6 9.e4 e5 10.d5 ♘b8 11.♘e2. It seems that in a blocked position white's bishops are not of much value. However, they actually do have prospects. White plans to play on both flanks (b2-b4 and f2-f4) and he gained a small advantage in the game Smirnov – Vu Thanh Ninh (Ho Chi Minh 2016): 11...♘e8 12.0-0 f5 13.f4 fxe4 14.fxe5 ♖xf1+ 15.♕xf1 dxe5 16.♗b4 ♕f6 17.♘c3 a5 18.♗c5.

6.♕xd2

After 6.♘xd2 the knight's position usually turns out to be unjustified. However, that was not the case in the example Palatnik – Rowley (Philadelphia 1992): 6...d6 7.e4 e5 8.d5 ♘bd7 9.b4 a5 10.a3 0-0 11.♘e2 c6 12.♘c3 cxd5 (12...♘b6!?) 13.cxd5 b6 14.0-0 ♗a6 15.♖e1 ♖fc8 16.♕b3 ♗d3 17.♗f1 ♗xf1 18.♖xf1 ♘e8 19.♖ac1 g6 20.♘b5 f5? 21.♖c6 with murderous consequences of the rook's invasion.

KEY TIP. The exchange of black's passive queen's bishop in the Bogo-Indian Defense also has its downside – the weakening of the light squares. In the last example, the effect from ♖c1-c6 places a question-mark against the reasonableness of opening the c-file.

6...d6

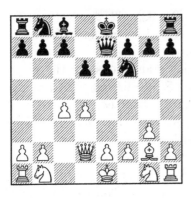

7.♘c3

Bogdanovich intends to push the e-pawn two squares. After 7.e3 e5 8.♘e2 0-0 9.♘bc3 black needs to accurately assess the structure's potential. The game Papaioannou – Kalesis (Porto Rio 2015) continued 9...exd4 10.exd4 c6 11.0-0 ♗f5 12.h3 ♘a6 13.♖fe1 ♕d7 14.g4 ♗g6 15.f4 h6 16.f5 ♗h7 17.♘g3 cutting the bishop out of play and hence with a clear advantage for white. It was better not to settle the tension in the center and to continue 9...♖e8 10.0-0 ♘bd7 11.♖ad1 ♘f8.

7...0-0

With an unsettled situation in the center, black in the game Kozul – Stanec (Austria 2019) got active on the queenside by a method untypical of the Bogo-Indian Defense. After 7...c6 8.e4 e5 9.♘ge2 0-0 10.0-0 ♖e8 11.h3 a6 12.♖fd1 b5 13.♖ac1 ♘bd7 14.cxb5 axb5 15.a3 ♖b8 16.dxe5 dxe5 17.♕d6 ♗b7 18.♕xe7 ♖xe7 19.f3 white's advantage was negligible.

8.e4 e5 9.♘ge2

If 9.d5 a5 10.♘b5 black is unable to develop his knight, whereas the immediate 9...♘bd7 allows the knight to jump to c5.

9...♗g4

The game Laznicka – Socko (Prague 2015) illustrates hand-to-hand combat on the queenside when the center is blocked: 9...c5 10.d5 ♘a6 11.0-0 ♘c7 12.a3 a6 13.b4 ♘d7 14.♘c1 b5!? 15.cxb5 ♘xb5 16.♘1e2 (16.♘b3!?) 16...♘xc3 17.♘xc3 a5 18.bxa5 ♖xa5 19.a4 ♗a6 20.♖fb1 ♖a8. The outside passer is totally blockaded and white essentially has no advantage.

10.f3 ♗e6 11.b3 a5 12.0-0 ♘a6 13.♘d5 ♗xd5 14.cxd5

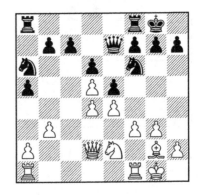

KEY TIP. This type of position is a frequent combination of two factors – the semi-open c-file with pressure on c7 and the ugly bishop stuck behind his own f3-e4-d5 pawn chain. With pressure against c7 it's convenient to put the bishop on h3, although it's problematic to integrate it into an attack on the kingside (as was seen in the game).

14...a4 15.♖ac1 axb3 16.axb3 ♕d7 17.f4 ♖fe8 18.fxe5 dxe5

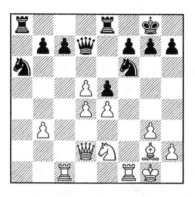

19.♖xf6?!

White can make progress even without the bishop's help, for example, via 19.dxe5 ♖xe5 20.♕f4 ♖ae8 21.♘d4 ♘xe4 22.♘e6! The exchange sacrifice is dubious, all the more so given that white plays inaccurately from hereon.

19...gxf6 20.♖f1 ♕d6 21.♗h3?!

After 21.♕h6 f5 22.♕h4 ♕e7 23.♕h5 white avoids the exchange of queens and is ready to plant his bishop on h3.

21...♔g7 22.♖f5 ♘b4?!

22...h6 23.♖h5 ♖h8 reliably plugs the attack. That's why white should not have allowed the king to move to g7.

23.♖h5 ♔f8 24.♖xh7 ♖a1+ 25.♔f2 ♖a2 26.♕h6+ ♔e7 27.♗e6 ♖f8 28.♕g6

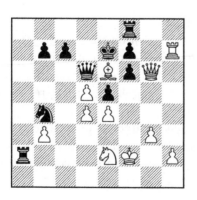

28...♕d8?

Without a computer it's not easy to find that after 28...♔d8! 29.♖xf7 ♖xf7 30.♕xf7 ♕e7 31.♕g8+ ♕e8 32.♕g7 black is not forced to submit to the "stepladder" (32...♕e7? 33.♕h8+!), but instead forces a draw through perpetual check with 32... ♖xe2+! 33.♔xe2 ♕h5+.

29.♗xf7 ♖h8 30.♖g7?!

30.♔f3!! unpins the knight favorably, which is important in the variation 30...♖xh7 31.♕xh7 ♔d6 32.♘c3. These events are most entertaining, albeit untypical for the Bogo-Indian Defense.

30...♔d6   31.♔f3   ♖xe2! 32.dxe5+?!

Whose king stands worse? The variation 32.♔xe2 ♖xh2+ 33.♔f1 exd4 34.♔g1 ♖e2 35.♖g8 ♕d7 36.♕xf6+ ♔c5 37.♖d8 ♖e1+ suggests that both are "worse"! So the game would end in perpetual check, whereas in the actual game the black monarch immediately runs away from the enemy army while the white king faces tough times.

32...♔c5   33.♔xe2   ♖xh2+ 34.♔e3 ♘c2+ 35.♔f3

35...fxe5

Unlike a human, a computer can see how to add the queen to the attack with a decisive effect – 35...♘d4+! 36.♔e3 (36.♔g4 ♕h8!) 36...♕a8! 37.♖h7 (37.♕xf6 ♖e2+ 38.♔d3 ♕a2) 37...♖e2+ 38.♔f4 ♖f2+ 39.♔g4 ♕a1!

36.♗e8 ♔d4 37.d6!? cxd6 38.♖d7 ♕a5?

Now Bogdanovich's queen has her say. The correct continuation was 38...♕b8 39.♕xd6+ ♕xd6 40.♖xd6+ ♔c3, and the endgame is defendable.

39.♕xd6+ ♔c3

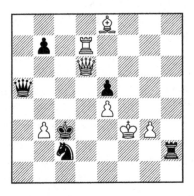

40.♖c7+?!

White doesn't want this fantastic game to be over! The study-like move 40.b4!! (distracting the queen from the e5 pawn) would have ended black's resistance.

40...♔b2 41.♔g4 ♘d4 42.♗g6 ♕b5 43.♖c4 ♖d2 44.♔h5 ♖d3 45.♖c5 ♕xb3 46.♕xe5 ♕d1+?!

After a faultless fragment black makes another error. Given the possible exchange of queens black should have pushed his passer – 46...b5 47.♔h6 b4.

47.♔h6?! b6?

Bogdanovich ignored the cover 47.g4, and black could have escaped at the death – 47...♕d2+ 48.♔h7 ♕h2+ 49.♔g7 ♕xg3. In the game black also captures on g3, but the remaining passer storms towards the back rank.

48.♖b5+ ♖b3 49.♖d5 ♔c3 50.♕c7+ ♔b2 51.♕d6 ♕d2+ 52.♔h7 ♕h2+ 53.♔g7 ♘f3 54.e5 ♕xg3 55.e6 ♕xd6 56.♖xd6 ♖e3 57.♔f8 ♘e5 58.e7 ♘xg6+ 59.♖xg6 b5 60.♖b6

Black resigned.

No. 13 A. Sarana - Liu Yan
Moscow 2018

1.d4 ♘f6 2.c4 e6 3.g3 ♗b4+ 4.♗d2 ♕e7 5.♗g2 ♘c6

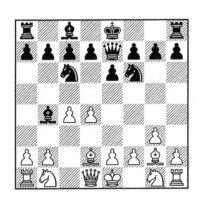

6.e3

The pawn on d4 is under attack, and white has to do something about it (6.♘f3 transposes to the main system and hence isn't reviewed here).

The charge 6.d5 restricts the range of the light-squared bishop, and concessions in the center would be required to reanimate it: 6...♘e5

7.♕b3 ♗xd2+ 8.♘xd2 d6 9.dxe6 fxe6 10.e3 ♘ed7 11.♘e2 a5 12.♕c2 0-0 13.♘c3 ♘c5 14.♘b3 ♘fd7 15.♘xc5 ♘xc5 16.♘e4 (Bacrot – Lenic, Moscow 2010) 16...♘xe4 17.♗xe4 h6. White has nothing to get his teeth into and the position is equal.

If 6.a3 ♗xd2+ 7.♕xd2 white can go without playing e2-e3, but after e6-e5 in order to fight for the d4 square he needs a knight on f3 (and, therefore, a transposition to a "normal" Bogo-Indian Defense). The draw in the game Svane – Anand (Douglas 2018) was only interesting in that Anand was unable to come up with anything constructive against a run of the mill GM: 7...0-0 8.e3 d6 9.♘e2 e5 10.0-0 ♖e8 11.d5 ♘b8 12.e4 a5 13.♘bc3 ♘a6 14.b4 ♘d7 15.♖ab1 ♖b8 16.♘c1 axb4 17.axb4 c5 18.dxc6 bxc6 19.♘d3 ♘c7 20.♖fc1 ♘e6 21.♘e2 ♘c7 22.♘c3 ♘e6. Black has also tried 7...e5!? 8.d5 ♘d4 9.♕d1 d6 10.e3 ♘f5 11.♘c3 ♗d7 and he came away without any defects in his position.

6...e5

After the exchange of bishops with 6...♗xd2+ 7.♕xd2 black should probably play 7...d5 to steer the game in a Catalan direction. The weakness of the move 7...e5 becomes apparent in the next note, while if 7...d6 8.♘c3 0-0 9.♘ge2 e5 10.d5 ♘b8 the plan with castling long is promising for white – 11.h3 a5 12.g4 ♘a6 13.♘g3 ♘c5 14.0-0 ♘e8 15.f4 f5 16.g5 ♗d7 17.h4. Black is cramped and has virtually no counterplay (Brunello – Karason, Porto Mannu Palau 2015).

7.d5

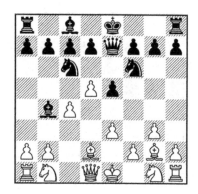

7...♘b8

The addition of 7...♗xd2+ 8.♕xd2 ♘b8 allows the standard push in the center: 9.d6! ♕xd6 10.♕xd6 cxd6 11.♘c3 ♘a6 12.0-0-0 ♔e7 13.♘f3 ♘c7 14.♖d2 (Cheparinov – Dimitrov, Pleven 2015). Passive defense of the d6 pawn was unattractive to black, but 14...d5?! 15.cxd5 d6 16.♘xe5! dxe5 17.d6+ ♔d8 18.dxc7+ ♔xc7 19.♘b5+ ♔b6 20.♘d6 ♗e6 21.b3 ♖ab8 22.♖hd1 ♘e8 23.♘e4 only made his difficulties worse.

8.♘c3

White is determined to gain the advantage of the bishop pair, counting on eventually breaking through the pawn walls.

8...0-0 9.a3

In the game Laznicka – Hracek (Hustopece 2011) white prepared a new shift worker: 9.♘ge2 d6 10.a3 ♗xc3 11.♘xc3 a5 (11...e4!?) 12.e4 ♘a6 13.b4 ♗d7 14.♖b1 axb4 15.axb4 c5!? 16.bxc5 ♘xc5. Laznicka's second try in this line and his second victory! However, the opening had nothing to do with that outcome.

9...♗xc3 10.♗xc3 d6 11.e4 a5 12.b3 ♘bd7 13.♘e2 ♘c5 14.♕c2 ♗d7 15.0-0 b5

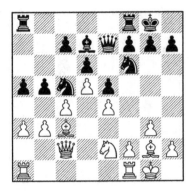

As a result of natural action by both sides, white has finally completed his development, while black has extended territory under his control on the queenside. In order to give his bishops a chance, Sarana engages in a square-off.

16.b4 axb4 17.axb4 ♘a4 18.♗d2 bxc4 19.♕xc4 ♖fc8 20.♖fc1 ♕e8

The Chinese player skillfully operates on the queenside, and white's hopes of an advantage have disappeared. The d5-e4 wedge is fine, but the white bishop is bored behind them!

21.♗g5 ♗b5 22.♕c2 ♘d7 23.♗e3 c6 24.dxc6 ♖xc6 25.♕d2 ♘db6

Black has got rid of his backward pawn, while putting up decent resistance against his opponent on the open file. The game approaches its logical and peaceful conclusion.

26.♗xb6 ♖xb6 27.♗f3 g6 28.h4 h5 29.♖c7 ♖c6 30.♖xc6 ♕xc6 31.♖c1 ♕d7 32.♕g5 ♕d8 33.g4 ♕xg5 34.hxg5 h4 35.♔h2 ♖b8 36.♖c7 ♗e8 37.♘c3 ♘xc3 38.♖xc3 ♖xb4 39.♔h3 ♖b2 40.♗d1 ♗b5 41.♗c2 ♖b4

Draw agreed.

Due to the many opportunities for transposition to the main Bogo-Indian Defense setups the practical value of this chapter is quite specific. The universal setup with e2-e4 and ♘g1-e2 recommended by Avrukh against both 4...a5 and 4...c5 doesn't look as promising as when there is an exchange on d2, but that's a minor matter. Material in this chapter is useful for players who play 3.g3 to avoid the Queen's Indian Defense but who are willing to fight against 3...c5. So your repertoire is key here.

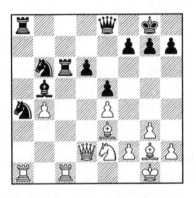

Part II

System with 3.♘f3 ♗b4+ 4.♘bd2

Introduction

1.d4 ♘f6 2.c4 e6 3.♘f3 ♗b4+ 4.♘bd2

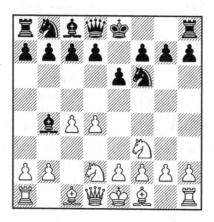

We encountered this block in game 2 of the historical introduction. In chapter 3 we review black's second-rate replies, while in chapter 4 we analyze 4...d5, in chapter 5 we learn 4...0-0, and in chapter 6 we consider 4...b6.

Chapter 3

Miscellaneous black replies

In game 14 we review 4...a5 (as well as 4...♘c6 and 4...♘e4 in the notes), while in game 15 we analyze 4...d6, and in games 16-18 we review 4...c5.

No. 14 M. Krasenkow – J. Riff
Mulhouse 2011

1.♘f3 ♘f6 2.d4 e6 3.c4 ♗b4+ 4.♘bd2

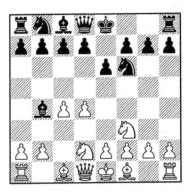

4...a5

A second-rate reply. This move should not be rushed. The group of inferior replies also includes 4...♘c6 such as Kuzubov – Markocic (Porticcio 2016): 5.a3 ♗xd2+ 6.♕xd2 d6 7.♕c2 ♕e7 8.b4 e5 9.d5 ♘b8 (suggesting the knight developed on c6 too early) 10.e4 ♘bd7 11.♗e2 0-0 12.0-0 a5 13.♗e3 b6 14.♘d2 axb4 15.axb4 ♗b7 16.f3 ♖fc8 17.♖fb1 ♕f8 18.♖xa8 ♖xa8 19.c5. This standard break fixes white's advantage, which increased after 19...bxc5 20.bxc5 ♗a6 21.♗xa6 ♖xa6 22.c6 ♘c5 23.♗xc5 dxc5 24.♘c4 to a decisive one.

A totally separate approach involves 4...♘e4 counting on

simplifying the defense of a cramped position with a double exchange. The forcing move 5.a3 guarantees white a small advantage, but he's far from required to settle the situation. In reply to 5.e3 the Dutch-style strengthening of the knight with 5...f5 is insufficient for equality – 6.♗d3 b6 7.a3 ♗xd2+ 8.♘xd2 ♗b7?! (it was better to exchange on d2) 9.♗xe4 fxe4 10.♕g4 0-0 11.♘xe4 h5 12.♕g6 ♕h4 13.♘g3 ♗xg2 14.♖g1 ♕xh2 15.♘e2 ♖xf2 16.♔xf2 ♗e4+ 17.♖g2 ♗xg2 18.♕xg2 ♕h4+ 19.♕g3 ♕e4 (Vukovic – Alekhine, Vienna 1922) 20.♗d2 ♘c6 21.♖g1, and there is no compensation for the piece. The future world champion's risky venture resulted from an eccentric opening – 1.d4 ♘f6 2.♘f3 e6 3.c4 ♘e4?! 4.♘bd2 f5 5.e3 ♗b4, and then as per the above.

5.a3

If 5.e3, then black should activate in the center via 5...d6 6.♗d3 e5. The a5 pawn protects the bishop from ♕d1-a4+, while 7.dxe5?! dxe5 8.♘xe5 ♕d6 9.f4 ♘c6 allows black to regain material in an advantageous situation. 7.0-0 ♕e7 8.♘e4! has also been played (the b4 bishop is still in danger, and hence it would have been useful to add the exchange 7...♗xd2 8.♘xd2) 8...♘xe4 9.♗xe4 exd4 10.♕xd4 0-0 11.b3 ♘c6 12.♕d3 f5 13.♗d5+ ♔h8 14.♗xc6 bxc6 15.♗b2 ♗d7 (Kempinski –

Vlassov, Cappelle la Grande 1998) 16.a3 ♗c5 17.♖fe1 followed by b3-b4 which is better for white.

5...♗xd2+ 6.♗xd2

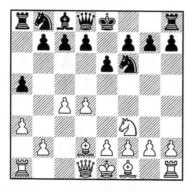

6...d6

KEY TIP. The exchange is frequently accompanied by a queenside bind with a5-a4. This standard ploy in the Bogo-Indian Defense has, however, a mixed reputation. On the one hand, it fixes the hole on b3, and white's queenside pawn chain has lost its elasticity. On the other hand, pawns cannot move backwards, and the pain of having to protect the pawn on a4 frequently leads black to regret his aggression.

If 6...a4 then 7.♕c2 followed by e2-e4 looks attractive. In the game Gelfand – Jobava (Plovdiv 2010) white's classical play didn't prevent his inventive opponent from launching counterplay: 7.♗g5 d6 8.e3 ♘bd7 9.♗d3 h6 10.♗h4 b6 11.♗e4 d5!? 12.cxd5 g5 13.dxe6 ♘xe4 14.exd7+ ♕xd7 15.♗g3 ♕b5 – the white king isn't comfortable.

7.♗g5

TRANSPOSITION ALERT. The position after 7.♕c2 ♕e7 8.♗c3 ♘bd7 is most often arrived at after 4.♗d2 a5 5.♘c3 d6 6.♕c2 ♕e7 7.a3 ♗xc3 8.♗xc3 ♘bd7. In the game Lysyj – Maletin (Nizhny Tagil 2005) white won back space in the interest of his bishop pair: 9.b4 e5 10.e3 0-0 11.♗e2 e4 12.♘d2 axb4 13.axb4 ♖xa1+ 14.♗xa1 ♖e8 15.d5. Nevertheless, black's position was very solid.

7...h6 8.♗h4 ♕e7 9.e3 g5 10.♗g3 ♘e4 11.♗d3 ♘xg3 12.hxg3

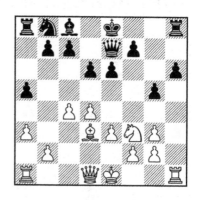

Black has deprived his opponent of the bishop pair advantage, but has still not equalized. Krasenkow, having sensibly waited with castling short, instead shelters his king on the queenside, and the h-file now works for him.

12...♘d7 13.♕c2 a4 14.0-0-0 ♖a5
Prophylaxis masked as activity. 14...b6?! would be met with 15.♗e4.

15.♘d2 b6 16.♘b1 ♘f6 17.♘c3
The knight is useless on f3, but from c3 it attacks the a4 pawn and controls the important b5 and d5 squares.

17...♗d7 18.♔b1 h5 19.e4

19...e5?!

The medicine to counter e4-e5 turns out to be worse than the illness.

20.♘d5 ♘xd5 21.exd5 ♚d8 22.♖de1 f6 23.f4 gxf4 24.gxf4 c6 25.c5

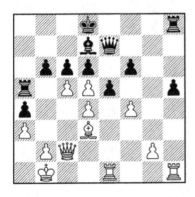

The white army is beyond doubt much better placed than black's, and the opening up of the position brings the denouement closer.

25...bxc5 26.♕c3 ♖a7 27.dxc5 cxd5 28.cxd6 ♕xd6 29.fxe5 fxe5?

He should have played the intermezzo 29...d4, preventing white from building a battery on the e-file.

30.♖xe5 d4 31.♕e1 ♖b7 32.♖exh5 ♖e8 33.♖h8 ♕b6 34.♕f2 ♖xh8 35.♖xh8+ ♚c7 36.♗e4 ♕b3 37.♕f4+ ♚b6 38.♕d6+

Black resigned.

No. 15 A. Moiseenko – M. Turov
Sochi 2008

1.d4 ♘f6 2.c4 e6 3.♘f3 ♗b4+ 4.♘bd2 d6

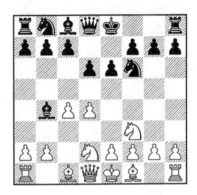

This move is seen in GM play from time to time. As a rule, black intends e6-e5.

5.a3

Forcing the exchange of the bishop. Black will then try to blockade the position to prevent white's bishops from sweeping across the board.

Occasionally, the pawn chain gets fixed via c7-c5, such as in the approximate line 5.♕c2 ♘bd7 6.e4 c5 7.e5 dxe5 8.dxe5 ♘g8 9.a3 ♗xd2+ (9...♗a5!?) 10.♗xd2 ♕c7 11.♗c3 ♘e7. The e5 pawn cramps black, while liquidating it may give the white bishops a free rein.

5...♗xd2+ 6.♕xd2

In the game Asadpour – Taimanov (Stockholm 2001) black worsened his pawn chain thanks to a bishop maneuver: 6.♗xd2 ♕e7 7.♗g5 e5 8.e3 ♗g4 9.♗e2 ♘bd7 10.h3 ♗h5 11.g4 ♗g6 12.♘h4 h6 13.♘xg6 fxg6 14.♗xf6 ♕xf6 15.dxe5 ♘xe5.

However, black's knight is more powerful than the bishop, and his rooks will comfortably sit on the e and f files.

6...♘bd7

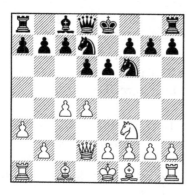

7.e3

If white deploys an extended fianchetto to establish control over e5, then black gains counterchances on the queenside: 7.b4 a5 8.♗b2 axb4 9.axb4 ♖xa1+ 10.♗xa1 b5!? 11.cxb5 ♗b7 12.e3 ♕a8 13.♕d1 ♕a3 (Goldin – Benjamin, Philadelphia 2001). Black's powerful blockade with greatly placed pieces more than compensates for the absence of a pawn.

7...e5 8.dxe5

Moiseenko varies play from an earlier game by Turov: 8.♕c2 0-0 9.b3 ♖e8 10.♗b2 exd4 11.♘xd4 ♘g4 12.♗e2 ♘de5 13.h3 ♕h4 14.0-0 ♘f6 (Kozul – Turov, Kusadasi 2008). Black's kingside play forced Kozul to seek simplifications – 15.♘f3 ♘xf3+ 16.♗xf3 ♕g5 17.♖ad1 ♗f5 18.♕c1 ♗e4 19.♗xf6 ♕xf6 20.♗xe4 ♖xe4 21.c5 dxc5 22.♕xc5 ♕e7 23.♕xe7, draw agreed.

8...dxe5 9.b4

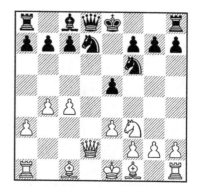

9...e4

Later, Turov advanced that pawn in a different variation: 9...a5 10.♗b2 axb4 11.axb4 ♖xa1+ 12.♗xa1 e4 13.♘e5 0-0 14.♗e2 ♕e7 15.♘xd7 ♗xd7 16.0-0 ♖a8 17.♖d1 ♗a4 18.♖c1 ♖d8 19.♕c3 (19.♗d4!?) 19...♕d6 20.h3 ♕d2 21.♗f1 ♕xc3 22.♗xc3 ♖d1 23.♖xd1 ♗xd1 (Fressinet – Turov, Nancy 2011). White has retained a small advantage, but predictably this was insufficient for a win. Note that replacing 13.♘e5 with 13.♘d4 would have reverted to the analyzed game.

10.♘d4 a5

GMs Browne and Yermolinsky twice tried 10...♘e5 11.♗b2 0-0. Their second game continued 12.♘b5 ♕e7 13.♕c3 ♘c6 14.♗e2 a6 15.♘d4 ♘xd4 16.♕xd4 ♖d8 17.♕c3 (Browne – Yermolinsky, San Francisco 2002) – it's not easy to neutralize white's slight advantage. Following an exchange of pawns and rooks, Turov counted on gaining attacking targets.

11.♗b2 axb4 12.axb4 ♖xa1+ 13.♗xa1 0-0 14.♗e2 ♘e5 15.h3 ♘e8

16.0-0

Black's plan proves justified after 16.♕c2 ♕g5 17.♕xe4 ♘d6 18.h4 ♕e7 19.♕c2 ♘dxc4! or the simpler 16...♕d6. Moiseenko ignores the pawn on e4, and he is probably right to do so.

16...♕g5 17.♔h2 ♕h6 18.♘f5 ♕e6 19.♕c3 ♘f3+!?

This is to shake up the white king's bunker and gain reciprocal chances.

20.♗xf3 exf3 21.g4 f6 22.♕d4

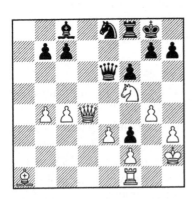

22...g6?!

He should only have chased the knight away after opening the h-file – 22...h5!? 23.c5 hxg4 24.hxg4 g6.

23.♖g1 ♔f7 24.♘h4

Now the queenside pawns really become vulnerable, rather than in the

hidden line with 16.♕c2. Moiseenko would have retained an advantage after 24.♘h6+ ♔g7 25.♕f4 with an approximate continuation 25...♘d6 26.c5 ♘e4 27.♘f5+ ♔g8 28.♘g3 ♘xf2 29.♕xf3 ♘d3 30.♘e4.

24...♕d6+ 25.♖g3 ♕xb4 26.♘xf3 ♕d6 27.♕c3 b6 28.e4 ♗b7 29.e5 fxe5 30.♘xe5+ ♔g8 31.♘d3 ♕f6 32.♖e3

Draw agreed.

16 H. Banikas – G. Vlassis
Kavala 1996

1.c4 e6 2.d4 ♘f6 3.♘f3 ♗b4+ 4.♘bd2 c5

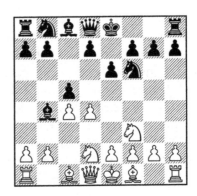

Due to the closing of the d-file white's impact on the center is weakened, and black immediately attacks d4. The drawback of this move is that the bishop's route back to base is cut off and it is often forced to exchange itself for the knight.

5.e3

The exchange 5.dxc5 ♗xc5 is logical if white plans an extended fianchetto. After 6.e3 b6 7.a3 ♗e7 prophylaxis is required, as 8.b4 is undermined by 8...a5, deforming the white pawn chain.

After 5.g3 cxd4 6.♘xd4 ♘c6 we reach a position from Aronian – Carlsen (Bilbao 2008), which began as an English Opening. Now keeping the knight in the center via 7.a3 ♗e7 8.♘2f3 (or 8.♘b3) is hit by the break d7-d5. Aronian continued 7.♘c2 ♗e7 8.♗g2 0-0 9.0-0 ♖b8 10.♘e4 b5!? 11.cxb5 ♖xb5 12.♘d6 ♗xd6 13.♕xd6 ♗b7 14.♘a3 ♖b6 15.♗e3!? ♖xb2 16.♗c5 ♖e8 17.♖ab1 ♖xb1 18.♖xb1 ♗a6 19.♘b5 ♗xb5 20.♖xb5 and gained compensation for the sacrificed pawn, but Magnus stood his ground and won. Interestingly, Aronian himself preferred 6...♕b6 7.a3 ♗c5 8.♘2b3, though that has never been tested.

5...d6

Black plays this opening very modestly, giving respect to his far stronger opponent. A reasonable alternative was 5...cxd4 6.exd4 0-0 7.a3 ♗e7 (so the bishop managed to return to base). The continuation 5...b6 6.♗d3 ♗b7 is reviewed via a different move order in game 28.

6.♗e2 ♘bd7 7.0-0

7...♗xd2

Not a moment too soon, otherwise the bishop will become a burden. After 7...0-0 8.♘b3 e5 9.h3 e4 10.♘h2 white can strengthen with ♕d1-c2 and ♖f1-d1, whereas it's hard to recommend anything for black.

8.♕xd2 ♕c7?!

He should have begun 8...b6, in order to take control over e4 more quickly.

9.b3 0-0 10.♖d1 b6 11.dxc5 dxc5 12.♗b2 ♗b7 13.♕d6

13...♕c6?

Vlassis didn't anticipate white's retreat after its invasion. The defensive setup 13...♖ac8 14.♖d2 ♕xd6 15.♖xd6 ♘b8 is hard to break through.

14.♕g3! ♔h8?!

14...♘e8 can be met by the strong 15.♘g5 ♘df6 16.♗f3 ♕c8 17.e4 h6 18.e5 ♘h7 19.♘xh7 ♔xh7 20.♖d3, and then ♖a1-d1. With the immediate doubling of rooks the game is over in a few moves.

15.♖d6 ♕c8 16.♖ad1 e5 17.♘xe5! ♘e4

18.♘xf7+! ♖xf7   19.♕xg7+!
♖xg7 20.♖xd7

For an instant white only has a few pawns for his queen. However, black's queen now disappears in thin air, while the extra pawns remain.

20...♕c6   21.♖d8+   ♕e8
22.♖xe8+ ♖xe8 23.♖d7

Black resigned.

No. 17 L. Van Wely – R. Hess
Berkeley 2011

1.d4 ♘f6 2.c4 e6 3.♘f3 ♗b4+
4.♘bd2 c5 5.a3

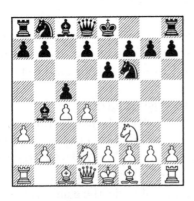

5...♗xd2+

LANDMINE. The pin 5...♕a5? will leave the black king stuck in the

center for a long time, and maybe forever, after 6.♖b1! ♗xd2+ 7.♗xd2 ♕c7 8.dxc5 ♕xc5 9.♗b4.

6.♗xd2

Van Wely had already captured twice with the bishop in previous games, so his opponent was prepared for this.

6...cxd4

If 6...d6 7.dxc5 dxc5 8.♗c3 white has a small but stable advantage. At first it's useful to dispute the open file, and then to decide where the light-squared bishop should stand (e2 or g2). A quiet and equal position arose after 6...b6 7.♗g5 ♗b7 8.e3 h6 9.♗h4 d6 10.♗e2 ♘bd7 11.0-0 ♕e7 12.♕a4 0-0 13.♖fd1 ♖fd8 14.♖ac1 g5 15.♗g3 ♘e4 16.♘d2 ♘xg3 17.hxg3 ♘f6 18.♗f3 e5 19.♗xb7 ♕xb7 20.dxe5 dxe5 (Volodin – Miezis, Finland 2009). Grandmaster Miezis is a big expert on the Bogo-Indian Defense, so it's worth taking a look at his harmonious setup.

7.♘xd4

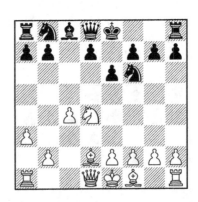

7...♘c6

After 7...d5 8.cxd5 ♕xd5 9.e3 ♗d7 10.♖c1 ♘c6 11.♘b5 ♖c8

12.♗b4 ♛xd1+ 13.♖xd1 ♘e4
14.♗d6 a6 15.♗d3 ♘f6 16.♘c3 ♘a5
17.a4 ♘c4 18.♗xc4 ♖xc4 19.f3 (Van
Wely – Rozentalis, France 2010) the
Dutchman took advantage of the
better position of his pieces. With
the stronger 10...0-0 11.♛b3 ♛xb3
12.♘xb3 black still has to reckon
with the pair of white bishops.

8.♗c3

Van Wely diverts from his earlier
game: 8.♘xc6 dxc6 9.♗b4 ♛xd1+
10.♖xd1 ♘e4 11.a4 a5 12.♗a3
b6 13.g4 ♗b7 14.♗g2 c5 (Van
Wely – Short, Sestao 2010). Black
successfully locked up the position,
and the bishop pair proved to be of
low value.

8...0-0 9.e3 ♘e4 10.♖c1

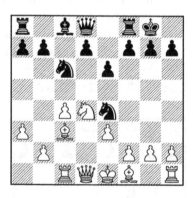

10...♛h4

Later Hess would also send his
queen to the kingside, whereas Jan
Timman placed his strongest piece on
her own flank. After 10...♛b6 11.♗d3
♘xc3 12.♖xc3 ♘xd4 (12...♛xb2??
13.♖b3 ♛a2 14.♗b1) 13.exd4 d6
14.0-0 h6 15.b4 e5 16.c5 dxc5 17.dxc5
♛c7 18.♛e2 ♗e6 19.♖e1 f6? 20.♛e4
(Kasparov – Timman, Brussels
1987) the world champion gained a

decisive advantage along the light
squares. Obviously, after 13...g6 the
weakening of the dark squares is less
substantial.

11.g3 ♘xc3

In the game Cheparinov – Hess
(Moscow 2011) the American
sensibly chose simplifications: 11...
♛f6 12.♛c2 ♘xc3 13.♛xc3 ♘xd4
14.♛xd4 ♛xd4 15.exd4 b6 16.♗g2
♖b8 17.♔d2 ♗b7 18.♗xb7 ♖xb7
19.b4 d6. Cheparinov only won the
rook ending due to his opponent's
errors.

**12.♖xc3 ♛e4 13.f3 ♛g6 14.♘b5
b6 15.♔f2 ♗b7 16.♘d6 ♖ab8**

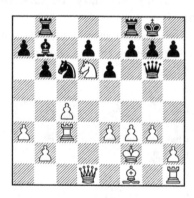

The black queen's travels have
caused virtually no damage to her
opponent's kingside, whereas the
invasion on d6 has fixed white's
advantage.

**17.♗e2 ♗a8 18.h4 ♛f6 19.g4
♘e7 20.♛d2 e5**

Instead of chasing the knight
away (20...♘c8 21.♘b5 ♗c6) Hess
continues to harass the enemy king.
Given that the latter carelessly
wanders onto the third rank, the plan
is justified.

21.♔g3?! h5 22.♖d1 ♛g6 23.e4

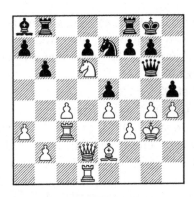

23...f5! 24.exf5 ♖xf5! A round of applause! Thanks to this rook sacrifice it's a black knight that will occupy a great central outpost.

25.♘xf5 ♘xf5+ 26.♔h3 ♘d4 27.♕e3 ♖f8 28.♖xd4 exd4 29.♕xd4 ♕b1

The queen invasion would be more effective after an exchange on g4.

30.gxh5

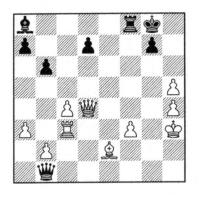

30...♖e8?

The continuation 30...♕xb2 31.♕e3 ♕a1 promised sufficient counterplay thanks to white's broken pawn structure and vulnerable king. Hess chases the bishop to its optimal square, an irreversible blunder.

31.♗d1 ♕xb2 32.h6 ♖e7 33.c5! ♕b5 34.cxb6 ♕f1+ 35.♔h2 ♖e2+

36.♗xe2 ♕xe2+ 37.♔g3 ♕e1+ 38.♔g4 ♕e6+ 39.♔g3 ♕e1+ 40.♔g4 ♕e6+ 41.♔f4 ♕xh6+ 42.♔g3

Black resigned.

By the time of the following exhibition match Short's career was already waning, while Kasparov had long retired. The players almost certainly hadn't taken a deep-dive in theory to prepare, and mostly relied on their accumulated experience.

No. 18 G. Kasparov – N. Short
Saint Louis match (rapid) 2015

1.d4 e6 2.♘f3 ♘f6 3.c4 ♗b4+ 4.♘bd2

Garry used to alternative between 4.♘bd2 and 4.♗d2, but in his last proper game when facing the Bogo-Indian Defense (also against Short) he switched to a Nimzo-Indian with 4.♘c3.

4...c5 5.a3 ♗xd2+ 6.♕xd2

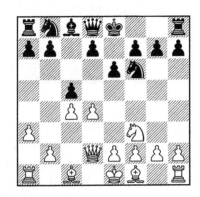

6...cxd4

LANDMINE. 6...b6? leads to the loss of a pawn due to the typical double attack 7.dxc5 bxc5 8.♕g5.

Even Boris Spassky once fell for this trick!

7.♘xd4

After 7.♕xd4 ♘c6 any queen retreat is met by the break d7-d5 (if 8.♕d6 then black first plays 8...♘e4). Here black has gained decent results. White occasionally goes for an extended fianchetto here, on the assumption that black's pawn won't make any progress. After 7.b4 a5!? 8.♗b2 axb4 9.axb4 ♖xa1+ 10.♗xa1 d5 (Werle – Timman, Amsterdam 2008) 11.c5 ♘e4 12.♕xd4 f6 13.e3 ♘c6 14.♕b2 e5 black is again fully equal.

7...0-0 8.e3

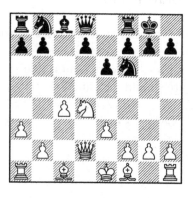

8...d5 9.cxd5

Here an extended fianchetto has been tried three times against Grandmaster Eingorn, and the third time he chose the optimal response: 9.b4 a5 10.cxd5 ♕xd5 11.b5 (this surrenders the c5 square to the knight) 11...♘bd7 12.♘f3 b6 13.♕xd5 ♘xd5 14.♘d2 ♘c5 15.♗b2 ♗d7 16.♗d4 ♖fc8 with equality (Bukal – Eingorn, Austria 1999).

9...♕xd5 10.♘b5 ♕c6!?

Black had drawn all previous games in the database with 10...♘c6, and but lost both when the queen moved to c6. Nevertheless, the move played is no worse. It's easiest to chase away the b5 knight with queens on the board than without them.

11.f3 a6 12.♘c3 e5 13.e4 ♘bd7

The knight rushes to b3, but the hole tempts not only a knight (13...♗e6!?). The choice here is a matter of taste.

14.♕f2 ♘c5 15.♗e3 ♘b3 16.♖d1 ♗e6 17.♗e2 ♖fd8 18.0-0

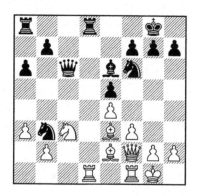

18...♘e8

Short strives to create a strong pawn chain that will imitate his opponent's. However, the plan with f3-f4 now gains momentum, and it was objectively stronger to play 18...♖xd1 19.♖xd1 ♖c8 with reasonable play without the initiative.

19.♕g3 f6 20.f4 ♘d4 21.♗h5!

With the aim of gobbling up the e5 pawn without giving up the one on e4.

21...♗c4

Interestingly, 21...♗b3 is also nicely met by the exchange sac – 22.fxe5! ♗xd1 23.♗xd1 ♔h8

24.♘d5 ♘e6 25.♗g4. Despite his age Kasparov had not lost his phenomenal sense of dynamism and would surely have played this sac.

22.fxe5! ♗xf1 23.♖xf1 ♔h8

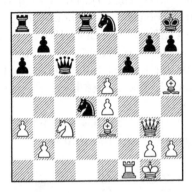

24.♘d5

It was more precise to play 24.♕f2 ♘e6 25.♘d5, as white would meet the reciprocal sac 25...♖xd5 26.exd5 ♕xd5 with the exchange 27.♗xe8 ♖xe8 and then come crashing down on f6.

24...♖xd5 25.exd5 ♕xd5 26.♕f2 fxe5 27.♕f8+

If 27.♗xd4 black saves the day with the intermezzo 27...♘f6! It's possible that from afar Kasparov had not spotted this unexpected resource (after all, they were playing a rapid game) and hence decided to deliver another surprise.

27...♕g8 28.♕e7 ♘f6 29.♖xf6!? gxf6 30.♗h6 ♘f5 31.♕xf6+ ♘g7 32.♕xe5

The pair of bishops together with the queen pin down black's army, but this is only sufficient for a draw.

32...♖c8 33.♗f3 ♕f7 34.h3 b5 35.♗e4 ♖e8 36.♕d4 ♕e7 37.b4 ♕e5 38.♕d7 ♕a1+ 39.♔h2 ♖xe4 40.♗xg7+ ♕xg7 41.♕d8+ ♕g8 42.♕f6+ ♕g7 43.♕d8+ ♕g8

Draw agreed.

Given that after 4...c5 5.a3 ♗xd2+ 6.♗xd2 playing Miezis style (6...b6) promises black a comfortable game, white should seek an advantage with 6.♕xd2. However, any advantage will be very small.

Chapter 4

4...d5 variation

Various white replies are reviewed in games 19-21, while the main continuation 5.♕a4+ is the subject of games 22-24.

No. 19 V. Potkin – V. Iordachescu
Serpukhov 2008

1.d4 ♘f6 2.c4 e6 3.♘f3 ♗b4+ 4.♘bd2 d5

This was the third game of the final match of the Russian Cup. In this position, Iordachescu castled in the first game.

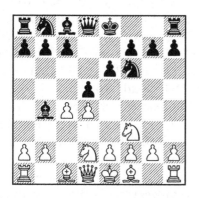

This aggressive fight back in the center may lead to a number of transpositions to other lines and openings (Catalan Opening, Queen's Indian Defense and even the Tarrasch Defense). I only highlight those that are material but unobvious.

5.a3

TRANSPOSITION ALERT 1. Reciprocal activity in the center 5.♕c2 0-0 6.a3 ♗e7 7.e4 is analyzed in games 37 and 38 via the move order 4...0-0 5.a3 ♗e7 6.e4 d5 7.♕c2 (the third most frequent move in this line).

TRANSPOSITION ALERT 2. The nature of the battle after 5.g3 dxc4 6.♗g2 is very close to the Catalan Gambit, though after 1.d4 d5 2.c4 e6 3.♘f3 ♘f6 4.g3 dxc4 5.♗g2 ♗b4+ the blocking move 6.♘bd2 is rarely played.

TRANSPOSITION ALERT 3. In reply to 5.g3 the game often continues 5...0-0 6.♗g2 b6 7.0-0 ♗b7. For this, see my book on the Queen's Indian Defense (after 1.d4 ♘f6 2.c4 e6 3.♘f3 b6 4.g3 ♗b7 5.♗g2 ♗b4+ 6.♘bd2 0-0 7.0-0 d5).

TRANSPOSITION ALERT 4. After 5.g3 0-0 6.♗g2 c5 7.dxc5 ♗xc5 8.0-0 ♘c6 we get to a position that can be reached via a number of openings. In particular, this is considered a line of the Tarrasch Defense usually reached with 1.d4 d5 2.c4 e6 3.♘f3 c5 4.g3 ♘f6 5.♗g2 ♗e7 6.dxc5 ♗xc5 7.0-0 ♘c6 8.♘bd2 0-0.

This impressive list of transpositions shouldn't deflate the reader's desire to learn the lines in this book. After reaching a certain level, a chess player needs to learn how to master transpositions. In the 2nd transposition here it is useful for him to assess whether the knight on d2 is in the right place in a sharp line of the Catalan Gambit. In positional lines, we first need to consider metamorphoses of strategic elements, above all, of pawn structures. Don't forget to count tempos, to check whether, in comparison with well-known lines, you haven't received a gift of one or gifted one to your opponent. Finally, at the other end of the board you have an opponent who may or may not be happy with the transposition (and you might know this already).

Let's return to the game.

5...♝e7

5...♝xd2+ is best met by capturing with the bishop, and then developing it to g5, and if black tries ♘f6-e4 then place the bishop on f4.

6.g3

In reply to 6.b4 black should take counteraction on the adjacent files – 6...a5!? 7.b5 c5!? In the rapid game Karpov – Kogan (Canada de Calatrava 2007) the ex-world champion played with purely positional methods: 8.bxc6 bxc6 9.e3 0-0 10.♕c2 ♘bd7 11.c5 a4?! 12.♝d3 ♕a5 13.0-0 ♝a6 14.♝xa6 ♕xa6 15.♝b2 ♖ab8 16.♝c3 ♘e8 17.♘e1 ♘c7 18.♘d3 f5 19.♖fb1 ♖xb1+ 20.♖xb1 ♘b5 21.♖b4, and black was almost completely outplayed already. The pawn on a4 is vulnerable, while the b4 square

has turned into a great outpost. Black should have played the same way but without a5-a4.

6...0-0 7.♝g2

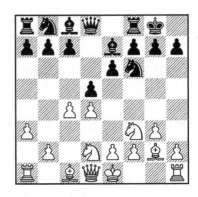

7...a5

It was perfectly acceptable to head for a position with a safely protected isolated pawn: 7...c5 8.dxc5 ♝xc5 9.0-0 a5 10.cxd5 exd5 11.♘b3 ♝b6 12.♝g5 ♘c6 13.♖c1 h6 14.♝f4 ♖e8 15.♘bd4 ♘xd4 16.♘xd4 (Laznicka – Mudrak, Czech Republic 2012) 16...♝g4 17.♖e1 ♖c8 18.♖xc8 ♕xc8. On the other hand, the blockade of the isolani would put a stop to black's efforts at activity. The move in the game prevents white from playing b2-b4 and for now leaves the situation in the center unsettled.

8.b3 ♘bd7 9.0-0 c6

This position is typical for closed systems of the Catalan, but it cannot be reached via a classical Catalan. Hanging pawns were created in the game Prusikin – Korchnoi (Fuegen 2006) after 9...c5 10.♝b2 b6 11.cxd5 exd5 12.dxc5 bxc5. Korchnoi countered the attack on his pawn pair energetically and precisely. The players' resources soon ran out:

13.e4!? dxe4 14.♘g5 ♖b8 15.♘gxe4 a4 16.♘xf6+ ♗xf6 17.♗xf6 ♘xf6 18.bxa4 ♗a6 19.♖e1 ♖b2 20.♘e4 ♘xe4 21.♕xd8 ♖xd8 22.♖xe4 g6 23.♗f1 ♗xf1 24.♔xf1 ♖c2 25.a5 ♖c3 26.♖a4 ♖d4 27.♖xd4 cxd4, draw agreed.

10.a4

Just in case, Potkin prevents the possibility of a5-a4 and b6-b5.

10...♘b8!?

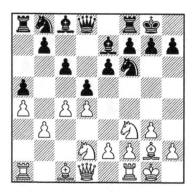

The transfer of the knight via a6 to the exposed square b4 is a feature of several closed openings, but not normally of the Bogo-Indian Defense.

11.♗b2 ♘a6 12.♘e5 ♘b4 13.e4 b6 14.♕e2 ♗a6 15.♖fd1 ♖c8 16.♖ac1 ♖e8 17.♕e3 ♘a2 18.♖a1 ♘b4 19.♖ac1 ♘a2

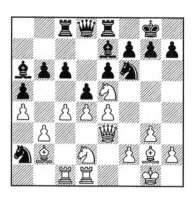

20.♖b1

The players have completed their development and their pieces are all nicely set up. Black now effectively offered a draw by move repetition. However, white wanted to continue the game.

20...♘b4 21.♗c3 ♗b7 22.♘d3 c5

This frees up not only black's pieces, but the c3 bishop as well. Therefore, the knights get swapped off.

23.♘xb4 axb4 24.♗b2 ♗f8 25.e5 ♘d7 26.♖bc1 ♖c7 27.f4

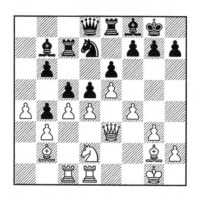

27...♘b8!?

In the heat of the battle the second knight retreats to base. It wants to develop on c6, from where it can pressurize the b4 pawn.

28.cxd5 exd5 29.h3 ♘c6 30.♔h2 ♘xd4 31.♗xd4 cxd4 32.♕xd4 ♖c5 33.♘f1 ♕c7 34.♕d2 ♖c3!

This shields the b4 and d5 pawns from nasty threats and fully equalizes.

35.♘e3 d4 36.♘d5 ♗xd5 37.♗xd5 ♖d8 38.♗c4

Draw agreed.

No. 20 A. Manea – D. Rogozenco
Mamaia 2015

1.d4 ♘f6 2.c4 e6 3.♘f3 ♗b4+
4.♘bd2 d5 5.e3 0-0

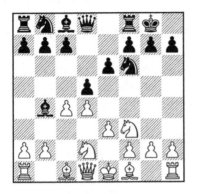

6.a3

White should not rush with mobilizing his kingside. If 6.♗d3 dxc4 7.♗xc4 c5 8.a3 ♗xd2+ 9.♕xd2 cxd4 10.♕xd4 ♕xd4 11.♘xd4 b6 black has fully equalized.

6...♗e7 7.b4

White plans to extract the maximum from 6.a3, carrying out a pawn charge on the queenside. 7.♗d3 is played in the next game.

7...b6

7...a5 8.b5 c5 9.bxc6 bxc6 is analyzed via a different move order in the notes to game 19.

8.c5

In QID-type positions pushes on the queenside after 8.cxd5 are of little effect due to the "bad" knight on d2. For example, 8...exd5 9.♕c2 ♗b7 10.♗d3 ♘bd7 11.♖b1 ♗d6 12.0-0 ♕e7 13.♘b3 ♖ab8 14.♗b2 ♘e4 15.♖fc1 c6 (Dizdar – Hulak, Pula 1999) – the knight has moved to b3, yet it is still out of the action. There

is no time to execute the typical improvement ♘d2-b1-c3 (11.♘b1?! c5).

8...a5

Rogozenco undermines the pawn chain first on the queenside, and then in the center. The blockade of light squares in the variation 8...bxc5 9.bxc5 ♘e4 10.♘xe4 dxe4 11.♘d2 ♗b7 12.♖b1 ♗d5 13.♕c2 f5 is insufficient for equality.

9.♗b2

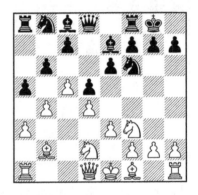

9...c6

A **historical interlude.** The position on the diagram occurred in the game Mackenzie – Tarrasch (Hamburg 1885) long before the Bogo-Indian Defense was invented. The actual move order was 1.d4 d5 2.♘f3 ♘f6 3.e3 e6 4.c4 ♗d6 (the decisive mistake according to Tarrasch!) 5.c5 ♗e7 6.b4 b6 7.♗b2 0-0 8.♘bd2 a5 9.a3, and now 9...♘fd7 (with the obvious idea e6-e5) 10.♕c2 c6 11.♗d3 axb4 12.axb4 ♖xa1+ 13.♗xa1 bxc5?! 14.dxc5 f5 15.♘d4 ♘f6 16.0-0 ♕c7 17.f4 with a dominant position. Instead of exchanging on c5, 13...h6 14.0-0 ♗a6 was stronger.

The game Simagin – Gipslis (Moscow 1964) reached the position on the diagram via the Bogo-Indian Defense. Just like the commentator, Boris Voronkov, they were unaware of the precedents that were hidden by being classified as Queen's Gambits. The game continued 9...axb4 10.axb4 ♖xa1 11.♕xa1 bxc5 12.dxc5 ♗b7 13.♗e2 ♘bd7 14.0-0 c6 15.♕a4 (15.♕a7 ♕c7 16.♖a1 ♖a8 17.♕xa8+ ♗xa8 18.♖xa8+ ♗f8 19.♗a6, is less convincing according to Simagin) 15...♕c7 16.♕c2 ♖b8 17.♖a1 ♗c8 18.♗c3 e5 19.♖a4 ♘e8 20.♕a2 ♗f6 21.♘b3 h6 22.♕a1 with pressure on two files. Rogozenco plays more in Tarrasch style, achieving the potential of the position that the classic player had missed. Still, as he told the publisher of this book, he was unaware of the classical predecessor game.

10.♗e2 ♘fd7 11.0-0 e5 12.dxe5 bxc5 13.bxc5 ♘xc5 14.♕c2

14...♗g4?!

The bishop on e2 isn't yet performing brilliantly, but given its potential black should have preferred to exchange it via ♗c8-a6 (immediately or after 14...♕c7).

15.♘g5! ♗xg5 16.♗xg4 ♗e7 17.f4 ♘ba6 18.♖f3 ♖e8?

Instead of any sensible move (18...♘c7, 18...♖b8, 18...a4...) the experienced grandmaster has left f7 without protection and turned a questionable position into a hopeless one.

19.♖h3

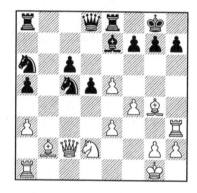

19...g6

19...h6 loses to 20.♖xh6! gxh6 21.e6 ♖f8 22.exf7+ ♖xf7 23.♕g6+ ♔f8 24.♗h5. The light-squared bishop found a role for itself!

20.f5 ♖a7 21.♖f1 ♗f8 22.e6! fxe6

After the exchange 22...♗g7 23.♗xg7 ♔xg7 white can choose whether to destroy the defense along the light squares (24.exf7 ♖xf7 25.♖xh7+) or the dark squares (24. fxg6 fxg6 25.♕c3+ ♔g8 26.♖f7).

23.fxg6 h6 24.♖f7 ♖c7 25.♗e5 ♕g5 26.♗xc7 ♕xg4 27.♖g3 ♕e2 28.g7! ♘xc7 29.♕h7+!

Black resigned.

No. 21 C. Sandipan – N. Short
Mumbai 2006

1.d4 ♘f6 2.c4 e6 3.♘f3 ♗b4+ 4.♘bd2 d5 5.a3 ♗e7 6.e3 0-0 7.♗d3

7...c5

> **TRANSPOSITION ALERT.** The main continuation 7...b6 8.0-0 ♗b7 leads to the Queen's Indian Defense (1.d4 ♘f6 2.c4 e6 3.♘f3 b6 4.e3 ♗b7 5.♗d3 ♗b4+ 6.♘bd2 0-0 7.0-0 d5 8.a3 ♗e7). Dreary play usually follows, whereas with an early conflict in the center (the move played in this game) play is more lively.

8.dxc5

Castling is found rarely. After 8.0-0 dxc4 9.♘xc4 cxd4 10.exd4 it's hard for white to gain an initiative in return for the isolani, in particular, after 10...♗d7 and 11...♗c6.

8...a5

Otherwise, white carries out the extended fianchetto with tempo and gains an advantage through simple means: 8...♗xc5 9.b4 ♗e7 10.♗b2

a5 11.b5 ♘bd7 12.0-0 ♘c5 13.♗c2 (Volodin – Miezis, Finland 2011). Now 13...♘fe4 would restrict one of the "Horwitz bishops" but after 14.♗d4 its colleague is beautifully placed.

9.cxd5

White shouldn't insist here on b2-b4, as after 9.♖b1 ♗xc5 10.b4 axb4 11.axb4 ♗e7 the pawn is vulnerable, while the a8 rook will have a decent job to do without having to leave its base. After 10.0-0 ♘c6 11.♕c2 ♕e7 12.cxd5 exd5 13.e4 h6 14.exd5 ♘xd5 15.♖e1 ♗e6 (Bogdanovich – Kuzubov, Lvov 2014) there has been nothing gained from ♖a1-b1 and the position is equal.

9...♕xd5

Short doesn't agree to an isolani, as after 9...exd5 10.♕c2 ♕c7 11.b3 ♕xc5 12.♕xc5 ♗xc5 13.♗b2 white has a stable advantage thanks to the exchange of queens.

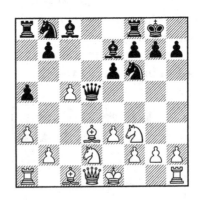

10.♗c4

In the 1980s Grandmaster Kurajica defended black's honor in this position, losing to Portisch, but holding against Timman. After 10.♕e2 ♖d8 11.♗c4 ♕xc5 12.0-0

a4 13.e4 ♕h5 14.e5 ♘fd7 15.♗b5
(Timman – Kurajica, Sarajevo 1984)
it's sensible to play the "provocation"
15...♘c6 16.♖e1 ♖a5!? 17.b4 axb3
18.♘xb3 ♖a8, and a target has
appeared in white's camp.

10...♕xc5 11.b4 ♕c7

It was also worth considering 11...
♕h5 12.b5 b6 13.♗b2 ♗b7 14.♗e2
♕g6.

12.b5 ♖d8 13.♗b2 a4

With a double aim – to separate
the white pawns and free up the a5
square for the queen.

**14.0-0 ♘bd7 15.♖c1 ♘c5
16.♕e2 b6 17.♘e5 ♗b7 18.f4 ♖f8
19.♘df3**

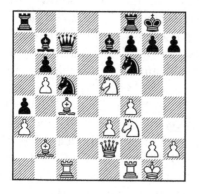

19...♘fe4?!

This direct defense to the
sortie ♘f3-g5 is unreliable. The
continuation 19...♗d6 20.♘g5 ♗xe5
21.♗xe5 ♕e7 at first glance looks
dangerous, but it allows the black
pieces to use the e4 hub at a more
convenient moment.

20.f5 ♗d5 21.♘xf7!?

Sandipan takes a tactical approach,
although the positional continuation
21.♗xd5 exd5 22.♖cd1 ♘f6 23.♘c6
is objectively stronger.

21...♖xf7 22.fxe6

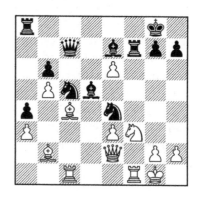

22...♗xc4

The variation 22...♖f5 23.g4 ♗xc4
24.♕xc4 ♘d6 25.♕d4 ♗f6 26.gxf5
♗xd4 27.exd4 ♘xf5 28.dxc5 would
be scary for either side without
computer help. The lack of material
compensation for the queen is made
up by the initiative.

23.♕xc4 ♖xf3 24.♖xf3 ♕d6

The "nail" on e6 is best extracted
via 24...♘g5 25.♖f5 ♘gxe6 and an
approximately equal position.

25.♖f7 ♘f6 26.♗xf6 ♗xf6

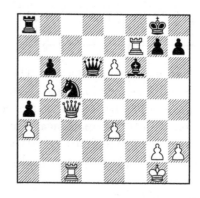

27.♖d7

The Indian grandmaster had at
his disposal a more promising line:
27.♖a7! ♖e8 28.e7+ ♕e6 (28...♘e6?

29.♕c8!) 29.♕xe6+ ♘xe6 30.♖c6 ♘c5 31.♖xb6, and although 31...♗xe7 liquidates the pawn it leaves white with an advantage. Compared with the actual game the advantage of retaining the extra rook pair is obvious.

27...♕xe6   28.♕xe6+   ♘xe6 29.♖d6 ♘c5 30.♖xb6 ♗g5 31.♖c3 ♖e8 32.♖c6 ♖xe3 33.♖xe3

Draw agreed.

No. 22 E. Najer – V. Shinkevich
Sochi 2018

1.d4 ♘f6 2.c4 e6 3.♘f3 ♗b4+ 4.♘bd2 d5 5.♕a4+

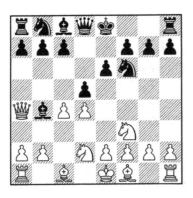

The main continuation, whose authorship is ascribed to Tigran Petrosian, though in fact it was played earlier, notably by Capablanca. White lures the enemy knight to c6 and then attempts to exploit the drawbacks of its position.

5...♘c6 6.♘e5

White usually plays here 6.a3 (games 23 and 24), but less frequently 6.e3 (which normally transposes into 6.a3 lines).

6...♗d7

7.♘xd7

A historical interlude. Ever since the game Petrov – Keres (Munich 1936) it has been known that the exchange 7.♘xc6?! leads to a worse position for white due to his lag in development despite the advantage of the bishop pair: 7...♗xd2+ 8.♗xd2 ♗xc6 9.♕c2 dxc4 10.♕xc4 ♘e4 11.♗f4 ♕f6 12.♗e3 ♘d6 13.♕c3, and now 13...0-0-0! 14.♕a5 ♘c4 15.♕xa7 ♘xe3 16.fxe3 ♕h4+ 17.♔d2 e5! with a nasty initiative. Note that the game began with the Vienna Variation of the Queen's Gambit – 1.d4 e6 2.♘f3 ♘f6 3.c4 d5 4.♗g5 ♗b4+ 5.♘bd2?! (a third-rate move) 5...dxc4 6.♕a4+ ♘c6 7.♘e5 ♗d7 8.♘xc6 ♗xd2+ 9.♗xd2 ♗xc6 10.♕xc4 and so on.

7...♕xd7

If 7...♘xd7 black maintains equality in a quiet game after 8.e3 ♘b6 9.♕c2 dxc4 10.♗xc4 ♘xc4 11.♕xc4 ♕d5 12.♕xd5 exd5 or in more exciting play after 8...♕g5!?

8.e3

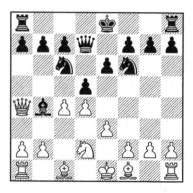

8...0-0

It would be interesting to learn what Najer planned in response to 8...e5!? (which was once tried in a club-level game). The computer doesn't really like white's position after 9.dxe5 ♘e4 10.♕c2 ♘xe5 11.a3 ♗xd2+ 12.♗xd2 0-0-0, and, given black's better development, a human should not argue against this assessment.

A simplifying strategy is also fine: 8...♘e4 9.♕c2 ♘xd2 10.♗xd2 ♗xd2+ 11.♕xd2 0-0 12.b4 ♖ad8 13.♖d1 a6 14.a4 dxc4 15.♗xc4 (Fridman – Heinz, Nuremberg 2006). Now we return to the central break: 15...e5! 16.0-0 exd4 17.♕b2 ♕g4 18.♗e2 ♕h4 19.b5 axb5 20.axb5 ♘e7 21.g3 ♕f6 22.♖xd4 ♖xd4 23.♕xd4 ♕xd4 24.exd4 ♖d8 – white has won back the pawn, but he won't get more than a draw out of this game.

9.a3 ♗xd2+ 10.♗xd2 ♘e4 11.♖d1

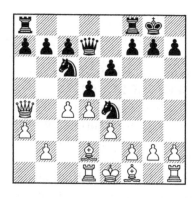

11...e5

This was not the best way to play the break, as white manages to close the position. Moving either rook to d8 was more accurate.

12.cxd5 ♕xd5 13.♗c4 ♕d6 14.d5 ♘e7 15.♗b4 ♘c5 16.♕c2 a5 17.♗c3

The exchange on c5 is unlikely to be stronger, as the light-squared bishop is inferior to the knight.

17...♘d7 18.0-0 f5 19.b4 a4?

Beginning an exchange of errors. Black should have played 19...b6, retaining pressure over b4.

20.f3?

If 20.b5! b6 21.♗b4 ♘c5 22.♖c1 black cannot avoid losing a pawn.

20...♔h8 21.♗a2 ♕b6 22.♔h1

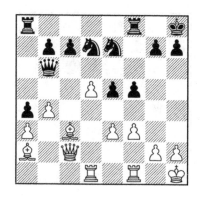

22...♕xe3?

He should have called Najer's bluff, leaving the pawn alone and choosing 22...♘g6 23.f4 ♕d6, maintaining pressure over e5 with all his might.

23.f4! ♘f6 24.♖f3!

The best continuation. The rook is improved and additionally protects the bishop.

24...♕e4 25.♕b2?!

Najer doesn't play this game with consistency, alternating great moves with poor ones. After 25.♕d2! ♖ad8 26.♗xe5 ♘exd5 27.♖d3 c6 28.♖d4 the queen perishes, trapped among the white pieces.

25...♘exd5?

Shinkevich has played this game badly. At the very end he chose the wrong knight – 25...♘fxd5 26.♗xe5 ♘f6 avoided an immediate defeat.

26.fxe5 ♘xc3 27.exf6
Black resigned.

No. 23 D. Rogozenco – L. Nisipeanu
Germany 2015

1.d4 ♘f6 2.c4 e6 3.♘f3 ♗b4+ 4.♘bd2 d5 5.♕a4+ ♘c6

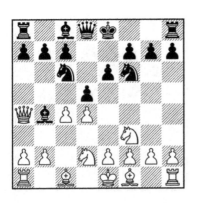

6.a3 ♗xd2+

In about half of games black makes this capture, and in the other half he retreats his bishop to e7.

7.♗xd2 ♘e4

If 7...0-0, then 8.♗g5 is good, exchanging the bishop and creating a dark-squared pawn chain. Black could continue 8...h6 9.♗xf6 ♕xf6 10.e3 dxc4 11.♕xc4 ♗d7 12.♗e2 ♖ac8 13.♖d1 ♖fd8 14.♕c5 with a stable advantage (Volodin – Tominga, Tallinn 2016).

8.♖d1

After 8.♗f4 the game Ivanchuk – Short (Galeta 2011) turned out to be very exciting: 8...g5!? 9.♗e3 f5 10.g3! 0-0 11.♖d1 ♔h8 12.♗g2 f4 13.♗c1 g4 14.cxd5 exd5 15.♘e5! f3 (15...fxg3 16.hxg3 ♘xf2 17.♗f4! guarantees a powerful initiative after all captures) 16.exf3 gxf3 17.♗xf3! ♘xe5 18.dxe5 ♘c5 (18...♖xf3? 19.♕xe4 dxe4 20.♖xd8+ ♔g7 21.♗g5) 19.♕d4 ♖xf3 20.♕xc5 c6 21.0-0, and white gradually converted his extra pawn. Instead of the risky 8...g5 castling is safer. The move in the game is more precise than 8.e3 ♘xd2 9.♘xd2, and the knight has to return to f3.

8...0-0

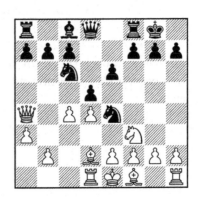

9.e3

9.g3 doesn't cramp the bishop, however, after 9...♘d6 10.c5 ♘f5 the white bishops are passive in this closed position.

9...♗d7

An expert in this system Bojan Kurajica has tried here 9...♘d6 with the idea of forcing white to settle the center. After 10.♕c2 ♘xc4 11.♗xc4 dxc4 12.♕xc4 ♕d5 13.♖c1 ♖d8 14.h3 ♗d7 15.0-0 ♗e8 16.♕e2 f6 17.♖c5 ♕b3 18.♗c3 ♖d5 19.♖xd5 exd5 black had no problems (Jovanic – Kurajica, Sarajevo 2006).

10.♕c2 ♗e8

Sometimes black continues 10...a5 (intending a5-a4) or 10...f5, but the bishop move is the most flexible one.

11.♗d3

This forces f7-f5, whereas after 11.♗e2 black can play 11...f6. In the game Schiendorfer – Korchnoi (Switzerland 2010) the position remained about equal: 12.0-0 ♗g6 13.♕b3 ♖b8 14.♘h4 ♗f7 15.cxd5 exd5 16.♘f5 ♕d7 17.♘g3 ♘xd2 18.♖xd2 ♘e7 19.♖c1 c6 20.♕d1 ♘c8 21.♗d3 ♘d6, although Korchnoi eventually won due to his superior ability.

In the game Dreev – Safarli (Wijk aan Zee 2016) white attacked on the queenside but could not choose a square for his bishop. This led to equality and a quick draw: 11.b4 a6 12.♖c1 f5 13.b5 ♘xd2 14.♕xd2 axb5 15.cxb5 ♘e7 16.♖c3 c6 17.bxc6 ♘xc6 18.♗e2 ♘a5 19.♕b2 b5 20.♗xb5 ♕b6 21.a4 ♘c4 22.♕c1 ♗xb5 23.axb5 ♕xb5.

11...f5 12.cxd5 exd5

13.♘e5?!

This change in structure is not to white's advantage. He should have begun with 13.♖c1 and then continued depending on black's plans. White can no longer claim any opening advantage.

13...♘xe5 14.dxe5 ♗h5 15.♖c1 ♕g5 16.♔f1 ♘xd2+ 17.♕xd2 f4! 18.exf4 ♖xf4 19.g3

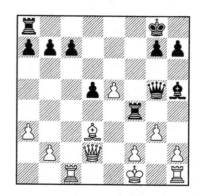

19...♖xf2+! 20.♕xf2 ♖f8?!

Nisipeanu misses the strongest continuation 20...♕xc1+ 21.♔g2 ♕c6 22.♖f1 ♖e8, where white has no compensation for the pawn.

21.♗xh7+! ♔xh7 22.♕xf8 ♕xc1+ 23.♔g2 ♕c2+ 24.♔h3??

As compensation for the exchange, black has a great position and only he can win after 24.♔f1? ♝e2+! 25.♔g1 ♝d3! (protecting the king from checks along the b1-h7 diagonal). However, after 24.♔g1! ♕e4 25.♔f2! it's hard for black to strengthen his position.

24...♕e4 25.♖g1 ♝g4+ 26.♔h4 ♕g6

White resigned.

No. 24 S. Drygalov – S. Bogdanovich
Moscow 2019

1.d4 ♘f6 2.c4 e6 3.♘f3 ♝b4+ 4.♘bd2 d5 5.♕a4+ ♘c6 6.a3 ♝e7

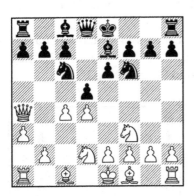

7.e3

The sortie 7.♘e5 (with the aim of gaining the advantage of the bishop pair) is stronger here than on move six, but 7...♝d7 8.♘xd7 ♕xd7 promises black easy development and the possibility to play the standard break e6-e5.

If 7.g3 0-0 8.♝g2 then 8...a5!? is good, and the queen will have to cede the square to the rook's pawn. For example, 9.0-0 ♝d7 10.♕c2 a4

11.cxd5 exd5 12.b4 axb3 13.♘xb3 ♖e8 14.♘e5 ♝d6 15.♘xd7 ♕xd7 16.e3 (S. Ernst – Janssen, Boxtel 2011) 16...♕e7 17.a4 ♘b4 18.♕b1 c6 and black's army stands somewhat better.

7...0-0

Here 7...a5 can be met by the promising 8.b4 (which would be no good with the bishop on g2 because of d5xc4 with d4 hanging). If 8...0-0 9.c5 ♘b8 10.♝d3 c6 (Jakovenko – Nisipeanu, Foros 2008) the occupied territory works to white's advantage after 11.♘b3!? b5 12.cxb6 ♝a6 13.b7! (but not 13.♝xa6?! axb4!) 13...♖a7 14.♘e5! axb4 15.axb4.

8.♕c2

When evaluating the move 8.b4 we should trust the judgement of Predrag Nikolic. The attack on the queenside is slightly premature: 8...♝d7 9.♕c2 a5 10.b5 ♘a7 11.♖b1 dxc4 12.♝xc4 c6 13.b6 ♘b5 14.a4 ♘a3 15.♝xa3 ♝xa3, and 16.e4?! only provoked black's bishops – 16...c5 17.dxc5 ♖c8 18.0-0 ♝xc5 (Dinstuhl – Nikolic, Germany 2013).

Nikolic found himself countering a pawn storm in an earlier game as well: 8.♝d3 a5 9.b4 dxc4 10.♝xc4 ♝d7 11.b5 ♘a7 12.♘e5 ♝e8 13.0-0 ♘d5 14.♕b3 (because of the threat of 14...♘b6 the queen has to evacuate from a4) 14...a4 15.♕b2 ♘c8 16.♘e4 ♘d6 17.♝d3 f6 18.♘xd6 cxd6 19.♘c4 f5 20.♝d2 (Von Herman – Nikolic, Germany 2012). Black looks solid, but has no counterplay, so it was worth considering 13...c6 (like in the game with Dinstuhl).

8...a5 9.b3

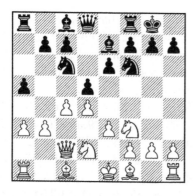

9...♘b8

Thanks to the closed nature of the position, black can spend tempi on improving his knight without being punished for it. He could also switch to a Dutch structure: 9...♘e8 10.♗d3 f5 11.♗b2 ♗d7 12.♘b1 ♘f6 13.cxd5 exd5 14.♗xf5 ♗xf5 15.♕xf5 ♘e4 16.♕e6+ (16.♕g4!?) 16...♔h8 17.♘c3 (Mareco – Delgado Ramirez, Sao Paulo 2015) 17...♘b4 18.axb4 ♗xb4 19.♖c1 ♖a6 20.♕g4 ♖g6 21.♕h3 ♖h6 and a repetition of moves. The sacrifice of the f5 pawn is sometimes seen in the Dutch Defense; white should seek improvements in this line both before and after the sacrifice.

10.♗b2 b6 11.♗d3 ♗b7 12.0-0 ♘bd7 13.♘e5 h6 14.cxd5 ♘xe5 15.dxe5 ♘xd5

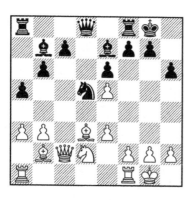

16.♘e4

The players were probably aware of a predecessor game Wojtaszek – Granda (Tromso 2014). After 16.♖ad1 ♕d7 17.♘e4 ♖fd8 18.♕e2 ♕e8 19.♕g4 ♕f8 20.♘f6+ ♔h8 21.♕e4 ♘xf6 22.exf6 (22.♕xb7 ♘d7 23.♕e4 ♕g8 24.♕c6 ♖ac8 25.♗b5 ♘b8 26.♕b7 ♕f8 doesn't leave white any evident targets) 22...♗xe4 23.fxg7+ ♕xg7 24.♗xg7+ ♔xg7 25.♗xe4 ♖xd1 26.♖xd1 ♖d8 27.♖xd8 ♗xd8 the total simplifications led to a draw.

16...a4! 17.bxa4 ♖a5 18.♘g3 ♕a8 19.♘h5 ♖d8

If 19...♖xa4!? 20.e4 the knight has nowhere to retreat, but it may be sacrificed – 20...♗c5 21.exd5 ♗xd5 22.♖fe1 ♗xg2 23.♘g3 ♖f4 24.♗e4 ♗xe4 25.♘xe4 ♖g4+ 26.♘g3 ♖f4 with an initiative sufficient for a draw.

20.♖ad1 ♖c5 21.♕b3 ♕a5!?

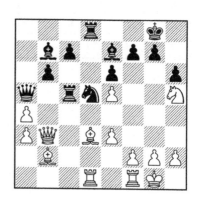

22.♗b5

Bogdanovich is not afraid of losing the exchange: 22.♗d4 ♘c3 23.♗xc5 ♕xc5 24.♖d2 ♕xe5 25.♘g3 ♖a8 with a powerful bishop pair and obvious compensation for the material.

22...♘c3   23.♖xd8+   ♗xd8 24.♗c4?!

Now the slight complications prove to be to black's advantage. Although exchanging on c3 would also have left him a small advantage.

24...♕xa4 25.♗xe6 ♕e4?

The right continuation was 25...♕xb3 26.♗xb3 ♘e2+ 27.♔h1 ♖b5 28.♖e1 ♖xb3 29.♖xe2 c5, and it's not easy for white to draw this ending.

26.♗xf7+   ♔f8   27.f3   ♕xe3+ 28.♔h1   ♕xe5   29.♗c4   ♕xh5 30.♗xc3 ♗e7 31.♗b4 ♗d6 32.g3 ♗xg3 33.♗xc5+ bxc5 34.♖f2 ♗xf2 35.♕xb7

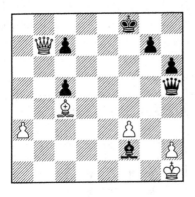

The players have played the last ten moves inventively and skillfully. The rest of the game is less interesting, as the opposite-colored bishops are set to deliver a draw.

35...♕e5 36.♕b1 ♔e7 37.♕f1 ♕c3 38.♔g2 ♗e3 39.a4 ♔f6 40.♕d3 ♕xd3 41.♗xd3 ♗d2 42.♔f2 ♔e5 43.♔e2 ♗a5 44.h4 ♔d4 45.♗c2 ♔c3 46.♔d1 ♔b2 47.h5 c4 48.♗e4 c3 49.♗c2 c5 50.♗e4 ♔b3 51.♗c2+ ♔b4 52.♔e2 ♔a3 53.♔d1 ♔b2 54.♗e4 ♔b3 55.♗c2+ ♔c4 56.g6 ♔d4 57.♔c2 c4 58.♗f7 ♔e5 59.♗g6 ♔f4 60.♗e4 ♔e3

Draw agreed.

I'm not sure that it's best for white to select 5.♕a4+ ♘c6 as the main continuation. In this line, centralizing the knight on e5 is not recommended, but after 6.a3 ♗e7 the queen will be chased from a4 with accurate play. The charge on the queenside is more attractive with the move order 5.a3 ♗e7 6.e3 0-0 7.b4 (game 20).

Chapter 5

4...0-0 variation

Black makes a useful move in castling, postponing his choice of pawn setup for another move. 5.g3 is the subject of games 25-27, 5.e3 is analyzed in games 28-31, and 5.a3 is covered in games 32-40.

No. 25 B. Socko – N. Miezis
Sweden 2019

1.d4 ♘f6 2.c4 e6 3.♘f3 ♗b4+ 4.♘bd2 0-0

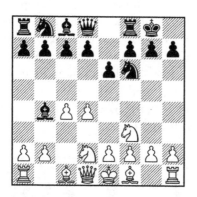

5.g3 d5

The continuation 5...b6 6.♗g2 ♗b7 is covered in my book on the Queen's Indian Defense via the move order 3...b6 4.g3 ♗b7 5.♗g2 ♗b4+ 6.♘bd2 0-0. After 5...d5 the game merges into a Catalan with the relatively rare position of the knight on d2.

If 5...c5 6.a3 ♗xd2+ 7.♕xd2 cxd4 there is an important nuance to note. After 8.♘xd4 d5 9.cxd5 ♕xd5 10.♘f3 the white queen looks clumsy, while black has the interesting alternatives 10...♕b5!? and 10...♕c4!? It's hence more precise to play 8.♗g2 d5 9.cxd5 ♕xd5 10.♕xd4, and black has to

agree to an exchange of queens in a slightly worse position.

6.♗g2

If 6.♕c2, then 6...c5, and white has to ramp up his vigilance – neither 7.♗g2?! cxd4 8.♘xd4 e5 9.♘4b3 ♕c7, nor 9.♘b5 d4 are attractive. After 7.dxc5 e5!? white must avoid 8.♘xe5?! ♖e8 9.♘ef3 d4 10.♕d1 (10.♕b1 ♘e4!) 10...♗f5 11.a3 ♘a6 12.♗g2 (Naumkin – Lomasov, Moscow 2017), and now black would have won with 12...♗c2! 13.♕xc2 d3.

6...c5

Here, attacking d4 is not the main line. 6...b6 again leads to the Queen's Indian Defense, while 6...dxc4 is analyzed in games 26 and 27.

7.cxd5

It makes sense to castle and thereby relieve the knight's pin prior to resolving the tension in the center. After 7.0-0 cxd4 8.♘xd4 ♘c6 (8...e5?! 9.♘c2 ♗xd2 10.♗xd2 dxc4 11.♗b4 provokes the bishops in an open position) 9.♘2f3 ♘xd4 10.♛xd4 b6 11.♗g5 ♗e7 12.cxd5 white has a more pleasant position in his battle against the isolani (12...exd5), as well as after 12...♘xd5 13.♗xe7 ♛xe7 14.♖fd1 ♗b7 15.♖ac1.

7...exd5

After 7...♛xd5 white should probably maintain a minimal advantage via 8.a3 ♗xd2+ 9.♛xd2. If 8.0-0 cxd4 9.♘b3 d3 10.exd3 ♛d8 (as Grandmaster Harikrishna has played as black) problems with the "Catalan" bishop on c8 are balanced by the odd pawn on d3.

8.a3

> **TRANSPOSITION ALERT.** After 8.0-0 ♘c6 9.dxc5 ♗xc5 we have reached a main line of the Tarrasch Defense – 1.d4 d5 2.c4 e6 3.♘f3 c5 4.cxd5 exd5 5.g3 ♘c6 6.♗g2 ♘f6 7.0-0 ♗e7 8.dxc5 ♗xc5 9.♘bd2 0-0 (similar to transposition 4 in the notes to game 19).

8...♗xd2+ 9.♗xd2

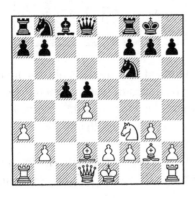

9...cxd4

The sad statistics with 9...c4 shouldn't frighten black. In the Tarrasch Defense (whose structure is now on the board) this is a standard advance. The addition of a2-a3 is not to white's advantage, and he would need to aim to open the position via b2-b3 (before black occupies the hole on b3).

10.♘xd4 ♘c6

After 10...♛b6 11.♗e3 ♛xb2 12.0-0 ♘c6 13.♘xc6 bxc6 14.♗d4 ♛b7 15.♗xf6 gxf6 16.e4 white has a decent initiative for the pawn, although black should hold on. 11.♗c3 ♘e4 12.0-0 ♘xc3 13.bxc3 is also to white's advantage – the maneuver ♖a1-b1-b5 should give the d5 pawn a red card.

11.♘xc6 bxc6 12.♖c1 ♗d7 13.0-0 ♖e8 14.♗e3

Black has not managed to convert his duet with a backward pawn into a hanging pair, and so he lacks full equality. Now, Miezis makes the mistake of waiting with a7-a5-a4, and white's advantage hence grows.

14...♛e7 15.♖e1 h5 16.♛d4 ♘e4 17.♗f4 a5

Given that black has pushed h7-h5, he should now consider pushing the pawn further – h5-h4-h3.

18.h4 a4 19.f3 ♘d6 20.e4 ♘b5 21.♕b6 ♕d8

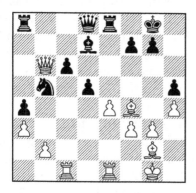

22.♕c5

How can white avoid frittering away the advantage that he has earned? Maybe he should not have left his queen in the enemy camp, and instead withdrawn her to f2?

22...dxe4 23.♖ed1 ♕c8 24.fxe4 ♗g4 25.♖d2 ♖d8 26.♕xc6 ♕xc6 27.♖xd8+

Now black sends his rook into enemy lines, and, attacking b2, it basically equalizes the position. 27.♖xc6 ♖xd2?! 28.♗xd2 ♖d8 29.♗b4 would look similar to the moves in the game, but would actually favor white. However, black should instead go for 27...♘d4 28.♖d6 ♖xd6 29.♗xd6 ♘f3+ 30.♗xf3 ♗xf3 and the opposite-colored bishops would lead to a draw.

27...♖xd8 28.♖xc6 ♖d1+ 29.♔f2 ♖b1 30.♖c2 ♘d4 31.♖d2 ♘b3 32.♖d8+ ♔h7 33.♗e5 ♖c1 34.♗f1 ♘c5 35.♖d4 ♖c2+ 36.♔e3 ♖xb2 37.♗c4 f6 38.♗f4 ♖c2 39.e5 ♖c3+

40.♔d2 ♖xa3 41.exf6 gxf6 42.♗d6 ♘b3+ 43.♗xb3 ♖xb3 44.♖xa4

Draw agreed.

No. 26 F. Caruana – A. Naiditsch
Baden Baden 2019

1.d4 ♘f6 2.c4 e6 3.g3 d5 4.♗g2 ♗b4+ 5.♘d2 0-0 6.♘gf3

White doesn't have to offer a gambit even with the moves ♘b1-d2 (instead of ♗c1-d2) in a Catalan move order. However, 6.♕c2 should be met by the obvious 6...c5, all the more so as the knight on g1 has not yet taken up its role of protecting d4.

6...dxc4

We begin our excursion into the Catalan Gambit over two games.

7.0-0

In the following game we review 7.♕c2.

7...b5

Obviously, white has to prepare against 7...c3 8.bxc3 ♗xc3 9.♖b1 when black gains a second pawn. White has clear compensation, though – 9...♗xd4 10.♗a3 ♖e8 11.♘c4 ♗b6 12.♕c2 ♘fd7 (freeing up the square for the queen) 13.♖fd1

♛f6 14.♝b2 ♛g6 (Tari – Antipov, Puna 2014) 15.e4 f6 16.♘xb6 cxb6 17.♛e2, and then e4-e5. To suffer so much in a dangerous position for just one pawn (if black rejects 9...♝xd4) doesn't suit everybody.

8.a4 c6

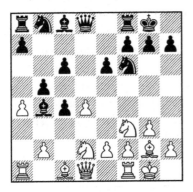

9.b3

Caruana played this move twice in 2009-10 and now reverted to it a decade later. Direct play against the king in game three of a friendly match Ivanchuk – Hou Yifan (Shenzhen 2017) led to perpetual check – 9.axb5 cxb5 10.♘g5 ♘d5 11.e4 ♘e7 12.e5 ♘d5 13.♘xh7 ♚xh7 14.♛h5+ ♚g8 15.♘e4 f6 16.♘xf6+ gxf6 17.♛g6+ ♚h8 18.♛h5+ ♚g8. As he was leading in the match Ivanchuk chose not to torture his Chinese opponent and try, for example, 13.♘de4!? Note that black should have retreated her knight to c7, thereby not blocking the d8-h4 diagonal.

An attack on b5 with 9.♘e5 takes that square away from white's pawn, while the knight risks getting exchanged on d7 as well as attacked from f7-f6. If 9.♘e1 ♘d5 10.e4 ♘b6 11.a5 ♘6d7 12.e5 ♝xa5 13.♘e4

♝b4 14.♛h5 ♝e7 15.♘f3 (Janik – Jarmula, Lviv 2019) white is at the door of the enemy king at the cost of a second pawn (which the computer assesses as 0.0).

If white postpones the break by one move with 9.♛c2 ♝b7 10.b3 black is not forced to capture on b3 (though we can count that as a small moral victory for white). Via 10... c3 he returns to the variation in the analyzed game.

9...c3 10.♘b1 ♝b7 11.♛c2 c5

11...♘bd7 12.♘xc3 ♜c8 from the game Caruana – Almasi (Reggio Emilia 2009) has not since been tried – probably due to 13.♘e5 ♛b6 14.♘xd7 ♘xd7 15.♜d1 c5 16.♝xb7 ♛xb7 17.♛e4! ♛xe4 18.♘xe4 with a comfortable ending. 11...bxa4 12.♜xa4 c5 13.♘xc3 a5 from the games Kveinys – Gelfand (Dresden 2008) and Caruana – Gelfand (Amsterdam 2010) has earned a decent reputation, but Fabiano must have prepared something new here.

12.♘xc3

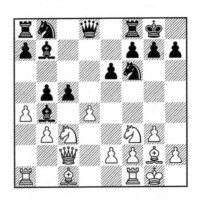

12...cxd4

The game Landa – Movsesian (Czech Republic 2015) continued

12...bxa4 13.dxc5 axb3 14.♕xb3 a5 15.♗f4 ♘bd7 16.♗d6 ♖e8 17.♖fd1 ♕c8, and it was time for white to simplify with 18.c6 ♗xc6 19.♗xb4 axb4 20.♕xb4. Naiditsch however follows a different plan, one which failed to do itself justice.

13.♘xb5 ♘c6 14.♕c4 ♕e7 15.♘bxd4 ♘a5 16.♕b5 ♖fd8 17.♗f4 ♗c3?

Now black will find himself a pawn down without compensation. The clumsy position of white's queen would have been highlighted by the temporary piece sac 17...♘xb3! 18.♘xb3 ♖d5 19.♘c5 (19.♕c4?! ♖c8) 19...♗xc5 20.♕b3 ♖dd8 with an equal position.

18.♖ac1 a6 19.♕e5 ♗xf3 20.♗xf3 ♗xd4 21.♕xa5 ♘d5 22.♗c7 ♖d7 23.e3 ♕f6 24.♗xd5 ♖xd5 25.♕b4 ♗b2 26.♖c2 h5 27.♕b7 ♖f8 28.♕xa6 h4 29.♕c4 h3 30.♕g4 ♖d3 31.b4 ♖b3 32.♕xh3 ♖a8 33.b5

Black resigned.

No. 27 Yu Yangyi – S. Ganguly
China 2018

1.d4 ♘f6 2.c4 e6 3.g3 d5 4.♗g2 ♗b4+ 5.♘d2 0-0 6.♘gf3 dxc4 7.♕c2

7...b5

This is far more interesting than 7...c5 with the approximate line 8.dxc5 c3 9.bxc3 ♗xc5 10.♘b3 ♗e7 11.0-0 ♘c6 12.♘fd4 ♗d7 13.♘xc6 ♗xc6 14.♗xc6 bxc6 – white is ready to continue to squeeze water from stone for a long time to come.

There have been a lot of games with 7...♘c6 8.♕xc4 ♕d5 9.0-0 ♗xd2 10.♕xd5 exd5 11.♗xd2 (and then 11...♗g4 or 11...♖e8). However, this line isn't exciting either, with few opportunities for white and virtually none for black.

These boring lines are losing adherents, whereas the move 7...a5 has become more popular. Black starts to uncoil after 8.♕xc4 b6 (9.a3 ♗e7 10.♘e5 ♖a7 with the idea of c7-c5), while after 8.0-0 b5 the opportunity to move his rook from a8 is also to his advantage. Another trendy variation is for white to play a pawn down along the lines of Shevchenko – Beliavsky (Kiev 2017): 8.a3!? ♗xd2+ 9.♗xd2 b5 10.a4 c6 11.e4 ♘a6 12.axb5 cxb5 13.e5 ♘d5 14.♘g5 g6 15.0-0 ♖a7 16.♘e4 ♘ab4 17.♕d1 – white plans the attack b2-b3, an invasion on d6 or aggression on the kingside. Direct action against the black king with 11.h4!? has been tried, but without any clear assessment.

8.a4 ♗b7

LANDMINE. After 8...c6?! 9.axb5 cxb5? 10.♘g5 the black knight is overworked and cannot block the long diagonal. The strong Hungarian chess master Schneider once fell for this trap.

The capture 8...bxa4 voluntarily breaks up the pawn chain, and white is guaranteed a small advantage. For example, 9.0-0 ♗b7 10.♘xc4 ♘bd7 11.♘ce5 ♗e4 12.♕xa4 a5 13.♘c6 ♕e8 14.♘fe5 ♘xe5 15.♘xe5 (15.dxe5!?) 15...♗xg2 16.♔xg2 c5 17.dxc5 ♗xc5 18.♗g5 ♘d5 19.♘d3 ♗b6 20.♖fc1 (Ni Hua – Wang Yi Ye, China 2016).

9.axb5

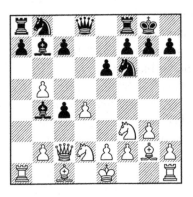

9...a6

It is worth considering 9...♕d5 10.0-0 ♕xb5 11.♕xc4 a6, so that after the exchange of queens black can at least formally connect his dispersed pawns in a chain. Black is close to equality here.

10.bxa6 ♖xa6 11.♖xa6 ♗xa6 12.0-0 ♘c6

White has completed his development and clearly stands better. An earlier game went 12...♕d5 13.e4 ♕h5 14.e5 ♗xd2 15.♗xd2 c3 16.bxc3 ♗xf1 17.♔xf1 ♘fd7 18.♘g5 (Baryshpolets – Jedynak, Krakow 2013) with more than enough compensation for the exchange.

13.♖d1

White does not have to give up the central pawn: 13.♕a4 ♗b7 14.♘xc4

was a more convincing continuation.

13...♘xd4   14.♘xd4   ♕xd4 15.♘e4 ♕b6?!

After 15...♕e5 16.♘xf6+ gxf6 the pawn structure deformation is forced (16...♕xf6? 17.♕a4), but at least the black queen is close to her king.

16.♘xf6+ gxf6

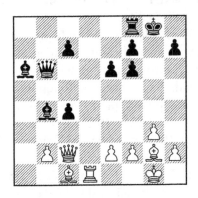

17.♗h6?!

The Chinese grandmaster lets the lion's share of his advantage slip away. The right continuation was 17.♕e4! ♗e7 18.♕g4+ ♔h8 19.♗h6 ♖g8 20.♕h5 ♖g6 21.♖d7 with a forced transition (after 21...♕b5) to a very tough ending.

17...♖b8?

On move 23 it transpires that the rook is vulnerable here and black should have moved it to c8.

18.♕e4 ♗f8 19.♕g4+ ♔h8 20.♕h4 ♕xb2 21.♗e4 ♗xh6 22.♕xh6 f5 23.♖b1 ♕xb1+ 24.♗xb1 ♖xb1+ 25.♔g2 ♖b8 26.♔f3!

The white king embarks on a hostile visit to his counterparty. Without His Majesty's intervention white cannot win the game!

26...♔g8 27.♕f6 ♖b3+ 28.♔f4 c3 29.♔g5 ♔f8 30.♕d8+ ♔g7

31.♕d4+ e5 32.♕xe5+ ♔f8 33.♕xc7
♔g7 34.♕e5+ ♔g8 35.♕e8+ ♔g7
36.♕c6 ♗b7 37.♕f6+ ♔f8 38.♕d8+
♔g7 39.♕d4+

Black resigned.

No. 28 T. Likavsky – B. Jobava
Austria 2012

1.d4 ♘f6 2.c4 e6 3.♘f3 ♗b4+
4.♘bd2 b6 5.e3

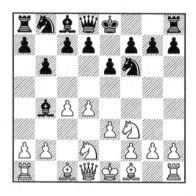

White makes kingside
mobilization his priority. A logical
and popular plan.

5...0-0 6.♗d3

Developing the bishop on e2
doesn't help in challenging for e4, and
it seems to have no merits. The game
could continue 6.♗e2 ♗b7 7.0-0 ♗e7
8.b3 c5 9.♗b2 cxd4 (9...♘c6) 10.♘xd4
♘c6 11.♘xc6 ♗xc6 12.♖c1 ♕c7 13.e4
♕b7 14.e5 ♘e4 15.♘f3 ♘g5 16.♖c3
♘xf3+ 17.♗xf3 ♖fd8 18.♕e2 (Miles
– Andersson, Linares 1983). After 18...
d5 19.exd6 ♖xd6 the bishop on b2 has
improved, and with it white's overall
position, albeit only slightly. The
continuation 18...a6 and then b6-b5
would have retained equality.

6...♗b7

TRANSPOSITION ALERT. This
position also arises in the Queen's
Indian Defense via the move order
3...b6 4.e3 ♗b7 5.♗d3 ♗b4+
6.♘bd2 0-0. There are two reasons
to review several games. The move
5...♗b4+ is not in the top three by
popularity, while I didn't cover
the 4.e3 system in my book on the
Queen's Indian Defense.

7.0-0

7...c5

7...d5 is analyzed in games 29-31.
The exchange 7...♗xd2 has also been
played with the idea of planting
the knight on e4 and transposing
to Dutch structures. White faces
a choice – to tackle the knight via
8.♗xd2 ♘e4 9.♗b4!? d6 10.♘d2
or to prevent its appearance on that
square by playing 8.♘xd2, as first
played by Bogoljubov himself (the
position had risen via a QID move
order). The game could continue
8...d6 9.b3 e5 10.♗b2 ♘bd7 11.♕c2
♕e7 12.♗f5 ♖fe8 13.♖ae1 c5 14.d5
b5 15.e4 bxc4 16.bxc4 a5 17.g3 a4
18.f4 ♖a6 19.♘f3 ♗c8 20.♕c3
(Vidit – Pountzas, Vrachati

2013), when black was devoid of counterplay.

8.a3

After 8.dxc5 ♗xc5 9.a3 d5 10.b4 ♗e7 11.♗b2 ♘bd7 we reach a position from the game Smith – Efimenko (Rogaska Slatina 2011) arrived at via the Queen's Indian Defense (3...b6 4.a3 ♗a6 5.e3 d5 6.♘bd2 c5 7.dxc5 ♗xc5 8.b4 ♗e7 9.♗b2 0-0 10.♗d3 ♘bd7 11.0-0 ♗b7). Black has no problems, and, due to the premature centralization of the white knight, he sought out the weakness on c3 in the enemy camp and grabbed the initiative – 12.♕b1 h6 13.♗d4 ♗d6 14.cxd5 ♘xd5 15.♘c4 ♗c7 16.♖d1 ♖e8 17.♘ce5 (17.♕b2!?) 17...♘xe5 18.♗xe5 ♗xe5 19.♘xe5 ♕g5 20.♘f3 ♕f6.

8...♗xd2 9.♗xd2

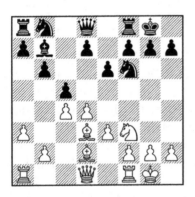

9...d6

Many famous chess players have reached this position, beginning with Keres. The sortie 9...♘e4 isn't very safe here, as the Dutch Defense with the pawn push c7-c5 is strategically dubious. In the game Ofitserian – Paravyan (St. Petersburg 2016) these young talents refreshed

theory: 10.♕c2 ♘xd2 11.♘xd2 cxd4 12.♗xh7+ ♔h8 13.♗e4 d5 14.cxd5 exd5 15.♗d3 dxe3 16.fxe3 ♘d7 17.♘f3 ♖c8 18.♕a4 ♖c6 19.♘d4 ♖h6 with decent counterplay due to white's rejection of the similar rook venture with 17.♖f3 and ♖f3-h3.

10.b4

In the final game of the Smyslov – Ribli candidates match (London 1983) Smyslov made do with pushing the pawn one square. After 10.♗c3 (the starting move order was different) 10...♘bd7 11.♕e2 ♖c8 12.♖fd1 cxd4 13.exd4 ♖e8 14.♖ac1 ♕c7 15.b3 a5 16.h3 h6 17.♗b2 ♕b8 18.♕e3 ♗c6 19.a4 ♖cd8 20.♗a3 ♗b7 21.♗b1 he outplayed his opponent and accepted a draw in a winning position (which was sufficient for him to progress to the candidates final against Kasparov). I consider b2-b4 and its rejection to be about equal and a matter of taste.

10...♘bd7 11.♗c3 ♕e7

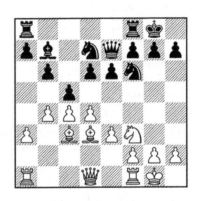

12.dxc5

Likavsky considered this exchange to be a passive route to a draw. In the game Smyslov – Kosten (Hastings 1989) the ex-world champion prepared to play e3-e4: 12.♖e1 ♗e4 13.♗f1 ♖ac8 14.♘d2 ♗b7 15.e4 cxd4 16.♗xd4 e5 17.♗b2 ♖c7 18.f3 ♕e6 19.♖c1 ♖fc8 20.♕b3 ♘h5 21.♕e3. White plans to strengthen via a3-a4-a5, while black has created no threats on the kingside.

12...dxc5 13.♗e2

The idea is to free up the file to exchange rooks. 13.♕c2 was more ambitious, without fearing deformation of his pawn structure – given the chance white will exploit the semi-open g-file to his ends.

13...♘e4 14.♗b2 ♖fd8 15.♕b3 ♘df6 16.♖ad1 ♖xd1 17.♗xd1 ♖d8 18.h3 h6 19.♗c2 ♘h7

The naturally enterprising Jobava isn't satisfied with a solid knight outpost and plans to demonstrate play on the kingside.

20.♖d1 ♘hg5 21.♖xd8+ ♕xd8 22.♘xg5 ♕xg5 23.♕d3

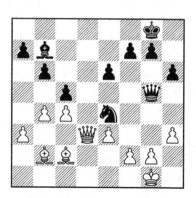

Baadur hasn't made much progress, and had white played 23.♕a4!? Baadur would have needed to seek compensation for the loss of the pawn on a7. Tomas's less aggressive move wouldn't promise an advantage were black to reply with

the normal 23...♕h4, however, the Georgian grandmaster preferred to bluff.

23...♘d2?! 24.g4?

White would have won with 24.♕h7+ ♔f8 25.♕h8+ ♔e7 and only now 26.g4 with the threats 27.♗xg7 and 27.♕b8.

24...♘f3+ 25.♔f1 ♗e4! 26.♕c3 ♗xc2 27.♕xc2 ♕h4 28.♔e2 ♕xh3 29.♕e4 ♘h2

With a smart exchange of bishops, Jobava gains some pawns and easily converts his advantage.

30.♕a8+ ♔h7 31.♕e4+ f5 32.gxf5 ♕f1+ 33.♔d2 ♕xf2+ 34.♔c1 exf5 35.♕f4 ♕xf4 36.exf4 ♘f1 37.♔c2 h5 38.bxc5 bxc5 39.♔d3 h4

White resigned.

No. 29 D. Jakovenko – N. Vitiugov
Novosibirsk 2016

1.d4 ♘f6 2.c4 e6 3.♘f3 ♗b4+ 4.♘bd2 0-0 5.e3 b6 6.♗d3 ♗b7 7.0-0 d5

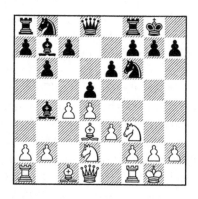

8.b3

8.a3 followed by an extended fianchetto is reviewed in games 30 and 31. The bishop's home diagonal c1-h6 opens up for it in the variation 8.♕c2 ♘bd7 9.e4 dxe4 10.♘xe4 ♘xe4 11.♗xe4 ♗xe4 12.♕xe4 with a minimal advantage typical of this structure. However, in complex play after 8...c5!? the c-file may open, which is uncomfortable for white's queen (if it is faced by a rook on c8). The equivalent ploy with 8.♕e2 (here the queen stands a little better) cannot be executed after 8...♘e4!?

8...♘bd7 9.♗b2 ♖c8

Vitiugov plans c7-c5, but begins with the rook move to retain the possibility of the bishop retreating to base in the event of 10.a3. 9...♘e4 is played more frequently, and if 10.a3, then Geller in his book on the Queen's Indian Defense (Batsford 1982, first published in Russia in 1981) recommends 10...♗d6 (protecting the c7 pawn, controlling e5 and leaving e7 free for the queen). The upcoming transposition to a Dutch setup requires care from black, as proved in the example Mamedyarov – Idani (Baku 2015): 10.♖c1 ♗d6 11.♕c2 f5 12.♖fd1 ♕e7 13.cxd5 exd5 14.♘e5 c5?! (14...♖c8 is solid) 15.♘xe4! fxe4 16.♗xe4! dxe4 17.♘xd7 ♕xd7? (17...♖f5! with the approximate variation 18.dxc5 bxc5 19.♖xd6 ♕xd6 20.♘xc5 ♖c8 21.b4 leaves black still in the game) 18.dxc5 ♗xh2+ 19.♔xh2 ♕c7+ 20.♔g1 – white is a good pawn up. It's not out of place to note that Mamedyarov was a fan of the Zukertort setup in the Queen's Pawn Opening and

in this game only played c2-c4 on move nine.

10.♕e2 c5 11.a3 ♗xd2 12.♘xd2 cxd4 13.exd4 ♕c7

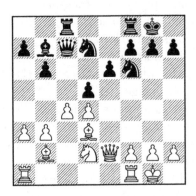

White has the bishop pair and the computer's favor, but this isn't enough to score a full point. So what should he do now? If he wants to strengthen the b2 bishop after 14.a4, then the knight heads via b8 to b4. Jakovenko pushes his f-pawn forwards and hence surrenders the e4 square to the other enemy knight.

14.f4 ♖fe8 15.♖ae1 ♘f8 16.♘f3 ♘e4 17.♗xe4

A commitment that fails to justify itself in the game. Seeing as the knight previously on d7 has moved further away from b4 he should have thought about 17.a4 and ♗b2-a3.

17...dxe4 18.♘e5 f6 19.♘g4 ♘g6 20.♕f2

Following 14.f4 it's logical to play 20.f5!? with a tactical nuance: 20...exf5 21.♖xf5 ♖cd8 22.♖xf6!? Perhaps white didn't fancy the unclear line 22...♘f4 (22...gxf6?? 23.♘xf6+ ♔g7 24.d5) 23.♖xf4 ♕xf4 24.d5.

20...b5! 21.cxb5 ♕c2

22.b4

It's no problem for white to achieve a draw with opposite-colored bishops after 22.♕xc2 ♖xc2 23.♖f2 ♖xf2 24.♘xf2 ♘xf4 25.g3 ♘d3 26.♘xd3 exd3 27.♖d1, but Jakovenko somewhat unjustifiably seeks more.

22...♕d3 23.♘e3 ♘e7 24.♕e2 ♘d5 25.f5 ♘xe3 26.♕xe3 ♖c2 27.♖f2?!

Black's rook on the second rank has got on white's nerves, as a result of which he fails to play the best move, 27.♗c1.

27...♕xe3 28.♖xe3 ♖xf2 29.♔xf2 exf5 30.d5 f4 31.♖e1 ♗xd5 32.♗d4 e3+ 33.♔g1 ♖e4 34.♗xa7 ♖c4 35.g3 g5 36.gxf4 gxf4 37.♖d1 ♗f3 38.♖f1 ♗b7 39.♖d1 ♗f3 40.♖f1 ♗b7 41.h3 ♔f7 42.♗c5 ♔g6 43.a4 ♔g5 44.♖e1 ♔h4 45.a5

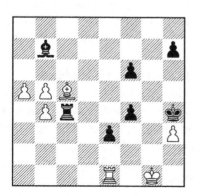

45...♔g3?

To Vitiugov's misfortune, he still needs to calculate accurately when the ending is winning. The correct continuation was 45...♗d5! 46.a6 ♖c2 47.♗xe3 ♖g2+ 48.♔f1 ♔xh3! (the bishop has shifted to d5, which threatens the fatal check on c4) 49.♖c1 fxe3 50.♖c3 ♖a2 51.♖xe3+ ♔g4, and white is out of moves.

46.a6! ♗d5 47.♗xe3 ♖c2

If 47...fxe3 48.♖xe3+ ♔f4 (48...♗f3 49.♖xf3+ ♔xf3 50.b6) 49.♖a3 ♖xb4 50.a7 ♗a8 51.♖c3 ♖xb5 52.♖c8 the extra pawn is insufficient to win the rook ending.

48.♗xf4+ ♔xf4 49.♖d1 ♗f3 50.b6 ♔g3 51.b7 ♖g2+ 52.♔f1 ♖f2+ 53.♔g1 ♖g2+ 54.♔f1

Draw agreed.

No. 30 E. Alekseev – I. Rozum
Skopje 2019

1.d4 ♘f6 2.c4 e6 3.♘f3 ♗b4+ 4.♘bd2 0-0 5.e3 b6 6.♗d3 d5 7.0-0 ♗b7 8.a3

The attack on the bishop is seen more often in this line than all the other moves together.

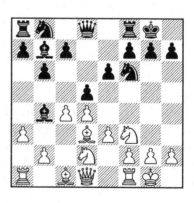

8...♗e7

If black goes for the exchange 8...♗xd2 then a good example of play for simplifications and a draw is the game Stocek – Romanishin (Hoogeveen 2014): 9.♗xd2 dxc4 10.♗xc4 ♘bd7 11.♕e2 ♘e4 12.♖fd1 ♘xd2 13.♖xd2 ♗xf3 14.♕xf3 ♘e5 15.♕e2 ♘xc4 16.♕xc4 c5 with peace agreed soon after. White can avoid this script (with no guarantee of even a tiny advantage) via 11.b4 ♘e4 12.♗e1 or capturing 9.♘xd2.

The retreat 8...♗d6 is less flexible. After 9.b4 white wants to play c4-c5 with a tempo, while the line 9...c5 10.cxd5 ♘xd5?! 11.bxc5 bxc5 12.dxc5 ♗xc5 13.♕c2 allows white to win a pawn (whereas with the bishop on e7 black has 12...♘xe3!).

9.cxd5

The immediate 9.b4 is the subject of the next game.

9...exd5 10.b4 ♘bd7

10...c5 is less precise due to 11.bxc5 bxc5 12.♖b1. The game Dreev – Goldin (Novosibirsk 1995) continued 12...♕c7 13.dxc5 ♘bd7 14.♘b3 ♘xc5 15.♘xc5 ♗xc5 16.♗b2 ♘e4 17.♘d4 ♗xd4 18.♗xd4 with a large advantage for white, partly because the queen is lured to the vulnerable c7 square. The drawbacks of her position are equally obvious after 17...g6 18.♕g4!? ♘d2 19.♘f5 f6 20.♖fc1 ♘xb1 21.♗d4.

11.♗b2

If 11.♖b1, then it's useful for black to switch to preparing a7-a5 along the lines of Prizant – Maletin (Dombai 2013): 11...♗d6 12.♕c2 ♕e7 13.♗b2 a5 14.♖fc1 axb4 15.axb4 c6 16.♗c3 ♖fe8 17.♗f1 ♖a7 18.b5 c5 19.♖a1 ♖aa8 20.♖xa8 ♖xa8 21.♖a1 ♕e8 22.♕b2 ♖xa1 23.♕xa1 ♗b8. This position is approximately equal, as it has been since move 11.

11...c5 12.dxc5 bxc5 13.bxc5 ♘xc5

14.♘b3

Previously the bishop would retreat to e2, but after 14...♘fe4 15.♘d4 ♗f6 it's far from easy to convert this powerful blockade into a real profit. Alekseev doesn't see any advantage in having the bishop pair in blockaded positions, which is logical.

14...♘xd3   15.♕xd3   ♕b6 16.♖fb1 ♗a6

Rozum doesn't prevent the queen from invading on f5 (which he could have done with 16...♘e4), but his opponent also considered 17.♕f5 to be harmless.

17.♕d1 ♗c4 18.♘bd4 g6

The players are being careful. Alekseev is offered the chance to play 19.♘e5 (which he ignores), which after 18...♘e4 would have been countered by the maneuver ♕b6-f6.

19.♗c3 ♛c7 20.♗b4 ♘e4
21.♗xe7 ♛xe7 22.♖b2 ♛d6 23.♘d2
♖ab8 24.♖xb8 ♖xb8 25.♘xe4 dxe4
26.♛a4 ♛a6 27.♛xa6 ♗xa6 28.g4

Now the kings join the battle far
more effectively than their subjects.
Nevertheless, they cannot avoid the
game ending in a draw.

28...♔g7 29.♔g2 ♖c8 30.♔g3
♗d3 31.h4 h6 32.♔f4 ♔f6 33.g5+
hxg5+ 34.hxg5+ ♔g7

Draw agreed.

The young Peruvian grandmaster
Jose Eduardo Martinez Alcantara
had already chalked up draws as black
with the strong Russians Epishin
and Demchenko, but Kramnik was
on another level. Nevertheless, the
Peruvian didn't change his favorite
opening.

No. 31 V. Kramnik –
J.E. Martinez Alcantara
Batumi 2018

1.d4 ♘f6 2.♘f3 e6 3.c4 ♗b4+
4.♘bd2 0-0 5.e3 b6 6.♗d3 ♗b7
7.0-0 d5 8.a3 ♗e7 9.b4

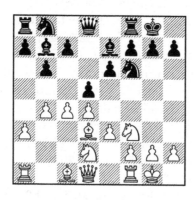

9...c5

KEY TIP. The creation of a strong
pawn (and a potential passer) in the
variation 9...dxc4 10.♘xc4 ♘bd7
11.♗b2 c5 12.dxc5 bxc5 13.b5 is a
typical white ploy in many closed
openings. As a rule, it is to white's
advantage and shouldn't be left
to rust without application in the
arsenal of technical weapons.

After 9...♘bd7 10.c5 a5 11.♗b2
white will enjoy a long-lasting
advantage. In the standard structure
that arises, the position of the knight
on d2 is valuable because it allows
white to control e5 without challenge.

The continuation 9...a5 10.b5
isn't particularly attractive for black
either. If black makes a break from
his cramped position via c7-c5 an
exchange follows on c6, and the b6
pawn turns into a target.

10.bxc5

This is not the only way to unravel
the tricky standoff of pawns. Unlike
the variation from the previous
annotation, 10.dxc5 bxc5 11.b5
doesn't work due to 11...a6, and the
pawn on b5 can only be saved at the
cost of allowing black to create a
threatening pawn chain in an extended
center. The tricky line 10.cxd5 ♘xd5
11.♛c2 cxb4 12.♗xh7+ ♔h8 13.♗d3
♘d7 14.♘c4 ♖c8 15.♛b3 a5 16.♗d2
(An. Bykhovsky – Arlinsky, Petakh
Tikva 2008) should be continued 16...
bxa3 17.♘xa3 ♘b4, and the position
remains unsettled.

10...bxc5

10...dxc4!? 11.♘xc4 bxc5 12.♖b1
♗d5 has good statistics and a nice
position for black. It's hard for white

to find something useful for his c1 bishop to do. Hence it's surprising that black doesn't choose this move more frequently.

11.♖b1

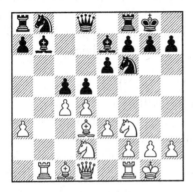

11.cxd5 exd5 12.♖b1 matches the recipe from the notes to game 30 (Dreev – Goldin), but 11...♕xd5 looks stronger. Kramnik's move order also enables black to diverge from Dreev – Goldin.

11...♕c8

The main continuation 11...♗a6 is considered sufficiently solid. In the game Ginsburg – A. Moiseenko (Viernheim 2018) after 12.♕c2 ♘bd7 13.♘e5 cxd4 14.♘c6 ♕e8 15.exd4 dxc4 16.♘xc4 ♘b6 17.♘xb6 ♗xd3 18.♕xd3 axb6 19.♘xe7+ ♕xe7 20.♖xb6 white won a pawn, but with careful defense he should not be able to convert it into a full point. Black does not have to force play, as after 13...♖c8 14.♕a4 cxd4 15.exd4 ♗xc4 16.♗xc4 dxc4 the knight's invasion of c6 promises only equality at best.

12.cxd5 ♘xd5

Thanks to the threat ♘d5-c3 black manages to complete his development and equalize.

13.♕c2 ♘f6 14.dxc5 ♘a6 15.♗b2 ♘xc5

If the bishop now moves to e2 or c4, then loss of control over e4 will end white's ambitions. Kramnik instead finds an extraordinary reply! He carries out a drawing combination, but refuses to deliver perpetual check, preferring to bluff.

16.♗xf6 gxf6 17.♗xh7+ ♔g7

18.♖fc1

The bishop retreat doesn't change the assessment of this position as drawing – 18.♗d3 ♘xd3 19.♕xd3 ♗a6 20.♕e4 ♗xf1 21.♕g4+. Perpetual check is now harder to deliver, but it was never part of Kramnik's plans anyway.

18...f5 19.♗xf5 exf5 20.♘d4 ♗e4 21.♘xe4 fxe4 22.♕e2?!

If white needed to achieve the unwanted draw, he would have started with 22.♖b5 and then tread a narrow path – 22...♖h8 23.♖xc5 ♗xc5 24.♕xe4 ♖h5 25.♕f3 ♕h8 26.♕g3+ ♔h7 27.♕f3 ♕e5 28.♖xc5 ♕xh2+ 29.♔f1 ♖xc5 30.♕xf7+.

22...♖h8 23.♖b5 a6 24.♕b2 ♔g8 25.♖b6

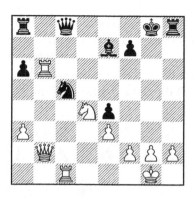

25...♘d3?

A cowardly move of an inexperienced (albeit rather strong) player. After 25...♕g4! black creates counter threats, and white's pair of extra pawns is no compensation for the missing bishop.

26.♖xc8+ ♖xc8 27.♕d2 ♖c1+ 28.♕xc1 ♘xc1 29.♖xa6

After the exchange of queens, white has captured a third pawn for the piece and faces virtually no risk of losing while retaining the right to rely on his advantage in both chess level and experience.

29...♖h5 30.♖a8+ ♗f8 31.a4 ♘d3 32.g4

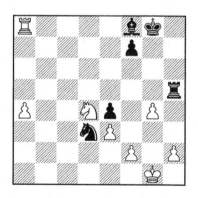

32...♖c5?

He could have drawn with 32...

♖h4 33.h3 ♖xh3 34.a5 ♖h6 35.a6 ♘b4 36.a7 ♖a6 37.♔g2 ♔g7 38.♘f5+ ♔g8 39.♘e7+ ♔g7 – as white has to give checks due to the unpinned bishop.

33.♔g2 ♖c4 34.a5 ♘f4+ 35.♔g3 ♘e6?!

Black is helpless against the pair of passed pawns. In any case, attempts at salvation such as via the variation 35...♘d5 36.h4 ♖c5 37.h5 ♘c7 38.♖c8 ♖xa5 39.♘c6 ♖c5 40.♘e7+ ♔g7 41.h6+ ♔xh6 42.♖xf8 ♔g7 43.♖b8 ♘e6 are most painful.

36.♘xe6 fxe6 37.g5 ♔f7 38.h4 ♗d6+ 39.♔g4 ♖c1 40.a6 ♖a1 41.♖a7+ ♗e7 42.♔h5 ♔e8 43.♔h6 ♗f8+ 44.♔g6 ♗e7 45.♖a8+ ♗d8 46.h5 ♖a5 47.♖xd8+

Black resigned.

No. 32 P. Svidler – A. Moiseenko
Dagomys 2009

1.d4 ♘f6 2.c4 e6 3.♘f3 ♗b4+ 4.♘bd2 0-0

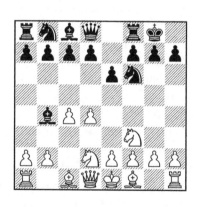

5.a3

By far the most frequent move here. Before we study the retreat to e7 (games 34-40), we have to review the exchange without moving onto chapter six's territory (4...b6).

5...♝xd2+ 6.♕xd2

Capture by the bishop is reviewed in game 33.

6...d6

Apart from 6...b6 (the topic of chapter 6) it's important to note the Dutch-style continuation 6...♘e4 7.♕c2 f5. The exchange of the dark-colored bishop for the knight is typical in the Dutch Defense, but white gets an easy game in the present version (with the black knight ensconced in the center at the cost of development). For example, 8.g3 d6 9.♝g2 ♘d7 10.0-0 ♕e7 11.b4 a5 12.b5 e5 13.e3 c5 14.♝b2 ♖b8 15.dxe5 dxe5 16.♖ad1 b6 17.♕d3 ♔h8 18.♘h4 ♘df6 19.f3 ♘g5 20.♘xf5 winning a pawn and the game (V. Mikhalevsky – Marsili, Antalya 2017). White's advantage increased like a natural process, and it's hard to find better moves for black in this line.

7.e3 ♕e7 8.b4

If white completes his kingside development via 8.♝e2 e5 9.0-0, then he has to reckon with 9...e4 10.♘e1 a5 11.b3 d5. There's no obvious way to punish black for his territorial expansion.

8...e5

Let's also look at the opening of the a-file with a switch to a Dutch-type structure: 8...a5 9.♝b2 axb4 10.axb4 ♖xa1+ 11.♝xa1 ♘e4 12.♕c2 f5 13.♝e2 ♘c6 14.b5 ♘d8 15.♘d2 ♘f6 16.0-0 ♘f7 17.♝b2 c6 18.bxc6 bxc6 (Esen – Kurajica, Sarajevo 2011). Black is actually not as bad as the computer thinks, and the vastly

experienced Grandmaster Kurajica eventually gained a draw. Black's counterplay around the enemy king should not be underestimated.

9.dxe5 dxe5 10.♝b2 ♘bd7

The position on the diagram has been reached via various opening move orders but the stats for black are disappointing.

11.♕c3

After 11.♝e2 e4 12.♘d4 ♘e5 13.h3 ♝d7 14.♕c3 ♖fe8 15.0-0 ♖ad8 16.♖fd1 c6 17.♖d2 ♝c8 18.♖ad1 (Markus – Rasovic, Niksic 2016) doubling rooks on the opening file enabled white to make progress on the queenside, while black has no chances on the kingside.

11...♖e8 12.c5 e4

In the game D. Berczes – Jurcik (Brno 2006) the Slovak master playing black built defensive ramparts along the long diagonal, but that didn't help much: 12...♘e4 13.♕c2 ♘g5 14.♘d2 f6 15.♝c4+ ♘f7 16.0-0 ♘f8 17.f4 ♝e6 18.fxe5 ♘xe5 19.♝xe5 fxe5 20.♖f5 ♘g6 21.♖af1. Only a miracle enabled black to escape defeat.

13.♘d2

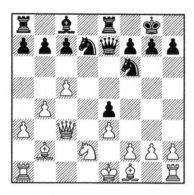

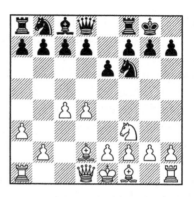

13...a5

Moiseenko diverges from the previous game Browne – Agdestein (Gjovik 1983): 13...♘e5 14.♘c4 ♘g6 15.♗e2 ♗e6 16.♖d1 ♖ad8 17.0-0 ♖d5 18.♖xd5 ♗xd5 19.♖d1 ♕e6 20.b5. The battery on the diagonal prevents black from carrying out counterplay on the kingside.

14.♗b5 axb4 15.axb4 ♖xa1+ 16.♗xa1 ♖d8

Whites next moves should be obvious – castling, retreating the bishop to e2, and ♖f1-d1. The exchange of a pair of rooks has made black's defense easier, but he still had to work hard to draw. However, as a result of Svidler's next action chances instantly equalized.

17.g4?! b6 18.cxb6 cxb6 19.g5 ♘e8 20.♖g1 ♗b7 21.♗b2 ♖c8 22.♕d4 ♖d8 23.♕c3 ♖c8 24.♕d4 ♖d8

Draw agreed.

No. 33 K. Piorun – B. Socko
Gorzow Wielkopolski 2013

1.d4 ♘f6 2.c4 e6 3.♘f3 ♗b4+ 4.♘bd2 0-0 5.a3 ♗xd2+ 6.♗xd2

6...♘e4

Just like in game 14 (after 4... a5 5.a3 ♗xd2+ 6.♗xd2 d6), 6...d6 can be met with 7.♗g5. White has an easy game on a decent strategic foundation. See for example Graf – Babar (Bad Wiessee 2012): 7...h6 8.♗h4 ♕e7 9.e3 ♘bd7 10.♗e2 e5 11.♕c2 ♖e8 12.0-0 e4 13.♘d2 g5 14.♗g3 ♘f8 15.♖ae1 ♘g6 16.f3 ♗f5 17.fxe4 ♗xe4 18.♕c3 – white has prospects on the queenside and the f-file, while black has nothing but weaknesses.

7.♗f4

A decent reply to 7.♗e3 is 7...d5, and the white bishops lack space to operate. After that, the queen's knight develops on c6, while the centralized knight can head via d6 (from where it attacks c4) to settle on f5.

If 7.g3 then the continuation 7... ♘xd2 8.♕xd2 d6 9.♗g2 ♕e7 with e6-e5 to come doesn't promise black full equality but nevertheless is more promising than the more popular Dutch setup. It's also worth reviewing the fragment Xiu Deshun – Torre (Subic Bay 2007): 7...d6 8.♗g2 ♘d7 9.0-0 f5 10.♗e3 ♘df6 11.♘e1 ♘g4 12.♗c1 ♘g5 13.e4 ♘h6 14.exf5 ♘xf5

15.h4 ♘f7 16.♘f3 ♕f6 17.b4 ♗d7 18.♖a2 ♖ae8 19.♖e1 b5 20.♖c2 bxc4 21.♖xc4 c6 22.♖c3 ♘e7 23.♕a4 with pressure on the queenside weaknesses. This was the second and last attempt by the Filipino grandmaster with 6...♘e4, and later he chose other setups.

7...d6 8.e3

The g-pawn charge that is an unusual visitor in grandmaster games did not find any followers in this line: 8.♕c2 f5 9.g4? ♘xf2! 10.♔xf2 fxg4 11.e3 gxf3 12.h4 e5! 13.dxe5 ♗f5 14.e4 (Krasenkow – Kveinys, Zakopane 2000), and the easiest way for black to win was with 14...♗e6 15.♗g5 ♕d7 16.exd6 ♘c6. White just gets harmed by his pieces hanging on the f-file and his exposed king.

8...b6

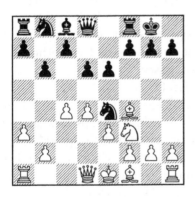

9.♗d3

There was an interesting game S. Ivanov – Cs. Berczes (Stockholm 2009): 9.♕c2 ♗b7 10.♖d1 f5 11.♗e2 ♘d7 12.0-0 g5 13.♗g3 ♘df6 (13...h5 14.h4 g4 15.♘d2 ♘xg3 16.fxg3 merely provides the white king with a cozy bunker with no consequences from the messed up pawn structure) 14.c5 ♗d5 15.♗c4 ♕e7 16.♗xd5

♘xd5 17.♖fe1!? bxc5 18.dxc5 ♘xc5 19.♘d4 a5 20.f3, and after the best moves 20...♘f6 21.b4 axb4 22.axb4 ♘a6 23.♕c4 d5 24.♕c6 white wins back the material with some advantage. Evidently, black should not have given up his wonderful blockade for the sake of a pawn.

9...♗b7 10.♕c2 f5 11.h3

This Dutch structure that has arisen is dangerous for black due to white's possibility of launching a direct king hunt. After 11.♖g1!? ♘d7?! 12.g4 ♕e8 13.gxf5 exf5 14.0-0-0 ♕h5 15.♘g5 ♖ae8 16.f3 ♘xg5 17.♖xg5 ♕xf3 18.♖f1 ♕h3 19.♖fg1 (Ikonnikov – Holzbauer, Werfen 1991) the opening of the g-file led to white gaining a decisive advantage. Instead of 11...♘d7 black should have retreated his knight to f6, when he would have still been somewhat worse.

11...♘d7 12.0-0-0 ♕e7 13.♖he1

With the queen on e7 it's much harder for white to switch to attack. For example, after 13.g4?! e5! 14.♗h2 exd4 15.♘xd4 fxg4 the f2 square is falling apart.

13...c5 14.♔b1 ♖ac8 15.♕e2 a5 16.♗c2 d5 17.♘e5

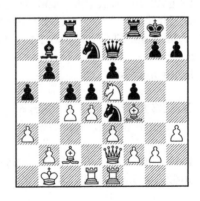

The nature of the battle has totally changed due to the heightened tension in the extended center. Socko's inaccurate play again prompts white to turn his attention to the kingside. If 17...♗a6 here black would be no worse.

17...♘df6 18.f3 ♘d6 19.g4 ♗a6?! 20.gxf5

Both players had missed the unpleasant reply 20.♕h2!

20...♘xf5 21.♗xf5 exf5 22.♕c2 ♕e6 23.♖g1 ♗xc4 24.♖g5 cxd4 25.♕g2 ♘e8 26.♖g1 ♕e7 27.exd4 ♗b3

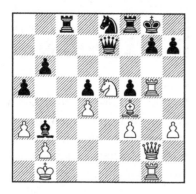

28.♖xg7+?!

This exchange operation gives black the initiative. I expect white was rushing the attack due to the invasion ♖c8-c2, but if 28.h4 ♖c2 29.♕f1 ♖f6 30.h5 he would still be dominant.

28...♘xg7 29.♗h6 ♖c7 30.♗xg7 ♕xg7 31.♕f1 ♖fc8 32.♘d3 a4 33.♖xg7+ ♖xg7 34.♕e1 ♔f8

Socko plans a king march to the queenside, where he will be better protected by pawns should he launch a decisive attack with his rooks. White didn't immediately figure out his opponent's brilliant plan, otherwise he would have replied 35.♕e3.

35.♘f4?! ♖e7 36.♕h4 ♖c6 37.♕f2 ♔e8 38.♕g1 ♔d7 39.♕f1 ♔c8 40.♕f2 ♖c2 41.♕f1 ♖c6 42.♘d3 ♔b7 43.♘b4 ♖ce6 44.♘d3 ♖e2 45.♔c1 ♖7e3 46.h4 ♗c4 47.♕g1 ♗xd3 48.♕g7+ ♖e7

White resigned.

No. 34 Wang Hao – M. Antipov
Abu Dhabi 2016

1.d4 ♘f6 2.c4 e6 3.♘f3 ♗b4+ 4.♘bd2 0-0 5.a3 ♗e7 6.e4

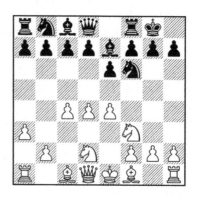

6...d6

This usually involves black playing e7-e5, or less frequently c7-c5. It most often leads to structures from well-known openings, although sometimes the lines are more original.

7.♗e2

In game 35 we review 7.♗d3. The advance b2-b4 is part of white's plans, but somewhat premature right here. After 7.b4 a5 8.b5 e5 black easily gains control over c5, while if 8.♗b2 axb4 9.axb4 ♖xa1 10.♕xa1 d5 the pawn on b4 is left hanging.

7...a5

Antipov immediately acts aggressively on the queenside. In the game Levin – Askerov (St. Petersburg 2019) after 7...♘bd7 8.0-0 e5 9.♕c2 exd4 10.♘xd4 ♖e8 11.b3 ♗f8 12.♗b2 ♘c5 13.f3 ♗d7 a typical four ranks versus three position arose, where black was solid but had no counterplay.

The same Chinese grandmaster had played this position as black and chose the rare move 7...♘fd7, which allowed him to carry out both standard pawn breaks mentioned above – 8.b4 e5 9.d5 a5 10.♗b2 c5 11.dxc6 ♘xc6 12.♗c3 ♕c7 (the white knights are too far from the b5 and d5 squares and hence won't harass the queen) 13.0-0 ♘b6 14.♕b3 ♗e6 15.♖ab1 axb4 16.axb4 ♖fc8 17.♖fc1 ♗f6 (Esipenko – Wang Hao, Moscow 2018). Given the chance, black will plant a knight on d4, while the weakness on d6 is no more painful than that on c4. Chances are approximately equal.

8.0-0

Antipov has played this position many times as black. His first attempt turned pear shaped: 8.♕c2 a4?! 9.e5! dxe5 10.dxe5 ♘fd7 11.♘e4 ♘c6 12.♗f4 ♖a5 13.0-0-0 ♕e8 14.h4 ♘dxe5 15.♘xe5 ♖xe5 (15...♘xe5 16.♕c3) 16.♗xe5 ♘xe5 17.f4 ♘c6 18.♘g5 f5 19.♕xa4 with no compensation for the material (Gelfand – Antipov, Moscow 2015). Later, he twice prepared a break in the center via 8...♘c6 (9.e5?! dxe5 10.dxe5 ♘g4 11.♕e4?! ♘cxe5!

12.♘xe5 f5). In the game Duzhakov – Antipov (Sochi 2017) after 9.b3 ♘h5!? 10.♗b2 ♘f4 11.♗f1 e5 12.d5 ♘b8 13.g3 ♘h3 14.♗g2 c6 15.♘f1 cxd5 16.cxd5 ♘a6 the black knights are placed oddly, but in return the white king is stuck in the center.

8...a4

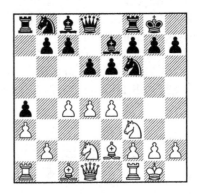

9.♗d3

The bishop heads to challenge the pawn that has dared to cross the demarcation line. In the game Hammer – Antipov (Gjakovo 2016) the Norwegian grandmaster followed Gelfand's example with less success, as black managed to control the d4 square: 9.e5 dxe5 10.dxe5 ♘fd7 11.♘e4 ♘c6 12.♗f4 ♘c5 13.♕c2 ♘d4 14.♘xd4 ♕xd4 15.♘xc5 ♕xf4 16.♘d3 ♕f5. The e5 pawn cramps black but the bishop pair provide compensation.

9...♘fd7 10.♗c2 ♘b6 11.e5 ♘8d7

A sensible alternative strategic idea is to transfer the bishop via d7 to c6, exchange it on f3, and then play d6-d5.

12.♕e2 ♖e8 13.♘b1

13...♘f8 14.♘c3 ♗d7 15.♗e3 d5 16.c5 ♘c4 17.♗d3

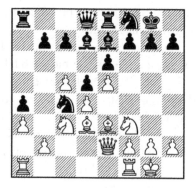

17...♘xe3

Opening the f-file is risky. It was safer to play 17...♘a5 18.♘d2 ♗c6 and then defend the still intact kingside. Black's lack of space would be uncomfortable, but not fatal.

18.fxe3 b6! 19.cxb6 c5! 20.b7 ♖a7

Antipov cleverly creates counterplay, although after 21.♗c2 (with action in two directions) white has better prospects. The exchange of bishops is somewhat weaker.

21.♗b5 ♕a5?!

The queen and then the bishop are distracted from the g5 square, where the enemy knight will appear. Black had to play 21...c4.

22.dxc5 ♗xc5 23.♗xd7 ♘xd7

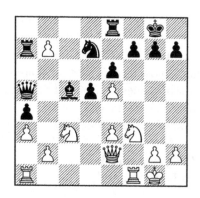

24.♘g5! ♘xe5 25.♘xf7! ♘xf7 26.♖xf7 ♕b6

Antipov was worried about the fate of his king in the variation 26...♔xf7 27.♕h5+ ♔e7 28.♕xe8+ ♔xe8 29.b8=♕+ ♔d7 30.♖f1.

27.♖af1

The computer recipe 27.♕h5! ♖d8 28.♔h1 ♗xe3 29.♘xd5!! exd5 30.♖e7! was too hard even for such a strong player as Wang Hao to spot.

27...♖xb7 28.♘xa4

It was better to capture the pawn after the exchange on b7.

28...♕b5 29.♕h5 ♗xe3+ 30.♔h1 ♗d4 31.♘c3 ♗xc3 32.bxc3 ♕d3 33.h3

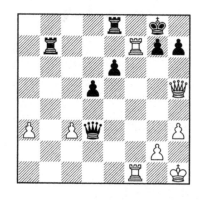

The players are no longer competing on the same level, and

the creation of this languid luft underscores this. Instead of the careful 33...♖be7 Antipov makes a sharp movement and gets mated by the white queen with modest support from its pinned rook.

33...♖b1?? 34.♖xg7+! ♔xg7 35.♕f7+ ♔h6 36.♕f4+ ♔h5 37.♕g4+ ♔h6 38.♕h4+

Black resigned.

No. 35 I. Sokolov – J. Timman
Amstelveen (rapid) 2018

1.d4 ♘f6 2.c4 e6 3.♘f3 ♝b4+ 4.♘bd2 0-0

In a similar competition two years earlier, Timman had chosen 4...b6 (and lost), then a year later he switched to the Queen's Indian Defense (with the same unfortunate outcome), and now returns to the Bogo-Indian Defense with a different variation.

5.a3 ♝e7 6.e4 d6 7.♝d3

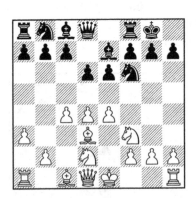

7...♘bd7

Earlier, Sokolov had faced 7...c5 8.d5 e5 (the main structure of a classical Benoni) 9.h3 ♘bd7 10.g4 ♘e8 11.♘f1 g6 12.♘g3 (the problem

knight has now found a job to do...) 12...♘g7 13.♝h6 ♘f6 14.♕c2 ♔h8 15.♝d2 a6 16.♘f1 ♝d7 17.♘e3 (... well, now it's changed its mind) 17...b5 18.♝c3 ♘ge8 (I. Sokolov – Stillger, Netherlands 2018). After that, the game grew more complicated and to black's advantage, but up to this point it mostly comprised long maneuvers. Both Sokolov and Timman have deep experience in the Bogo-Indian Defense.

The move 7...♘c6 quickly fell out of practice, as the moves 8.b4 e5 9.d5 ♘b8 10.♘b3 demonstrate the advantage that white gained from playing both a2-a3 and ♘b1-d2. It makes more sense to try a7-a5, restricting white on the queenside. The game Rodshtein – Eingorn (Cappelle la Grande 2013) arrived at a KID structure with equal chances: 7...a5 8.0-0 e5 9.b3 exd4 10.♘xd4 ♘fd7 11.♖b1 ♝f6 12.♘e2 ♘c6 13.♘f4 g6 14.♘d5 ♝g7 15.♝c2 ♘d4 16.♘f3 ♘xc2 17.♕xc2 c6 18.♘c3 ♖e8.

8.0-0

Here 8.b4 is not as strong as against 7...♘c6. The example Nakamura – Caruana (Saint Louis 2016) despite being a blitz game demonstrated excellent play in the opening – 8... e5 9.d5 a5 10.♖b1 (the drawback of playing 10.♝b2 is the loss of control over f4 after 10...♘h5!?) 10...axb4 11.axb4 c6 12.0-0 cxd5 13.cxd5 ♘b6 14.♘b3 ♘bxd5!? 15.exd5 e4 16.♖e1 exd3 17.♕xd3 ♖e8 18.♝g5 h6 19.♝h4 ♝d7. It's hard for the players to strengthen their positions.

8...e5

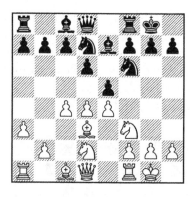

9.d5

In the game Hedman – Stefansson (Reykjavik 2016) after 9.b3 black went for a KID setup similar to the Rodshtein – Eingorn example, but without the slowing move a7-a5. As a result, Stefansson found himself in difficulties: 9...♖e8 10.♗b2 ♗f8 11.♖e1 g6 12.♗f1 ♗g7 13.♕c2 b6 14.♖ad1 ♗b7 15.dxe5 dxe5 16.c5! ♘xc5 17.♘xe5 ♕c8 18.b4 ♘cd7 19.♘df3.

9...♘c5 10.♗c2 a5 11.b3 c6

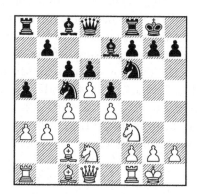

KEY TIP. Black's arsenal in the Bogo-Indian Defense includes pawn advances which aim to ruin white's strong pawn chain and slightly free up the black position.

12.♗b2 cxd5

A sensible exchange, which black delayed in vain in the game Forcen Esteban – Salgado Lopez (Madrid 2015). After 12...♕b6 13.♗c3 ♗g4 14.h3 ♗h5 15.b4 axb4 16.axb4 ♖xa1 17.♕xa1 ♘a6 18.dxc6 bxc6 19.♖b1 white is ready to extract an advantage from pushing c4-c5.

13.cxd5 ♗d7 14.b4 axb4 15.axb4 ♘a6 16.♗c3

16...♕b8

Timman wants to activate his dark-squared bishop, but the more active setup 16...♗b5 17.♖e1 ♕b6 and ♖f8-c8 looks preferable.

17.♗d3 ♖c8 18.♕b3 ♗d8 19.♖a3 ♘c7

Black doesn't hurry to move his bishop to b6 due to ♘d2-c4 and cedes the a-file. Both sides are now playing to win.

20.♖xa8 ♕xa8 21.♖a1 ♕b8 22.b5 ♘xb5 23.♗xe5 dxe5 24.♗xb5 ♕c7 25.♗xd7 ♘xd7

The protected passed pawn is clearly stronger than the outside passer, which is far from its queening square. White now needs to strengthen his position with moderate steps.

26.g3 ♗e7 27.♔g2 g6 28.♕b5 ♘f6 29.♖a4 ♗c5 30.♖c4 b6 31.♕b2 ♘d7 32.♘b3 ♕d6

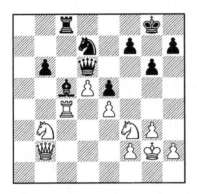

33.♘c1 ♖a8?!

Given that black has totally barricaded the c-file, white should have moved his rook to the a-file on his last move. Transferring the knight via c1 to d3 is useful in principle, but that allowed Timman to activate with 33...f5 34.exf5 ♕xd5 35.♕b3 ♖f8, after which it's time for white to trade queens.

34.♘d3 f6 35.♕b5 f5?!

The following queen invasion proves decisive, so 35...♖c8 would have resisted better. Then, the white rook would return to the a-file.

36.♕c6 ♕xc6 37.dxc6 fxe4 38.♖xe4 ♘f6 39.♘xc5 bxc5 40.♖xe5 ♖c8 41.♖xc5 ♔f7 42.♘d4 ♘e8 43.♘b5 ♔e7 44.♖e5+ ♔f6 45.♖xe8 ♖xe8 46.♘d6

Black resigned.

No. 36 T. Gareev – I. Rozum
Chennai 2018

1.d4 ♘f6 2.c4 e6 3.♘f3 ♗b4+ 4.♘bd2 0-0 5.a3 ♗e7 6.e4

Previous games involving Gareev (on either side) were all in the 4... b6 variation. Rozum had previously castled in this line, while as white he preferred 6.b4.

6...d5 7.♗d3

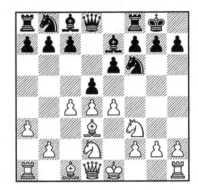

Games 37 and 38 continued 7.♕c2, while games 39 and 40 feature 7.e5. The variation in the current game can be reached through both 7.♗d3 and 7.e5.

7...c5

Just like in the 7.♕c2 line, this is the right way for black to seek counter chances. Otherwise he will be forced to engage in depressing defense, as in the case Tihonov – Stupak (Minsk 2011): 7...dxe4 8.♘xe4 ♘bd7 9.♘c3 b6 10.0-0 ♗b7 11.♖e1 c5 12.♗e3 a6 (12...h6 is interesting in order to prevent white's knight from getting to g5) 13.h3 ♕c7 14.♕e2 ♖ac8 15.♖ad1 ♖fe8 16.♘g5 h6 17.♘ge4 cxd4 18.♗xd4 e5 19.♗e3 ♘xe4 20.♗xe4 ♗xe4 21.♘xe4 ♘f6 22.♘xf6+ ♗xf6 23.b3.

8.e5

If 8.dxc5 dxe4 9.♘xe4 ♘xe4 10.♗xe4 ♕xd1+ 11.♔xd1 black is not forced to regain the pawn only to be chased with b2-b4. After 11...f5 12.♗c2 ♗f6 13.♖b1 ♖d8+ 14.♔e2 e5 15.♖d1 ♖xd1 16.♔xd1 ♘c6 (Gelfand – Tomashevsky, Rogaska Slatina 2011) he has achieved so much in the center that white cannot do anything with his queenside pawn majority.

8...♘fd7

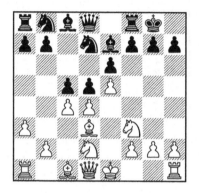

9.h4

The continuation 9.♕c2 is reviewed in game 40 via 7.e5. Gareev switches to a decisive attack on the kingside based on the advanced e5 pawn. However, his opponent has planned counterplay to prevent his plan from being achieved.

The variation 9.cxd5 exd5 10.0-0 ♘c6 11.♖e1 is well-known from Yusupov's games for both colors. The game Moiseenko – Korobov (Lviv 2014) tested the rare and ambitious continuation 11...♕b6!? There followed 12.♘f1 ♘xd4 13.♘xd4 cxd4 14.b4 a5 15.♘g3 g6 16.♖b1 axb4 17.axb4, after which 17...♘b8!? (improving the knight and opening up a path for the bishop) makes it questionable whether there is compensation for the pawn. The main

moves 11...♖e8 (and then ♘d7-f8 or ♗e7-f8) and 11...a5 have disappeared from serious practice without any definitive evaluation. In the example Kempinski – Petrik (Czech Republik 2015) play continued 11...a5 12.♗c2 ♖e8 13.h3 h6 14.♘b3 c4 15.♘bd2 b5 16.♘f1 ♘f8 17.♘g3 – the knight's maneuver has removed tension from the d4 square, and now each player will attack on opposite sides with unclear consequences.

In recent years, well-known grandmasters have sought chances in the center, where you would think it hard to gain the upper hand over black. In the highly complex game Gelfand – Dominguez (Khanty-Mansiysk 2015) the war theater shifted to the queenside: 9.0-0 ♘c6 10.♖e1 a5 11.♗c2 ♕c7 12.dxc5 ♘xc5 13.♘b3 ♘xb3 (the variation 13...dxc4 14.♘xc5 ♖d8 15.♕e2 ♗xc5 16.♕xc4 ♘d4 17.♘xd4 ♖xd4 18.♕b3 b6 leaves the position still quite unclear) 14.♕d3 g6 15.♗xb3 ♖d8 16.♗f4 a4 17.♗a2 dxc4 18.♕xc4 b5!? (18...♕b6!? strengthens control over d4) 19.♕xb5 ♖a5 20.♕f1 ♘d4 21.♘xd4 ♖xd4 22.♖ec1 ♕b8 with tangible compensation for the pawn.

9...h6

The continuation 9...f5 10.cxd5 exd5 11.♕c2 g6 protects black from difficulties on the b1-h7 diagonal, but after 12.h5 cxd4 13.♘b3 ♘c6 14.hxg6 hxg6 15.♗f4 and long castling he faces a catastrophe on the h-file. Instead of 11...g6? he should have played the stronger 11...♘c6, and white's outside pawn has nothing to grasp hold of.

If 9...g6 10.h5 cxd4 11.♕c2, the best move is 11...♘c5, chasing the bishop from d3 and thereby weakening pressure on g6. The precise and exciting play by both sides in the game Navara – Najer (Jerusalem 2015) led to a peaceful outcome: 12.♗f1 a5 (12...d3 13.♗xd3 ♘xd3+ 14.♕xd3 after the exchange of queens grants white a lasting advantage) 13.♘xd4 dxc4 14.♘2f3 g5!? 15.♗xc4 g4 16.♗a2! ♘bd7 17.♘g5!? ♗xg5 18.♗b1 f5 19.exf6 ♘xf6 20.♗xg5 ♕xd4 21.♗e3 ♕e4 22.♕xc5 ♕xg2 23.♖f1 ♕d5 – the bishop pair in an open position compensate for the lack of a pawn.

10.♗b1

White sets up an ideal battery with the queen in front of the bishop. A pawn storm no longer works here: 10.g4?! cxd4 11.g5 h5 12.g6 ♘c6 13.♕e2 fxg6 14.cxd5 exd5 15.e6?! ♘c5 16.♗xg6 ♗xe6 17.♘g5 ♗xg5 18.hxg5 ♗g4 19.f3 ♕d6 (Hayrapetyan – Goganov, Yerevan 2014) and white resigned – the opening of play in the center worked against his own king.

10...♖e8

This frees up the square for the knight. Naturally, the knight could protect h7 from f6 in the variation 10...cxd4 11.♕c2 f5 12.exf6 ♘xf6. In practice, white doesn't exchanged on f6, preferring blockade play: 12.cxd5 exd5 13.♘b3 ♘c6 14.♗f4 ♕b6 15.♗a2 ♖e8. In the highest-level game in this line, Wojtaszek – Korobov (New Delhi 2012), white castled long, aiming to attack the enemy king, but failed in his efforts. In general, thanks to the strengthened pawn on e5 and his territorial advantage, white's chances are somewhat better.

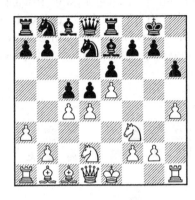

11.♘g5!?

A novelty. Previously, games continued 11.♕c2 and after 11...♘f8 the players switched their attention to the other side of the board. After 12.dxc5 a5 13.0-0 ♘a6 14.♖d1 ♘xc5 15.♗a2 ♗d7 16.cxd5 exd5 17.♘f1 (Khairullin – Alekseenko, Khanty-Mansiysk 2015) the isolation of his central pawn doesn't threaten black with disaster thanks to the maneuver 17...♗a4 18.b3 ♗c6. It wasn't by chance that Alekseenko waited to win back the pawn, as after 12...♗xc5?! 13.cxd5 ♕xd5 14.♘e4 the retreat 14...♗e7? is directly refuted – 15.♗xh6! gxh6 16.♖h3 (Kacheishvili – Shahade, Saint Louis 2011). After the stronger 14...♘bd7 15.0-0 ♗e7 16.♖d1 ♕a5 17.♗d2 ♕a6 the sac 18.♗xh6! (18...gxh6 19.♖d4!) doesn't win but promises a strong initiative.

11...cxd4

Here after 11...♘f8?! the f7 square collapses – 12.♘xf7! ♔xf7 13.♕h5+ ♔g8 14.♘f3 with the idea of a new sac 15.♗xh6!

12.f4 ♘c6

He cannot play 12...dxc4?
13.♗h7+ ♔f8 14.♕h5 ♗xg5 15.hxg5
♔e7 16.♘xc4, but it was worth
considering 12...♕c7!?, when it's
unclear whether there is anything
better than repeating moves with
13.♕h5 ♖f8 14.♗h7+ ♔h8 15.♗b1
♔g8 16.♗h7+.

**13.♕h5 ♖f8 14.cxd5 exd5 15.0-0
♕e8 16.♘df3**

16...d3?!

Obviously, black being a pawn up
he needs to consolidate his position,
and f7-f5 with the exchange of queens
is the right approach. He should
have taken e6 under control via 16...
♘b6 or 16...♘c5, and black's chances
would have been no worse.

**17.♗xd3   f5   18.♕xe8   ♖xe8
19.♘e6   ♗c5+   20.♘xc5   ♘xc5
21.♖d1 ♘xd3 22.♖xd3 ♗e6**

Black's gains do not justify the
return of the pawn. A comparison of
the d5 and e5 passers clearly doesn't
favor the former.

**23.♗e3   ♖ec8   24.♖c1   ♔f7
25.♖dc3 ♔e8 26.♔f2 ♔d7 27.b4 b6
28.h5 ♗f7??**

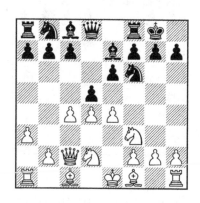

All black had to do was retreat
♘c6-e7 and force the exchange of
rooks, after which the opposite-
colored bishops would have allowed
him to hold on. Instead he made a
terrible blunder.

29.e6+!

Black resigned due to 29...♗xe6+
30.♖xc6.

No. 37 B. Gelfand – D. Bocharov
Sochi 2007

**1.d4   ♘f6 2.c4 e6 3.♘f3   ♗b4+
4.♘bd2 0-0 5.a3 ♗e7 6.e4 d5 7.♕c2**

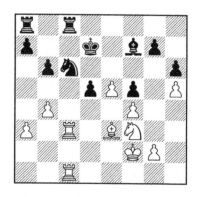

This line can also be reached
after 4...d5 5.♕c2 0-0 6.a3 ♗e7 7.e4.
Dmitry Bocharov is a specialist in
this variation.

7...c5

Gelfand had also faced this line twice in his younger days. The immediate surrender of the center with 7...dxe4 is reviewed in the next game.

> **KEY TIP.** In both the orthodox Queen's Gambit and Catalan Opening the advance c7-c5 is a typical way to attack d4 once it is no longer protected by white's queen. It's the same in the Bogo-Indian Defense.

8.dxc5

8.e5 ♘fd7 9.♗d3 would create a battery that is harmless for black's king. After 9...h6 10.0-0 ♘c6 11.♖e1 a5 white cannot play b2-b4 as a follow-up to d4xc5, while 12.♘b3 a4 unwinds the tension in the center with no problems for black.

8...dxe4 9.♘xe4 ♘xe4 10.♕xe4

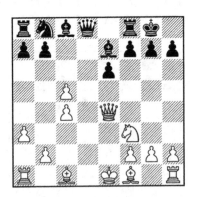

10...♘c6

Bocharov plans to return the pawn at the most appropriate moment. An interesting alternative is 10...♗xc5 11.b4 ♕f6!? 12.♖b1 ♗e7 13.♗b2 ♕f5 14.♕xf5 exf5 with counterplay in the form of a7-a5. White's pawn majority on the queenside is more threatening after 13.♗d3 ♕g6 14.♕xg6 hxg6 15.0-0.

11.♗f4

If 11.b4 f5 12.♕e3 ♗f6! 13.♖a2 e5 and then e5-e4 black controls the center, and he has obvious compensation for the material.

11...♗xc5?!

It was hard to foresee that this was the wrong way to win back the pawn. The correct continuation was 11...f5! 12.♕c2 ♕a5+ 13.♗d2 ♕xc5 with the important subtlety 14.b4 ♘d4! 15.♘xd4 ♕xd4 16.♗c3 ♕f4.

12.♖d1

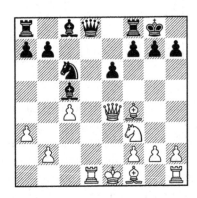

12...♕b6

12...♗xf2+ 13.♔e2 ♕b6 leads back to the actual game, while 13...f5 14.♖xd8 fxe4 15.♖xf8+ ♔xf8 16.♗d6+ ♔g8 17.♔xf2 exf3 18.gxf3 grants white the advantage of the bishop pair in the endgame.

13.b4 ♗xf2+ 14.♔e2 f5

If 14...e5 15.c5 ♗xc5 16.bxc5 ♕xc5 17.♗e3 ♕xa3 18.♔f2 (Gelfand) the mathematical count of material isn't valid. The bishop is stronger than four pawns, which are far from the queening square.

15.♕c2 e5 16.c5 ♕c7

16...♗xc5 17.bxc5 ♕c7 leads to more open play. Analysis by Golubev shows that the centralized white king avoids difficulties: 18.♕b3+ ♚h8 19.♘xe5! ♘xe5 20.♕e3 ♕f7 21.♗xe5 f4 22.♕d4 ♗g4+ 23.♚f2 ♗xd1 24.♗c4.

17.♚xf2 exf4 18.♗c4+ ♚h8

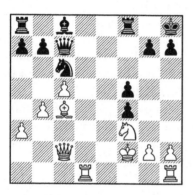

19.♕c3

The most natural move 19.♖he1, as is frequently the case, is also the best one. It's advisable to calculate the pretty variation 19...♗d7 20.♘g5! h6 21.♖d6! hxg5 22.♕c3.

19...♗d7 20.♖he1 ♖ae8 21.♖d6 ♖xe1 22.♕xe1 ♖f6 23.♘g5 h6?

The decisive blunder. After 23...♖xd6 24.♘f7+ ♚g8 25.♘xd6+ ♚f8 26.♕d2 white regains the pawn with an excellent position, but he isn't yet winning.

24.♘f7+ ♚h7 25.♖xf6 gxf6 26.♕d1!

The invasion squares along the e-file are covered, but the d-file and d1-h5 diagonal have plenty of room!

26...♕c8 27.♕d6 ♚g6 28.b5 Black resigned.

No. 38 E. Schiendorfer – D. Sengupta
Biel 2012

1.d4 e6 2.c4 ♗b4+ 3.♘d2 ♘f6 4.♘gf3 0-0 5.a3 ♗e7 6.e4 d5 7.♕c2 dxe4 8.♘xe4

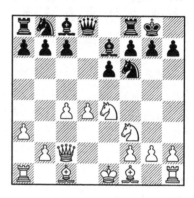

This is a "four versus three ranks" position. White can be proud of his greater freedom to maneuver, while black enjoys a solid position.

8...♘bd7

After 8...♘xe4 9.♕xe4 ♘d7 10.♗d3 ♘f6 11.♕e2 b6 12.0-0 ♗b7 13.♖d1 black's minor pieces are mobilized but it's not so easy for him to find good squares for his major pieces.

Attacking the d4 pawn via 8...♘c6 will prove justified if black manages to capture it or gain coherent piece play. The latter is possible after 9.♗e3 ♘xe4 10.♕xe4 f5 11.♕d3 f4 12.♗d2 e5 13.dxe5 ♗g4, but Tisdall's recommendation 14.♕e4 is an attempt by white to retain an advantage.

9.♗d3

After 9.♘eg5!? h6 10.h4 the knight remains at the battlefront, but he has nobody to support him. After 10...c5 11.♗e3 cxd4 12.♗xd4 e5 13.♗c3 ♖e8 this complicated position hardly favors white.

9...♘xe4 10.♗xe4

10...f5!?

This is far more interesting than the banal 10...♘f6 11.♗d3 b6. The Indian grandmaster believes action in the center here to be justified even when he hasn't completed development.

11.♗d3 c5 12.♗e2

If 12.d5 exd5 13.♗xf5 ♘f6 14.0-0 ♗xf5 15.♕xf5 d4 black at least has no cause to complain about his pawn structure.

12...cxd4 13.♘xd4 ♘f6 14.♘f3 ♕c7 15.0-0 ♗d7 16.b3

In itself, the bishop will be on an excellent square on b2. However, it has lost touch with its own king. It was preferable to play 16.♖d1 and then develop the bishop on d2 or g5, depending on black's play.

16...♗c6 17.♗b2 ♘g4 18.g3 ♗e4

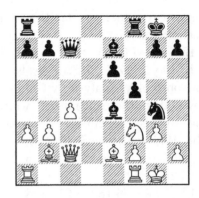

19.♕c1

The apparently dangerous continuation 19.♕c3 ♗f6 20.♘d4 ♖ad8 21.♖ad1 is actually acceptable for white. The retreat to c1 misses a tactic.

19...f4! 20.♘d4?

In reply to the more stubborn 20.b4 black has a number of good continuations. The simplest one is doubling rooks on the f-file.

20...♘xf2! 21.♖xf2 fxg3 22.♖g2 ♗xg2 23.♔xg2 ♖f2+ 24.♔g1 ♗c5 25.♕e3 e5 26.hxg3 ♖f6

White resigned.

No. 39 Y. Shulman – A. Lenderman
Wheeling 2011

1.d4 ♘f6 2.c4 e6 3.♘f3 ♗b4+ 4.♘bd2 0-0 5.a3 ♗e7 6.e4 d5

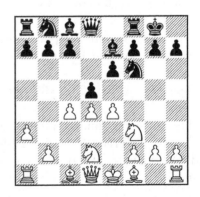

7.e5

This commits white to playing energetically and precisely. The advanced pawn may easily become a target of attack.

7...♘fd7

After 7...♘e4?! 8.♕c2 f5 9.exf6 ♘xf6 black faces problems with the e5 square and the e6 pawn. In the game Volkov – Iliushkin (Taganrog 2015) these problems quickly became unsolvable: 10.♗d3 b6 11.0-0 c5 12.dxc5 bxc5 13.b3 ♕c7 14.♗b2 h6 (14...d4 15.b4) 15.♗e5 ♗d6 16.♖fe1 ♘c6 17.♗xd6 ♕xd6 18.cxd5 exd5 19.♖ad1 ♘d7 20.b4! (20...cxb4 21.♘e4!). The exchange 8...♘xd2 9.♗xd2 doesn't create any obvious strategic defects, but black gains nothing in return for conceding space.

8.b4

The extended fianchetto is a logical continuation of 5.a3. The continuation 8.♗d3 is reviewed in game 40.

8...a5

After 8...b6 9.cxd5 exd5 10.♕b3 ♗b7 11.♗d3 pressure on the c-file doesn't promise dividends, whereas after h2-h4 and ♘d2-f1 exciting prospects open up on the kingside.

9.b5 c5

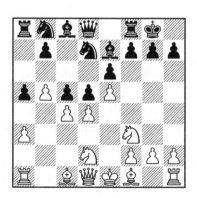

A pretty structure resembling a ladle (from a5 to h7). Now white will either resolve the tension in the extended center or provide black with that opportunity.

10.♗b2

There have been many games with 10.cxd5 exd5 11.♗d3 cxd4 12.♘b3 a4 13.♘bxd4 ♘c5. The pawn structures of both sides are smashed up, the pieces don't yet create any threats, and only the blockade on d4 accords white a slim advantage. The example Fressinet – Yusupov (Germany 2010) continued 14.♗c2 ♗g4 15.0-0 ♘bd7 16.h3 ♗h5 17.♖e1 ♖e8 18.♘f5 ♗f8 19.g4 ♗g6, and after 20.♕xd5 ♘b6 21.♕a2 ♕d7 22.♗e3 ♕xb5 winning back the pawn fails to ensure complete equality.

10...cxd4 11.♗xd4 ♘c5 12.♕c2

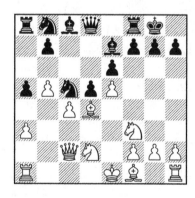

12...b6

Lenderman leaves the c8-h3 diagonal free and later uses it to develop his bishop. After 12...♘bd7 13.♗e2 b6 14.cxd5 exd5 15.0-0 ♗b7 16.♖fe1 ♘e6 17.♗b2 ♖c8 18.♕b1 ♘dc5 19.♘d4 ♘xd4 20.♗xd4 ♘e6 21.♘f3 ♗c5 22.♕b2 (Korobov – Zhou Jianchao, Khanty-Mansiysk

2011) white retained the blockade and a small advantage thanks to the bishop on b7 being stuck behind its own pawn.

13.cxd5 exd5 14.a4 ♗g4 15.♗e2 ♘bd7 16.0-0 ♖c8 17.♕a2 ♗f5 18.♖fe1 ♘e6

If 18...♕c7 or 18...♖e8 white still cannot capture the pawn on d5 due to 19...♗e6 trapping the queen. Now, though, the sacrifice transforms from an imaginary one into a real one. So far it's correct.

19.♕xd5

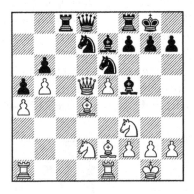

19...♘f4?

He had to play 19...♗c5 20.♗b2 before chasing the queen away. Shulman's strong bishop in the center allows him to consolidate.

20.♕b3 ♗c2 21.♕a2 ♗b4 22.♗f1 ♗xd2 23.♘xd2 ♘xe5 24.♗xe5 ♕xd2 25.♖ad1 ♘h3+ 26.gxh3 ♕g5+ 27.♗g3 ♗xd1 28.♖xd1

The computer doesn't accord white a decisive advantage, but a human should not doubt it. After the exchange of queens black cannot counter the bishop pair.

28...♖fd8 29.h4 ♕e7 30.♕b3 h5 31.h3 g6 32.♔h2 ♖xd1 33.♕xd1

♖d8 **34.♕c2 ♕e1 35.♗c4 ♔f8 36.♗b3 ♕e7 37.♕c3 ♔g8 38.♕c6 Black resigned.**

No. 40 Ding Liren – B. Amin
Tsaghkadzor 2015

1.d4 ♘f6 2.c4 e6 3.♘f3 ♗b4+ 4.♘bd2 0-0 5.a3 ♗e7 6.e4 d5 7.e5 ♘fd7 8.♗d3 c5 9.♕c2

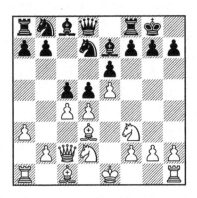

White builds a "wrong" battery, but its strength should not be underestimated.

9...g6

Grandmaster Ryazantsev questioned this defense, and 9...h6 is stronger. A typical position in this variation arises after 9...h6 10.0-0 ♘c6 11.♘b3 cxd4 12.♖e1 ♖e8 13.♗f4 dxc4 14.♗xc4 ♘b6 15.♗f1 ♘d5 16.♗d2 ♕b6. The d4 pawn is protected and has somewhat cramped white, but black's queenside remains undeveloped. The e5 pawn is strong, and the e4 square will become a hub for developing an initiative on the kingside. The example Sargissian – Papin (Beirut 2017) continued: 17.♗c4 ♗d7 18.♕e4 ♗f8 19.♕g4 f5 20.exf6 ♘xf6 21.♕h4, and the structure has evolved to white's advantage – black will not hang on to his extra pawn.

10.cxd5

He should have considered charging with Harry the h-pawn. After 10.h4!? ♘c6 11.h5 cxd4 12.hxg6 hxg6 13.♗xg6 ♘dxe5 14.♘xe5 ♘xe5 15.♗h7+ ♔g7 16.♘f3 ♘g4 17.♘e5! (Kunin – Noe, Schwaebisch Gmuend 2018) 17...♘xe5 18.♗h6+ ♔f6 19.♕d2! ♗b4 20.axb4 ♔e7 21.♕xd4 black's position is hopeless despite the material equality, and he needs to find a stronger defense. It was better to neutralize the d3 bishop via 10...cxd4 11.h5 ♘c5 with a highly complex position.

> **KEY TIP.** After the h-pawn is thrown forward, the bishop on d3 can be sacrificed to destroy the enemy king's bunker, and the maneuver ♘d7-c5 is an important defensive ploy.

10...exd5

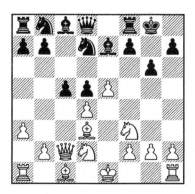

11.e6!

> **KEY TIP.** A purely tactical move, as is appropriate to this very sharp line: the pawn barrier on the light squares is blown apart.

11...fxe6   12.♗xg6!   hxg6 13.♕xg6+ ♔h8 14.♘e4!

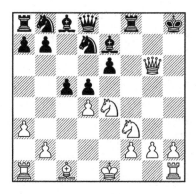

White opens a diagonal for his queen's bishop, sacking another piece.

14...dxe4?!

After 14...♕e8 15.♕h6+ ♔g8 16.♘fg5 ♗xg5 17.♕xg5+ ♔h7 18.♕h6+ ♔g8 19.a4! ♕e7 20.♖a3 ♖f7 21.♘d6! ♖g7 (Ryazantsev – Vokaturo, Jerusalem 2015) white eventually lost, but he had already carried out the hard work and all that was left was to harvest the fruit of his labor with 22.♖h3 ♕xd6 (22...♖h7 23.♘xc8) 23.♗g5!

The variation 14...♖f5!? 15.♕h6+ ♔g8 16.♕xe6+ ♖f7 17.♘fg5 ♗xg5 18.♘xg5 ♕f8 19.♕xd5 also appears on the surface to be to white's advantage, but this is probably the right way for black to save the day.

15.♕h5+ ♔g8 16.♗h6 ♖f6

If black brings his queen over to defend his king at the cost of material, he will lose due to the lack of

development of the rest of his army –
16...♖f7 17.♕g6+ ♔h8 18.♕xf7 ♕g8
19.♕xe7 exf3 20.gxf3 ♘c6 21.♕h4
♘xd4 22.0-0-0 ♕g6 23.♗e3+ ♕h7
24.♗xd4+ cxd4 25.♕xd4+.

**17.♕g4+ ♔f7 18.♘g5+ ♔g6
19.♘xe6+ ♔f7 20.♘xd8+ ♗xd8
21.♕g7+ ♔e8 22.0-0-0**

If we don't count the pawns, then
the three minor pieces ought to be the
material equivalent of the lost queen.
However, this isn't the case with
Amin's wretched army.

**22...♗e7 23.♗g5 ♗f8 24.♕h7
cxd4 25.♖xd4**

Black resigned.

Variations from game 40 show
convincingly that it's not very rational
for black to go for the complicated line
4...0-0 5.a3 ♗e7 6.e4 d5. He needs to
take onboard the scale of the danger
and be ready to transpose to a worse
but playable position. The truth is
that the Bogo-Indian Defense isn't
very appropriate if you want to grab
the initiative as black in the opening,
and the majority of sharp variations
are in white's favor. If in the above
chain of moves black replaces 6...d5
with 6...d6 (games 34 and 35), then
he has every chance to equalize using
standard methods.

Chapter 6

4...b6 variation

Black immediately opts for a QID setup, in order to establish control over e4.

No. 41 N. Chadaev – I. Gerasimov
Moscow 2012

1.♘f3 ♘f6 2.c4 e6 3.d4 ♗b4+ 4.♘bd2 b6

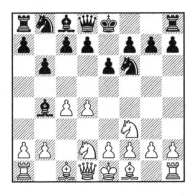

5.a3

Frequent alternatives are 5.e3 (reviewed in chapter 5) and 5.g3 (a variation of the Queen's Indian Defense).

5...♗xd2+

Strong players don't retreat the bishop here. After white takes control of the center with 6.e4 black has an unpleasant choice – accept a cramped game on three ranks without a hint of counterplay, or else go for 6...d5 7.cxd5 exd5 8.e5 ♘e4 9.♗d3. In a structure that is already good for white the addition of a2-a3 and b7-b6 is clearly an extra bonus.

6.♗xd2

The capture 6.♘xd2 is covered in game 2 of the historical introduction.

6.♕xd2 is reviewed in games 45-49.

6...♘e4

Apart from 6...♗b7 (games 42-44), occupying e4 is the most logical move. However, in terms of popularity the prophylactic 6...h6 is ranked between those two moves. Its idea is that after 6...♗b7 7.♗g5 black faces certain difficulties. After 6...h6 white has to choose between 7.g3, 7.e3 and 7.♗f4. That variation lacks dynamism, and the loss of a tempo is not significant.

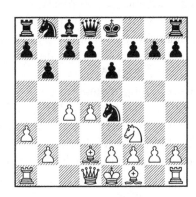

7.♗e3

After 7.♗f4 black will most probably select a Dutch setup in order to maintain the knight in the center. In the game Fier – Hoolt (Rome 2016) black didn't hurry to castle, and the game didn't merge with the respective variation of chapter 5. Play continued 7...d6 8.e3 ♗b7 9.♗d3 ♘d7 10.♕c2 f5 11.h3 (creating a safe luft for the king at the cost of weakening the kingside) 11...♕e7 12.♗h2 0-0

13.0-0 ♖f6 14.♘d2 ♘xd2 15.♕xd2
♖g6 16.f3 ♖f8 17.b4 e5 18.d5 ♗c8.
White's queen's bishop has found
a decent job to do, while black has
sufficient "Dutch" counterplay.

The bishop on d2 isn't so valuable
that white must avoid exchanging it.
A good example is the game between
two great strategic players Nikolic –
Andersson (Naestved 1985): 7.g3 ♗b7
8.♗g2 ♘xd2 9.♕xd2 d6 10.0-0 ♘d7
11.d5 e5 12.b4 0-0 (12...a5!?) 13.♘e1
♕e7 14.♘d3 ♖fc8 15.c5 bxc5 16.bxc5
♘xc5 17.♘xc5 dxc5 18.♖ab1 ♗a6!
19.d6 ♕xd6 20.♕xd6 cxd6 21.♗xa8
♖xa8 22.♖fd1 ♗xe2 23.♖xd6. Black
can hold this endgame despite the
lack of the exchange, but Andersson
played the ending too passively and
lost. In any case, Nikolic played well
and demonstrated that the plan with
c4-c5 promises a slight advantage.

7...♗b7 8.g3 a5

In the approximate line 8...0-0
9.♗g2 f5 10.0-0 (10.♘d2?! ♘c3!)
10...♕f6 11.♘d2 ♘d6 12.♗xb7
♘xb7 black will easily improve the
position of his knight, while the hole
in white's kingside bunker will be a
long-term factor.

9.♗g2 a4 10.0-0 0-0 11.♕c2

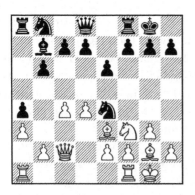

11...♖a7

If 11...♘f6 white would obviously
play 12.♗g5, and as a result of black
having played a5-a4 he can now play
12...♖a5!? The rook is active, but at
the same time it cannot detach itself
from the pawn on a4.

**12.♖fd1   d5   13.♖ac1   dxc4
14.♕xc4 ♗d5 15.♕d3 h6**

Black's play is not altogether
convincing, and he should definitely
have played 15...f6 here, preventing
white's knight from getting to e5.

16.♘e5 ♘f6 17.♗xd5 ♕xd5

Gerasimov won't accept defeat in
the strategic skirmish after 17...exd5,
but Chadaev nevertheless forces him
to make concessions.

**18.f3 ♖d8 19.♗f2 ♘fd7 20.♘c4
b5**

20...♕b5 would be met by 21.♖c3,
followed by 22.♕c2 and e2-e4.

21.♘e3 ♕b7

**22.d5! ♘f6 23.♕c3! exd5 24.♘f5
♖a6 25.♕xc7 ♕xc7 26.♖xc7**
Black resigned.

White's   gigantic   positional
advantage will definitely convert into
a material advantage (most probably
after 27.♖b7).

No. 42 L. Ftacnik – U. Boensch
Germany 2011

1.d4 ♘f6 2.♘f3 e6 3.c4 ♗b4+
4.♘bd2 b6 5.a3 ♗xd2+ 6.♗xd2
♗b7

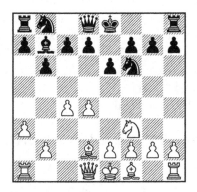

7.g3 0-0 8.♗g2

This merges with the line from the
Queen's Indian Defense 3...b6 4.g3
♗b7 5.♗g2 ♗b4+ 6.♘bd2 0-0 7.a3
♗xd2+ 8.♗xd2, which due to the
rare move a2-a3 has become a quite
unusual line. 7.♗g5 is covered in
games 43 and 44.

8...d6

It is worth considering 8...d5
9.cxd5 ♗xd5, and probably the only
way that white can challenge black's
hegemony on the light squares is
via the undesirable exchange of
light-squared bishops. After 10.0-0
♘bd7 11.♖c1 c5 12.dxc5 ♘xc5
13.♗b4 ♖c8 14.♘e5 ♗xg2 15.♔xg2
♕e7 16.♔g1 a5 17.♗xc5 ♖xc5
18.♘c6 ♕c7 19.♖xc5 bxc5 20.♕a4
(Gabuzyan – Swiercz, Moscow 2014)
black practically forced a draw with
20...♖c8! 21.♘xa5 ♖a8 22.b4 cxb4
23.axb4 ♘d5 and the unavoidable
regaining of the pawn.

9.0-0

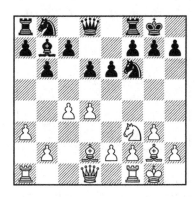

9...♘bd7

If 9...a5 it's best to reply 10.b4,
preventing white's pawn pair
from being cramped by a5-a4.
Here Grandmaster Boensch has
since played white and achieved a
comfortable position after 10...axb4
11.axb4 ♘bd7 12.♕c2 ♗e4 13.♕b3
♕b8 14.b5 ♕b7 15.♗b4 ♖fc8
16.♗h3 ♗f5 17.♗xf5 exf5 18.d5
♖xa1 19.♖xa1 ♖a8 20.♖a3 (Boensch
– Hoelzl, Austria 2015).

10.♖c1

10.♗c3 is featured in a large
number of games reached via the
Nimzo-Indian Defense (when
♗c1-d2 is followed by an exchange
on c3). Black achieves a decent
Dutch setup after 10...♘e4 and f7-f5.
The continuation 10.b4 looks more
precise, especially after 10...♕e7
11.♗c3 ♘e4 and in b2 the bishop
gains a good square to retreat to.

10...♕c8 11.b4 ♘e4 12.♗e3

From here the bishop will support
the standard push c4-c5. 12...c5 can
be met by 13.♕d3?, followed by
14.♖fd1 and the exchange d4xc5.

12...a5

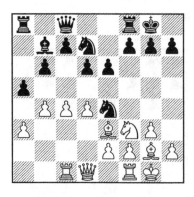

13.b5

White misses the right time to play d4-d5 and centralize the knight with ♘f3-d4 (13.d5 e5 14.♘h4 is clearly to white's advantage).

13...f5 14.♘e1 e5 15.♘d3 ♕e8

It was better to play 15...exd4 16.♗xd4 ♕e8 17.♘f4 ♕f7 18.♕c2 ♖ae8 – black has not only neutralized the break but has also gained a great hub for his knights.

16.c5   bxc5   17.dxc5   dxc5 18.♗xc5 ♖f7 19.♗e3 ♘b6 20.♕b3 ♗d5 21.♕b2 ♖e7

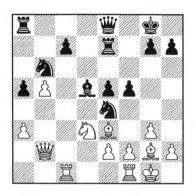

22.f3?

It's surprising that a strong grandmaster has made such a weak move. After 22.♗c5 ♘xc5 23.♗xd5+ ♘xd5 24.♘xc5 white is much better.

22...♘d6 23.♗g5 ♖e6 24.♖xc7 h6 25.♗e3 ♘bc4 26.♕c1 ♘xe3 27.♕xe3 ♘xb5

Boensch has won the pawn back and equalized. After this both sides played carefully and soon exhausted the opportunities to fight further.

28.♖c5 ♖d8 29.a4 ♘d4 30.♖xa5 ♗c4 31.♖xe5 ♖xe5 32.♘xe5 ♗xe2 33.♖e1 ♕xa4 34.♖xe2 ♘xe2+ 35.♕xe2 ♖d1+ 36.♗f1 ♕d4+ 37.♔h1 ♖xf1+

Draw agreed.

No. 43 M. Krasenkow – J. Duda
Montpellier 2015

1.d4 ♘f6 2.c4 e6 3.♘f3 ♗b4+ 4.♘bd2 b6 5.a3 ♗xd2+ 6.♗xd2 ♗b7 7.♗g5

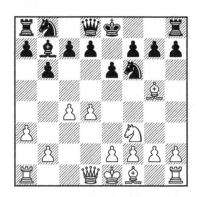

Before setting up a pawn chain d4-e3-f2, white dispatches his bishop beyond the barrier. After that he can castle long or short (the latter in the next game).

7...d6 8.e3 ♘bd7

We occasionally encounter the variation with the immediate exchange of white's bishop 8...h6 9.♗h4 g5 10.♗g3 ♘e4 11.♘d2

♘xg3 12.hxg3 ♘d7. Here we should trust the wisdom of the former world champion: 13.g4 c5 14.♘b1!? (to control d4 with his queen) 14...cxd4 15.♕xd4 ♕f6 16.♘c3 ♕xd4 17.exd4 ♘f6 18.f3 ♔e7 19.b4 with a small advantage (Karpov – Adams, Dos Hermanas 1995).

9.♕c2

Via 9.♘d2 h6 10.♗h4 ♕e7 11.f3 g5 12.♗f2 the bishop evades being exchanged, but black has got active in the center – 12...e5 13.d5 (13.dxe5 ♘xe5 14.e4 0-0-0 15.♗e2 g4 16.f4 ♘g6 clearly favors black) 13...e4!? 14.♘b3 (Burmakin – Othman, Oberwart 2002) 14...0-0-0 15.♘d4 exf3 16.gxf3 g4!? 17.fxg4 ♖de8 with compensation for the pawn.

9...h6 10.♗h4 g5 11.♗g3 ♘e4 12.♗d3

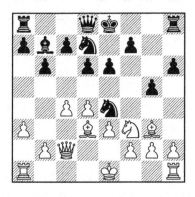

12...♘df6

No solution to the attacked knight is devoid of drawbacks. After 12...♘xg3 13.hxg3 the semi-open file works for white. Protecting it with 12...f5 isn't safe due to 13.d5! ♘dc5 (13...exd5 14.cxd5 ♗xd5 15.♘d4 ♕f6 16.♘b5 winning back the material with an advantage) 14.♘d4 ♕f6 15.♗xe4

fxe4 16.0-0 exd5 17.b4 ♘e6 18.♕a4+ (Watson – Lobo, San Francisco 1995) – the initiative more than compensates for the pawn.

13.0-0-0 ♕e7 14.d5! ♘c5

14...exd5 15.cxd5 ♗xd5? is catastrophic due to 16.♗b5+ ♔f8 17.♖xd5 ♘xd5 18.♕c6.

15.e4 e5 16.h4

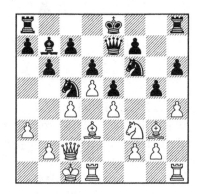

Now that the center is locked up it's time for white to get active on the kingside. The position on the board has occurred twice elsewhere.

16...g4

If 16...♘xd3+ 17.♕xd3 ♘h5 18.hxg5 hxg5 (Osterman – Hulak, Slovenia 2002) 19.c5!? ♕f6 20.cxd6 cxd6 21.♔b1 ♘xg3 22.fxg3 the knight is superior to the bishop, and white's chances are preferable.

17.♘d2

In the first game in this variation Grandmaster Viktor Mikhalevsky sent the knight via h2 and f1 to e3, whereas Krasenkow tests the g4 pawn a little earlier.

17...♘h5

If 17...h5 white will probably retreat his bishop to e2, then via f2-f3 will try to force the exchange g4xf3, g2xf3 and then transfer his bishop to h3. Well, talk is cheap – the success of such a venture is far from assured.

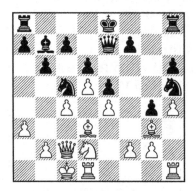

18.♝e2 ♝c8 19.b4 ♘d7!?

Black didn't want to retreat his knight to b7, so he gives up the pawn, counting on pressure along the g-file.

20.♝xg4 ♘xg3 21.fxg3 ♖g8 22.♝xd7+ ♝xd7 23.♕c3 ♕f6 24.♖df1 ♕g6 25.♖f3 ♝g4 26.♖e3

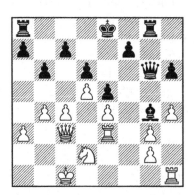

26...♖c8?! Duda has played nicely up until now, but this move is too timid. He should have gone for 26...a5 followed by opening the a-file and then ♚e8-e7. In the rooks battle white won't be calling the shots, as one of his rooks is stuck protecting the pawn on g3.

27.c5 ♚e7 28.♘c4 h5 29.♖f1 ♕h6 30.♚b2 ♖g6 31.♖ee1 a5 32.♘e3 axb4 33.cxd6+ cxd6 34.♕xb4 ♝d7 35.♕xb6 ♖xg3 36.♕a7! ♚e8 37.♖xf7! ♖xg2+ 38.♚a1 ♖d8 39.♖e7+! ♚f8 40.♖xd7 ♖c8 41.♖c7

Black resigned.

A great achievement by Krasenkow, who played the end of the game especially well.

No. 44 A. Rombaldoni – J. Hjartarson
Porto Mannu 2015

1.d4 ♘f6 2.c4 e6 3.♘f3 ♝b4+ 4.♘bd2 b6 5.a3 ♝xd2+ 6.♝xd2 ♝b7 7.♝g5 d6 8.e3 ♘bd7

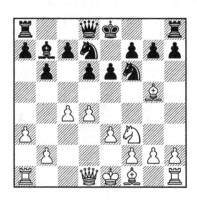

9.♝d3

After 9.♝e2 h6 10.♝h4 g5 11.♝g3 h5 12.h3 (there isn't full compensation for the material in the line 12.h4 g4 13.♘g5 ♝xg2 14.♖g1 ♝b7) 12...♘e4 13.d5 ♕f6 14.♕c2 ♘xg3 15.fxg3 0-0-0 16.e4 g4 17.♘d2 ♕e5 18.♕c3 (Markos – Davy, Tromso 2014) 18...♕xc3 19.bxc3 ♘e5 a draw for the grandmaster playing white (against a weaker opponent) would be the best he could hope for. In the battle against the pawn attack, white needs the bishop on d3.

9...h6 10.♗h4 ♕e7

In the principled variation 10...g5 11.♗g3 h5 12.h4 g4 13.♘g5 ♗xg2 14.♖g1 ♗b7 15.♕c2 ♕e7 16.0-0-0 0-0-0 17.b4 ♔b8 18.♔b2 e5 19.♗f5 ♖he8 (Gelfand – C. Hansen, Wijk aan Zee 1993) white gained active positions for his pieces at the cost of a pawn. Whether the initiative (or material) comes out on top depends on how the players continue in a highly complicated position.

11.0-0 g5

After 11...0-0 12.♘d2 black cannot exchange the bishop and in the game Wojtaszek – Kuzubov (Dresden 2007) he challenged for territory using his c-pawn – 12...c5 13.b4 ♖fd8 14.♕b3 ♗c6 15.♕b2 a5 16.h3 ♕f8 17.♗g3 axb4 18.axb4 ♖xa1 19.♖xa1 ♖a8 20.♖xa8 ♕xa8 21.♗xd6 ♗xg2 22.dxc5 bxc5 23.bxc5 ♗xh3. The black battery on the long diagonal is shooting blanks, and white's chances are preferable.

12.♗g3

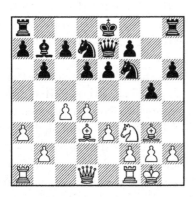

12...♘e4

If 12...h5?! 13.h4 g4 14.♘g5 e5 15.♗f5 then in comparison with the 10...g5 line white has planted a knight and bishop for free in the enemy camp.

13.♘d2

After 13.♗xe4 ♗xe4 14.♘d2 ♗b7 15.f3 f5 16.e4 0-0-0 17.exf5 exf5 18.d5 h5 19.♗f2 g4 white has locked in black's bishop, although black has counter chances on the kingside.

13...f5?!

After 13...♘xg3 14.fxg3 0-0-0 black has to contend with white's attack on the queenside, but unlike in the game he has counterplay.

14.♘xe4 fxe4 15.♗e2 0-0 16.b4 ♘f6 17.♖c1 ♖f7 18.c5 ♗d5 19.cxd6 cxd6

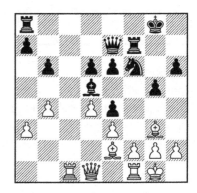

20.♗b5

Now Hjartarson gains counterplay, hence 20.h3 was stronger here.

20...h5 21.♗c6 h4

Instead of 21...♖d8 the Icelandic grandmaster preferred to pick up two pieces for his rook, a somewhat questionable decision.

22.♗xa8 ♗xa8 23.♖c8+ ♖f8 24.♖xf8+

This only works due to Hjartarson's mistakes. 24.♕c1 hxg3 25.fxg3 was objectively better.

24...♕xf8?!

After 24...♚xf8 25.♝e5 dxe5 26.dxe5 ♞d7 the knight is protected by the queen and is ready to capture on e5. The forced centralization of the knight as per the game is clearly weaker.

25.♝e5   dxe5   26.dxe5   ♞d5 27.♕h5 ♕e7 28.♕g6+ ♚f8

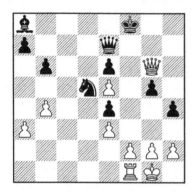

29.♕xe4

Rombaldoni in his euphoria grabbed a pawn and thereby dragged out the game for longer. The variation 29.f3! ♞xe3 30.♖c1 ♝b7 31.fxe4 was far more convincing.

29...♝b7

After 29...♕c7 30.f4 gxf4 31.exf4 ♕c6 32.f5 ♞e3 33.♕xc6 ♝xc6 black's chances of saving the game are very low, but he can still put up some fight.

30.♕g6 b5 31.h3 a6 32.♖d1 ♝c6 33.♖d4 ♝e8 34.♕h6+

Black resigned.

No. 45 P. Michalik – P. Haba
Czech Republic 2009

1.d4 ♞f6 2.♞f3 e6 3.c4 ♝b4+ 4.♞bd2 b6 5.a3 ♝xd2+ 6.♕xd2

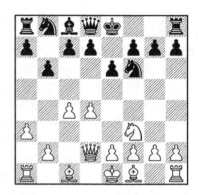

The capture by the queen involves white placing his bishop on the long diagonal.

6...♝b7

If black wants to avoid 7.b4, then he can play 6...a5. In the game Zubov – Enchev (Arad 2015) white put off mobilizing the kingside for some time. However, due to his opponent's blunders he won quite quickly – 7.b3 ♝b7 8.♝b2 0-0 9.♕c2 ♕e7 10.♖d1 d5 11.e3 ♖c8 12.cxd5 exd5 13.♝d3 ♝a6 14.♝xa6 ♖xa6 15.0-0 a4 16.bxa4 ♞e4?! 17.♕b3 c6 18.♞d2 ♞xd2 19.♖xd2 ♕a7?! 20.e4! dxe4 21.d5! cxd5 22.♖xd5 ♖a5? 23.♕c3! The move 16...♕e8 with the natural idea of winning back the pawn would have preserved an acceptable position.

7.g3

As a rule, 7.b4 merges into the lines 7.g3 or 7.e3, although that didn't happen in the following fragment: 7...a5 8.♝b2 (8.b5 is more ambitious) 8...♞e4 9.♕c2 axb4 10.axb4 ♖xa1+ 11.♝xa1 ♕e7 12.c5 (the following long, near forced line leads to an equal ending: 12.b5 d5!? 13.cxd5 ♕b4+ 14.♞d2 ♞xd2 15.♝c3 ♕xb5 16.♝xd2 exd5 17.♕xc7 ♕b1+ 18.♕c1 ♕xc1+ 19.♝xc1 ♞c6) 12...0-0 13.e3 f5

14.♗e2 (Ree – Andersson, Wijk aan Zee 1984), and the attractive (and admittedly standard) piece setup with 14...♗d5 and ♘b8-c6 promises black slightly better prospects.

7...0-0 8.♗g2 d6 9.0-0

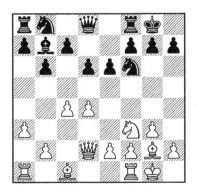

9...♘bd7

If 9...a5 10.b3 ♘bd7 white rarely plans b3-b4 – he usually prefers playing in the center and on the kingside. For example, 11.♖d1 ♗e4 12.♗b2 h6 13.♖ac1 ♖c8 14.♗h3 ♕e7 15.♘e1 ♖fe8 16.f3 ♗f5 17.♗f1 d5 18.♘g2 c6 19.e3 ♖ed8 20.♕f2 ♗h7 21.g4 with a small advantage (Mirzoev – Bellahcene, Marseille 2016).

KEY TIP. White has demonstrated a method typical of closed openings for neutralizing the enemy bishop along the long diagonal. The plan often ends with e2-e4, which in the last fragment is prevented by d6-d5.

10.b4 a5

It's hard for black to equalize with a Dutch setup: 10...♕e7 11.♗b2 ♘e4 12.♕c2 f5. He suffers from a tangible lack of space, while battle for territory via c7-c5 is strategically risky.

11.b5

In response to 11.♗b2 the pawn sac 11...axb4 12.axb4 b5!? needs to be tested. If white accepts it black gains clear positional compensation, while after 13.c5 ♘b8!? it's hard for white to prevent black rearranging his forces with ♗b7-d5 and ♘b8-c6.

11...c6!?

Haba makes a committal move. He could also have played 11...♖e8 with the idea of e6-e5, after which the pawn's moving from d4 grants the black knight the c5 square.

12.bxc6 ♗xc6

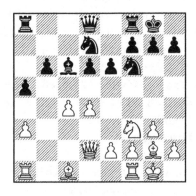

13.d5! exd5 14.♘d4 ♘e5

After 14...♗b7 15.♘f5 ♘e5 16.♕g5 g6 17.cxd5 ♗xd5 18.f4 ♘ed7 19.♘h6+ ♔g7 20.♗h3 white's initiative is too dangerous, and hence black needs to agree to the exchange of his bishop.

15.♕a2 ♖c8 16.♘xc6 ♖xc6 17.cxd5 ♖c7 18.a4 ♘c4

White's advantage is unstable, as the black knights still have outposts, and activing his heavy pieces will alleviate his defense. 18...♘fd7 with the idea of 19...♕f6 was interesting.

19.♗f4 ♖c5 20.♖ac1 ♕c7

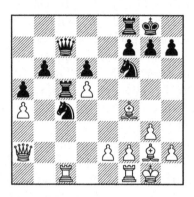

21.♖xc4?!

As a result of the exchange white is left with a light-squared bishop shooting into its own pawn, and his advantage disappears. He should have doubled rooks on the c-file.

21...♖xc4   22.♗xd6   ♖xa4 23.♕xa4   ♕xd6   24.♕c6   ♕b4 25.d6 ♖d8 26.e4 ♕d4 27.e5 ♕xe5 28.♕xb6

Draw agreed.

No. 46 B. Harsha – P. Kiriakov
Dubai 2018

1.d4 e6 2.c4 ♘f6 3.♘f3 ♗b4+ 4.♘bd2 b6 5.a3 ♗xd2+ 6.♕xd2 ♗b7 7.e3

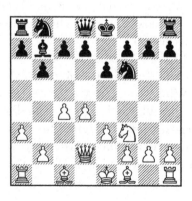

7...0-0

7...♘e4 8.♕c2 f5 is found in game 49, where it makes more sense to discuss possible divergences.

8.♗e2

The drawback of the reasonable continuation 8.♗d3 is that after the d-file opens the bishop is in the way. The example Grishchenko – Romanov, Sochi 2012, continued: 8...d6 9.♕c2 c5 10.dxc5 dxc5 11.b3 ♕e7 12.♗b2 a5 13.0-0 ♘bd7 14.♕c3 ♖fd8 15.♖fd1 ♘e8 16.♕c2 ♘f8 17.♗e4 ♘d6 18.♗xb7 ♕xb7, and chances are fully equal.

8...a5 9.b3

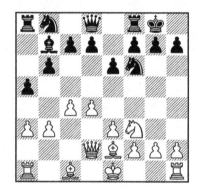

9...d5

Usually the pawn advances only one square (see game 47).

10.♗b2 c5

Kiriakov accepts that he will be saddled with hanging pawns, whereas after the more subtle move order 10...♘bd7 11.0-0 c5 if 12.dxc5 then 12...♘xc5 is good. Therefore, the tension in the center is not reduced immediately, and black demonstrates counterplay on the queenside: 12.♖fd1 ♕e7 13.♖ac1 ♖fd8 14.♕c2 a4!? 15.bxa4 ♗c6

16.a5 ♖xa5 17.♖e1 dxc4 18.♕xc4 ♗d5 19.♕c2 (Lenic – Kovacevic, Hungary 2018) 19...♘e4 20.♗d3 f5 with a powerful blockade and equality.

11.dxc5 bxc5 12.cxd5 exd5 13.♕c3 ♕b6 14.0-0 ♖e8 15.♗d3

Black has stubbornly refused to develop his knight to d7, and Harsha takes advantage of his opponent's inaccuracy. Now 15...d4?! 16.exd4 ♗xf3? would be met by the intermezzo 17.dxc5, which is harmless after 14...♘bd7.

15...♗a6 16.♖fd1 a4

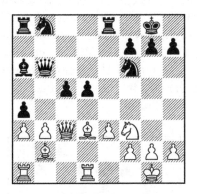

17.bxa4

17.b4 was also good, with the approximate variation 17...♘bd7 18.♗f5 d4 19.♕c2 ♕b5 20.bxc5 dxe3 21.♗d4 e2 22.♖e1 – the bishop pair is worth more than the passed pawn in this open game.

17...♗xd3 18.♖xd3 ♕d6 19.♖ad1 ♕f8 20.♕c2 ♘bd7 21.♖xd5! ♘xd5 22.♘g5 ♘7f6?

He should have stamped out white's initiative by exchanging queens. After 22...g6 23.♖xd5 ♕e7 24.♘xh7 ♕e4 25.♕xe4 ♖xe4 26.♖xd7 ♔xh7 27.♖xf7+ ♔g8

white cannot win, whether or not he captures on g6.

23.♖xd5 ♕e7 24.♗xf6 ♕xf6 25.♕xh7+ ♔f8 26.h3 g6

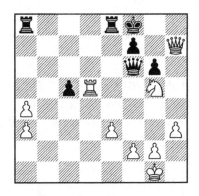

27.♕h4

The position is quite complicated for handling over the board, and so now the players exchange inaccuracies. It was stronger to continue 27.♖d7! ♖e7 (blocking the king's escape) 28.♖d6! ♕g7 29.♕h4 ♔g8 30.♖c6 gaining the c5 pawn and probably winning the game.

27...♔g8 28.♕h7+ ♔f8 29.♕h4 ♔g8

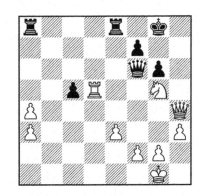

Now (and two moves earlier) if black's king heads to g7 this would revert to the variation from the previous note. After f7 falls the game finishes immediately.

30.♖d7 ♕a1+ 31.♔h2 ♕h8 32.♕c4 ♕f6 33.♖xf7 ♕a6 34.♖f8+ ♔xf8 35.♕f7#

No. 47 M. Yilmaz – J. Hjartarson
Reykjavik 2017

1.d4 ♘f6 2.c4 e6 3.♘f3 ♗b4+ 4.♘bd2 b6 5.a3 ♗xd2+ 6.♕xd2 ♗b7 7.e3 d6 8.♗e2 ♘bd7 9.0-0 a5 10.b3 0-0 11.♗b2

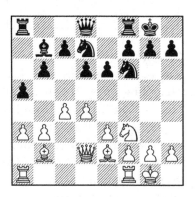

The moves to get to this position have many different orders. What's key is that black's d-pawn rationed himself to moving just one square on move 7, while his ninth move made the advance b2-b4 difficult.

11...♕e7

If 11...♘e4 12.♕c2 f5 then the principled move is 13.d5!? Now 13...exd5 14.♘d4 ♕e7 15.cxd5 ♗xd5 16.♖ad1 ♘dc5 17.♗b5 provides white with rich play along the light squares, while black (as in the game) is advised to strive for a battle of a more closed nature – 13... e5 14.♘d2 ♘xd2 15.♕xd2 ♕e7.

12.♖fd1

The subtle move 12.♕c2 involves the idea of moving the queen to c3 in response to 12...♗e4 and otherwise chasing the knight from e4 (12...♘e4 13.♘e1 and f2-f3). The game could continue 12...c5 13.♖fd1 h6 14.♖ac1 ♖fc8 (gunning for white's queen) 15.a4 cxd4 16.♘xd4 ♘c5 17.♗a3 ♘fe4 18.♘b5 d5 19.f3 ♘f6 20.♕b2 (Shankland – J. Polgar, Tromso 2014) 20...♗a6, and the exchange of white's strong knight makes chances equal.

12...♘e4

If black goes for an all-out win, then he needs to switch to a Dutch setup. Even the super-aggressive Korchnoi was unable to launch a fight with 12...♖fd8. White continued b3-b4, and all the major pieces got exchanged on the open a-file.

13.♕c2 f5

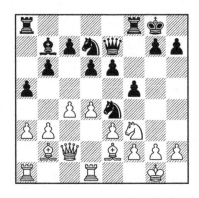

14.d5 e5

14...exd5 no longer wins a pawn – 15.cxd5 ♘df6 16.♖ac1 ♖ac8 17.♗xf6 ♘xf6 18.♗c4. But since the d5 pawn remains alive, black has no chance of equality.

15.b4 ♘g5 16.♗c3 ♘xf3+ 17.♗xf3 ♕h4 18.♗e2 ♘f6

The Icelandic grandmaster stakes on his attack, but white easily parries his threats.

19.♗e1 axb4 20.axb4 ♕g5 21.♕c3 f4 22.exf4 ♕xf4 23.f3 ♕f5 24.♗d3 ♕d7 25.♕c2 g6

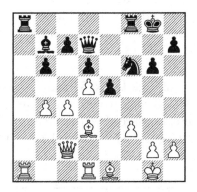

26.♗d2

The positions of the bishops have changed: while they carried out defensive functions on e2 and e1 they are now ready to attack.

26...♕f7 27.♗h6 ♖fb8 28.♖f1 b5

He should have stuck to a waiting game.

29.cxb5 ♗xd5 30.♖a5 ♖e8?

The decisive mistake in a difficult position. The right continuation was 30...♖c8 31.♖c1 ♘e8.

31.♖c1 ♖e7 32.b6 ♖xa5 33.bxa5 cxb6 34.♕c8+ ♖e8 35.♗b5! ♗b7 36.♗xe8 ♘xe8 37.♕d8

Black resigned.

No. 48 R. Wojtaszek – B. Jobava
Khanty-Mansyisk 2011

1.d4 ♘f6 2.c4 e6 3.♘f3 ♗b4+ 4.♘bd2 b6 5.a3 ♗xd2+ 6.♕xd2 ♗b7 7.e3 d6 8.♗e2 ♘bd7 9.0-0 0-0

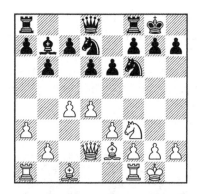

10.b4 ♘e4

The knight's sortie here involves the c7-c5 break, while in the next game it involves f7-f5. 10...c5 straight away is also possible, which is mostly likely to continue with the opening of the d-file and simplifications, as per the example Malakhatko – Filippov (Almaty 2017): 11.♗b2 ♕e7 12.♖fd1 ♖fd8 13.dxc5 dxc5 14.♕d6 ♕xd6 15.♖xd6 ♘e4 16.♖d3 ♘f8. White's advantage is tiny.

But why is 10...e5 11.dxe5 dxe5 with a similar structure found rarely? The reason is that the pawn on e5 becomes a target, and white is right to look after his queen and use his bishop pair as trump cards. For example, 12.♗b2 ♕e7 13.♖fd1 ♖ad8 14.♕c2 c5 15.♘d2 ♕e6 16.f3 h5 17.♗d3 with a tangible advantage (Laznicka – Zeng Chongsheng, Taizhou 2014).

11.♕c2 c5 12.♗b2

12.♘d2!? is also of interest, so that white immediately neutralizes the enemy bishop and uses his along the c1-h6 diagonal. The game Gelfand – Anand (Dortmund 1996) continued 12...♘xd2 13.♕xd2 ♕g5 14.f3 ♖fd8 15.♖d1 d5 16.♕b2 cxb4 17.♕xb4 ♗a6 18.e4 ♕g6 19.♕a4 ♗xc4

20.♗xc4 dxc4 21.♕xc4 ♘f8 22.♗e3 f5 23.exf5 with a draw. After 17.cxd5 bxa3 18.♕xa3 exd5 19.e4 ♕h4 20.e5 white's bishop pair compensates for the pawn, but does he have anything real?

12...♖c8

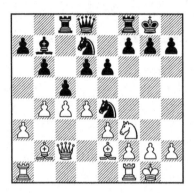

13.♖fd1

White had earlier played 13.♖ad1 cxb4?! 14.axb4 d5 15.c5 a5 16.bxa5 bxc5 17.a6 ♗a8 18.dxc5 ♖xc5 19.♕b3 ♕c7 20.♖c1 e5 21.♖xc5 ♘exc5 22.♖c1 ♕a7 23.♕c2 ♘xa6 24.♗a3 (Nyback – Jobava, Novi Sad 2009), and any rook retreat is crushed by 25.♕c8! Baadur attacked the strong pawn chain too early, and basically committed a number of blunders. The experience gained puts him on a different path this time.

13...♕e7 14.♕b3 f5

I'm sure the players knew about the game Gelfand – Eljanov (Wijk aan Zee 2008), although the predecessors were not easy to spot due to different move orders (d2-d4 was played as late as move 12!). After 14...♖c7 15.a4 d5 16.dxc5 bxc5 17.b5 ♘d6 18.cxd5 exd5 19.♖ac1 ♖b8

20.♕c2 ♖cc8 21.♗a3 h6 22.♗b2 ♕e6 23.♕c3 f6 24.h3 ♘b6 25.♕c2 ♘bc4 26.♗a1 white employed skillful maneuvers to shake down the black king's bunker and had a better position.

15.♘e1 ♕h4 16.g3 ♕e7

Jobava doesn't burn his bridges to take the sharp continuation 16...♕h6 17.f3 ♘g5 18.dxc5 ♘h3+ 19.♔g2 ♘e5.

17.f3 ♘g5 18.bxc5 bxc5

The struggle would take on quite a different nature after 18...dxc5.

19.h4 ♘f7 20.♕xb7 ♖b8 21.♕xa7 ♖xb2

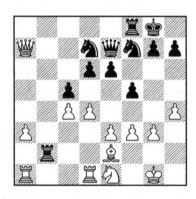

22.♔f1?! cxd4

Instead of 22.♗d3 Wojtaszek carelessly shifted his king's position, which would have cost him dear after 22...f4! 23.exf4 (23.♘d3 fxg3! 24.♘xb2 ♕xh4 25.♔e1 cxd4 26.exd4 ♕g5) 23...e5! 24.♘d3 (24.dxe5? ♘fxe5! 25.fxe5 ♕xe5) 24...exf4 25.♘xb2 fxg3. That said, it's hard to find these lines over the board.

23.♕xd4 ♖fb8 24.♘d3 e5 25.♕xb2

In a somewhat worse position after 25.♕c3 ♖2b3 26.♕e1 white's extra passed rook's pawn isn't worth much, but in the distant future it could prove decisive. Now the exchange of white's queen for two rooks encourages black's initiative on the kingside.

25...♖xb2 26.♘xb2 f4! 27.♔g2 fxg3 28.♔xg3?!

White has lost his way and is unable to set up a decent defense. He could have resisted better with 28.♖h1.

28...e4! 29.f4 ♘h6 30.♖d5 ♕f6 31.♖b1?

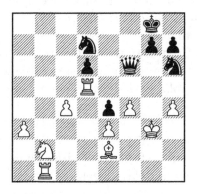

31...♕c3!

A wonderful alternative to winning the exchange after ♘h6-f5+. Unlike after 31.♖a2 white can no longer reply 32.♘d1 due to 32...♕e1+ winning the bishop.

32.♔f2 ♕c2 33.♖dd1 ♘g4+ 34.♔e1 ♕c3+ 35.♖d2 ♕xe3

White resigned.

No. 49 A. Esipenko – T. Gareev
Karlsruhe 2019

1.d4 ♘f6 2.♘f3 e6 3.c4 ♗b4+ 4.♘bd2 b6 5.a3 ♗xd2+ 6.♕xd2 ♗b7 7.e3 ♘e4

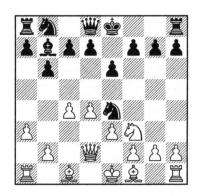

8.♕c2

Black immediately goes for a Dutch setup, whereas this is not mandatory after 8.♕d3. The queen proves to be placed awkwardly after 8...0-0 9.♗e2 d5 10.b3 a5 11.♗b2 a4 12.♖c1 ♗a6 13.♕c2 axb3 14.♕xb3 ♘c6 15.♗c3 (Yusupov – Nikolic, Barcelona 1989) 15...e5 16.cxd5 ♗xe2 17.♔xe2 exd4 18.♘xd4 ♘e5 – black has excellent play for the pawn.

8...f5 9.♗e2

After 9.♗d3 0-0 10.0-0 the frequently played transfer of the rook to the kingside doesn't look that solid – 10...♖f6 11.♘d2 ♖h6. The reason for playing it is perpetual check in the line 12.f3 ♕h4 13.fxe4 ♕xh2+ 14.♔f2 ♖g6 15.exf5 ♖xg2+ 16.♔e1 ♕g3+ 17.♔d1 ♕g4+. It's better for white to seek a tiny advantage with 12.♘xe4 ♕h4 13.h3 ♗xe4 14.♗xe4 ♕xe4 15.♕xe4 fxe4 or else continue 11.♖d1, leaving the knight on f3.

9...0-0 10.0-0 d6

Here it's useful to meet the black rook's maneuver with a break in the center – 10...♖f6 11.b4 ♖h6 12.d5! In the variation 12...exd5 13.♗b2 dxc4 14.♗xc4+ d5 15.♖ad1 ♖d6 16.♗a2 (D. Berczes – Wojtaszek, Stockholm

2008) white has active bishops, better development and great prospects.

> **KEY TIP.** Fans of the Dutch Defense will be aware that black always has to reckon with d4-d5 whether or not the pawn is being sacrificed. In the current line, the attack on black's pawn chain involves the undoubtedly correct sacrifice of the pawn.

11.b4 ♘d7

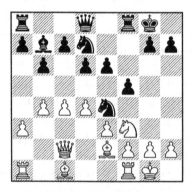

Interestingly, the position on the diagram has been reached many times via the Nimzo-Indian Defense with black to move (with the approximate move order 3.♘c3 ♗b4 4.♕c2 b6 5.a3 ♗xc3+ 6.♕xc3 ♗b7 7.♘f3 d6 8.e3 0-0 9.♗e2 ♘e4 10.♕c2 f5 11.0-0 ♘d7 12.b4). However, even with an extra tempo black is forced to fight for equality given white's dominance of space and bishop pair.

12.d5

The usual move 12.♗b2 is also followed by d4-d5 (sometimes with the addition of ♖a1-d1), but building a pawn barrier on the long diagonal also favors white: 12.♘e1 ♕h4

13.f3 ♘g5 14.c5 dxc5 15.dxc5 bxc5 16.bxc5 ♗c6 17.♗b2 ♖ab8 18.♘d3 ♗b5 19.c6 ♘b6 20.♗d4 (Belov – Wang Rui, Tianjin 2013). Black has no attack and his army is positioned worse.

12...e5

Accepting the sacrifice energizes white's initiative: 12...exd5?! 13.♘d4 ♕e7 14.cxd5 ♗xd5 15.f3 ♘g5 16.♘xf5 ♕e5 17.e4 ♖xf5 18.♗b2 ♗xe4 19.fxe4 ♖xf1+ 20.♖xf1 (Huzman – T. Hansen, Kallithea 2008) 20...♕xe4? 21.♕xe4 ♘xe4 22.♗c4+ ♔h8 23.♗d5 ♖e8 24.♗c6, and the snake-like bishop brings white an extra piece.

13.♘e1

In practice, white has much more frequently exchanged black's centralized knight. For example, 13.♘d2 ♘xd2 14.♗xd2 ♕e7 15.f3 c5 16.dxc6 ♗xc6 17.♖ad1 ♔h8 18.♗c3 ♖f6 19.♖f2 ♖af8 20.f4 ♖g6 21.♗f3 ♗xf3 22.♖xf3 with a minimal advantage (Wojtaszek – Quparadze, Doha 2016). More complicated variations arise in this game.

13...a5

Both players were familiar with this line; in particular, Timur Gareev had also played it as white: 13...♕e7 14.♗d3 ♘g5 15.f4 ♘e4 16.♗xe4 fxe4 17.♕xe4 ♘f6 18.♕c2 b5! with decent counterplay (Gareev – Christiansen, Saint Louis 2013). It's possible that Gareev didn't copy the play of his older colleague due to 15.♗xf5 e4 16.♗xd7 ♕xd7 17.♗b2 – and the compensation for the pawn may disappear.

14.f3 ♘g5 15.♖b1 axb4 16.axb4 ♕f6

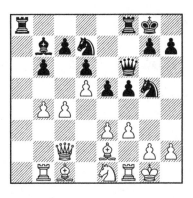

17.♘d3

It appears that black is fine, but in the open combat he will be missing the locked out bishop. It's no surprise that the computer recommends that black loosen his position with 17...c6 that frees up the bishop.

17...e4 18.fxe4 ♘xe4 19.♗b2 ♕e7

He should probably have placed the queen on g5, and the d7 knight on e5. Then the bishop would move to c8, without getting caught behind the knight.

20.♘f4 ♘g5 21.♗d4 g6 22.♕b3 ♖fe8 23.♖a1 ♘e4 24.♕b2 ♘e5 25.♖xa8 ♖xa8

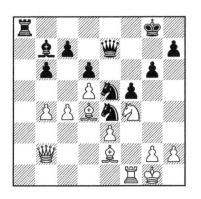

26.♖a1

So far white has been playing very well. Having placed his pieces optimally, he plans to take control of the open file.

26...♖xa1+ 27.♕xa1 c5 28.dxc6

Esipenko suggested that after 28.bxc5 bxc5 29.♗xe5 ♕xe5 30.♕xe5 dxe5 31.♘d3 the extra pawn is insufficient to win.

28...♘xc6 29.♘d5 ♕h4 30.♘f6+ ♘xf6 31.♗xf6 ♕e4 32.♗f3 ♕xe3+ 33.♔h1 ♘d8 34.♗xb7 ♘xb7 35.♗d4 ♕e4 36.♗xb6

White has gained a distant passed pawn, but it doesn't guarantee success even in the endgame due to the knight's ability to block it. Gareev reaches peaceful shores without the need to exchange queens.

36...f4 37.♕f1 d5 38.cxd5 ♕xb4 39.♕a6 ♘d6 40.♗g1 h5 41.♕c6 ♔g7 42.♕d7+ ♘f7 43.♕e6 ♕c4 44.h3.

Draw agreed.

Just like in chapter 5, after 4...b6 black faces a tricky psychological choice. As a rule, deeply defensive action allows him to demonstrate the solidity of his position, but getting active (here by switching to a Dutch setup) often proves to be unjustified. The combination b7-b6 and f7-f5 is not as effective as it looks.

Part III

System with 3.♘f3 ♗b4+ 4.♗d2

Introduction

1.d4 ♘f6 2.c4 e6 3.♘f3 ♗b4+ 4.♗d2

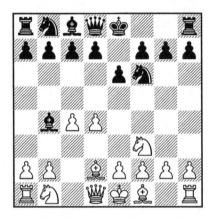

In chapters 7 and 8 we review the exchange 4...♗xd2+. The defense 4...c5 is the subject of chapters 9-11, 4...a5 is treated in chapters 12-15, and 4...♛e7 is covered in chapters 16-20.

The retreat 4...♗e7 is also met frequently, but it's not an independent line. After 5.g3 we reach a Catalan Opening, or 5...b6 is the Queen's Indian Defense. If 5.♘c3 d5 6.♗f4, 6.♗g5 or 6.cxd5 exd5 7.♗g5 various Queen's Gambit Declined variations appear. It is safe to ignore the small number of original lines from serious games.

Chapter 7

4...♗xd2+ 5.♘bxd2 variation

No. 50 M. Krasenkow – A. Kogan
Drancy 2016

1.d4 ♘f6 2.c4 e6 3.♘f3 ♗b4+ 4.♗d2 ♗xd2+ 5.♘bxd2

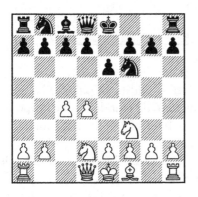

5.♕xd2 is played twice as frequently (games 53-57). However, the birth of the Bogo-Indian Defense proper (as we know from our historical introduction) was marked by this very capture.

5...d6

Variations involving d7-d5 are the subject of games 51 and 52. If 5...c5 6.dxc5 ♕a5 7.a3 ♕xc5 8.b4 ♕c7 9.c5 then white has an advantage on the queenside. If 5...b6 white is not forced to transpose to the Queen's Indian Defense via 6.g3 as he has the strong move 6.e4 available.

6.e4

TRANSPOSITION ALERT. If in reply to 6.g3 0-0 7.♗g2 black places his queen on e7 in order to support e6-e5 then we merge into a line of the 4...♕e7 system normally reached by the move order 5.g3 0-0 6.♗g2 ♗xd2+ 7.♘bxd2 d6. Preparing e6-e5 via ♘b8-c6 is found less often, although black has got some decent positions from it. If 6.g3 0-0 7.♗g2 ♘c6 8.0-0 e5 9.d5 ♘e7 10.e4 c5!? the knight on d2 is out of place both after 11.dxc6, and with a fixed center.

6...e5

Should black be worried about e4-e5? After 6...0-0 7.e5 dxe5 8.dxe5 ♘fd7 9.♕c2 ♘c6 10.♕c3 white's spatial advantage can be disputed by 10...f6!? 11.exf6 ♕xf6 12.♘e4 ♕xc3+ 13.♘xc3 ♘c5 and then e6-e5 with equality.

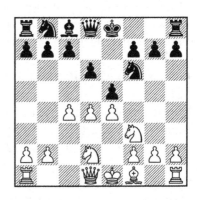

7.♗d3

One strong grandmaster offers a sac, and his opponent politely declines. If we take a look at the position arising after 7.dxe5 dxe5 8.♘xe5 ♕e7 9.f4 0-0, then it's evident that white has exposed himself and his king will not be totally safe anywhere. The black rook will move to d8, while the bishop will get to b7 (after b7-b6) and aim at the e4 pawn.

7...0-0 8.0-0

8...♖e8

An earlier game continued 8...♗g4 9.♕b3 ♘bd7 10.♗c2 ♖b8 11.♕a3 a6 12.b4 exd4 13.♘xd4 c5 14.bxc5 ♘xc5 15.♖ab1 ♕c7 16.♖fe1 ♘e6 17.♘xe6 ♗xe6 18.♗b3 ♘d7 19.♖e2 ♕c5 20.♕b2 ♘e5, draw agreed (Epishin – Andersson, Germany 2003). In the final position it's black who had the better chances.

9.d5 a5 10.♗c2 ♘a6 11.a3 ♗d7 12.♖e1

Transferring the knight via e1 to d3 is more in spirit with the position, and at the same time prevents 12...♘h5!? and then ♘h5-f4.

12...c6 13.♖b1 ♕b6

Black has no problems either after his queen excursion or after 13...cxd5 14.exd5 b5!? (a plan later carried out by Kogan).

14.b3 ♕c5 15.♕c1 cxd5 16.exd5 h6 17.♕b2 b5 18.cxb5 ♗xb5 19.♘e4 ♘xe4 20.♗xe4 ♕b6

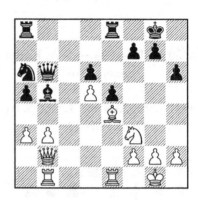

21.b4

He should have pulled his knight from f3 to d2 (for defensive purposes) or to h4 (with the imitation of an attack).

21...axb4 22.axb4 ♗d7 23.♘h4 ♖ab8?!

23...♖eb8 would have defused white's counterplay seen in the game.

24.♕a3 ♘xb4 25.♗f5 ♗xf5 26.♘xf5 g6

If 26...♔h7 27.♘xh6!? gxh6 (27...♔xh6 28.♖e4) 28.♕f3 ♕a7 29.♕f5+ ♔g7 30.♕g4+ ♔h8 31.♖xb4 ♕a5 black emerges a pawn up, but his exposed king will prevent him from winning.

27.♘xh6+ ♔g7 28.♘g4 ♕d4 29.♘e3 ♘xd5 30.♖xb8 ♖xb8 31.♕xd6 ♕c3 32.♘c2 ♖b2 33.♕xd5 Draw agreed.

No. 51 G. Gaehwiler – V. Kunin
Balatonszarszo 2017

1.d4 e6 2.♘f3 ♘f6 3.c4 ♗b4+ 4.♗d2 ♗xd2+ 5.♘bxd2

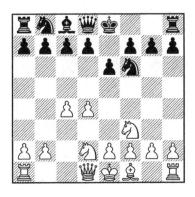

5...d5

In his commentary to the game Capablanca – Marshall (New York 1927) Alekhine placed a question-mark against this move. The freshly-crowned world champion's excessive categoricalness was built on the modest opening knowledge of the time. It's interesting that Marshall later played the same move against Vidmar (game 52), and that 5...d5 continues to be met today.

6.g3

The number of games here increases, thanks to the Catalan move order 1.d4 d5 2.c4 e6 3.♘f3 ♘f6 4.g3 ♗b4+ 5.♗d2 ♗xd2+ 6.♘bxd2. We consider 6.e3 in game 52.

6...0-0 7.♗g2

7...♘bd7

Black later played b7-b6, and it's a valid question why not start with that move? The sample game Nakamura – Giri (Biel 2012) continued 7...b6 8.0-0 ♗b7 9.cxd5 ♘xd5 (the structure without dark-squared bishops after 9...exd5 condemns black to a passive game) 10.♖e1 ♘bd7 11.e4 ♗b7 12.e5 (otherwise white cannot improve his d2 knight) 12...♘d5 13.♘e4 h6 14.♖c1 ♕e7 15.a3 a5 16.♘fd2 ♖ad8 17.♘c4 ♘b8 18.♘e3 ♘xe3 19.fxe3 c5 20.♕g4 ♗xe4 21.♗xe4 ♖c8. ♘b8-d7 and f7-f5 will cope with white's battery on the b1-h7 diagonal and chances are even.

8.0-0 b6

The continuation 8...c6?! has deservedly poor stats. In a standard Catalan position the absence of dark-squared bishops favors white – for example, after 9.♕c2 b6 10.e4 dxe4 11.♘xe4 ♘xe4 12.♕xe4.

After 8...c5 9.cxd5 exd5 10.dxc5 ♘xc5 11.♖c1 the isolated pawn ensures white a lasting but small advantage.

9.♖c1

It's worth reviewing the game Banusz – A. Saric (Zagreb 2011): 9.cxd5 exd5 10.b4 c5 11.♘e5 ♘xe5?! (a stronger continuation was 11...cxb4 12.♘c6 ♕e8 13.♘xb4 ♗b7 with the idea of establishing a knight on e4) 12.dxe5 ♘g4 13.bxc5 ♘xe5 14.♘b3 ♗e6 15.♕d4 ♘c6 16.♕a4 ♘e7 17.♖ac1 bxc5 18.♖xc5 – as well as white's better pawn structure his pieces are on better squares.

9...♗b7 10.cxd5 exd5

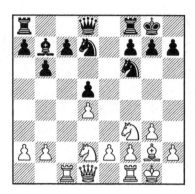

11.♘b1

The Swiss master playing white transfers his knight to a better square, although this was far from urgent. The knight could find another job to do: 11.♘e5 c5 12.♘xd7 ♘xd7 13.dxc5 bxc5 14.♘b3 c4 15.♘d4 ♕a5?! (the immediate 15...♖b8 was better) 16.b3 ♖ab8 17.♘f5 ♘f6 18.♖c2 ♖fd8 19.♕c1 h6 20.♕f4 cxb3 21.axb3 ♕b6 22.♖fc1 d4 23.♗xb7 ♖xb7 24.♖c6 ♕xb3 25.♖xf6 gxf6 26.♕xh6 (Mareco – Toth, Brazil 2012). Instead of creating hanging pawns black could have considered a stronger construction via 11... ♘xe5 12.dxe5 ♘g4 13.♘f3 c5.

11...♖e8 12.♘c3 a6 13.♘e1

The prophylactic move a7-a6 often precedes c7-c5, but Gaehwiler's maneuver prevents the creation of hanging pawns (the d5 pawn is left en prise after d4xc5), and Kunin didn't want to play with an isolani.

13...♕e7 14.♘c2 ♕d6 15.♕d2 ♖ac8

16.♕f4

The result of a lack of ideas. If white doubles rooks on the c-file the number of attackers will not exceed the number of defenders. The break e2-e4 is but a utopia, as the e4 square is controlled by four enemy units. After the exchange of queens Gaehwiler wants to send his knight to e5, which Grandmaster Mareco managed to do in a single move.

16...♕xf4 17.gxf4 ♘f8 18.♘b4 ♖cd8

A switch to a hanging pawns structure is enough for equality, as after 18...c5 19.dxc5 bxc5 the loss of the d5 pawn is compensated for by the liquidation of the one on e2. Kunin so far holds back from simplifications given he is facing a weaker opponent.

19.e3 a5 20.♘d3 ♗a6 21.♖fd1

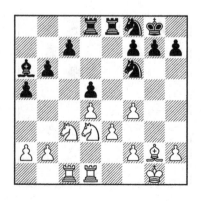

21...c5!? 22.♘e5

> **KEY TIP.** The pawn group d4-e3-f2-f4 is typical for closed openings. The attack on that group with c7-c5 is also typical. After the approximate variation 22.dxc5 d4 23.exd4 ♖xd4 24.♗f1 ♗xd3 25.cxb6 ♖xf4 26.♗xd3 ♖b4 the pawn quartet is liquidated and white will not hold on to his material advantage.

22...cxd4 23.♖xd4 ♘e6 24.♖dd1 d4 25.♘c6 dxc3 26.♘xd8 cxb2 27.♖b1 ♖xd8 28.♖xd8+ ♘xd8 29.♖xb2

The complications have led to an ending where it's not a good idea for black to lose his b6 pawn. Therefore, a draw by move repetition is logical.

29...♘d7 30.♖d2 ♗c8 31.♖c2 ♘c5 32.♖b2 ♘d7 33.♖c2 ♘c5 34.♖b2 ♘d7

Draw agreed.

No. 52 M. Vidmar – F. Marshall
New York 1927

1.d4 ♘f6 2.♘f3 e6 3.c4 ♗b4+ 4.♗d2 ♗xd2+ 5.♘bxd2 d5 6.e3

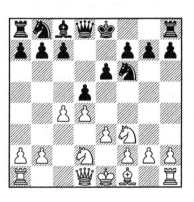

6...0-0 7.♕c2

In the game V. Moiseenko – Sarin (Moscow 2017) white preferred a Carlsbad setup. His opponent took control of e4 and gained equal chances: 7.cxd5 exd5 8.♕c2 ♖e8 9.♖c1 c6 10.b4 ♘e4 11.♘xe4 ♗f5 12.♘f6+ ♕xf6 13.♗d3 ♗e4 14.♘e5 ♕f5 15.♗xe4 dxe4 16.♕b3 ♕e6 17.♕xe6 ♖xe6. White should have fought for the central square via 9.♗d3 and then thought about the career of the passive knight on d2.

7...♘bd7 8.♗d3 h6

Like 5...d5, Alekhine assigned this move a question-mark in his annotations, as this prophylaxis created a hook to be attacked with. However, firstly, the approximate variation 9.♖g1 ♖e8 10.g4 e5 (a counterstrike in the center, just like the strategy textbooks tell us) 11.dxe5 ♘xe5 12.♘xe5 ♖xe5 13.♘f3 ♖e8 14.g5 hxg5 15.♘xg5 ♘g4 leads to an unclear position, and, secondly, this contrasted with Vidmar's sensible style (of which Marshall was aware).

9.0-0

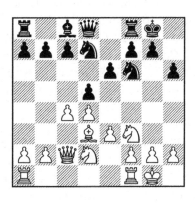

9...c5?!

Asking for trouble. After 9...c6 black has a passive but solid position.

10.cxd5 ♘xd5 11.dxc5 ♘b4 12.♝h7+ ♚h8 13.♕c4 ♘a6 14.♝c2 ♘dxc5 15.b4 ♘d7 16.♖fd1 ♘b6 17.♕b3 ♕d5

If 17...♕e7 18.♕d3 f5 19.♘e5 (Alekhine) 19...♚h7 20.a3 ♖d8 21.♕e2 ♝d7 22.♘xd7 ♖xd7 23.e4 g6 black has problems but he's not yet losing.

18.♕b2 ♝d7 19.♘e4 ♕b5 20.a3 ♝c6

21.♘d4?!

In exchanging the enemy bishop, Vidmar has sold himself short. Via 21.♝d3 ♘a4 22.♝xb5 ♘xb2 23.♝xc6 bxc6 24.♖dc1 white would win the c6 pawn and the game.

21...♕e5 22.f4 ♕c7 23.♘xc6?!

23.♖ac1 ♝d5 24.♝d3 ♕e7 25.♘c5 ♘xc5 26.bxc5 ♘c8 27.f5 retained the best chances for white due to the clumsy position of the black king.

23...bxc6 24.♝d3 ♘b8 25.♖ac1 ♘d5 26.♕f2 a5 27.b5 ♕b6 28.bxc6 ♘xc6 29.♘c5 ♖ad8 30.g4 ♘de7 31.h4 ♖d5 32.e4 ♖d4

33.f5?!

Vidmar surrenders the e5 square and gets into trouble. 33.g5 was far better.

33...exf5 34.gxf5 ♘e5 35.♝e2 ♖xd1+ 36.♖xd1 ♖d8 37.♖xd8+ ♕xd8 38.f6 ♘7c6

Back when they were watching the world go by from the a6 and b6 squares, black's knights didn't even dare to dream about the squares they have now reached. The white king's upcoming trip to h3 costs him the game

39.fxg7+ ♚xg7 40.♚g2 ♘g6 41.♚h3?! ♕d6 42.♚g2 ♘d4 43.♘b7 ♕e5 44.♚f1 ♘f4 45.♕g3+ ♚h7 46.♝d3 ♘de6 47.♝a6 ♕a1+ 48.♕e1 ♕b2 49.♕e3 ♕g2+ 50.♚e1 ♕c2 51.♕f3 ♘g2+ 52.♚f1 ♘ef4 53.♚g1 ♘xh4 54.♕f1 ♕xe4 55.♘c5 ♕e3+ 56.♚h1 ♕xc5 57.♝d3+ f5

White resigned.

I have to agree with Tartakower's description of the 5.♘bxd2 variation: "An underestimation of the nature of the knight, that is best placed on c3!" Black's best reply is 5...d6, without fearing the advance of white's e-pawn. White's spatial grab in this line isn't well supported by his pieces.

Chapter 8

4...♝xd2+ 5.♛xd2 variation

No. 53 E. Ghaem Maghami –
H. Toufighi
· *Amol 2018*

1.d4 ♘f6 2.c4 e6 3.♘f3 ♝b4+
4.♝d2 ♝xd2+ 5.♛xd2

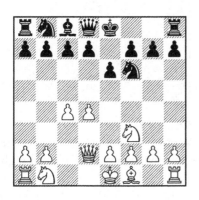

5...b6

Variations involving d7-d5 are reviewed in games 54-57. The continuation 5...d6 6.♘c3 0-0 was analyzed by Geller, and his assessments haven't changed. White immediately grabbing space in the center without the dark-squared bishops on the board is strategically unambitious. For example, 7.e4 ♘c6 8.0-0-0 ♛e7 9.h3 e5 10.d5 ♘b4 11.a3 ♘a6 12.♝d3 ♘c5 13.♝c2 a5 with approximate equality (Krasenkow – Meier, Germany 2005).

In reply to 7.g3 Geller suggests preparing the typical e6-e5 break not via 7...♘bd7, but via 7...♘c6 which at the same time pressurizes d4. After 8.♝g2 e5 there are two possible lines.

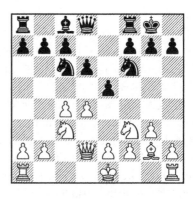

If 9.d5 ♘b8 white is not forced to place another pawn on light squares (e4). He retains chances of a slight advantage via 10.0-0 a5 11.♘e1 ♘a6 12.♘d3 with the idea of f2-f4. After 9.0-0 ♝g4 the push 10.d5 is again possible, as are the harmless exchange on e5 and 10.e3, maintaining tension in the center. In the latter case, the fragment Vl. Zakhartsov – Kazakovsky (Moscow 2017) is illustrative: 10...a5 11.h3 ♝f5 12.♘h4 ♝d7 13.f4 exd4 14.exd4 a4 15.♚h2 ♘a5 16.♛d3 ♝e6 17.d5 ♝d7 18.♘f3 c5 19.dxc6 ♝xc6. The knight on a5 has a job to do, keeping the c4 pawn under attack. Due to the idea of d6-d5 chances are equal.

6.♘c3 ♝b7

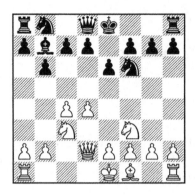

7.d5

7.g3 0-0 8.♗g2 is analyzed in my book on the Queen's Indian Defense via the move order 3...b6 4.g3 ♗b7 5.♗g2 ♗b4+ 6.♗d2 ♗xd2+ 7.♕xd2 0-0 8.♘c3. The move played in this game is one attempt to come up with original play, which is also the case after 7.♕f4!? The queen supports e2-e4 and takes aim at the c7 pawn (which is felt after 7...d5 8.cxd5 ♘xd5 9.♘xd5 ♕xd5). In the game Ragger – Danner (Graz 2014) the switch to a closed center ensured white the initiative on the kingside: 7...♗xf3 8.♕xf3 ♘c6 9.e3 0-0 10.♗d3 e5 11.d5 ♘e7 12.g4 d6 13.♖g1 ♘d7 14.g5 f5 15.gxf6 ♘xf6 16.0-0-0.

7...0-0

Without dark-squared bishops on board the idea of 7...d6 and e6-e5 is strategically justified, although it leaves the bishop on b7 without a job to do.

8.e4

In the game Kaidanov – Cherniaev (New York 1993) black pressed on d5 via queenside operations – 8.g3 exd5 9.cxd5 b5!? 10.♘xb5 ♗xd5 11.♗g2 a6 (11...♘a6!?) 12.♘c3 ♗b7 13.0-0 d6 14.♖ac1 ♘bd7 15.♘d4 ♗xg2 16.♔xg2,

and white's better pawn structure ensures him a slight advantage.

8...exd5 9.exd5 c6

Toufighi attacks the d5 pawn directly. Seeing as 10.d6 is dubious due to 10...c5, white completes his kingside development.

10.♗e2 cxd5 11.cxd5 ♘a6 12.0-0

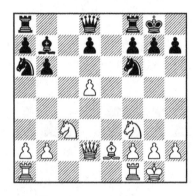

12...♘c7

White is somewhat better no matter which move the black knight makes. Black could also have played 12...♘b4 13.d6 ♘c6 or 12...♘c5 with the idea of settling into e4.

13.d6 ♘e6 14.♘e5 ♖c8 15.h3

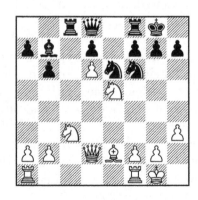

15...♖c5!?

The start of a complicated exchange operation with a chain of moves approved by the computer.

16.f4 ♘d5 17.♗f3 dxf4 18.♗xb7 ♖xe5 19.♖xf4 ♘xf4 20.♕xf4 f6

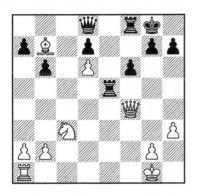

21.♖f1

Two minor pieces are a bit stronger than a rook and pawn. White dreams of exploiting the strength of the d6 pawn.

21...♕b8?!

A waste of time. He should have moved his king to h8 right now, and met 22.♕c4 with 22...♕e8.

22.♕c4+ ♔h8 23.♕c7 ♕e8 24.♗f3 ♕e6 25.♗d5!

Unwinding   the   material imbalance. In an ending with major pieces white gains chances of winning.

25...♖xd5 26.♘xd5 ♕xd5 27.♕xd7 h6 28.♖e1 ♕d4+ 29.♔h1

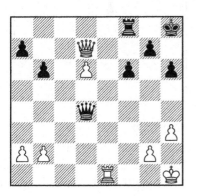

29...♕d5?!

If 29...♕d2 the rook's invasion is prevented due to perpetual check.

30.♖e8 ♖xe8 31.♕xe8+ ♔h7 32.♕e7 ♕d1+?

The right continuation was 32...♕c5 33.♕c7 ♕e5, preventing the passer from getting to the 7th rank.

33.♔h2 ♕d4 34.d7 ♕f4+ 35.♔g1 ♕c1+ 36.♔f2 ♕xb2+ 37.♔f3 ♕c3+ 38.♕e3

Black resigned.

No. 54 S. Ionov – I. Rozum
Sochi 2019

1.d4 ♘f6 2.c4 e6 3.♘f3 ♗b4+ 4.♗d2 ♗xd2+ 5.♕xd2 0-0 6.g3 d5

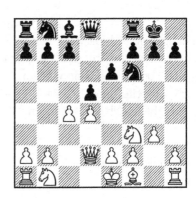

Thirty years ago, the Catalan Opening without dark-squared bishops could be found in battles between the world's best players, including Kasparov and Karpov. These days, the top players prefer other openings, and the level of players in this line is lower.

7.♗g2 c6

The frequent queen move to e7 is reviewed not here, but in the text on the 4...♕e7 system. 7...♘bd7 8.0-0 dxc4 is acceptable, after which either white's rook wins the pawn back (♖f1-c1xc4 with black planning e6-e5 in reply) or the knight wins it – 9.♘a3 e5!? 10.dxe5 ♘xe5 11.♕xd8 ♘xf3+ 12.♗xf3 ♖xd8 13.♘xc4 ♗e6 with gradual equality.

8.0-0 ♘bd7

If 8...b6 then 9.♘e5 ♗b7 10.♖c1 is logical, planning to fight for the c-file. After 10...♘bd7 11.cxd5 cxd5 12.♘c3 a6 13.♘a4 ♖c8 14.♕b4 ♘xe5 15.dxe5 ♘d7 16.♖xc8 ♗xc8 17.♕d6 b5 18.♘c5 ♘xc5 19.♕xc5 ♗b7 20.♖c1 (Li Chao – Moradiabadi, Jakarta 2011) black proved unable to neutralize his opponent's minimal advantage.

> **KEY TIP.** After the bishops are exchanged it is typical for white to quickly move his king's rook to c1. There is no rush to develop the knight on c3, but the queen's rook should support the march of the a-pawn.

9.♘a3
The next game reviews 9.♖c1.
9...b6

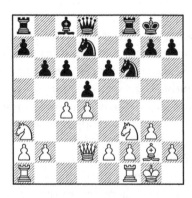

10.♘e5

Now white constantly needs to keep an eye on the possible exchange on e5. It was worth considering an attack on the queenside: 10.♖ac1 ♗b7 11.♖fd1 ♕b8 12.b4 ♖c8 13.♕b2 a5 14.b5 cxb5 (I. Sokolov – L'Ami, Amsterdam 2017) 15.cxd5 ♗xd5 16.♘xb5 with a small advantage.

10...♗b7 11.♖ac1 ♖c8

If 11...♘xe5 12.dxe5 ♘d7 13.f4 ♕e7 14.cxd5 exd5 15.b4 white is ready to strengthen his position via ♘a3-c2-d4 or via the committal e2-e4.

12.cxd5   exd5   13.♗h3   ♕e7 14.♕e3 ♖ce8?!

The players could have calculated the variations better. After 14...♖fe8 15.♘xd7 ♘xd7 16.♕xe7 ♖xe7 white has 17.e4!? with the idea of 17...dxe4?! 18.d5! cxd5 19.♖xc8+ ♗xc8 20.♖c1. However, after 17...♖ce8 18.exd5 cxd5 white has nothing in particular.

15.♘xc6 ♕d6 16.♘b5 ♕xc6

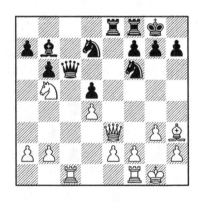

17.♕b3?!
Let's try the exchange of queens: 17.♖xc6 ♖xe3 18.♖c7 ♖xe2 19.♖xb7 ♖xb2 20.♘d6 ♖d8 21.♖xa7. White

has won the pawn back and seems set for more. Ionov played a weak move instead.

17...♘c5 18.dxc5 bxc5 19.♘xa7 ♕a6 20.♘b5 ♖xe2

Rozum plans play against the enemy king, not satisfied with equality after 20...c4 21.♕b4 ♖xe2 22.♘c3 ♖e5 23.♕c5.

21.♖xc5 ♘e4 22.♖cc1 ♕h6

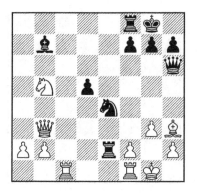

23.♘d4?

The right continuation was 23.♘c3. If 23...♘xc3 white captures the bishop, while if 23...♘c5 24.♕a3 ♖xf2 he captures the knight with approximate quality.

23...♖xf2! 24.♗g2?

After 24.♕xb7 ♕e3! 25.♖xf2 ♕xf2+ 26.♔h1 ♕xd4, white's position is awful despite the material equality, as his pieces are uncoordinated and his king exposed. Still, this was better than capitulating without a fight.

24...♕d2! 25.♗xe4 ♖xf1+ 26.♖xf1 ♕xd4+ 27.♖f2 dxe4 28.♕xb7 e3 29.♖f4 ♕d1+

White resigned, as he can only stop the passer at the cost of his rook.

No. 55 V. Kramnik – D. Andreikin
Moscow 2013

1.d4 ♘f6 2.c4 e6 3.g3 ♗b4+ 4.♗d2 ♗xd2+ 5.♕xd2 d5 6.♗g2 0-0 7.♘f3 c6 8.0-0 ♘bd7 9.♖c1

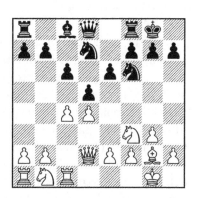

9...♕e7

Unlike the continuation 7...♕e7, this move does not belong to the 4...♕e7 line. In reply to 9...b6 white follows the standard plan of c4xd5, c6xd5 (Li Chao – Moradiabadi from the notes to game 54). Support of the b2-b4 break from the queen adds a different flavor to the game. After 10.b4 ♗b7 11.♕b2 ♖b8 12.♘bd2 ♕e7 13.e3 ♖fc8 14.♖c2 c5 15.bxc5 bxc5 16.♕a3 ♖c6 17.♖ac1 ♖a6 18.♕d3 h6 19.♕e2 dxc4 20.♕xc4 cxd4 21.♘xd4 ♖b6 22.♗xb7 ♖8xb7 (Topalov – Carlsen, Nanjing 2010) black created a lot of counterplay on the queenside and even managed to win thanks to his opponent's blunders.

If 9...a5 the b-pawn doesn't advance, but during the exchange on d5 black will recapture with his e-pawn. Therefore, in the game Sarana – Short (Moscow 2016) white focused on preparing e2-e4: 10.♕f4 b6 11.♘bd2 ♝b7 12.e4 dxe4 13.♘xe4 c5 14.♘d6 ♝c6 15.♖e1 ♕b8 16.♖ad1 ♘h5 17.♕g5 ♕xd6 18.♕xh5 ♖ad8 19.dxc5 ♕xc5 20.♕xc5 ♘xc5 21.♘e5 ♝xg2 22.♔xg2 ♘a4 – his advantage proved to be short-lived.

10.♕e3

Like ♕d2-f4 the idea of this move is to combat e6-e5, and the different queen moves may merge into the same line if black plays the break. If 10.♕f4 b6 it makes sense to capture on d5, and in the game Cheparinov – Gagunashvili (Legnica 2013) the queen successfully traveled along the fourth rank, exchanging for the black queen to some advantage – 11.cxd5 cxd5 12.♘e5 ♘xe5 13.dxe5 ♘d7 14.♘c3 ♝a6 15.♕a4 ♝b7 16.♕d4 ♝c6 17.♖c2 f6 18.exf6 ♘xf6 19.♖ac1 ♖ad8 20.f4 ♕c5 21.e3 ♕xd4 22.exd4 ♝d7 23.♝f1. It was also worth considering 10...dxc4 11.♖xc4 ♘d5, and the queen cannot escape to a3 as it does in this game.

10...dxc4

The variation 10...♖e8 11.♘bd2 e5 12.dxe5 ♘xe5 13.♘xe5 ♕xe5 14.♕xe5 ♖xe5 has been played often, starting with games by Karpov and Andersson. White has a great score here, with half of games being white wins and the other half being draws (out of 14 games in the database). At first, he stands slightly better due to his spatial advantage. It's noteworthy that Ulf Andersson, a big expert in this line, eventually switched to 10...dxc4.

11.♖xc4

In the game Bacrot – Andersson (Pamplona 1998) white dispatched

his knight to liquidate the pawn, after first preventing the defense b7-b5 – 11.a4 ♖e8 12.♘a3 e5 13.♘xc4 e4 14.♘fe5 ♘xe5 15.dxe5 ♘g4 16.♕xe4 ♘xe5 17.♖d1 f5 18.♕xe5 ♕xe5 19.♘xe5 ♖xe5 20.♖d8+ ♔f7 21.e4 ♖e8 22.♖xe8 ♔xe8. Black made the standard break e6-e5 and gained full equality.

11...♘d5

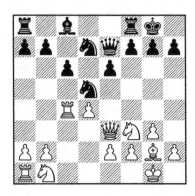

12.♕a3

An earlier game continued 12.♕e4 f5!? 13.♕d3 b6 14.♖c1 ♝b7 15.♘bd2 (Khairullin – Zvyagintsev, St. Petersburg 2012). Instead of the reasonable 15...c5!? black went for blowing up the blockade, and encountered difficulties after 15...e5?! 16.e4! fxe4 17.♘xe4 ♖ae8 18.♖e1 h6 19.♖e2 c5 20.♘xe5 ♘xe5 21.dxe5 (not 21...♕xe5?? due to 22.♘c3).

12...♖e8 13.♕xe7 ♖xe7 14.e4 ♘5b6 15.♖c2 e5

Andreikin didn't want to allow the bind e4-e5, that would have condemned him to a stodgy defense. I suspect that the players had both analyzed this position during their prep.

16.♘bd2 a5 17.a3 g6

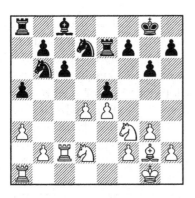

18.♖ac1

Kramnik didn't find 18.♘xe5 ♘xe5 19.dxe5 ♖xe5 20.♘b3 a4 21.♘c5 ♘d7 convincing. Andreikin instead settles matters in the center.

18...exd4 19.♘xd4 ♘e5 20.f4 ♖d7 21.♘e2 ♘g4

The outpost on d3 looks more appealing, but Dmitry doesn't want to risk too much here.

22.♘f1 ♖d8 23.h3 ♘f6 24.♖d2 ♗e6 25.♔f2

Kramnik plans to take a bumpy road. The spectacular battle of the greedy knights after 25.♘d4 ♘c4 26.♘xe6 ♘xd2 27.♘xd8 ♘xf1 28.♘xb7 ♘xg3 would have ended in a draw, and Kramnik cannot forgive himself for ignoring it.

25...♘a4 26.♖cc2 ♘d7

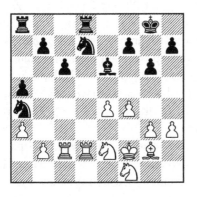

27.♔e3??

Instead of moving his e2 knight to d4 or c1 white walks into a trap.

27...♗b3 28.♖c1 ♘db6

This wins a pawn and the game.

29.♖d4 c5 30.♖xd8+ ♖xd8 31.e5 ♘c4+ 32.♔f3 ♘axb2 33.♘c3 ♘xa3 34.♘e3 b5 35.♘e4 ♘d3 36.♖h1 ♘c2 37.♘xc2 ♗xc2 38.h4 b4 39.h5 gxh5 40.♘f6+ ♔f8 41.♔e3 b3 42.♘d5

White resigned.

No. 56 E. Postny – S. Fedorchuk
Llucmajor 2017

1.d4 ♘f6 2.c4 e6 3.♘f3 ♗b4+ 4.♗d2 ♗xd2+ 5.♕xd2 0-0 6.♘c3 d5 7.e3

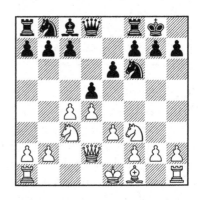

We already know this position from Alekhine versus Bogoljubov (game 1 of the historical introduction).

7...♕e7

Bogoljubov made do without moving his queen, preferring 7...♘bd7 and c7-c6. The move 7...b6 leads logically to play with hanging pawns, where the absence of dark-squared bishops somewhat favors white – 8.cxd5 exd5 9.♗d3 c5 10.0-0 ♗b7 11.dxc5 bxc5.

8.cxd5

The main move 8.♖c1 is met in the next game. Sometimes white immediately rejects the fight in favor of castling. After 8.♗d3 (e2) 8...dxc4 9.♗xc4 c5 10.0-0 ♖d8 11.♕e2 cxd4 12.exd4 all black has to do is to keep in mind the threat d4-d5 (12...a6? 13.d5) and protect his queen via 12...♘c6 with satisfactory play.

8...exd5 9.♗d3

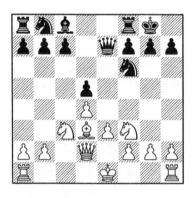

9...♘c6

Fedorchuk is trying to set up his pieces actively. Usually, though, black wants to set up a pawn chain with a7-b7-c6-d5, and to send his knight to d7. If black carefully prepares the exchange of light-colored bishops then he has nothing to fear from the pawn minority attack. For example, 9...c6 10.♕c2 ♘bd7 11.0-0 ♖e8 12.♘d2 ♘f8 13.h3 ♘e6 14.♘f3 g6 15.a3 ♘g7 16.b4 ♗f5 17.b5 cxb5 18.♗xf5 ♘xf5 19.♘xb5 ♖ac8 20.♕d3 (Faizrakhmanov – Khanin, Kazan 2019) 20...a6 21.♘c3 ♘d6, and then doubling rooks on the c-file.

10.h3

In the game Giri – Jobava (Melilla 2011) white didn't spend time on this prophylaxis and allowed the enemy bishop to get to g4: 10.0-0 ♖d8 11.a3 ♗g4 12.♘e1 ♗h5 13.b4 a6 14.f3 ♘a7 (obviously the knight will not stay here for long) 15.♘c2 ♗g6 16.a4 ♘c8 17.♖ae1 ♘d6 18.♗xg6 hxg6 19.♕d3 ♖e8. The e3-e4 break is feasible, but is hardly enough for an advantage.

10...♖d8 11.a3 ♘e4 12.♕c2 ♗f5

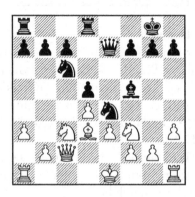

Black controls e4 and completes his development. An interesting battle awaits.

13.0-0

A year later, Postny immediately exchanged in the center: 13.♗xe4 dxe4 14.♘d2 ♖e8 15.♘e2 ♖ad8 16.♖c1 ♕g5 17.♕c5 h6 (17...♕xg2? 18.♖g1 ♕xh3 19.♘f4 ♕h2 20.♖g2 ♕h1+ 21.♔e2) 18.g4 ♗g6 19.♕xg5 hxg5 20.♖c5 f6 21.h4 gxh4 22.♖xh4 (Postny – Zysk, Greece 2018). His rejection of castling proved to help white, who gained a promising blockade-type endgame. As black's bishop became a bad one, it was preferable to capture with 13...♗xe4.

13...♗d6 14.♘d2 ♖e8 15.♗xe4 dxe4

Here the capture with the pawn is correct, as in the middlegame the bishop may be used for attacking.

16.♘e2

16.♖fd1 was more flexible, freeing up a square for the knight.

16...♕h4 17.♘g3

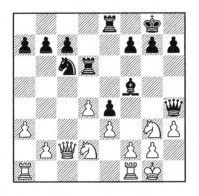

17...♗xh3!   18.gxh3   ♕xh3 19.♖fc1?

The Israeli grandmaster playing white had missed an important nuance. 19.♘dxe4? ♖g6 is bad for white, but via 19.d5! he would lure the rook to the fifth rank, and after 19...♖xd5 20.♘dxe4 the g-file isn't available.

19...h5 20.♕c5

If 20.♕d1 h4 21.♕f1 ♕g4 22.♕e2 ♕g6 black avoids the exchange of queens and wins back the piece with a clear advantage.

20...♖g6 21.♘df1 ♖ee6! 22.♖c2 h4 23.♕h5

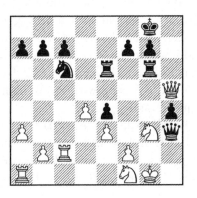

23...♖ef6!

Black has prepared the move 24...♖h6, which previously was no good due to ♕h5-f5. Postny adds a rook to the defense, but it's too late to save the day.

24.f3 ♖xf3 25.♖g2 ♘e7!

White is tied in knots and is forced to watch hopelessly as black's knight carries out a decisive maneuver.

26.♖c1   ♘f5   27.♕xg6   fxg6 28.♘xe4 ♖xf1+ 29.♖xf1 ♘xe3

White resigned.

No. 57 P. Tregubov – M. Nezar
Montpellier 2015

1.d4 ♘f6 2.c4 e6 3.♘f3 ♗b4+ 4.♗d2 ♗xd2+ 5.♕xd2 0-0 6.♘c3 d5 7.e3 ♕e7

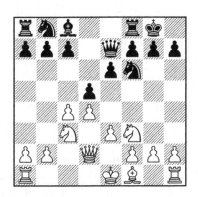

8.♖c1

The most common method of fighting for a tempo (i.e. if black plays d5xc4 then white captures with the bishop without moving it earlier). This is similar to the Queen's Gambit Declined (1.d4 d5 2.c4 e6 3.♘c3 ♘f6 4.♗g5 ♗e7 5.e3 0-0 6.♘f3 ♘bd7 7.♖c1) – the c-file is likely to become semi-open so it's good to have the rook there so early.

8...dxc4

The French master cedes the tempo immediately. Much more often, black challenges the white queen with 8...♖d8. Then, the exchange on d5 takes us to a position similar to that in game 56. In the game Hjartarson – Jobava (Helsingor 2018) after a prophylactic series of moves 9.♕c2 a6 10.a3 h6 white exhausted his resources in the battle for the tempo and exchanged on d5.

9.♝xc4 c5

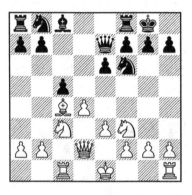

10.0-0

If 10.dxc5 ♕xc5 11.♝b3 the black queen comfortably moves to a5. Further play (which unfortunately takes us to a draw) is very simple – ♘b8-c6, ♖f8-d8, ♝c8-d7-e8 and exchanging all the major pieces on the d-file. In particular, this has been played by Grandmaster Zvyagintsev.

10...♖d8

After the variation 10...♘c6 11.♖fd1 ♖d8 12.♕e2 cxd4 13.♘xd4 ♝d7 14.♘xc6 ♝xc6 15.h3 ♖xd1+ 16.♖xd1 ♖d8 17.a3 h6 18.♖xd8+ ♕xd8 19.♕d3 ♕xd3 20.♝xd3 ♘d5 21.♘xd5 ♝xd5 (Tregubov – Fedorchuk, Montpellier 2015)

a whirlwind has blown across the board, sweeping away almost all the pieces and, with that, the slightest hint of intrigue.

11.♖fd1 cxd4 12.exd4

The knight can also take the pawn now (12...e5?? 13.♘f5), but given white's 229 higher Elo rating at the time he wasn't going to opt for mass exchanges.

12...♘c6 13.a3 ♝d7 14.h3

Tregubov wants to move his queen out of range of black's rook. To push her to e3 he first needed to prevent ♘f6-g4.

14...♖ac8 15.♝a2 ♝e8 16.♕e3 ♖c7 17.b4 b6 18.♕f4

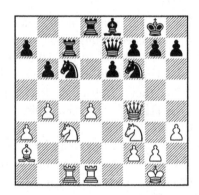

18...♘b8?!

Nezar was clearly worried about the d4-d5 break, but the knight's preventive retreat isn't a very good choice. After 18...♖dc8 the move 19.d5 would be met by 19...♘xb4 20.axb4 ♖xc3 21.♖xc3 ♖xc3 22.dxe6 fxe6 23.♕e5 ♕c7 with an exchange of queens and equality.

19.d5! exd5 20.♖e1 ♕d7?

Black didn't like the fact that his pawns were deformed after 20...♕d6 21.♕xd6 ♖xd6 22.♘xd5 ♖xc1

23.♘xf6+ gxf6 24.♖xc1. However, that was nothing important, whereas the exchange of queens was necessary.

21.♘e4! ♖c6 22.♖xc6 ♕xc6

He could have fought on more stubbornly with 22...♘h5 23.♘f6+ gxf6 24.♕h6 ♘xc6 25.♗b1 f5.

23.♘d4 ♘h5 24.♘xc6 ♘xf4 25.♘xd8 ♘d3 26.♘f6+

Black resigned.

If the 5...b6 line leaves white with two or three promising alternatives, then the more reliable 5...d5 should gradually equalize. It's very hard for black to count on anything more, but he has already limited his aspirations with the exchange on d2.

Chapter 9

Various after 4...c5

No. 58 C. Repka – J. Druska
Banska Stiavnica 2015

1.d4 ♘f6 2.c4 e6 3.♘f3 ♗b4+ 4.♗d2 c5

We encountered Alvis Vitolins's original idea in game 5 of the historical introduction. In the vast majority of cases, white immediately captures on b4. In the present game we analyze 5.e3 (with rarer moves in the notes), while game 59 covers 5.g3.

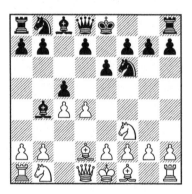

5.e3

Most often this results in a covert transposition to the Nimzo-Indian Defense (5.♘c3 is an overt transposition). 5.dxc5 ♗xc5 usually leads to a hedgehog that is pleasant for black. For example, 6.♘c3 0-0 7.a3 a6 8.b4 ♗e7 9.e4 d6 10.♗e2 b6 11.♗f4 ♗b7 12.♘d2 ♘bd7 13.0-0 ♖c8 14.♕b3 ♖e8 15.a4 (Erenberg – A. Moiseenko, Israel 2019) 15... d5! 16.exd5 exd5, and 17.cxd5? ♖xc3! tips the scales in black's favor.

White's dark-colored bishop is out of place both on d2 and f4.

After 5.a3 ♗xd2+ 6.♕xd2 cxd4 7.♘xd4 0-0 8.♘c3 the break d7-d5 is totally fine. Black has made exclusively useful moves, whereas a2-a3 is a waste. After that, white exchanges on d5 or else black exchanges on c4, and the position with two open files is equal.

5...♗xd2+

TRANSPOSITION ALERT. The continuation 5...0-0 6.♘c3 is identical to the well-analyzed variation of the Nimzo-Indian Defense 3.♘c3 ♗b4 4.♗d2 0-0 5.e3 c5 6.♘f3. Lines involving the exchange ♗b4xd2 usually comprise a separate branch. For example 5...0-0 6.♗d3 ♘c6 7.0-0 d6 8.a3 (8.♘c3 again leads to the Nimzo-Indian Defense) 8...♗xd2 9.♘bxd2 cxd4 10.exd4 e5 11.d5 ♘e7 12.♖c1 ♘g6 13.♗xg6 hxg6 14.♖e1 ♖e8 15.♘f1 ♗g4 16.h3 ♗xf3 17.♕xf3 (Neumeier – Nisipeanu, Magdeburg 2015). Black gains sufficient counter chances with 17...e4 (as in the actual game) or the maneuver ♘f6-h5-f4.

6.♘bxd2

After 6.♕xd2 cxd4 7.exd4 b6 8.♘c3 ♗b7 control over e4 promises black equality. After 7.♘xd4 the fianchetto is not such a good idea (7...b6 8.♘b5), whereas simplifications along the e1-a5 diagonal lead to equality – 7...♘e4

8.♕c2 ♕a5+ 9.♘d2 ♘xd2 10.♕xd2 ♕xd2+ 11.♔xd2 ♔e7 12.♗e2 d6.

6...cxd4

Black has the right not only to resolve the tension in the center but also to throw wood on the fire – 6...0-0 7.♗d3 d5!? If 8.dxc5, then 8...♘a6 and ♘a6xc5 with the idea of exchanging on d3.

7.exd4

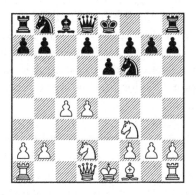

7...d5

In the game Neverov – Malakhatko (Mumbai 2017) black preferred the fianchetto – 7...0-0 8.♗d3 b6. Neverov launched a pawn charge on the queenside: 9.b4 ♗b7 10.0-0 ♘c6 11.b5 ♘e7 12.a4 ♖c8 13.♕c2 (13.♖c1 and then c4-c5 is interesting) 13...♘ed5 14.♖fb1 ♘f4 15.♗f1 ♕c7 16.♖c1 d6 17.♕b2 ♖fe8 18.a5. Counterplay in the center led to equality – 18...e5 19.axb6 axb6 20.g3 ♘g6 21.♗g2 ♕b8 22.♘f1 exd4 23.♕xd4 ♖c5.

8.c5

This change in pawn structure is unusual for the Bogo-Indian Defense. Given that one of the standard breaks, e6-e5, is prevented, while another, b7-b6, is of little effect, white has chances to gain an advantage.

8...0-0 9.♗d3 ♘c6 10.0-0 ♕c7 11.♖e1 b6

It's dangerous to put off queenside mobilization any longer. At the very least, b2-b4 has been excluded.

12.♖c1 bxc5 13.♖xc5 ♕d6 14.♘b3 ♗b7 15.♘e5

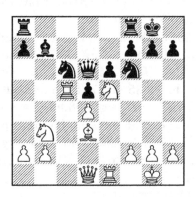

15...♘e4

Black decides to resist the attack on c5 and e5 not by passive defense (15...♖ac8), but by a pawn sac.

16.♗xe4 dxe4 17.♘c4 ♕e7 18.♖xe4 ♖fd8 19.d5?!

After 19.♘e3 ♘b4 20.♖g4 ♘xa2 21.♕e1! there is no road back for the knight, while after 20...♘d5 the blockade is hardly worth the sacrificed pawn.

19...♘b4 20.♘e3 ♘xd5 21.♘xd5

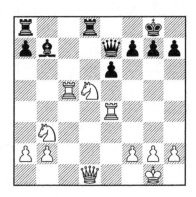

21...♕g5! 22.h4 ♖xd5 23.♕xd5 ♕xd5 24.♖xd5 ♝xd5 25.♖a4 ♝xb3 26.axb3

The series of moves with multiple captures and a pretty geometric pattern has led to a rook ending. White activates the rook and gains a three versus four pawns position in an ideal setup for defense.

26...♔f8 27.♖b4 ♖d8 28.g3 ♖d2 29.♖b8+ ♔e7 30.♖a8 ♖d7 31.♖b8 ♔f6 32.b4 ♖d2 33.b5 ♖xb2 34.♖b7 e5 35.♖xa7 ♖xb5 36.♖a6+ ♔f5 37.♖a7 ♔g6 38.h5+ ♔xh5 39.♖xf7 ♔g6 40.♖f8 h5 41.♔g2 ♔g5 42.♔f3 ♖b3+ 43.♔e4 ♔g4 44.♔xe5 g5 45.♔e4 ♖b1 46.♖g8 ♖e1+

Draw agreed.

No. 59 S. Laza – T. Banusz
Zalakaros 2015

1.d4 ♘f6 2.c4 e6 3.♘f3 ♝b4+ 4.♝d2 c5 5.g3

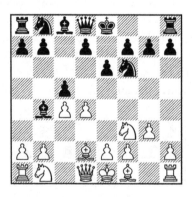

5...♕b6!

A curious case! This queen sortie has been played successfully since the 1980s, yet the number of players willing to continue g2-g3 without

exchanging on b4 hasn't declined. Moreover, these "masochists" include grandmasters, and even top ones! Hungarian amateur Szabolcs Laza (Elo 2192) is no big name, but in this game, against a grandmaster, he did his utmost to defend the reputation of the 5.g3 line.

Other black replies instead of 5...♕b6 are second-rate. For example, 5...0-0 6.♝g2 ♝xd2+ 7.♕xd2 ♘e4 8.♕c2 ♕a5+ 9.♘bd2 ♘xd2 10.♕xd2 ♕xd2+ 11.♔xd2 d6 12.dxc5 dxc5 13.♖hd1 ♘c6 14.♔c3 ♖b8 15.♖d6, and black needs to neutralize his opponent's domination of the central file.

6.♕b3

If 6.♝xb4 ♕xb4+ 7.♕d2 ♕xc4 8.♘a3 there is no point in the black queen protecting c5, as after 9.d4xc5 the queen cannot capture back. The right continuation was 8...♕a4 9.dxc5 ♘e4 10.♕d4 ♕xd4 11.♘xd4 ♘a6 12.♘db5 ♔e7 (Belzo – Efimov, Klaksvik 2018) – black nevertheless remains with the extra pawn.

> **TRANSPOSITION ALERT.** 6.♝g2 cxd4 7.♘xd4 leads to a complicated variation of the English Opening (1.c4 c5 2.♘f3 ♘f6 3.g3 e6 4.d4 cxd4 5.♘xd4 ♝b4+ 6.♝d2 ♕b6 7.♝g2). However, it's better to play 6...♘c6 and test what white plans to do with the d4 pawn. It has been demonstrated that after 7.d5 exd5 8.cxd5 ♘xd5 9.0-0 ♘de7 white has nothing for the pawn. The move 7.e3 prevents the loss, but the combination of e2-e3 and g2-g3

with the knight on f3 (rather than on e2) is undesirable.

6...♘c6

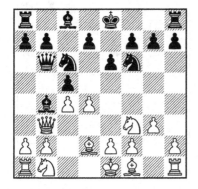

7.dxc5

After 7.♗xb4 ♕xb4+ white should exchange queens in a way to avoid obvious difficulties. After 8.♕xb4 ♘xb4 9.♘a3 there is a clear dissonance in the positions of the knights. 8.♘bd2 b6 9.♗g2 ♗b7 10.0-0 is more precise, and the players will fight out the endgame with equal chances.

7...♗xd2+

Before capturing on c5 with the queen, it's useful to first swap the bishops. After 7...♕xc5 8.♗xb4 ♕xb4+ white's queen's knight develops on c3, and then white's position is more pleasant. The continuation 7...♗xc5 8.♕xb6 axb6 9.♘c3 0-0 10.e3 d5 11.cxd5 exd5 12.♘b5 ♘b4 13.♗xb4 ♗xb4+ 14.♔e2 ♗d7 15.♘bd4 ♗c5 (Michalik – Romanishin, Presov 2010) doesn't leave white with any chances to demonstrate the merits of the knights in the blocked position. Here all the knights can do it block,

but the bishop pair will prevent them from attacking.

8.♘bxd2 ♕xc5 9.♗g2 b6 10.0-0 ♗b7 11.♖ac1 0-0 12.♕c3 ♖ac8 13.a3

13...a5

This weakens the b6 pawn, which Laza then exploited. It was worth considering 13...♘e7 14.b4 ♕c7 with a possible transposition to a nice hedgehog.

14.♘b3 ♕e7 15.♘bd4 ♗a6 16.♕e3

White is in a hurry to attack b6. After 16.♘xc6 ♖xc6 17.♘e5 ♖cc8 18.♖fd1 d5 19.♕e3 the queen has evaded the pin in good time, and white has a minimal advantage.

16...a4?

After 16...♘xd4 17.♕xd4 ♕c5 18.b3 d5 19.♕xc5 ♖xc5 20.cxd5 ♗xe2 21.♖xc5 ♗xf1 22.♖c6 ♗xg2 23.♔xg2 ♘xd5 24.♘e5 white's pieces have sufficient energy to draw at best, after winning back a pawn.

17.♘xc6 ♖xc6 18.♘e5 ♖c5 19.♘d3! ♖xc4 20.♕xb6 ♖xc1 21.♘xc1 ♗c4 22.♕a5

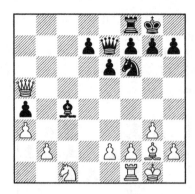

Without making a huge effort, white wins a pawn. Still, converting it into a win will be most difficult.

22...d5 23.♕xa4 ♖b8 24.b3 ♗b5 25.♕a5 ♕b7 26.a4 ♗e8 27.♕d2 ♘d7 28.♖e1

He cannot play e2-e4, but the rook move looks limp. After 28.♕d4 Banusz would be in difficulties.

28...♘c5 29.♕c3 ♖c8

The grandmaster bluff is impressive! Were he to capture on b3 he would be guaranteed a draw but with zero chances of winning against an opponent over 400 Elo points lower. Hence he temporarily reprieves the pawn, pinning his hopes on activating his forces.

30.♕e3 ♕b4 31.♖d1 ♘b7 32.♘a2 ♕a3 33.♖c1 ♖c5 34.♖xc5 ♘xc5 35.♕c1 ♕xb3 36.♕xc5 ♕xa2 37.a5 h5!?

If black captures on e2, then ♗g2-f1 will support a5-a6, and black's extra pawn will only suffice to draw. This second bluff is crowned with success.

38.♕c8 ♕a4 39.a6 ♔h7 40.a7 ♗b5

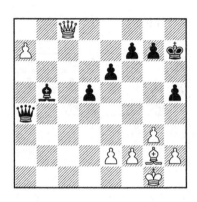

41.♗e4+?

Laza failed to notice the line 41.a8=♕! ♕d1+ 42.♗f1 ♗xe2 43.♕a1 ♕xa1 44.♕c2+ g6 45.♕xe2, where white would not lose with the extra bishop.

41...♕xe4 42.a8=♕??

He had to play 42.♕c1 d4 43.a8=♕ ♕xa8 44.♕b1+ g6 45.♕xb5, and white would probably have drawn despite being a pawn down.

42...♕b1+ 43.♔g2 ♗xe2
White resigned.

Obviously, this is just a miscellaneous chapter. In game 58 we saw a transposition to the Nimzo-Indian Defense, and in game 59 we encountered white's efforts to obtain equality after 5.g3 ♕b6! However, the structures in these games are different from the ones we will analyze in the following chapter.

Chapter 10

Various after 4...c5 5.♗xb4 cxb4

No. 60 A. Illner – L. Gonda
Budapest 2012

1.d4 ♘f6 2.♘f3 e6 3.c4 ♗b4+ 4.♗d2 c5 5.♗xb4 cxb4

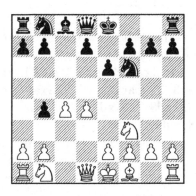

6.♕d3

The queen's sortie with the idea of supporting e2-e4 is not played often. However, 6.g4!? looks more eccentric. Still, in recent decades pushing the g-pawn two squares in closed openings has become epidemic, and in this position is justified by the c5-pawn leaving its square and exiting the extended center (which creates problems with counterplay for black). Black should be guided by Grandmaster Rozentalis's second attempt at combating 6.g4: 6...d5 7.e3 ♘c6 8.♘bd2 0-0 9.♖g1 ♖e8!? (freeing a square for the knight) 10.♗d3 ♘d7 11.h4 ♘f8 12.♕c2 ♗d7 13.♘g5 g6 14.♕b3 ♕e7 15.cxd5 ♘a5 16.d6 ♕xd6 17.♕d1 ♗c6 (Ezat

– Rozentalis, Reykjavik 2014), and a few moves later white offered a draw from a position of strength. Black can probably improve with 10... e5!? 11.♘xe5 ♘xe5 12.dxe5 ♖xe5 13.g5 ♘g4 14.♖xg4 ♗xg4 15.♕xg4 ♖xg5 16.♕f4 and a very complicated position.

6...0-0 7.e4 d6

After 7...d5 white has the following line at his disposal: 8.♘bd2 dxe4 (he mustn't allow 9.e5) 9.♘xe4 ♘xe4 10.♕xe4 ♗d7 11.♗d3 g6 12.♕f4 ♗c6 13.♗e4 ♗xe4 14.♕xe4 ♘c6. White has a small but stable advantage.

8.♘bd2

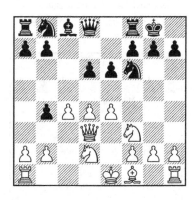

8...♘fd7

Black plans e6-e5 and in reply to d4-d5 has the a6 square for his queen's knight (enabling him to challenge properly for the c5 square), while if e5xd4 (as in the game) he can move it to c6. In reply to 8...♘c6 9.♗e2 e5 10.d5 ♘e7 the break 11.c5!? doesn't

promise any advantage due to 11...
♘g6 12.♕b5 a5! The best way to
fight for a small advantage in a more
maneuvering struggle is via 11.0-0
♘g6 12.g3 ♗g4 13.a3.

9.♗e2 e5 10.0-0 ♘c6 11.♖fd1 exd4

Against Epishin, two strong
grandmasters, Nisipeanu and Socko,
refused to concede the center and
allowed it to be locked up with d4-
d5. In the game Epishin – Socko
(Dresden 2007) the d5 pawn suddenly
stormed up the career ladder: 11...
♖e8 12.♕e3 ♘f6 13.♖ac1 ♗g4
14.d5 ♗xf3 15.dxc6 (after 15.♘xf3
♘e7 16.c5 ♘c8 the knight plans a
blockade on d6) 15...♗xe2 16.cxb7
♗xd1 17.bxa8=♕ ♕xa8 18.♖xd1
♕c6 19.f3 a5 20.b3 ♘d7 21.♘f1 ♘c5
22.♕d2 ♖e6 23.♘e3. The knight is
right by its desired d5 square, but
black is holding the defense.

12.♘xd4 ♘c5 13.♕e3 ♖e8

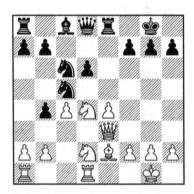

14.♘b5

Illner wants to highlight the
fragility of the c5 knight + d6 pawn
construction. After 14.a3 ♘xd4
15.♕xd4 ♕b6 16.axb4 ♕xb4
17.♕xd6 b6 white has won a pawn,

but the excellent position of black's
pieces gives him compensation for the
material.

**14...a6 15.♘xd6 ♕xd6 16.♘b3
♕f6 17.♘xc5 ♕xb2 18.♘a4 ♕e5
19.♘b6 ♖b8 20.f3**

The knight on b6 worked hard,
and from an exile transformed into
a powerful fighter. Now he's ready
to establish himself on d5, but black
launches counterplay.

20...f5 21.c5

21.♗d3 fxe4 22.♗xe4 ♗f5
23.♗d5+ ♔h8 24.♕xe5 ♘xe5 is only
sufficient for equality.

**21...fxe4 22.♘c4 ♕c3 23.♕xc3
bxc3 24.♖ac1 ♗e6 25.fxe4 ♖ed8
26.♖xd8+ ♖xd8 27.♖xc3 ♖d4
28.♘d6**

At last, the e-pawn is well
protected, however, the black rook's
invasion of the second rank places a
cross against white's efforts.

**28...♖d2 29.♗c4 ♗xc4 30.♘xc4
Draw agreed.**

No. 61 P.L. Basso – A.S. Samant
Cannes 2019

**1.d4 ♘f6 2.c4 e6 3.♘f3 ♗b4+
4.♗d2 c5 5.♗xb4 cxb4 6.a3**

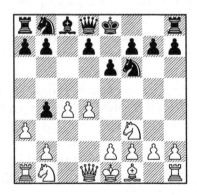

The feature of this attack is that after the pawn exchange the white rook will land on a3 and his knight on c3. How the kingside pieces will mobilize depends on the queenside setup.

6...bxa3

The defending move 6...♘c6 allows a white pawn to get to d6. With precise play, white gets to prove that his daring pawn is a strong point and no weakness: 7.d5 exd5 8.cxd5 ♘e7 9.d6 ♘c6 10.axb4 ♕b6 11.♘c3 ♕xb4 12.♕d2 0-0 (Mamedyarov – Fridman, Khanty-Mansiysk 2011, rapid) 13.♖a4 ♕c5 14.e3 b6 15.♗e2 ♗b7 16.0-0.

7.♖xa3

LANDMINE. White should not be tempted to build a long wall with 7.b4? due to 7...♘c6 8.b5 ♕a5+! 9.♕d2? ♘b4. White ends up the exchange down in a horrible position.

7...0-0 8.♘c3

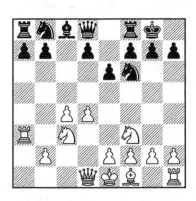

8...d6

In reply to 8...d5 it's premature to play 9.c5 due to 9...b6 10.b4 a5. After 9.e3 ♘c6 the break c4-c5 gains in strength, and black is better fighting for equality via 9...dxc4 10.♗xc4 b6.

9.e3

The Italian grandmaster postpones central operations until he completes his development. In the game Inkiov – Bagheri (Guingamp 2002) grabbing the center didn't bring white any real dividends: 9.e4 ♘c6 10.♗d3 e5 11.d5 ♘b4 12.♗b1 ♗g4 13.0-0 ♘d7 14.♘b5 ♘c5!? Bagheri sacrifices a pawn for the sake of a blockade on dark squares. Now 15.♖xa7 ♖xa7 16.♘xa7 f5 gives black the initiative on the kingside, while 15.♘xa7 ♕b6 16.♘b5 ♖xa3 17.bxa3 ♘ba6 and ♘a6-c7 probably gives him the initiative on the queenside.

9...♘c6 10.♗e2 a5

In this game, Samant didn't push his e-pawn, turning off the beaten path. The position with a tense center after 10...e5 11.0-0 ♗g4 12.h3 ♗h5 13.♕d2 ♖e8 is more promising for white.

11.0-0

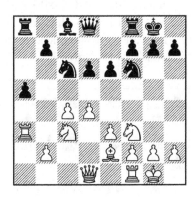

11...b6

Samant was probably unaware of the old game Granda – Nikolic (Habana 1987), in which after 11...♘b4 Granda organized pressure on the d6 pawn – 12.e4 ♘d7 13.♘b5 ♕e7 14.♕d2 b6 15.♕g5 ♕xg5 16.♘xg5 h6 17.♘f3 d5 18.cxd5 exd5 19.e5 ♗a6. White gained a pawn majority on the kingside, but no stable advantage.

By the time of the game Xiao Zhang – Samant (Ho Chi Minh City 2019) the Indian player had probably discovered that old grandmaster game and, like Nikolic, played 11...♘b4. Play continued 12.d5 e5 13.♘d2 b6 14.e4 ♘d7 15.♘b5 ♘c5 with the black knights standing impressively, and then 16.f4?! exf4 17.♖xf4 ♕e7 18.♖f1 ♗d7 made white's position worse.

12.d5 ♘b4 13.♘d4 exd5 14.cxd5 ♗b7

It was better to continue 14...♗d7 15.e4 ♕e7 16.f3 ♖fc8 – the rook is doing nothing on a3.

15.e4 ♘d7 16.♘cb5 ♘c5 17.♘f5 ♘xe4?!

The black bishop is blocked by enemy pawns, while the white cavalry are running amok. 17...♕f6 is insufficient due to 18.♘fxd6 ♕xb2 19.♖c3 or 18.♖f3 – but that was still better than allowing the queen to d4.

18.♕d4 ♘f6 19.♖g3 g6

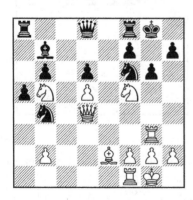

20.♘h6+?

The right continuation was 20.♘bxd6 but white found it a couple of moves later.

20...♔g7 21.♘f5+ ♔g8?

If 21...♔h8 then white will have to capture on d6 with the f5 knight, and then 22...♗xd5 almost evens up chances.

22.♘bxd6! ♗xd5 23.♕e5! ♘c6

23...♖a7 would be met by 24.♖d1! with the murderous threat 25.♘e4! The triumph of centralization!

24.♕c3 ♘b4 25.♖d1 ♖a7 26.♘c8

26.♘e4! was even more convincing, but this attack deep in enemy lines was enough. **Black resigned.**

No. 62 F. Urkedal – J. Tisdall
Norway 2017

1.d4 ♘f6 2.c4 e6 3.♘f3 ♗b4+ 4.♗d2 c5 5.♗xb4 cxb4 6.e3

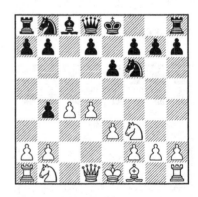

The d4-e3-f2 pawn chain doesn't cramp black's dark-colored bishop, as he has left the board together with his counterparty. White develops his light-colored bishop either on e2, as in this game, or on d3, as in the next game.

6...0-0 7.♗e2 d6

After this black often continues b7-b6 and ♗c8-b7, so the question is why not play the fianchetto first? Well, partially this is because after 7...b6 8.0-0 ♗b7 white gains the additional possibility to play 9.♘e5 d6 10.♗f3 and exchange the long-range enemy bishop. Unlike variations with 6.g3, the exchange doesn't create a hole in the white king's bunker. I have carried out this idea several times in my own games.

In the game Giri – David (Mulhouse 2011) black protected his b4 pawn, not rushing to develop his queen's knight. After 7...a5 8.a3 ♘a6 9.♘e5 d6 10.♘d3 bxa3 11.♘xa3 ♖e8 12.♘b5 ♘c7 white would have retained a small opening advantage with 13.♘c3 b6 14.0-0 ♗b7 15.♕b3 ♘d7 16.♖fd1.

KEY TIP. Transferring the knight from f3 to d3 is typical of this line. The knight continues to control e5, but in addition attacks the squares b4, c5 and f4. That said, the loss of influence over the d-file may make itself felt.

8.0-0

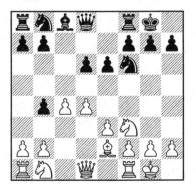

8...b6

The continuation 8...♘c6 9.a3 bxa3 10.♖xa3 e5 is another way to solve the problem of black's hemmed in bishop. The variation 11.♘c3 ♗g4 12.h3 ♗h5 13.♕d2 ♖e8 merges into one from the note to 10...a5 in game 61. If white wants to prevent the bishop from getting to g4, then he can play 11.h3 ♖e8 12.♘c3 ♗f5 (Laxman – Kunte, Lucknow 2016) 13.♘b5 ♕b8 14.dxe5 dxe5 15.♕d6 with better prospects after the exchange of queens.

9.a3

In itself, the early d7-d6 doesn't prevent white in the slightest from exchanging the second bishop pair. After 9.♘e1 white continues ♗e2-f3, and then might continue, ♘b1-d2 and ♘e1-d3, but what next? He will probably have to continue to attack the cramping b4 pawn.

9...bxa3 10.♘xa3

Urkedal's plan involves a pawn charge on the queenside, during which the f3 knight stays where it is as on d3 it would prevent its bishop from supporting the pawn push.

10...♘c6 11.♘c2 ♗b7 12.b4

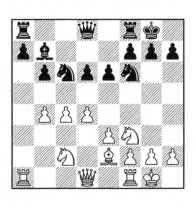

12...a5

12...a6 is also acceptable, setting up a kind of hedgehog. Tisdall, however, thinks that black is right not to restrict himself to defense on the queenside.

13.♖b1 ♘e4 14.♕d3 d5 15.♘d2 ♘d6 16.c5 ♗a6 17.b5 ♘xb5 18.♖xb5 bxc5

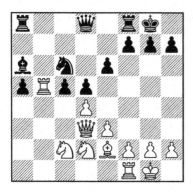

19.dxc5?!

Urkedal fails to calculate accurately and in sufficient depth. He stakes all on his planned 25th move, failing to spot his opponent's great reply. He had relatively better prospects from 19.♕c3 ♗xb5 20.♗xb5 cxd4 21.exd4 ♖c8 22.♕e3 (the rook and pair of pawns are only slightly stronger than the bishop and knight) or even 21.♕xc6 ♖c8 22.♘xd4 ♖xc6 23.♘xc6 ♕d6 24.♖a1 ♖a8 25.♗a4, and black's material advantage is probably insufficient to deliver a full point, despite the computer's contrasting evaluation.

19...♘a7 20.♘a3 ♘xb5 21.♘xb5 ♖b8 22.♖b1 ♕d7 23.♕c3?!

White still hasn't noticed the trick, otherwise he would have sought salvation via 23.♕c2 ♗xb5 24.♖xb5 ♖xb5 25.c6 ♖b2 26.♕xb2 ♕xc6.

23...♗xb5 24.♖xb5 ♖xb5 25.c6 d4! 26.♕c4 ♕d6?!

Now it was Tisdall's turn to make a mistake. 26...♕a7! 27.♕xb5 dxe3 28.♘f3 ♖b8 29.♕d3 exf2+ 30.♔f1 ♕c5 left white without chances of drawing.

27.♕xb5 dxe3 28.♘c4 exf2+ 29.♔xf2 ♕d4+ 30.♔g3 a4!?

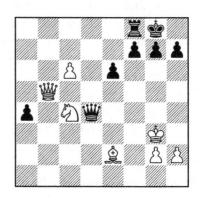

31.♗f3?

This gives Tisdall one more chance to win. White cannot take the pawn due to 31...g5!, but after 31.c7 a3 32.♕a5 or 31.h3 a3 32.♕a6 g5 33.♔h2 he would fight on as an equal.

31...a3 32.♕a6 g5 33.h3 h5?

This was the right time to bring the rook back into the game via b8. I think the players were in time trouble.

34.♘xa3 ♕f4+ 35.♔f2 g4 36.hxg4 hxg4 37.♕c4 ♕xc4 38.♘xc4 gxf3 39.♘d6 fxg2 40.c7 ♔g7 41.♔xg2 ♔f6 42.c8=♕ ♖xc8 43.♘xc8

Draw agreed.

No. 63 D. Hartl – S. Siebrecht
Austria 2012

1.d4 ♘f6 2.c4 e6 3.♘f3 ♗b4+ 4.♗d2 c5 5.♗xb4 cxb4 6.e3 0-0 7.♗d3

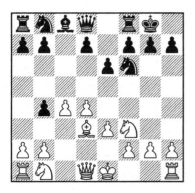

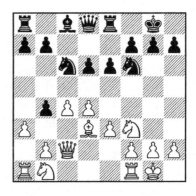

The bishop takes aim at the kingside, which is, however, strong enough not to shudder at the bishop's angry face. In addition, white shows he will fight for e4.

7...d6

In the game Fressinet – Akopian (Porto Carras 2011) white won the fight for the central square after 7...b6 8.♘bd2 (note that the actual move order was different) 8...♗b7 9.♕c2 d6 10.♘e4 ♘xe4 11.♗xe4 ♗xe4 12.♕xe4 ♘d7 13.0-0 (the queen's invasion of the enemy camp without support would be pointless) 13...♖c8 14.♕d3 ♕c7 15.♘d2 a5 16.a3 bxa3 17.bxa3 e5 18.♖ab1 ♖fe8 19.♖b5 exd4 20.♕xd4 ♖e5 21.♖fb1. White has a minimal advantage.

8.0-0 ♖e8

Black's main plan is unchanged – e6-e5. The black queen is also able to support that break. For example, 8...♕e7 9.♘bd2 e5 10.♘e4 ♘xe4 11.♗xe4 ♘d7 12.♗f5 ♘b6 13.♗xc8 ♖axc8 14.b3 ♘d7 with gradual equality (Sipila – Miezis, Vaxjo 2013).

9.a3 ♘c6 10.♕c2

10...bxa3 11.bxa3

> **KEY TIP.** It makes sense for white to recapture on a3 with his pawn when black has played a7-a5 and thereby weakened the b6 pawn. Then, white's queen's knight nicely sits on c3 with a guaranteed outpost on b5.

11...e5 12.♘c3 ♗g4 13.dxe5 dxe5

If 13...♘xe5 14.♘xe5 ♖xe5 the black pieces come alive at the cost of deforming his pawn structure. The latter isn't material, all the more so as the white pawns don't make up a strong and compact row either.

14.♘g5 h6 15.♘ge4 ♘xe4 16.♗xe4 ♖c8

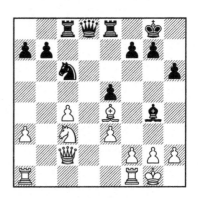

17.♗d5

The Austrian player increases his dominance of the center, however, this paradoxically does not improve his position overall. It was worth considering 17.h3 ♗e6 18.♘b5 with the threat that the knight would invade on d6.

17...♘a5 18.♕e4 ♕g5 19.♗xf7+

A blunder due to a terrible miscalculation. After 19.♘b5 ♖cd8 20.♘xa7 ♗f5 21.♕f3 ♗e6 black will restore the pawn balance thanks to his good pieces.

19...♔xf7   20.♕d5+   ♖e6 21.♕xa5??

I have the impression that white had by now noticed the threat of mate but gave up trying. However, he had two ways to save the game. The first was – 21.f4!? exf4 22.♖xf4+ ♔g8 23.♕xg5 hxg5 24.♖xg4 ♖xc4 25.♖xc4 ♘xc4 26.e4 with a drawish ending. The second, which was less certain, was to lure the bishop from covering f3 via 21.♕d7+ ♖e7 22.♕d5+ ♗e6 23.♕xa5 b6, and again transpose to an ending after 24.f4.

21...♗f3 22.g3 ♕g4
White resigned.

The continuations 6.♕d3 and, especially, 6.g4 (from game 60 and the notes to it) should be studied carefully. Black cannot apply standard methods and has to leave his comfort zone and think independently. At the same time, the lines 6.a3 bxa3 7.♖xa3 and 6.e3 are also sufficient to fight for a minimal advantage.

Chapter 11

4...c5 5.♗xb4 cxb4 6.g3 variation

No. 64 M. Al Sayed – B. Amin
Dubai 2015

1.♘f3 ♘f6 2.d4 e6 3.c4 ♗b4+ 4.♗d2 c5 5.♗xb4 cxb4

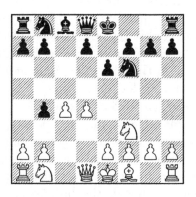

6.g3

In games 62 and 63 the light-squared bishop developed to e2 and d3, respectively, which didn't prevent it from occupying squares on the long diagonal, f3 and e4, when the chance arose. In a number of closed openings the g2 square is just right for the bishop, and the Vitolins Defense is no exception.

6...b6

In games 66-70 we review 6...0-0 and an early d7-d6.

7.♗g2 ♗b7

TRANSPOSITION ALERT. This position can be reached by the QID – 1.d4 ♘f6 2.c4 e6 3.♘f3 b6 4.g3 ♗b7 5.♗g2 ♗b4+ 6.♗d2 c5 7.♗xb4 cxb4.

8.0-0

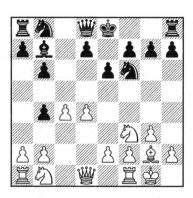

8...0-0

The drawback of playing 8...a5 9.a3 ♘a6 is that the knight is passive on a6 if white doesn't relieve the tension over a3-b4. The game Nihal – Karthik (Xingtai 2019) continued 10.♘bd2 0-0 11.♘e5 ♗xg2 12.♔xg2 ♕c7 13.e3 d6 14.♘d3 bxa3 15.bxa3 e5 16.♕b3 ♘b8 17.a4 ♘bd7. With the "correct" capture by white of the a3 pawn with his own pawn (see the earlier key tip on this) white has fixed the enemy pawn on b6. At the same time, white has transferred his idle knight from a6 to d7, covered his weakness and has a satisfactory position.

9.a3

The development of the queen to d3 is found in the next game (where the move 9.♕b3 is also covered in the notes). The continuation 9.♘bd2 merges into various other plans, in particular, into game 5 of the historical introduction.

9...bxa3

Hou Yifan has twice demonstrated an interesting idea – she played 9...♛e7 (as d7-d6 has not yet happened) and only exchanged on a3 after ♘b1-d2. Her second try was as follows: 10.♛b3 ♘c6 11.♘bd2 bxa3 12.♛xa3 (an unexpected piece lands on a3) 12...♘b4 13.♜ac1 ♘e4 14.♘xe4 ♝xe4 15.♘e5 ♝xg2 16.♚xg2 a5 17.♘d3 ♜fc8 18.♜fd1 ♚f8 19.♘xb4 ♛xb4 20.♛xb4+ axb4 with a drawish rook ending (Shen Yang – Hou Yifan, Qingdao 2011).

10.♜xa3

Capturing with the knight doesn't create much of an impression, while the string of pawns after 10.b4 will not last long. See for example Grinev – Matsenko (Konja 2017): 10...♘c6 11.♘e5 ♛c7 12.♘xc6 ♝xc6 13.♘xa3 ♝xg2 14.♚xg2 a5 15.bxa5 ♜xa5 16.♛d3 ♜fa8 17.♘c2 ♛c6+ 18.f3 ♜xa1 19.♜xa1 ♜xa1 20.♘xa1 d5 21.cxd5 exd5, and neither side has winning chances left.

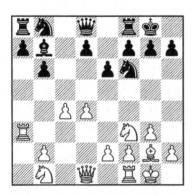

10...♛e7

Amin is Egypt's strongest grandmaster with experience of playing the 4...c5 system at top-level

chess. Therefore, we can assume that he had already analyzed this unusual black setup with a pawn still on d7.

Black usually prefers 10...a5 here, without being concerned at weakening b5. After 11.♘c3 ♘a6 12.♘b5 d6 the warring armies are positioned equally harmoniously and are ready for a tense battle.

11.♘bd2 ♘c6

The maneuver ♘b1-c3-b5 was not tried because at any moment black could chase the knight away with a7-a6. At the same time, Amin didn't play 11...a5 due to 12.♛b3.

12.♘e5 ♜fc8 13.♘xc6 dxc6

This leads to a structural advantage for white, albeit a minor one. After 13...♝xc6 14.e4 e5 15.d5 ♝b7 white gains territory with tempo, although the bishop on g2 will be no happier than its opposite number.

14.♛a1 a6

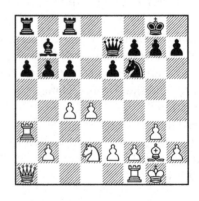

15.c5!?

Apart from this standard pawn sac, 15.♜b3!? is also attractive, and if 15...c5 (protecting the b6 pawn with the queen allows white to push c4-c5 without a sac) 16.♖xb6 ♗xg2 17.♔xg2 cxd4 white has created a passed pawn.

15...bxc5 16.dxc5 ♕xc5 17.♖c1 ♕e7 18.♘c4

Instead of this guaranteed way to regain the pawn the blockading maneuver ♘d2-b3-c5 was more promising.

18...♖ab8 19.♖b3 ♘d5 20.♘a5 ♘b4 21.♖bc3 h6 22.♗xc6 ♗xc6 23.♘xc6 ♖xc6 24.♖xc6 ♘xc6 25.♖xc6 ♕f6 26.♕xa6 ♕xb2 27.♖c8+ ♖xc8 28.♕xc8+ ♔h7 29.♕c4 ♕b1+ 30.♔g2 ♕b7+

Draw agreed as both players had run out of pieces.

No. 65 V. Babula – V. Akopian
Tromso 2014

1.d4 ♘f6 2.c4 e6 3.♘f3 ♗b4+ 4.♗d2 c5 5.♗xb4 cxb4 6.g3 b6 7.♗g2 ♗b7 8.0-0 0-0

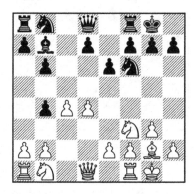

9.♕d3

It's useful to compare this queen sortie with the similar one in game 60 (when the white bishop's development isn't yet decided). The direct attack 9.♕b3 is seen frequently

with the continuation 9...a5 10.a3 ♘a6 11.♘bd2 d6. In the game Urkedal – A. Onischuk (Khanty-Mansiysk 2017) the Norwegian grandmaster again harvested on b4 and resolved the a3-b4 standoff to some advantage: 12.♖fd1 ♕e7 13.♘e1 e5 14.♗xb7 ♕xb7 15.♘c2 bxa3 16.bxa3 ♖fe8 17.♖ab1 ♖ab8 18.♘f3 exd4 19.♘cxd4.

9...d6 10.♘bd2 ♕c7

It's possible that black rejected 10...a5 so that after 11.a3 he would avoid placing his knight on the edge of the board (11...♘a6) as well as avoiding ending up with a vulnerable pawn on b6 (11...bxa3 12.bxa3). However, in recent games grandmasters as white have continued 11.e4 e5 12.♘e1 with the knight transferring to c2. Then it's better for both players to maintain tension in the game: black should not capture e5xd4 as that would allow pressure on d6, while white should avoid d4xe5, as that would concede the d-file.

11.♖fd1

White is not forced to exchange the second bishop pair. In the game Carlsen – Epishin (Tromso 2007) the future world champion immediately set up a barrier on the long diagonal: 11.e4 ♘bd7 12.♘e1 a5 13.♘c2 e5 14.♘e3 exd4 15.♕xd4 ♖ae8 16.f3 ♖e5 (the knight is better on this square) 17.♖fd1 ♘c5 18.♘df1 ♘e8 19.♖ac1 g6 20.♘g4 ♘e6 21.♕d2 ♖c5 22.♘fe3 h5 23.♘f2 ♕e7 24.a3 bxa3 25.bxa3. Now black has a second pawn weakness and white plans f3-f4 – black has a difficult position.

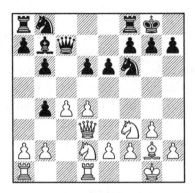

11...♖e8

Two months before this game Akopian got into trouble: 11...♘bd7 12.♘e1 ♖fe8 13.♘c2 a5 14.e4 e5 15.f3 b5?! 16.cxb5 d5 17.♘e3 ♕b6?! 18.exd5 ♘xd5 19.♘dc4 ♕xb5 20.♘d6 ♕xd3 21.♖xd3 (Cheparinov – Akopian, Albena 2014). This adventure was hardly forced. Against Babula the Armenian grandmaster playing black at least rushed to exchange bishops.

12.♘e1 ♝xg2 13.♔xg2 a5 14.e4 e5 15.♘c2 ♘c6 16.f3 ♘d7

The e4 pawn is strongly protected, and the knight now seems to be seeking a new job to do. In reality, though, Akopian has planned a sacrifice so that his rook can invade the second rank.

17.♘f1

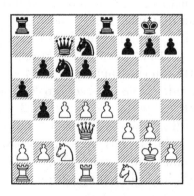

17...f5!?

Let's try sending the knight to pressurize d4 – 17...♘f8 18.♘fe3 ♘e6!? 19.dxe5 dxe5 20.♕d7 ♖ac8 21.♕xc7 ♖xc7. Black is close to equalizing.

18.exf5 exd4 19.♘xd4 ♘xd4 20.♕xd4 ♖e2+ 21.♔h3

In the variation 21.♔h1 ♕b7 22.♕f4 ♖xb2 23.♖xd6 ♖e8 white closes the second rank with his rook or knight. That said, black has evident compensation for the pawn, as white's pawn structure is broken, while his king still isn't safe.

21...♘f6?!

Black failed to notice the drawish character of the endgame after 21...♕c6 22.♕xd6 ♕xf3 23.♕d5+ ♕xd5 24.♖xd5 ♘c5 (or 24...♘f6) 25.♖d2 ♖xd2 26.♘xd2.

22.♖d2 ♖ae8

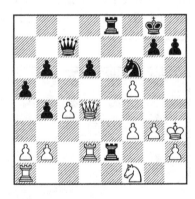

23.♕d3?!

A poor move that ensures the game ends in a draw. He first had to play 23.♖ad1 and only then ♕d4-d3.

23...♖xd2 24.♘xd2 ♕c5 25.♘e4 ♕xf5+ 26.♔g2 ♘xe4 27.♖e1 ♕f6 28.♖e2 h6 29.fxe4 ♖f8 30.♖d2 a4 31.♕e2 ♖e8 32.♖d5 a3 33.bxa3 bxa3 34.♖d3 ♕b2 35.♕xb2 axb2 36.♖b3

♖xe4 37.♖xb2 ♖xc4 38.♖xb6 ♖c2+ 39.♔g1 ♖xa2 40.♖xd6
Draw agreed.

No. 66 E. Postny – S. Maze
Andorra 2005

1.d4 ♘f6 2.c4 e6 3.♘f3 ♗b4+ 4.♗d2 c5 5.♗xb4 cxb4 6.g3 0-0 7.♗g2

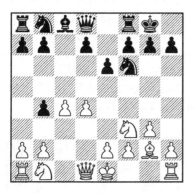

7...d6

This is the main continuation. Black prepares e6-e5 and then the development of his bishop along the c8-h3 diagonal.

7...d5 doesn't help to develop the bishop, or the queenside as a whole. White easily gains an advantage, such as in the example Ivanchuk – Gulko (New York 1988): 8.♘bd2 ♘c6 9.0-0 b6 10.♖c1 ♗b7 11.e3 ♕d6 12.♕a4 ♖fc8 13.♖c2 ♖c7 14.♖fc1 ♖ac8 15.cxd5. Now 15...exd5? 16.♗h3 ♘d7 17.♘e5 led to material gains for white, but 15...♘xd5 16.♘e5! wouldn't have saved black from difficulties (he cannot accept the pawn sac due to the threat of mate on the back rank).

8.♘bd2

Postny carries out the old idea of Yuri Dokhoyan – to transfer the knight via f1 to e3. Delaying castling isn't dangerous for white, as the armies have not yet engaged in battle.

8...♖e8

The lengthy knight maneuver is more often played after 8...♘c6. The game Chernin – A. Moiseenko (Spain 2005), despite the early draw, created intrigue after 9.♘f1 e5 10.♘e3 ♘g4 11.♘d5 f5!? 12.a3 e4 13.♘d2 bxa3 14.♖xa3 ♗e6 15.h3 ♘h6 16.♘f4 ♗f7 17.e3 ♘b4 18.h4 a5 with two strongly entrenched knights and equal chances. Seeing as white could also fight for an advantage via the solid 12.e3, it made sense for black not to weaken e5 and to find a different way to bring his bishop into play. In practice, black has equalized here with 9...♗d7 10.♘e3 ♘e7 11.0-0 b5 12.c5 ♗c6, though ♗d7-c6 is also good on move 11.

Obviously, white doesn't let his opponent know in advance whether 8.♘bd2 will be accompanied by the knight's further journey or whether castling has simply been postponed for one move. Hence it's useful for black to take note of white's flexibility of choice here.

9.♘f1

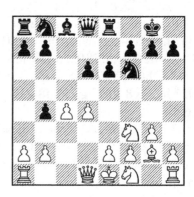

9...♛c7

The queen proactively protects b7 in order to prepare the fianchetto. Petursson's old recipe is also good here – 9...a5 10.♘e3 ♘a6 11.0-0 ♝d7. Further, the Icelandic grandmaster placed his bishop on c6 and easily solved his opening problems. The knight on e3 has to make do with the role of protecting the c4 pawn.

10.♘e3 b6 11.0-0 ♝b7 12.d5 e5 13.♛d2 a5 14.♘f5 ♘bd7

The queen's development to c7 left the knight on f6 without protection, and Maze rushes to fix that.

15.♛g5 g6 16.♝h3

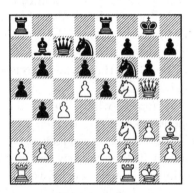

16...♚h8

The engine assesses the position after 16...♛xc4 17.♘xd6 ♛xe2 18.♘xe8 ♜xe8 19.♘h4 ♛xb2 as totally zero. It's better for white to win the exchange with the addition of 18.♘d2!? ♝xd5 19.♜fe1 ♛a6.

17.♘h6 ♚g7 18.♘f5+ ♚h8 19.♛h6 ♜g8 20.♘g5 ♜af8 21.♘e3 ♜g7!

This counters the deadly threat 22.♝xd7! ♛xd7 23.f4! by overprotecting h7 and freeing up the g8 square for the knight.

22.a3!? b3?!

Black has not met the sudden change in war theater in the best way. He would have built a safe defensive setup after 22...bxa3 23.♜xa3 ♘g8 24.♛h4 ♘df6.

23.♜ac1?!

The right continuation was 23.♝xd7!, and if 23...♛xd7 white after 24.a4! wins the pawn on b3. If 23...♘xd7 (to protect the b3 pawn from c5) white continues 24.♜ac1 with the idea of ♘e3-g4 and he still wants to follow up with f2-f4.

23...♘g8 24.♛h4 ♘c5 25.f4 exf4 26.♛xf4 ♜e8 27.♜c3

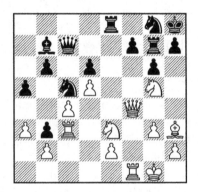

27...f5?!

He should have protected f7 with the simple 27...♜e7 and then transferred his bishop from b7 to c8 in order to exchange his bad piece.

28.♝xf5! gxf5 29.♘xf5 ♜xg5

29...♜g6? is refuted by 30.♘xd6! ♜xd6 31.♘f7+.

30.♛xg5 ♝c8?

The worst time to activate the bishop. Black should have defended via 30...♘e4 31.♛e3 ♜e5, and the computer recommendation

32.♘xd6!? ♕xd6 33.♖xb3 doesn't show any clear advantage.

31.♖e3! ♗xf5

If 31...♖xe3 white wins with the pretty 32.♘h6!

32.♖xe8

Black resigned.

No. 67 Z. Gonzalez Zamora – Y. Quezada

Merida 2008

1.d4 ♘f6 2.c4 e6 3.♘f3 ♗b4+ 4.♗d2 c5 5.♗xb4 cxb4 6.g3 0-0 7.♗g2 d6 8.0-0

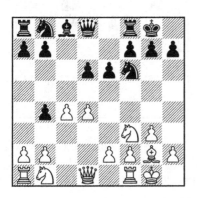

8...a5

In the following games black pushes his e-pawn, but here he starts by shoring up his queenside. The d6-e6 pawn pair temporarily remain in their flexible formation.

9.a3 ♘a6

Developing the knight to c6 harms the pawn structure: 9...♘c6 10.d5 exd5 11.cxd5 ♘e7 12.axb4 ♘exd5 13.♖xa5 ♖xa5 14.bxa5 ♕xa5. Black would then have to defend an unpleasant position without counterplay.

10.axb4 ♘xb4 11.♘c3

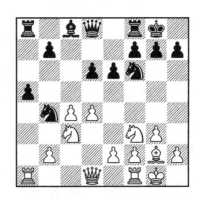

11...b6

Later black tended to revert to the plan with e6-e5. After 11...♕c7 12.b3 ♗d7 13.e4 e5 14.♕e2 ♗g4 15.♖fd1 ♘c6 16.♘b5 ♕b6 17.♕e3 exd4 18.♘bxd4 ♘e5 19.h3 ♘xf3+ 20.♗xf3 ♗xh3 21.♘f5 ♕xe3 22.♘xe3 (Costachi – Rogozenco, Mamaia 2015) the bishop has feasted on a pawn, but given the threat g3-g4 black cannot retain the material and white has a small advantage.

12.♘e1

In reply to 12.♘e5!? black is advised not to capture the knight. In any case, after 12...dxe5 white should continue not 13.♗xa8 exd4 14.♘b5 e5 15.♗g2 ♕e7 16.♕d2 ♗e6 17.b3 ♘d7 and black has compensation for the exchange (Kunte – Kasimdzhanov, Pune 2004), but 13.dxe5! ♖b8 14.exf6 ♕xf6 15.♕d6. The reply 12...♖b8 forces the knight to retreat to d3 with an insignificant advantage.

12...d5

As we know, this is a principally poor continuation in the Vitolins Defense. In the game Kunte – A. Moiseenko (Montreal 2006) black preferred to play against the e4 pawn: 12...♖b8 13.♘d3 ♘xd3 14.♕xd3 ♝a6 15.b4 ♕c7 16.♘b5 ♝xb5 17.cxb5 axb4 18.♝c6 d5 19.♖fb1 ♕e7 20.♖a4 ♘e4 21.♖axb4. White won the pawn back but achieved nothing else.

13.♘c2 ♝a6

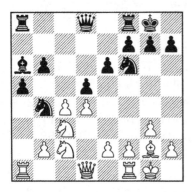

14.cxd5

Gonzalez Zamora immediately resolves the tension in the center. Now both players have a clearer idea of how the piece setups will evolve. In the game between the more illustrious grandmasters Dzhumabayev – Akopian (Moscow 2012) the exchange in the center happened later: 14.♘e3 ♝b7 15.♕d2 ♖b8 16.♖fd1 ♕d7 17.cxd5 ♘fxd5 18.♘cxd5 ♘xd5 19.♘c4 ♖fc8 20.♖ac1 ♝a6 21.♘e5 ♕d6 22.h4 f6 23.♘d3 ♖xc1 24.♖xc1 ♖c8 25.♖xc8+ ♝xc8 26.e4 ♘e7 27.♕c3 ♝b7 28.♘f4. White gained an insignificant advantage in the center but would have gained none at all had Akopian played 18...♝xd5! 19.♘xd5 exd5 with a favorable balance of minor pieces in a blockaded structure.

14...♘bxd5 15.♘xd5 exd5 16.♕d2 ♕d7 17.♖fc1 ♕b5 18.♝f3 ♖ac8 19.b4

In an equal position (19.♘e3 with an exchange of rooks on the c-file was logical here) the Mexican grandmaster playing white strives to use the better position of his rooks.

19...a4 20.♘a3 ♕d7 21.♕b2 ♝b5 22.e3 ♝d3 23.♕d2 ♕f5 24.♝g2

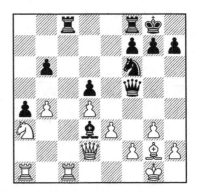

24...♘e4! 25.♕xd3 ♕xf2+ 26.♔h1 ♖xc1+ 27.♖xc1 ♕b2 28.♖f1 ♘f2+ 29.♖xf2 ♕xf2 30.♝xd5 ♖e8 31.e4

Quezada had the foresight to provoke a skirmish. Black has a rook for two minor pieces, but keep watching the outside passer and the white king's lack of safety.

31...♖d8 32.b5?!

He should have focused on how the black rook would move along the 6th rank. The right continuation was 32.h4 ♖d6 33.♕c2, and after the exchange of queens the rook wouldn't manage to support the passers.

32...♖d6 33.♘c4 ♖h6 34.h4 ♖g6 35.♕e3

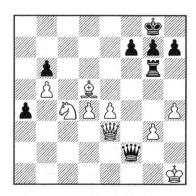

35...♕f1+?!

The Cuban playing black heads for an endgame without having carefully calculated the variations. The right way to carry out the exchange was 35...♕xe3 36.♘xe3 ♖xg3 37.♘c4 ♖b3 38.♘xb6 ♖b1+ 39.♔g2 a3 40.♘a4 ♖xb5 41.♘c3 ♖b2+ 42.♔f3 ♖h2.

36.♕g1 ♕xg1+ 37.♔xg1 a3 38.♘e5 ♖xg3+ 39.♔f2 ♖c3 40.♗xf7+ ♔f8 41.♗d5 ♔e8 42.♔e2 a2 43.♗xa2 ♖c2+ 44.♔d3 ♖xa2 45.♘c4?!

Now it's white's turn to err. 45.d5 ♖a3+ 46.♔d4 collects all the white forces into a powerful phalanx. He threatens d5-d6 and ♔d4-d5 – black doesn't have time to grab the h-pawn and needs to make do with a draw after 46...♖b3.

45...h5 46.♘d6+ ♔f8 47.e5? g5 48.♘f5 ♖f2

Now it's clear why white needed to push his d-pawn and not its neighbor. The knight has no protection, and the newly-baked outside passer decides the outcome.

49.♘e3 gxh4 50.♘d1 ♖a2

White resigned.

No. 68 A. Rasmussen –
L. Nisipeanu
Germany 2012

1.d4 ♘f6 2.c4 e6 3.g3 ♗b4+ 4.♗d2 c5 5.♗xb4 cxb4 6.♗g2 0-0 7.♘f3 d6 8.0-0

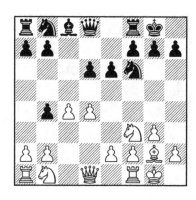

8...♖e8

Supporting e6-e5 via 8...♘c6 is reviewed in separate games (69 and 70). 8...♕c7 is weaker. If 9.a3 bxa3 10.♖xa3 e5 11.♘c3 the knight will be ready to move to d5 with tempo, while after 9...♘a6?! 10.♕b3 bxa3 11.♖xa3 black has two awkwardly placed pieces.

9.♕d3

The main continuation here is 9.a3 ♘c6 10.axb4 ♘xb4 11.♘c3 ♗d7, which takes the game along lines fairly similar to those in game 67, especially after 12.♕b3 a5. If 10.d5 exd5 11.cxd5 ♘e7 12.axb4 ♘exd5 13.b5 ♗d7 14.♘d4 ♕b6 (Garcia Padron – Korchnoi, Las Palmas 1991) the b5 pawn is under attack.

9...a5

This move together with black's following non-standard move had already been deployed by Nisipeanu in a rapid game against Dreev. 9...♘c6 isn't safe due to 10.d5 exd5 11.cxd5, and 11...♘e7 delivers nothing (white's e-pawn, protected by its queen, will beef up its neighbor) and it also gets in the way of the rook.

10.e4

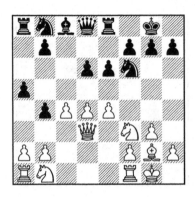

10...♘fd7!?

Black insists on preparing the e6-e5 break, but maybe it was already time to play it? The engine approves the sac 10...e5!? 11.dxe5 dxe5 12.♕xd8 ♖xd8 13.♘xe5 ♗e6, then ♘b8-a6-c5. White really has problems with his queenside, but this line has never been tried.

11.a3

The Danish grandmaster playing white plays more dynamically than in the game Cebalo – Nisipeanu (Saint Vincent 2004). After 11.♘bd2 ♘c6 12.♖fe1 e5 13.♖ad1 ♕f6 (the incessant pressure on d4 opens the door for the d7 knight to get to c5) 14.dxe5 dxe5 15.♘f1 ♘c5 16.♕e3 b6 17.♕g5 ♕xg5 18.♘xg5 ♘d4 the position is more pleasant for black, and Cebalo failed to hold the slightly worse ending.

11...♘c6 12.♘bd2

It was worth considering 12.♖d1!?, and the move in keeping with the plan 12...e5?! leads to difficulties after 13.d5 ♘c5 14.♕e3 ♘a7 15.axb4 axb4 16.♘e1.

12...bxa3 13.♕xa3

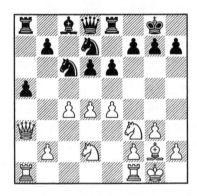

13...♘b4

Let's look at the immediate 13...e5!? If 14.♕xd6?! ♘b4 15.♘xe5 ♖a6 16.♘xf7 ♖xd6 17.♘xd8 ♖xd4 18.♘b3 ♖d3 19.♘xb7 ♗xb7 the piece is stronger than the three pawns. Hence white should seek an advantage via 14.c5!? dxc5 15.dxc5 ♕e7 16.♖fc1 with the idea of ♘d2-c4.

14.♖fc1 e5 15.c5!?

KEY TIP. The plan with c4-c5 is the main way for white to develop an initiative on the queenside in such closed openings. Here the c5 pawn disconnects the enemy pair on a5-b7 which is in white's favor.

15...dxc5 16.dxc5 ♕e7 17.♕e3 ♘b8!

The idea is to support the other knight from c6, and if the chance arises then to move to d4. Black's position is gradually improving.

**18.♘c4 ♘8c6 19.♘b6 ♖b8
20.♘d2**

Rasmussen sends his knight to hunt the a5 pawn. However, as Nisipeanu finds sufficient resistance, white should have considered transferring his passive bishop on g2 via f1 to c4.

20...♗e6 21.♘dc4 ♘d4 22.♖xa5 ♘bc6 23.♖aa1 ♕xc5 24.♘d5

24...♕f8

After skillfully repositioning his knights, black has won back the pawn and now it would have been useful to challenge for the a-file via 24...♖a8. Instead, the queen's modest retreat provokes a flash of complications.

25.♘xe5! ♗xd5 26.♘d7 ♕d6 27.♘xb8 ♕xb8 28.♖d1

The other way to highlight the loose nature of the black pieces was via 28.♖a4. The game could have continued 28...♘b3 (28...♘b5? 29.♕d3) 29.♖c3 b5 30.♖a3 ♘cd4 (30...♘bd4? 31.exd5 b4 32.dxc6 ♖xe3 33.♖xe3 bxa3 34.c7! ♕f8 35.♖xa3 leads to a winning ending for white) 31.exd5 ♖xe3 32.♖xe3 b4 33.♖axb3 ♘xb3 34.♖xb3 with a balance of forces that should lead to a draw.

28...♘c2 29.♕c3 ♗xe4 30.♗xe4 ♘xa1 31.♗xc6 bxc6 32.♖xa1
Draw agreed.

No. 69 A. Bachmann – C. Valiente
Asuncion 2014

1.♘f3 ♘f6 2.c4 e6 3.d4 ♗b4+ 4.♗d2 c5 5.♗xb4 cxb4 6.g3 0-0 7.♗g2 d6 8.0-0 ♘c6

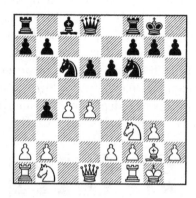

9.♘bd2

The evaluation of the principled move 9.d5 has been clarified. After 9...exd5 10.cxd5 ♘e7 11.♘e1 ♕b6 12.♘c2 ♗f5 13.♘e3 ♗d7 14.♘d2 a5 15.♘dc4 ♕a6 16.♕d4 ♗b5 (P. Nikolic – Kurajica, Jahorina 2012) the unhurried maneuvers of the white knights allowed black to set his army up quite nicely. Were white to push his e-pawn forward, that would provide black the time to set up his army ideally – 12.e4 ♗d7 13.♘c2 ♖ac8 14.♘e3 ♘g6 and ♘g6-e5.

9...e5 10.d5 ♘e7

The knight much more frequently retreats to its starting square, so that it can be redeployed to a6 from where it controls b4 and c5. The game Pantsulaia – A. Moiseenko (Kocaeli

2002) continued 10...♘b8 11.a3 ♘a6 12.♘e1 ♕b6 13.♘d3 ♗f5 14.e4 ♗g4 (the bishop maneuver takes control of d4) 15.♗f3 ♕d4!? (Ivanchuk here immediately exchanged bishops, which is also fine) 16.♕e2 ♗xf3 17.♕xf3 ♖fc8 18.♖fd1 ♘c5 19.♘xc5 ♕xc5 20.axb4 ♕xb4 with equality.

11.♘e1 ♗f5 12.e4 ♗g4 13.f3 ♗d7

The three-stage movement of the bishop not only brought Valiente the d4 square, but also provoked the white pawns to crowd the long diagonal. The bishop on g2 has transformed into a tall pawn, and white should think about redeploying it to another diagonal via 14.♖f2 and ♗g2-f1.

14.♘d3 a5

The queen will not get to control d4 – 14...♕b6+?! 15.c5! dxc5 16.♘c4 ♕d8 17.♘dxe5. Moreover, she has no chance of landing there herself (15. ♖f2 ♕d4? 16.♗f1 with the idea of c4-c5).

15.♖c1 b6 16.f4 ♘g6 17.♕f3

Creating a passer with 17.fxe5 ♘xe5 18.♘xe5 dxe5 doesn't promise any advantage. Black neutralizes the break c4-c5 via ♖a8-c8 or ♕d8-c7 (or

both), while the f6 knight heads via e8 to d6.

17...exf4 18.gxf4 ♗g4

Black needs to counter e4-e5, but he has not chosen the ideal method. 18...♖e8 19.♖fe1 ♘g4 20.h3 ♘h6 was preferable, in order to meet e4-e5 with placing his knight on f5.

19.♕f2 ♘d7 20.h3 ♗h5

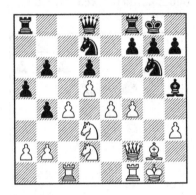

21.♘b3

The knight is heading for d4. This is a reasonable move, but 21.e5!? dxe5 22.fxe5 promised more (22...♘dxe5? 23.♘xe5 ♘xe5 24.♕f5).

21...♘c5 22.♘bxc5 bxc5 23.f5! ♘h4 24.♗h1

Bachmann pushed the f-pawn just when the black knight was unable to occupy e5 due to the loss of the c5 pawn. The pawn cannot move further, as after 24.f6 ♕xf6 25.♕xf6 gxf6 26.♖xf6 ♘xg2 27.♔xg2 ♗g6 black mounts a successful defense.

24...♖e8?!

The black knight needed additional protection with 24...g5. Valiente prevents e4-e5, but f5-f6 contains a greater threat.

25.♖ce1 ♖c8 26.♕g3

Black cannot reply 26...♗e2, so the game is over. Black's minor pieces have got in each other's way on the rook file.

26...♔h8 27.f6 ♘g6 28.♕g5 gxf6 29.♕xh5 ♖g8 30.♔h2

Black resigned.

No. 70 R. Zhumabaev – I. Lysyj
Nizhny Tagil 2007

1.d4 ♘f6 2.c4 e6 3.♘f3 ♗b4+ 4.♗d2 c5 5.♗xb4 cxb4 6.g3 0-0 7.♗g2 d6 8.0-0 ♘c6 9.a3

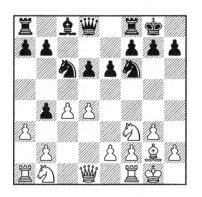

We have seen plenty of evidence that the b4 pawn cramps white. The attack on this harmful pawn is by far the most popular move here.

9...bxa3

9...♕b6 protects b4, but the queen is vulnerable here. For example, 10.axb4 ♘xb4 11.♘c3 ♗d7 12.e4 ♖fd8 13.♕e2 h6 14.♖ad1 ♖ac8 15.♖fe1 a5 16.e5 dxe5 17.♘xe5 ♘c6 18.c5 ♕b4 19.♘c4 ♗e8?! (19...♖b8!?) 20.d5! exd5 21.♘d6 (Kuzubov – Fedorchuk, Brest 2018), and black thought it best to give up the exchange at this point.

10.♘xa3

In the main line 10.♖xa3 e5 11.♘c3 ♗g4 a decision needs to be made on the d4 pawn. If white advances it further, then after 12.d5 ♘b4 (or 12...♗xf3 13.♗xf3 ♘b4) the white bishop turns bad, with no dynamism in compensation. If white exchanges on e5 then he is a bit better. In the game Banikas – Amin (Khanty-Mansiysk 2010) his advantage grew: 12.dxe5 dxe5 13.♕b3 ♕e7 14.e3 ♖fd8 15.♖fa1 ♗xf3 16.♗xf3 e4 17.♗g2 b6 18.♘d5 ♘xd5 19.cxd5 ♘a5 20.♕a2 ♖ac8 21.♖a4 f5 22.♗f1 – the bishop comes into play and is clearly better than the knight. After the stronger 15...♖ab8 white is still guaranteed a slim advantage with his knight invading on d5.

10...e5

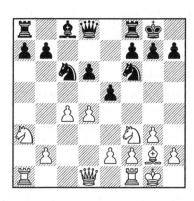

11.♘b5

Without doubt the knight mustn't idle on the edge of the board. Ideally it will get to d6.

11...a6

In the game Sara – Petkov (Palma de Majorca 2009) black sacrificed a pawn to send white's knight back to the edge: 11...♗g4!? 12.d5 ♘b4

13.♖xa7 (13.♘xa7 ♕b6 14.♘b5 ♖xa1 15.♕xa1 ♘bxd5) 13...♖xa7 14.♘xa7 ♗d7 15.♕b3 ♕a5 16.♕a3, and here 16...♕xa3 17.bxa3 ♘c2 leaves white with very little hope of an advantage.

12.dxe5

Beliavsky in this position chose more closed play without open files. After 12.d5 ♘b4 13.♕d2 a5 14.♘e1 ♕b6 15.♘d3 he eventually outplayed a weaker opponent, but so far this fairly plain position is about equal.

12...dxe5 13.c5

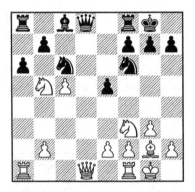

13...♗h3!

This is a spectacular discovery by Petursson from way back in 1994, obviously found without an engine. It's the optimal way to fight the knight's invasion.

14.♗xh3

After 14.♕xd8 ♖fxd8 15.♘d6 ♗xg2 16.♔xg2 ♖ab8 17.♖fd1 h6 18.♘d2 ♔f8 19.♘b3 ♘e8 20.♘c4 f6 21.e3 ♖xd1 22.♖xd1 ♖d8 23.♖xd8 ♘xd8 (Miljkovic – Drasko, Plovdiv 2010) white's attempt to win an equal ending was in vain. Note that Milan Drasko is quite an expert in the Vitolins Defense, and in the 8...♘c6 line in particular.

14...axb5 15.♖xa8 ♕xa8 16.e3 ♖d8

There was an interesting struggle in Van Der Sterren – Petursson (Reykjavik 1994): 16...♕a2!? 17.♕e2 ♕d5 (a strong and wide-reaching maneuver) 18.♖c1 ♖d8 19.♘e1 b4 20.♗f1 e4 21.♕c4 b3 22.♕c3 ♕d2 23.♗c4 ♘g4 24.♕xd2 ♖xd2 25.♗xb3 ♖xb2 26.♗d5 ♘xf2 27.♖c2 ♖xc2 28.♘xc2 ♘d3 29.♗xe4 ♘xc5 with a draw as white was going to win the pawn back. Black had the initiative and white had to play along, though he tried hard.

17.♕c2 ♕a4

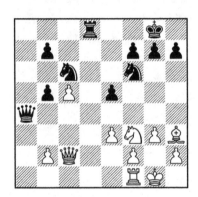

18.♖c1?!

After 18.♕xa4 bxa4 19.♖a1 it's equally good for black to occupy e4 with his pawn or knight. Nevertheless, the queens don't stay on the board for long, which can only please black.

18...e4 19.♘e1 ♘e5

A somewhat timid move without creating any direct threats. A stronger continuation was 19...♕b4! 20.♕c3 ♕xc3 21.bxc3 ♖d5 22.♖a1 g6 23.♘c2 ♖xc5 24.♘d4 ♖xc3 25.♘xb5 ♖d3, and white should draw despite being a pawn down.

20.♕c3 ♕c4 21.♗f1 ♕xc3 22.bxc3 ♖d2 23.♖b1 h5 24.h3

After 24.♖xb5 ♖d1 25.♘c2 ♘f3+ 26.♔g2 ♖c1 27.♘d4 ♘e1+ we reach a draw in the same way as in the actual game.

24...♘fd7

Zhumabaev's inaccuracy could have allowed his opponent to torture him more with 24...♘d5 25.♖c1 ♖b2. Note that 25.♖xb5? doesn't work due to 25...♖d1 26.♘c2 ♘f3+ 27.♔g2 ♖d2.

25.♖xb5 ♖d1 26.♘c2 ♘f3+ 27.♔g2 ♘de5 28.♖xb7 ♖c1 29.♘d4 ♘e1+ 30.♔g1 ♘1f3+ 31.♔g2 ♘e1+ Draw agreed.

There is no simple way to classify the g2-g3 lines due to the multiple move orders. Usually white comes to the conclusion that the b4 pawn is cramping him and resorts to attacking it with a2-a3. Hence you should review the numerous games with an early a2-a3...

I believe that the Vitolins Defense doesn't as a whole contain serious opening risks for either player. The opening up of the game is usually postponed until the middlegame, and therefore the outcome of the battle is usually determined by the players' overall ability (rather than by their better memorization of concrete lines). As in other Bogo-Indian Defense systems, the evaluation of the position is usually stable and doesn't diverge much from a minimal advantage for white.

Chapter 12

Various after 4...a5

No. 71 E. Postny – M. Brown
Greensboro 2018

1.d4 ♘f6 2.c4 e6 3.♘f3 ♗b4+ 4.♗d2 a5

We touched upon this reply briefly in game 4 of the historical introduction. In this chapter we review miscellaneous moves by white (5.♕c2 – game 72, 5.a3 – game 73, 5.♘c3 – games 74 and 75), while in chapters 13-15 we cover the main line, 5.g3.

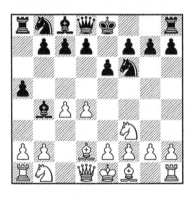

5.e3

The main difference between 4...a5 and 4...c5 is that white mustn't exchange bishops. After 5.♗xb4?! axb4 the black rook is very powerful on its home file, attacking the a2 pawn. If needed, black can protect the b4 pawn with a knight on c6 and his queen on e7.

5...b6

The fianchetto seems more precise than the plan with d7-d6. The game

Shankland – Gareev (Saint Louis 2019) continued 5...0-0 6.♗d3 d6 7.0-0 ♖e8? 8.♗c1! e5 9.a3 ♗c5 10.dxc5 e4 11.cxd6 exd3 12.dxc7 ♕xc7 13.♕xd3 – black's activity compensates for one pawn, but not for two. He should have made the concession of exchanging with 7...♗xd2.

> **KEY TIP.** Gareev ignored a well-known feature of such positions – the bishop on b4 is on an awkward square if its counterparty has the opportunity to avoid exchanging after castling. We will see examples of that later here and in the chapters on 4...♕e7.

6.♗d3 ♗b7 7.♘c3

In the game Houska – Cramling (Tromso 2014) white retreated her bishop to its starting square even when her opponent had a good square for her own retreat: 7.0-0 0-0 8.♗c1 d5 9.a3 ♗e7 10.♘c3 ♘bd7 11.b3 ♘e4 12.♗b2 f5 13.♘e2 ♗d6 14.♘e5 ♗xe5 15.dxe5 ♘dc5 16.♘f4 ♘xd3 17.♕xd3 ♘c5 18.♕c2 dxc4 19.bxc4 ♗e4 20.♕e2 ♕e8. Cramling has successfully switched to a Dutch setup, and is already slightly better.

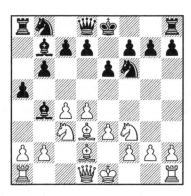
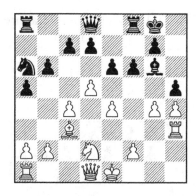

7...♗xc3

The position on the diagram more often occurs via 5.♘c3. The game could also continue 7...d6 8.♕c2 ♘bd7 9.e4 e5 10.♘d5 ♗xd2+ 11.♕xd2 exd4 12.♘xd4 ♘c5 13.0-0 0-0 14.♖fe1 ♖e8 15.f3 c6 16.♘c3 ♕c7 17.♗f1 ♖ad8 18.♖ad1 d5 (Kasparov – Tal, Niksic 1983) – black has successfully freed himself and has equalized. Overall white has a modest advantage in space. Brown preferred to exchange two pairs of minor pieces.

8.♗xc3 ♘e4 9.♗xe4 ♗xe4 10.♘d2

Another version of breaking in the center is also possible – 10.d5 f6 11.♕d4 ♗g6 12.h4 h5 13.♖d1 (Istratescu – Megalios, London 2018). Now 13...e5? 14.♘xe5! fxe5 15.♕xe5+ ♕e7 16.♕xc7 grants white a fourth pawn for the piece. Instead, though, the position of the queen on d4 enabled black via e6-e5 to close the position with reasonable prospects.

10...♗g6 11.d5 f6 12.h4 h5 13.♖h3 0-0 14.e4 ♘a6 15.g4

The Israeli grandmaster playing white takes full advantage of his rejection of castling. In reality, the success of white's attack should be quite doubtful given his king's exposed position.

15...♕e8 16.♖e3 ♘c5 17.♗d4 exd5 18.cxd5 ♕f7 19.f4?! ♘xe4?

Instead of exchanging on h5 white has played overly riskily, in response to which black sacrificed a piece. This was a poor response, if for no other reason than after 19...hxg4 20.♕xg4 f5 21.♕g5 fxe4 black has a better position.

20.♘xe4 ♗xe4 21.♖xe4 ♖ae8?!

Why exchange pieces when a bishop down? After 21...♕xd5 22.♕e2 c5 23.♗c3 hxg4 24.♔f2 the king finds refuge on g3, and the bishop is stronger than the three pawns, but there is plenty of fight left in the game.

22.♖xe8 ♖xe8+ 23.♔f2 ♕xd5 24.gxh5 ♕f5 25.♕f3 ♕c2+ 26.♔g3 ♖e6 27.♗c3 a4 28.a3 c6 29.♖d1 d5 30.♕d3 ♕b3 31.h6 gxh6 32.♕g6+ ♔f8 33.♕xh6+ ♔e7 34.♕h7+ ♔d6 35.♕d3 c5 36.f5 ♖e8 37.♔f4 d4 38.♗xd4 ♕xd3 39.♖xd3 cxd4 40.♖xd4+

Black resigned.

No. 72 A. Balleisen – A. Ramirez
Greensboro 2016

1.d4 e6 2.c4 ♗b4+ 3.♗d2 a5 4.♘f3 ♘f6 5.♕c2

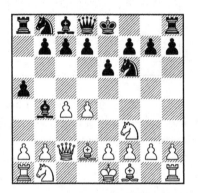

With the overt plan of playing e2-e4. Black has to decide whether or not to allow this pawn advance.

5...d5

Ramirez undermines white's plan. After 5...0-0 6.e4 white would continue e4-e5 and grab territory to his advantage. For example, 6...♗xd2+ 7.♘bxd2 d6 8.e5 dxe5 9.dxe5 ♘fd7 10.♗d3 ♘c6 11.♗xh7+ ♔h8 12.♗e4 ♘cxe5 13.♘xe5 ♘xe5 14.♕c3 ♘g4 15.♘f3 (Iskusnykh – Nozdrachev, Samara 2016) – the exchange of pawns leaves black's king exposed.

If 5...d6 white's pawn will not make it to e5 (6.e4 e5 7.dxe5 dxe5 8.♘xe5?! ♕d4). So white would have to choose a more restrained setup with ♘b1-c3 and e2-e3.

6.a3

This game is not very typical, whereas after white's more usual setup black can prepare e6-e5: 6.e3 0-0 7.♗d3 ♘c6 8.♘c3 ♗d6 9.a3 dxc4 10.♗xc4 e5 11.d5 ♘e7 (Stefansson –

Kharitonov, Heraklion 2011). In such a structure it's hard for either side to find an active plan.

Dreev suggests 6.g3!? and transposing to Catalan-type positions with the somewhat superfluous move a7-a5. Nevertheless, this just leads to a well-known variation via a different move order: 5.g3 d5 6.♕c2 (chapter 14).

6...♗e7

If black exchanges bishops then white will revert to playing e2-e4. After 6...♗xd2+ 7.♘bxd2 0-0 8.e4 dxe4 9.♘xe4 ♘c6 10.0-0-0 white's chances are probably better, while after 7...♘c6 8.e3 it's hard for black to play the e6-e5 break.

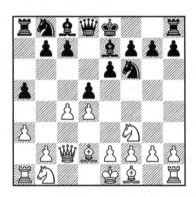

This is a structure from the Queen's Gambit Declined with the addition of a2-a3 and a7-a5, which slightly favors white. The position of the white queen on c2 eases the c7-c5 break for black. If white wants to give his queen's bishop his freedom and then play e2-e3, the best square for the bishop is g5.

7.♗f4 c5 8.cxd5 exd5

The use of the pawn being on a3 is obvious after 8...♘xd5 9.♗xb8 ♖xb8 10.e4 ♘f6 (the b4 square is unavailable) 11.dxc5 0-0. However, after ♕d8-c7 it's risky for white to try to hold on to the pawn.

9.e3 b6

It was worth considering 9...c4 10.b3 cxb3 11.♕xb3 ♘c6 and then, most probably, a5-a4.

10.♗xb8 ♖xb8 11.♘e5 ♕c7

Ramirez is unwilling to concede the advantage of the bishop pair that he gained so easily and agrees to castle artificially. The continuation 11...♗d7 was sufficient for approximate equality.

12.♗b5+ ♔f8 13.♘d2

The pressure on c5 hasn't brought white anything, and so he should have developed his knight to c3.

13...g6 14.0-0 ♗f5 15.♕c3 ♔g7 16.♖ac1 ♗d6

17.f4?! Black's reply cramps white so much that he should have preferred 17.b3.

17...c4 18.♖ce1 ♘e4 19.♘xe4 ♗xe4 20.♘f3 ♖a8 21.♗a4?

This wasn't the right time to find the bishop a job. He should have admitted his rooks were on poor squares and played 21.♖c1.

21...b5! 22.♗xb5 a4 23.♘d2 ♗d3 24.e4 ♗xf1 25.♖xf1 ♖hb8 26.e5 ♗f8

27.f5 ♖xb5 28.♕f3 gxf5 29.♕xf5 ♖a6 30.♘f3 ♗e7 31.♕xf7+ ♔xf7

White resigned. Eventually white went crazy, but prior to then he should have paid more attention to the unresolved structure in the center.

No. 73 T. Sanikidze – L. Paichadze
Tbilisi 2018

1.d4 ♘f6 2.♘f3 e6 3.c4 ♗b4+ 4.♗d2 a5 5.a3

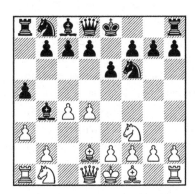

This is played to make black commit, after which white can select a setup in response to black's decision.

5...♗xd2+

As noted earlier, 5...♗e7 6.♘c3 d5 with the bishop moving to f4 or g5 leads to the Queen's Gambit with the extra pawn moves that favor white. The a7 pawn would normally have made a more modest move to support the b7-b5 break after black concedes the center.

6.♕xd2

Stats are very bad for white if he captures with the knight. For example, after 6.♘bxd2 d6 7.e3 ♕e7 8.♗e2 e5 9.dxe5 dxe5 10.♕c2 ♘bd7

11.♘e4 ♘xe4 12.♕xe4 f6 13.h3 ♘c5 14.♕c2 a4 15.♖d1 0-0 16.0-0 b6 (Costin – Svetushkin, Arad 2019) white is slightly worse. The a-pawn gives white problems, and he will need to exchange his passive knight.

6...b6

After 6...d6 7.♘c3 ♘bd7 8.♖d1 in the game Sarkar – Fressinet (Caleta 2017) the French grandmaster playing black changed his mind and decided not to prepare e6-e5, instead going for a fianchetto – 8...b6 9.e3 ♝b7 10.♝e2 ♘e4 11.♘xe4 ♝xe4 12.0-0 0-0 13.♕c3 f5 14.♘d2 ♝b7 15.♝f3 ♝xf3 16.♘xf3 ♘f6 17.♘d2. In a typical Dutch position white plans f2-f3 and e3-e4 with slightly better chances.

Black has also tried 6...d5 7.♘c3 0-0 8.e3. Here his counter chances (following Cheparinov's recipe) promise a tense center after 8...b6, ♝c8-b7 and c7-c5.

7.♘c3 ♝b7

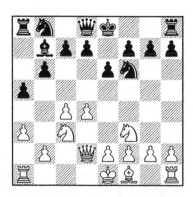

8.♕f4!?

Now, unlike after 8.♕c2, it's not advisable to prevent e2-e4 via 8...d5 due to 9.♘b5, luring the enemy knight to a6. 8.e3 is best met by simplifying – exchanging knights with 8...♘e4.

8...0-0 9.e4 d5

It would seem that 9...d6, ♕d8-e7, ♘b8-d7 and e6-e5 is a safer formation, especially as the last move also attacks the white queen.

10.cxd5 exd5 11.e5 ♘e4 12.♝d3 f5

Paichadze didn't fancy the exchanges after 12...♘xc3 13.bxc3 ♝a6 14.♝xa6 ♘xa6, as they would allow his opponent to take advantage of his pawn majority in the center unhindered.

13.exf6 ♘xf6 14.0-0 c5

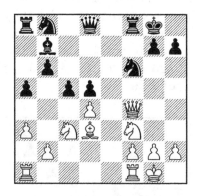

15.♖ae1

Maybe white shouldn't have been worried about f2. After 15.♖fe1 ♘c6 16.dxc5 bxc5 17.♖ad1 his rooks are on ideal squares, and black's position isn't appealing.

15...♘c6 16.♕h4 ♝a6 17.♝xa6 ♖xa6 18.♖e6 ♕d7 19.♖fe1 ♖aa8 20.dxc5 bxc5 21.♘a4 ♘e4 22.♘g5 h6 23.♘b6 ♕d8

23...hxg5?! is weaker due to 24.♕xe4! Paichadze has been defending excellently, and now it's his opponent who blinks first.

24.♘xa8?

White should have opted for 24.♖xc6 hxg5 25.♕g4 ♖f6 26.♖xf6

♕xf6 27.♖xe4 ♕xb6 28.♖e1 ♕f6, though it won't deliver more than a draw.

24...♘xg5   25.♕a4   ♘xe6 26.♕xc6 ♘f4 27.g3 ♘h3+

After 27...♕xa8 28.♕xa8 ♖xa8 29.gxf4 a4 black would have had to seek a draw in a rook ending (or on the next move, in a slightly favorable position). Black overestimated his threats to the enemy king.

28.♔g2   ♖xf2+? 29.♔xh3 ♕g5 30.♕e6+ ♔h7 31.♖e5 ♕c1 32.♕xd5 ♕f1+ 33.♔g4 ♖f6 34.♖e6 ♖xe6 35.♕xe6 ♕d1+ 36.♔h3

The players were probably in time trouble by now. If 36.♔f4 ♕f1+ 37.♔e5 ♕e2+ 38.♔d5 the king easily evades the checks. At best, black can feast on white's queenside pawns, but that is not enough to draw.

36...♕f1+ 37.♔g4 ♕d1+ 38.♔h3 ♕f1+

Draw agreed.

No. 74 V. Keymer – P. Eljanov
Skopje 2019

1.d4 ♘f6 2.c4 e6 3.♘f3 ♗b4+ 4.♗d2 a5 5.♘c3

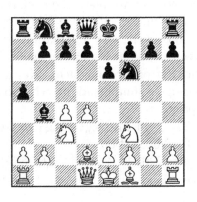

"This is the Leningrad variation of the Nimzo-Indian Defense in a version favorable for black. His move a7-a5 is much more useful than white's ♗c1-d2" (Geller). However, the Leningrad variation occurs after 3.♘c3 ♗b4 4.♗g5, and after 4...h6 the bishop is normally retired not to d2, but to h4. It's more logical to compare this line with the moves 3.♘c3 ♗b4 4.♗d2 a5 5.♘f3, where the knight's development is more useful.

5...d5

Here I agree with Geller: in Queen's Gambit-type setups a7-a5 is pointless for black. However, many games have been played by strong players in this line, so we need to analyze it.

6.e3

If 6.cxd5 exd5 7.♗g5 it's acceptable to select the setup from the game Kosteniuk – Zhao Xue (Tromso 2014): 7...h6 8.♗h4 ♕d6 9.♘d2 (9.♗g3 ♕e7) 9...♘bd7 10.a3 ♗xc3 11.bxc3 c5 12.e3 0-0 13.♗b5 b6 14.0-0 ♗a6 15.♗xa6 ♖xa6 16.a4 ♖aa8. Black has a solid position, but we cannot see any active plans for her.

6...0-0 7.a3

If 7.♗d3 b6 8.0-0 then apart from 8...♗b7 a decent alternative is 8...♗a6, pinning the c4 pawn. The game Jakovenko – Vokaturo (Germany 2015) continued 9.♕e2 ♘bd7 10.a3 ♗xc3 11.bxc3 ♘e4 12.♖fd1 ♘d6 13.cxd5 ♗xd3 14.♕xd3 exd5 15.a4 ♖e8 16.♗c1 ♖e6 17.♗a3 ♘c4 18.♘d2 ♘xd2 19.♖xd2 ♖c6 20.♖c2 ♖c4. The subsequent e3-e4-e5 didn't deliver any clear dividends for white – as black had mounted a successful blockade on c4. In the current game, Eljanov organized a more typical blockade on the long diagonal.

7...♗xc3 8.♗xc3

In the game Fridman – Romanov (Germany 2015) white captured with the pawn and immediately improved his structure: 8.bxc3 b6 9.cxd5 exd5 10.c4 ♗a6 11.♕c2 c5 (an unexpected transposition to hanging pawns) 12.dxc5 bxc5 13.♗d3 d4 14.0-0 ♘c6 15.exd4 ♘xd4 16.♘xd4 cxd4 17.♗f4 and white has the advantage of the bishop pair and a clear advantage. The pawn sac 12...♘bd7!? 13.cxb6 ♕xb6 is interesting, granting black the initiative in return for the material.

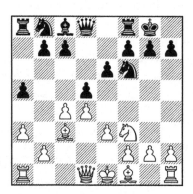

8...b6

Switching to Dutch lines via 8...♘e4 9.♕c2 b6 10.♗d3 f5 looks unappealing. The holes in the black walls are not compensated for by initiative.

9.cxd5 ♕xd5 10.♗e2 ♗b7 11.0-0 ♘e4 12.♕c2 ♘d7 13.♖fd1 ♗a6

Via a different move order we reach the game Schenk – Romanishin (Lippstadt 2003), when after 13...♖fc8 14.♖ac1 h6 15.♗f1 ♕h5 16.♕e2 ♗a6 17.♕e1 ♗b7 18.♘d2 ♘xd2 19.♕xd2

♕g6 20.♕d3 f5 21.♔h1 ♗d5 22.f3 c6 the players agreed a draw. Romanishin strictly adhered to a blockading strategy, whereas Eljanov's actions are somewhat eclectic.

14.♗xa6 ♖xa6 15.♘d2 f5 16.♖ac1 b5 17.f3 ♘ef6 18.b4

Now, the enemy knight will settle into c4, hence it made sense to consider e3-e4 either immediately or after b2-b3.

18...a4 19.♕d3 ♖c6 20.e4 fxe4 21.fxe4 ♕h5 22.♘f3 ♘b6

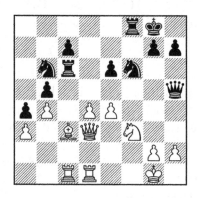

23.♘e5

After 23.♖f1 ♘fd7 24.e5 (24.h3!?) 24...♘d5 25.♕xb5 ♘xc3 26.♕xc6 ♘e2+ 27.♔f2 ♘xd4 28.♕xd7 ♖xf3+ the game will end in perpetual check. However, after 23.♖e1 black has no counterplay. The closing of the fifth rank then threatens the b5 pawn with liquidation. It's possible that in his battle against a much stronger opponent Keymer considered simplifications to be more appropriate.

23...♘g4 24.♘xg4 ♕xg4 25.♖f1 ♖xf1+ 26.♖xf1 h6

After 26...♘c4 27.e5 ♕g6 28.♕f3 ♕e8 29.h3 black has no time to capture on a3 due to the d4-d5 break. Keymer urgently redeploys his bishop.

27.♖f3 ♕g5 28.♗d2 ♕h5 29.h3 ♘c4 30.♗f4 e5!

This temporary pawn sac more or less forces a drawn ending.

31.dxe5 ♕e8 32.♕d4 ♔h7 33.♖d3 ♖e6 34.♕c5 c6 35.♗g3 ♘xe5 36.♗xe5 ♖xe5 37.♕c2 ♕g6 38.♖c3 ♖e6 39.♖c5 ♔h8 40.e5 ♕xc2 41.♖xc2 ♖xe5

Draw agreed.

No. 75 I. Khenkin – D. Anton
Don Benito 2012

1.d4 ♘f6 2.c4 e6 3.♘f3 ♗b4+ 4.♗d2 a5 5.♘c3 b6

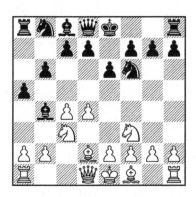

6.♗g5

The continuation 6.e3 ♗b7 7.♗d3 is reviewed in game 71 via a different move order. 6.g3 is often played, but the fianchetto is reviewed in the next three chapters.

6...a4!?

This should be considered carefully for two reasons: 1) the bishop has moved twice, leaving the knight without a defender; 2) to avoid a4-a3 it's best for white to stop the pawn, and as a result white ends up with an unfavorable, deformed pawn chain.

Khenkin has also played this line as black, but differently: 6...♗b7 7.♘d2 h6 8.♗h4 ♘c6 9.a3 ♗xc3 10.bxc3 ♘e7 11.f3 ♘g6 12.♗f2 ♕e7 13.e4 e5 14.g3 0-0 15.♗d3 (Georgiev – Khenkin, Plovdiv 2012), and now instead of the risky 15...d5?! 16.cxd5 ♘xd5 17.0-0 ♘f6 18.♘c4 the move 15...d6 would have left black with a passive but solid position.

7.a3

In the game Jojua – Deak (Jerusalem 2015) after 7.♖c1 a3 8.b3 ♗b7 9.e3 h6 10.♗xf6 ♕xf6 11.♗e2 ♘a6 12.0-0 ♗xc3 13.♖xc3 ♘b4 14.♕d2 c5 15.♖d1 ♗xf3 16.♗xf3 ♖d8 17.♖cc1 0-0 black totally blocked up the queenside and experienced no problems. Even the exchange of good bishops came in handy.

7...♗xc3+ 8.bxc3 ♗b7

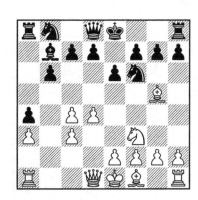

9.♘d2

Khenkin knew of the game Khalifman – Aleksandrov (St. Petersburg 1996), which continued 9.e3 ♖a5 10.♗h4 d6 11.♘d2 g5

12.♗g3 ♘bd7 13.f3 ♖g8 14.♗e2 h5 15.e4 h4 16.♗f2 ♕e7 with a very complicated position that was acceptable to black. Instead, white wants to place the pawn on e4 in a single move, and Anton rejects a flank attack in favor of reciprocal action in the center.

9...h6 10.♗h4 d6 11.f3 e5 12.e4 ♘c6 13.c5

The a4 pawn is nevertheless vulnerable, as can be seen after 13.d5 ♘b8 14.c5 bxc5 15.♗b5+ c6 16.♗xa4 0-0 17.c4. However, white's passer is too modest so far to act as a foundation of future success.

13...dxc5

The Spanish grandmaster playing black is willing to go for what is at least an interesting pawn sac. That said, the highly complicated variation 13...exd4 14.cxd4 ♘xd4 15.cxb6 0-0 still looks more promising.

14.dxc5   0-0   15.cxb6   ♘a5 16.♕xa4 cxb6 17.♕b4 ♕c7 18.♗b5 ♖fd8

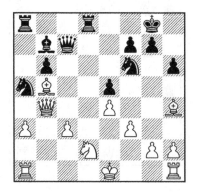

19.c4

White should have preferred the maneuver ♘d2-f1-e3 without worrying about losing the pawn on c3.

19...♖d3 20.0-0 ♖ad8 21.♖a2 ♖8d6 22.♖c1 ♕d8

Instead of this ostentatious display of architecture, 22...♗c6 23.a4 ♗xb5 24.axb5 ♘h5 with the subsequent ♘h5-f4 was stronger.

23.♘f1 ♗c6 24.♗xc6

If 24.a4!? the knight's relocation via b3 to d4 is harmless for white, as it unloads the "Alekhine's Gun".

24...♘xc6

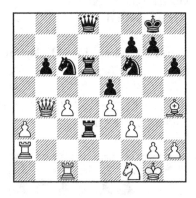

25.♕b5?

This is part of a miscalculation. The right continuation was 25.♕e1, as after 25...♖d1 26.♖xd1 ♖xd1 27.♖d2 ♖xd2 28.♕xd2 ♕xd2 29.♘xd2 ♘d7 30.♘f1 black is not ensured a draw.

25...♖d1 26.♖xd1 ♖xd1

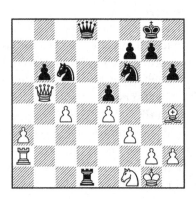

27.♕xc6??

After 27.♖f2 ♕d4 28.g4 the luft preserves approximate equality on the board.

27...♕d4+! 28.♗f2

Oddly enough, white had failed to notice in time that he would be mated after 28.♖f2 ♖xf1+!

28...♕d3 29.h3 ♕xf1+ 30.♔h2 ♕h1+ 31.♔g3 ♔h7 32.♕c8 g6 33.♗xb6 ♘h5+ 34.♔h4 ♕h2 35.♕g4 ♘f6

White resigned.

Of the various setups for white reviewed in this chapter, the most solid seems to be the system with e2-e3, ♗f1-d3 and ♘b1-c3. In that case it's hard for black to extract any use from the pawn on a5.

Chapter 13

4...a5 5.g3 d6 variation

No. 76 H. Banikas – M. Turov
Paleohora 2009

1.d4 ♞f6 2.c4 e6 3.♞f3 ♝b4+ 4.♝d2 a5 5.g3

This chapter considers the reply 5...d6, while chapter 14 analyzes 5...d5, and chapter 15 covers 5...b6. The early castling with 5...0-0 cannot mask black's plans, since the logical continuation 6.♝g2 will force black to reveal his hand.

5...d6

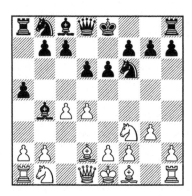

We first came across this line in game 4 of the historical introduction. Black immediately plans to challenge for the center with e6-e5.

6.♝g2 ♞c6

In games 77-79 we analyze the move 6...♞bd7. The knight's development on c6 was often played by International Master Nikolai Vlassov, then the married pair Grandmaster Maxim Turov and International Master Irina Turova took it up. The knight doesn't get in the way of the bishop's development and puts pressure on d4.

It's very rare for black to castle on this move – it happens more often via 5...0-0 6.♝g2 d6. After 6...0-0 7.0-0 ♝xd2 8.♛xd2 ♞bd7 9.♞c3 e5 10.dxe5 ♞xe5 (10...dxe5 11.♞b5!) 11.♞xe5 dxe5 12.♛xd8 ♖xd8 13.♖fd1 ♝d7 14.♞b5 black has problems, so he needs to take a more fundamental approach to preparing e6-e5 – adding 9...♖e8 and sometimes ♛d8-e7 as well.

7.0-0 e5 8.♝g5

In the game Kasimdzhanov – Turov (Nancy 2011) white's play against black's pawn weaknesses failed to deliver a result – 8.d5 ♞e7 9.♝xb4 axb4 10.♛d2 c5 11.dxc6 ♞xc6 12.♖d1 ♝e6 13.b3 ♞e4 14.♛e3 ♞c5 15.♞bd2 0-0 16.♞e4 ♞xe4 17.♛xe4 ♛e7. White also provides black with a target (on a2), and chances are approximately equal.

8...exd4

It's worth pointing out again the threat of a2-a3, which here forces black to concede the center. This is the flip side of the move 6...♞c6 – the knight is left hanging and needs to be redeployed.

9.♞xd4

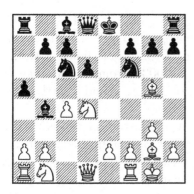

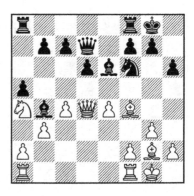

9...♘xd4

Vlassov preferred 9...♘e5. Here is a fragment from one of his games: 10.a3 ♗c5 11.♘c3 ♘eg4 (if black instead castles he needs to contend with 12.♘b3, whereas now this would be a bad move due to 12...♘xf2!) 12.♘d5 h6 13.♗xf6 ♘xf6 14.b4 ♘xd5 15.bxc5 ♘f6 16.♘b5 dxc5 17.♕xd8+ ♚xd8 18.♖fd1+ ♘d7 (Krylov – Vlassov, Moscow 2005). Black has won a pawn and exchanged queens, yet his position is unappealing.

10.♕xd4 h6 11.♗f4

Several games have seen 11.♗xf6 ♕xf6 12.♕xf6 gxf6. After 13.a3 ♗c5 14.♘c3 c6 15.e3 ♚e7 16.♘a4 h5 17.h4 ♖g8 18.♖fc1 ♖a7 19.♗f3 ♗g4 20.♗xg4 ♖xg4 21.♔f1 ♖a8 22.b3 ♚e6 23.♘c3 (Giri – Ivanchuk, Reggio Emilia 2012) white prepared and carried out b3-b4 and won a complicated endgame. Nevertheless, it's hard to consider that black's doubled pawns should lead to a white victory.

11...0-0 12.♘c3 ♕e7 13.e4 ♗e6 14.b3 ♕d7 15.♘a4

15...♗xc4

This exchange operation significantly shakes up the game. However, given the threat of a2-a3 Turov had no choice.

16.♕xc4 b5 17.♕c1 bxa4 18.e5 dxe5 19.♗xe5

After 19.♗xa8 exf4 20.♗c6 ♕e6 21.bxa4 h5 black threatens to bomb the enemy king's bunker and he has obvious compensation for the exchange.

19...♖a6 20.♕xc7 axb3 21.axb3 ♕d3 22.♖fd1 ♕xb3 23.♗f1 ♘e8!

When planning his expedition to grab the b3 pawn, Turov had foreseen this intermezzo. He has now equalized.

24.♕c8 ♖a7 25.♖d8 ♖e7 26.♗d4 ♕e6 27.♗c5

Draw agreed.

After the simplifications, the crumbs of initiative still in white's hands are sufficient only to capture the a-pawn.

No. 77 F. Gheorghiu – M. Prusikin
Switzerland 2016

1.d4 ♘f6 2.c4 e6 3.♘f3 ♗b4+ 4.♗d2 a5 5.g3 d6 6.♗g2 ♘bd7 7.0-0 e5

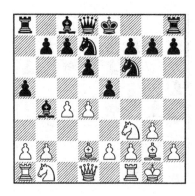

8.♝g5

White has tried many different moves in this tabiya, though not all of them deserve separate games (or even mention). Above all, we need to review bishop moves from d2 with the threat of 9.a3. Igor Zaitsev has even recommended 8.♝h6!? gxh6 9.a3, though here it's hard to argue against Geller – after 9...♝c5 10.dxc5 ♘xc5 white will have to overcome black's strong center if he wants to attack black's weaknesses.

Apart from 8.♝g5 a frequent move is 8.♝e3 (game 78). The retreat 8.♝c1 appears a waste of time, as the bishop will still have to be developed. For example, 8...exd4 9.♘xd4 0-0 10.♘c2 ♜e8 11.a3 ♝c5 12.♘c3 a4 13.♘b4 ♘b6 14.♝g5 h6 15.♝xf6 ♛xf6 16.♘bd5 ♘xd5 17.♘xd5 ♛d8 18.e3 ♝e6 (Irwanto – Tkachiev, Jakarta 2012) – black is fine here.

The continuation 8.♝xb4 axb4 9.♛b3 has attracted the attention of Nikolic – a grandmaster with a wonderful feel for openings. However, his Serbian colleague played skillfully here: 9...exd4 10.♘xd4 0-0 11.♘c2 ♜e8 12.♜e1 c5 13.a3 ♛b6 14.♘d2

bxa3 15.♜xa3 ♜xa3 16.♘xa3 ♛a5 17.♘ab1 ♘e5 18.♘c3 (18.♝xb7?! ♘xc4!) 18...♘c6 (Nikolic – Markus, Serbia 2003). From its new square the knight aims at b4 and d4 and chances are equal.

An interesting plan was tried by Vladimir Burmakin – a grandmaster with a creative approach to openings. The game Burmakin – A. Smirnov (Schwaebisch Gmuend 2016) continued 8.dxe5 dxe5 9.♛a4!? (instead of the banal 9.♘c3) 9...♛e7 (the exchange on d2 would be to some extent a concession) 10.♝xb4 ♛xb4 11.♛c2 0-0 12.♘fd2! c6 13.a3 ♛e7 14.♘c3 ♘c5 15.b4 ♘e6 16.c5 ♘g5 17.♘c4 ♘h3+ 18.♝xh3 ♝xh3 19.♜fd1 axb4 20.axb4 ♜xa1 21.♜xa1 h5 22.♘e4. White has a colossal strategic advantage, while black has no attack and it will be very hard for him to equalize. In the approximate line 12...♘c5 13.a3 ♛b6 14.♘c3 c6 15.b3 white plans ♜a1-b1 and b3-b4, and after black's knight retreats to e6 the move e2-e3 will cramp it.

The move 8.e3 is covered in the historical introduction, while 8.♘c3 is played in game 79.

8...exd4 9.♘xd4

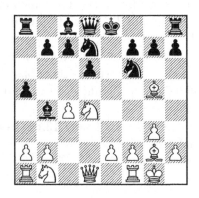

9...0-0

Sometimes black first forces white to redeploy his bishop. In the game Evdokimov – Venkatesh (Moscow 2012) after 9...h6 10.♗f4 0-0 11.♕c2 ♞e5 12.♖d1 ♕e7 13.♞c3 ♞g6 14.♗e3 ♗c5 15.h3 c6 16.♖ac1?! the bishop would have felt uneasy had black found 16...♞h5! with the idea of f7-f5. If 16.b3 however, the reply 16...♞h5 is punching thin air due to 17.♗c1! and ♗c1-b2. Instead of 11...♞e5 Bachmann had an interesting idea 11...a4!? 12.♖d1 ♞b6. This doesn't prevent 13.♞c3 (13...♞xc4 14.♞db5), but later the c4 pawn will require protection.

10.a3

In the game Swinkels – Kveinys (Ohrid 2009) black skillfully forced useful exchanges: 10.♞c2 ♗c5 11.♞c3 h6 12.♗e3 ♞g4 (attacking the bishop) 13.♗d4 ♞ge5 14.b3 ♖e8 15.h3 ♞c6 (again attacking the bishop) 16.♗e3 ♞b4 (attacking the bishop's protector) 17.♗xc5 ♞xc2 18.♕xc2 ♞xc5 19.♔h2 ♗d7 20.♖ad1 ♗c6 21.♞d5, draw agreed.

10...♗c5 11.♞c3 h6 12.♗xf6 ♞xf6 13.♖c1

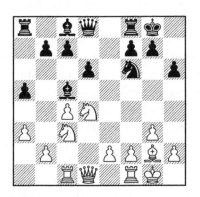

13...c6

After the exchange on f6 it's not a good idea for black to play 13...a4 due to the simple 14.e3 (forcing an awkward protection of the pawn by the queen). After 12.♗f4 white cannot protect his knight with his pawn (as the bishop gets into trouble), and 12...a4 would be recommended for black.

14.e3 ♕e7 15.♞a4 ♖e8 16.♕c2 ♕e5 17.♞xc5 dxc5

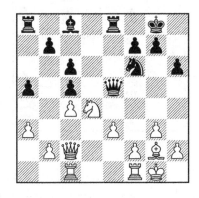

This change in structure favors white if he can exploit his pawn majority. Here, though, that is unlikely given black's strong control over e4.

18.♞e2 ♗f5 19.♕c3 ♕e7

Black can also play as equals without queens (19...♞d7!?).

20.♖fd1 ♖a6

A nice move! If 21.a4 ♖b6 the rook is ready to occupy b4, while in the game it managed to entrench itself even deeper!

21.♞f4 a4 22.♞d3 h5 23.♖e1 ♗xd3 24.♕xd3 ♖b6 25.♖e2 ♖d8 26.♕c2 ♖b3 27.♖d1 ♖xd1+ 28.♕xd1 g6 29.♖d2 ♕e5

Prusikin gradually outplays his opponent, but here instead of the maneuver ♘f6-g4-e5 (and then b7-b5) he over-rates the march of his h-pawn.

30.♕c2 h4 31.♗f3?!

The "ugly" capture of the pawn would have maintained equality.

31...h3 32.♔f1 ♔g7 33.♔e2 g5 34.♔d1 g4 35.♗h1 ♔h6 36.♔c1

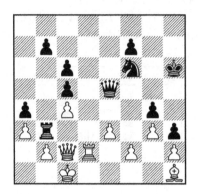

36...♔g5?!

After 36...♕e6 37.♖d8 ♘d7 38.♖h8+ ♔g5 the rook invasion no longer leads to perpetual check.

37.♖d3?

White should have played 37.♖d8, and if 37...♘d7 the rook heads to a8 and captures the a4-pawn.

37...♖xd3 38.♕xd3 ♕f5 39.♕c2 ♕xc2+ 40.♔xc2 ♘d7?!

He would have won immediately with 40...♔f5 41.♔d3 ♘d7 42.♔c3 ♘e5 43.b3 axb3 44.♔xb3 b5.

41.b3 ♘e5 42.bxa4 ♘xc4 43.♔c3 ♘e5 44.a5 ♔f5 45.a4

White should have tried his luck with 45.♔c2 ♔e6 (45...♘c4? 46.a6) 46.♗e4 ♔d6 (after 46...f5?! white retreats his bishop and then plays e3-e4) 47.♗f5 ♔c7 48.♔d1 ♔b8 49.f3 gxf3 50.♗xh3. Now the passed h-pawn will prevent the black king

from attacking the white a-pawns, but the king's retreat will retain the advantage. Whether that is still enough to win is questionable.

45...♔e6 46.♔b3 ♔d6 47.♗e4 ♔c7 48.♗f5 ♔b8 49.♔c3 ♔a7 50.f4 gxf3 51.♗xh3 f2 52.♔d2 ♘f3+ 53.♔e2 ♘g1+ 54.♔xf2 ♘xh3+ 55.♔g2 c4

White resigned.

No. 78 L. Van Wely – H. Nakamura
Wijk aan Zee 2013

1.d4 ♘f6 2.c4 e6 3.♘f3 ♗b4+ 4.♗d2 a5 5.g3 d6 6.♗g2 ♘bd7 7.0-0 e5 8.♗e3

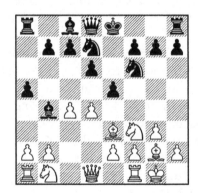

Van Wely varies play compared with game no. 79 (which took place earlier). Now, as a result of the inevitable exchange on d4 (if 8...0-0 9.a3 it takes place one move later) the bishop occupies the central square. It will most likely be exchanged.

8...exd4 9.♗xd4 0-0

If 9...a4 10.♘c3 a3 11.b3 0-0 12.♖c1 the pawn on a3 is more of a weakness than a strong point. White can be recommended the maneuver ♘f3-e1-c2-e3.

10.a3

White is not forced to chase the bishop away to the detriment of his pawn chain. Here is an example from the current world champion's early career: 10.♘c3 ♗c5 11.♕c2 ♗xd4 12.♘xd4 c6 13.♖ad1 ♘c5 14.♖d2 ♕e7 15.♖fd1 g6 16.b3 ♗d7 17.♕b2 ♖fd8 18.♘c2 ♗e6 19.♘e3 h5 20.♖d4 ♖d7 21.♕d2 ♘e8 (Carlsen – Paehtz, Lausanne 2005). Black protected her weak pawn, but white then strengthened on the kingside. If black avoids c7-c6, then the white bishop aims at the b7 pawn, and black has to deal with ♘c3-d5.

10...♗c5 11.♘c3

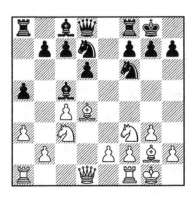

11...♖e8

The typical plan of counterplay on the queenside was successfully carried out in the later game Cornette – Romanov (Doha 2014): 11...♗xd4 12.♘xd4 (12.♕xd4!?) 12...♘b6 13.b3 (13.♕d3 ♘fd7) 13...a4!? 14.♘xa4 ♘xa4 15.bxa4 ♘d7 16.♖b1 ♘c5 17.♖b4 c6 18.♕c2 ♕e7. White couldn't think up anything and the game soon ended in a draw.

12.♕c2 c6 13.♖fd1 ♕e7 14.h3 ♘e5

Here it was worth considering ♘d7-b6, provoking b2-b3 and hooking on to that pawn via a5-a4.

15.♗xc5 ♘xf3+ 16.♗xf3 dxc5 17.♗g2 ♕e5 18.e4 g5 19.♕d2 g4

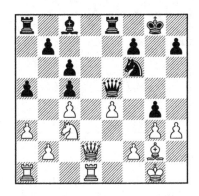

20.h4

Black pushed his g-pawn so that any exploitation of white's pawn majority would entail the opening of the kingside. After 20.hxg4 ♗xg4 21.f3 ♗e6 22.f4 ♕h5 23.e5 ♘g4 24.♗f3 white's advantage is marginal.

20...♘d7

Instead of the normal 20...♗e6 Nakamura plans to transfer his knight to e6 but in doing so complicates his own position.

21.♘a4 ♘f8 22.♕d6 ♕xd6 23.♖xd6 ♘e6 24.e5 ♔g7 25.♖e1 ♖a6 26.♖e4 h5 27.f3 gxf3 28.♗xf3 ♖h8 29.♗e2

Van Wely prevents b7-b5; at the same time, the continuation 29.♖e3!? b5 30.cxb5 cxb5 31.♘b6 ♖a7 32.♗xh5 was clearly in his favor.

29...b6 30.♔f2 ♘d4 31.♗d1 ♘e6

The e6 square attracts the knight like a magnet, though once again it was more appropriate for the bishop – 31...♘f5 32.♖f6 ♗e6 33.b3 ♘e7.

32.♗e2 ♘d4 33.♗d1 ♘e6 34.♘c3 ♖a7

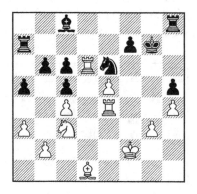

35.♘e2?!

Due to time-trouble the Dutch grandmaster failed to calculate the line 35.♗a4 ♘d4 36.♗xc6 ♘xc6 37.♖xc6 ♗b7 38.♖c7 to the end, and this allowed black to simplify play.

35...♖d7 36.♖xd7 ♗xd7 37.♘f4 ♘xf4 38.gxf4 ♗f5 39.♖e3 ♖d8 40.♗xh5 ♖d2+ 41.♗e2 ♖d4 42.♔g3 ♖xc4?!

He had to play 42...b5 – then white's pawns would have remained immobile.

43.♗g4 ♗d3 44.♖e3 ♖d4 45.h5 c4 46.f5 ♖d8 47.f6+ ♔h6 48.e6 fxe6 49.♖xe6 ♔g5 50.f7?!

The pawn heads off to die, whereas after 50.♖xc6! ♗e4 51.♖e6! ♖d3+ 52.♔f2 ♗d5 53.f7 it would have triumphed.

50...♖f8 51.♖xc6 ♖xf7 52.♖xb6 ♖f1 53.♖b5+ ♔h6 54.♖xa5 ♖b1 55.♔f4 ♖xb2 56.♖a6+ ♔g7 57.♔e3 ♖g2 58.♗f3 ♖g3 59.a4 ♔h7?

One more exchange of errors before the curtain falls. Nakamura misses the theoretical draw after 59...

c3! 60.♔xd3 ♖xf3+ 61.♔c2 ♖f2+ 62.♔xc3 ♖f3+.

60.♖c6?

In his turn, Van Wely fails to notice the pretty transposition to a bishop versus rook ending, and he should have won after 60.a5.

60...♗c2! 61.♖xc4 ♗d1 62.♖f4 ♖xf3+ 63.♖xf3 ♗xa4 64.♖f6 ♗e8 65.h6 ♗g6 66.♖xg6 ♔xg6 67.h7 ♔xh7

Draw agreed – a game not without mistakes, but meaty and of theoretical significance.

No. 79 L. Van Wely – V. Babula
Warsaw 2005

1.d4 ♘f6 2.c4 e6 3.♘f3 ♗b4+ 4.♗d2 a5 5.g3 d6 6.♗g2 ♘bd7 7.0-0 e5 8.♘c3

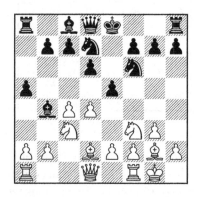

8...0-0

Previously, the Czech grandmaster had played 8...c6 with the idea of gaining a strong pawn pair in the center. After 9.a3 ♗xc3 10.♗xc3 e4 11.♘e1 d5 12.cxd5 cxd5 (Hirneise – Babula, Germany 2011) white can hope for an advantage (especially with the maneuver ♘e1-c2-e3), but the "plug" on the open file is not in his favor. Therefore, the variation 9.♕c2 (9...♗xc3 10.♗xc3 e4 11.♘h4 d5 12.♘f5) seems more accurate.

If 8...exd4 9.♘xd4 0-0 the sortie 10.♘d5 is an independent line. However, the knight will get chased away, while the d6 pawn will be safely protected – 10...♗xd2 11.♕xd2 c6 12.♘c3 ♘c5 13.♘b3 ♗e6 14.♖fd1 ♘xb3 15.axb3 ♕b6 16.♕c2 ♖fd8 with equality (Sargissian – Spraggett, Moscow 2014).

9.♕c2

Here, the sortie 9.♘d5 has poor stats, although the blunders occurred later. For example, 9...♗xd2 10.♕xd2 ♖e8 11.dxe5 dxe5 12.♖fd1 ♘xd5 (this unforced exchange is accompanied by the idea of e5-e4) 13.cxd5 ♘f6 14.♘g5?! e4 15.d6 cxd6 16.♕xd6 ♕xd6 17.♖xd6 h6 18.♘h3 ♖a6 19.♖ad1 ♖xd6 20.♖xd6 ♗e6 21.b3 ♖c8 22.♘f4 ♖c1+ 23.♗f1 ♗d7, and white is already outplayed (Murshed – Bu Xiangzhi, Abu Dhabi 2016). Obviously, 14.♘e1 e4 15.♘c2 (and ♘c2-e3) would have resolved all his problems.

9...♖e8

Here I quote the beginning of the famous example Polugaevsky – Smyslov (Moscow 1979), which was incorrectly analyzed by Geller: 9...exd4 10.♘xd4 ♘e5 11.♗g5 h6 12.♗xf6 ♕xf6 13.♘d5 ♕d8 14.♘xb4 axb4 15.c5 dxc5! (15...c6?! 16.♖fd1 d5 17.e4 as Smyslov played was really in white's favor) 16.♕xc5 ♘d7 17.♕c2 c6 18.a3 ♘f6 19.e3 bxa3 20.♖xa3 ♖xa3 21.bxa3 ♕a5 (Beikert – Ksieski, Germany 1996). White

hasn't a crumb of an advantage, and he should have abandoned his plan of c4-c5 and instead conserved the little pluses that he had via 15.♖fd1.

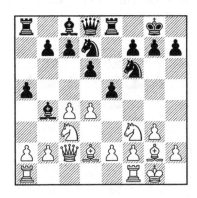

10.e4

In the game Zontakh – Kryakvin (Samara 2014) white preferred to change the structure – 10.dxe5 dxe5 11.♖ad1 c6 12.a3 ♗f8 13.♗e3 ♕e7 14.♘g5 h6 15.♘ge4 ♕e6. This is almost a standard setup where white employs the fianchetto against the KID, but white's pawn group on the queenside lacks flexibility, while black has obviously managed without g7-g6.

10...exd4 11.♘xd4 ♘e5 12.b3

Later, Van Wely chose 12.♗g5 in a rapid game, but I don't think he had any advantage after 12...h6 13.♗xf6 ♕xf6 14.♘d5 ♕d8. Black has quite a busy bishop pair, while if pieces are exchanged on b4, then white will have to worry about his a-pawn.

12...a4

More often, black asks questions of the white knight with 12...♗c5, which doesn't rule out counterplay with a5-a4 later. For example, 13.♘f5 ♗d7 14.♖ad1 a4 (A. Filippov –

Sedlak, Bol 2014) 15.♗g5 h6 16.♗xf6 ♕xf6 17.♘d5 ♕d8 18.b4 ♗a7 with an unclear position.

13.♖ad1 axb3 14.axb3 ♗d7 15.h3 ♘c6 16.♘db5 ♗c5 17.♗g5 ♘b4 18.♕d2

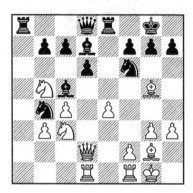

18...♗xb5 19.cxb5

In reply to 19.♘xb5 black parries the threat of 20.♗xf6 with the ugly-looking move 19...♖e6. If 20.e5!? ♖xe5 21.♗xb7 ♖a2 22.♕f4 ♕e7 black is no worse.

19...h6 20.♗f4 ♕e7 21.♖fe1 ♘d7 22.♘a4 ♘e5 23.♕c3 b6 24.♗e3 ♘a2 25.♕d2 ♘b4 26.f4 ♖xa4!? 27.♗xc5

The Dutchman rejects a draw by move repetition, and the game livens up. If 27.bxa4 ♘c4 28.♗xc5 ♘xd2 29.♗xb4 ♘c4 30.e5 ♕d8 31.♗c6 ♖e7 32.♗d5 ♘a5 it's hard for either side to strengthen.

27...♖a2 28.♕xb4 bxc5 29.♕c3 ♘g6

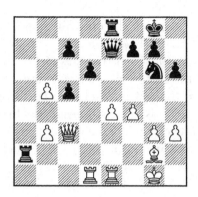

30.♖a1

If white wants to blow up his opponent's pawn trio, then the computer shows a draw – 30.b4 ♖ea8 31.e5 ♖8a3 32.exd6 ♖xc3 33.dxe7 ♘xe7 34.♗e4 ♖xg3+ 35.♔f1 f5 36.♗b1 ♖f3+.

30...♖ea8 31.♖xa2 ♖xa2 32.♖a1 ♖xa1+ 33.♕xa1 ♕e8 34.♕a6 ♘f8 35.♕b7 ♘e6 36.♗f1 g5

The white king is too exposed to hope for progress on the queenside. Perpetual check is the logical outcome.

37.♗c4 gxf4 38.gxf4 ♕d8 39.♔f1 ♘xf4 40.b6 ♕g5 41.bxc7 ♕g2+ 42.♔e1 ♕g3+ 43.♔d1 ♕f3+ 44.♔c2 ♕f2+ 45.♔b1 ♕e1+ 46.♔b2 ♕d2+ 47.♔a3 ♕a5+ 48.♔b2

Draw agreed.

The line 5...d6 6.♗g2 ♘c6 is acceptable for black, but the variation 6...♘bd7 7.0-0 e5 is a matter of debate. To fight for the advantage in the latter line, we can recommend that white try the well-known lines 8.♗e3 and 8.♘c3, as well as Burmakin's little-known idea 8.dxe5 dxe5 9.♕a4. In any case, the plan with the early e6-e5 has not been refuted.

Chapter 14

4...a5 5.g3 d5 variation

No. 80 G. Tunik – P. Maletin
Moscow 2006

1.d4 ♘f6 2.c4 e6 3.♘f3 ♗b4+ 4.♗d2 a5 5.g3 d5

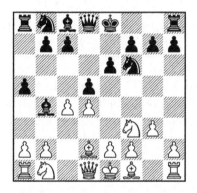

This is a hybrid of the Bogo-Indian Defense and Catalan Opening, where black strives to prove that the pawn on a5 is useful. After 6.a3 ♗e7 we reach a fashionable line of the Catalan normally reached after 1.d4 d5 2.c4 e6 3.♘f3 ♘f6 4.g3 ♗b4+ 5.♗d2 ♗e7 with the addition of a2-a3 and a7-a5, which is more to black's advantage.

6.♕c2

The move 6.♗g2 only leads to variations considered later via a different move order, or to lines of the Catalan Opening. If 6...dxc4 we arrive at very modern lines in the Catalan Gambit.

6...♘c6

The beginning of a plan tried by Taimanov back in 1981 and which

became well-known after Smyslov's success with it a year later. On the eve of the new century grandmasters tried 6...c5 (game 82).

Players from Belarus introduced the setup 6...c6 7.♗g2 b6 8.0-0 ♗a6 attacking c4. However, in the 21st century that is no longer played – after 9.♗xb4 axb4 10.♘bd2 ♘bd7 11.a3 bxa3 12.♖xa3 ♗b7 13.♖fa1 ♖xa3 14.♖xa3 0-0 15.b4 the bishop is locked out of the game, and black has an overall passive position.

7.♗g2

Here in response to 7.a3 black should aim for a break in the center – 7...♗d6 8.♗g2 0-0 9.0-0 dxc4 10.♕xc4 e5 11.d5 ♘e7. If 9.c5 ♗e7 then black is advised to choose a Dutch setup with ♘f6-e4 and f7-f5.

7...dxc4 8.♕xc4 ♕d5

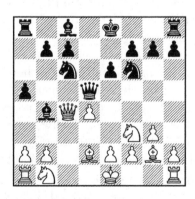

Compared with other Bogo-Indian Defense positions the black army is bursting with energy! White has to choose between exchanging queens and retreating with 9.♕d3 (in the next game).

9.♕xd5 exd5

Via the move order 6...0-0 7.♗g2 ♘c6 8.0-0 dxc4 9.♕xc4 ♕d5 10.♕xd5 exd5 we would reach the same position with the addition of castling for each side. This addition is definitely better for white, as the unpinned bishop can move to f4 and attack the pawn on c7.

10.0-0

In the game Browne – Smyslov (Las Palmas 1982) the ex-world champion gained an initiative on the queenside after 10.♘c3 ♗e6 11.♖c1 a4 12.♘b5 ♗xd2+ 13.♔xd2 ♔d8 14.♘e5 ♖a5! 15.♘xc6+ (if 15.♖xc6 ♖xb5 16.♖xe6 fxe6 17.♘f7+ ♔e7 18.♘xh8 ♖xb2+ 19.♔d3 c6 only white is at risk) 15...bxc6 16.♘c3 ♔e7 17.♘d1 ♔d6 18.f3 c5 19.dxc5+ ♖xc5 20.♖xc5 ♔xc5 21.♘c3 ♔b4 22.♖c1 c5 23.e3 d4 24.exd4 cxd4, although after 25.♘e2 ♗xa2 26.♗f1, which Smyslov failed to show in his notes, white should still draw. Today players don't strive to save a tempo by not castling.

10...♗f5

The main continuation here is 10...♗g4, tried by Taimanov with some fantastic results. That said, sometimes he got lucky: 11.♗e3 ♘e7 12.♗f4 0-0-0 13.♖c1 ♘e8 14.♘e5 ♗e6 15.♘c3 f6 16.♘d3 g5 17.♗d2 ♘c6 18.a3 ♗e7 19.♘b5 ♘d6 20.♘xd6+ ♗xd6 21.e3 ♔d7 22.♘c5+ ♗xc5 23.♖xc5 b6 (Gaprindashvili – Taimanov, Elista 2002) 24.♖c2 ♘e7 25.b4 axb4 26.♗xb4 ♖c8 27.♗f1 – white has a stable advantage. Maletin

places his bishop differently, in order to support the centralized knight.

11.♗f4 0-0-0

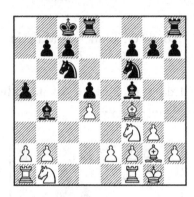

KEY TIP. This is one of the few lines in the Bogo-Indian Defense where black frequently castles long. This is the most natural way to protect the pawn on c7.

12.a3 ♗e7 13.♘c3 ♘e4 14.♘b5 ♖d7 15.♖fc1

I won't quote the game Novikov – Kochyev (Beltsy 1981) with the move 15.♖fe1 due to the very weak play by the future grandmaster Igor Novikov. The computer's recommendation 15.♘e5 ♘xe5 16.dxe5 is unappealing to a human, as it ruins the pawn chain without visible reasons.

15...g5 16.♗e3 f6 17.♘d2

So far, neither player can be faulted. White wants to get rid of black's troublesome knight.

17...♖e8 18.♘xe4 dxe4 19.♖d1 ♖ed8 20.♖ac1 ♔b8 21.h3

In an approximately equal position Tunik starts to meander. He should have played 21.f3 exf3 22.exf3, and the h3 square may later become available for his bishop.

21...h5 22.♔h2 ♗g6 23.f3 exf3 24.♗xf3 ♘a7

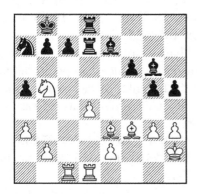

25.♘c3

White would have gained an almost impregnable position via 25.♘xa7 ♔xa7 26.♗d2 b6 27.b4 a4 28.e3.

25...♗d6 26.♔g2 ♖e8 27.♗f2

Why not move to d2, in order to keep the g5 pawn under attack?

27...f5 28.e3 g4 29.hxg4 hxg4 30.♗e2 ♗e7 31.e4?

Tunik had obviously not calculated the variation 31.♗d3 ♗g5 32.♘e2 ♗xe3 33.♗xe3 ♖xe3 34.♘f4 ♗h7 35.♖e1 – white is a pawn down but doesn't risk losing.

31...♗g5 32.♖a1 fxe4 33.♗xg4 ♖d6 34.♗e1 e3 35.♗f3 ♖b6 36.b4 axb4 37.axb4 e2! 38.♘xe2 ♗c2 39.d5 ♗xd1 40.♖xd1 ♘b5

Maletin has spectacularly won the exchange and confidently converts his material advantage. This isn't one of those positions where the bishop pair could stop black's progress.

41.♖a1 ♗f6 42.♖a2 ♘d4 43.♘xd4 ♖xe1 44.♘c2 ♖b1 45.♗e4 ♖b3 46.g4 ♗e5 47.♔f1 ♖h6 48.♖a3 ♖b1+ 49.♔e2 ♖h2+ 50.♔d3 ♖b2

51.♔c4 ♖bxc2+ 52.♗xc2 ♖xc2+ 53.♔d3 ♖g2

White resigned.

No. 81 J. Thybo – E. Tomashevsky
Skopje 2019

1.d4 e6 2.c4 ♗b4+ 3.♗d2 a5 4.♘f3 d5 5.♕c2 ♘f6 6.g3 ♘c6 7.♗g2 dxc4 8.♕xc4 ♕d5 9.♕d3

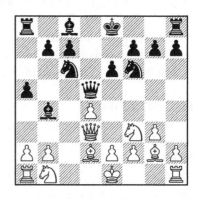

9...♕e4

Black has also proposed exchanging queens on f5. After 9... ♕f5 10.♕xf5 exf5 11.0-0 ♗e6 12.♖c1 ♗d5 13.e3 ♘e4 14.♗e1 0-0 15.♘fd2 ♖fe8?! 16.♘c3 ♘xc3 17.bxc3 ♗xg2 18.cxb4 ♗d5 19.b5 ♘b4 20.a3 ♘d3 21.♖c3 ♘xe1 22.♖xe1 c6 23.♖b1 (Giri – Landa, Mulhouse 2011) white outplayed his opponent, but 15...♘f6 would have been a clear improvement. The two queen moves are probably of equal strength.

Smyslov suggested that black could search for counter chances via 9...0-0 10.♘c3 ♕h5 11.0-0 ♖d8. Oddly enough, white can consider exchanging queens via 12.♗g5 ♗e7 13.♕b5 – and he has a minimal advantage.

10.♕xe4 ♘xe4 11.e3

The change in structure after 11.♗xb4 axb4 doesn't look appealing for white (although grandmasters have played it). The main move here is 11.a3, and after the sample continuation 11...♘xd2 12.♘bxd2 ♗e7 13.♖c1 0-0 14.0-0 a4 15.e3 ♗d7 16.♖c3 ♖fb8 17.♖fc1 ♗d8 18.♘e4 ♗e8 19.♘c5 ♖a7 (Sasikiran – Zhang Zhong, Zaozhuang 2012) black confidently held the defense. Our game features a similar pattern, with the main difference being that black's king comfortably remained in the center.

11...♗d7 12.0-0

12.♘c3 was weaker due to the exchange on d2. If white recaptures with his knight, then black plays the immediate 13...e5, while if he recaptures with his king then black plays first 13...f6, and then e6-e5.

12...♔e7   13.♖c1   ♘xd2 14.♘bxd2 a4

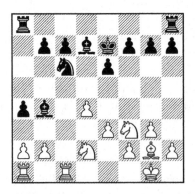

Crossing the demarcation line is a universal idea in variations where the queen is exchanged. Black has both dynamic advantages (a4-a3), and static ones (control over b3 if white

plays a2-a3, and freeing up the a5 square for the rook).

15.a3 ♗d6 16.♘c4 f6 17.♘fd2 ♖hb8 18.♘xd6 cxd6 19.d5 exd5 20.♗xd5 ♖a5

Thanks to a5-a4 the rook has gained the chance to operate along the fifth rank. Black's extra pawn island isn't a problem, as it's easy to protect.

21.♗c4 ♘e5 22.♗e2 ♖d5 23.♘f3 ♘xf3+ 24.♗xf3 ♖c5 25.♖c3 b5 26.♖ac1

26.♖d3 was more accurate, in order to cramp his opponent's activity by pressing on d6. 26...♖c2 is met by 27.b4.

26...b4 27.♖xc5 dxc5 28.♖xc5 bxa3 29.bxa3 ♖b3 30.♔g2 ♖xa3

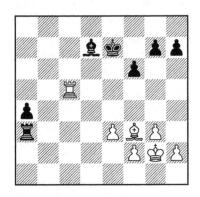

31.♖c4?

The young Danish master playing white (who already had a grandmaster rating of 2525 at the time (black was 2705 by the way)) let in a soft goal in a simple ending. If white places his rook behind the passer, and his bishop on d5, then black has no way to win.

31...♖d3   32.♗c6   ♗xc6+ 33.♖xc6 ♖d6 34.♖c2 ♖a6 35.e4 a3 36.♖a2 ♔d6 37.f4 ♔c5 38.♔f3

♚b4 39.e5 f5 40.♚e3 ♚c3 41.g4 g6 42.♚f3 ♚b3 43.♖a1 a2 44.♚g3 ♚b2 45.♖xa2+ ♚xa2 46.gxf5 gxf5 47.♚h4 ♖g6

White resigned.

No. 82 I. Farago – M. Tratar
Graz 2011

1.d4 ♘f6 2.c4 e6 3.♘f3 ♗b4+ 4.♗d2 a5 5.g3 d5 6.♕c2 c5

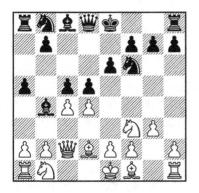

This is a relatively new idea (dating back to 1996), regularly played by Grandmaster Eingorn. That said, black frequently raises the tension in the center in this way in similar positions in reply to ♕d1-c2.

7.cxd5

White sometimes also plays 7.dxc5 d4 8.♗xb4 axb4 9.♗g2 ♘c6 10.♘bd2 0-0 11.0-0. This geometrically pleasing but unusual position is not simple to assess. In the game Berkes – Dzhumabayev (Martuni 2009) after 11...♕e7 12.♘b3 e5 13.e4 dxe3 14.fxe3 ♘d7 15.♚h1 h6 16.♘h4 ♘xc5 17.♗d5 (Dzhumabayev had also played 17.♘g6 fxg6 18.♘xc5 as white, which is weaker) 17...♘e6 18.♘f5 ♕g5 19.♕f2 white grabbed

the initiative, but the players' choices can vary on just about every move.

7...cxd4 8.♘xd4 0-0 9.♗g2 ♕b6!?

This is a good intermezzo with the aim of creating disharmony in white's army. He should avoid 9...e5?! 10.♘b5 ♘xd5 11.0-0 ♘c6 12.♖d1 ♗e6 13.a3 ♗e7 14.♗e1 ♕b6 15.♗xd5 ♕xb5 16.♗xe6 fxe6 17.♘c3 ♕c5 18.e3, and black has no compensation for his broken pawn structure (Bunzmann – Kosten, Austria 2008).

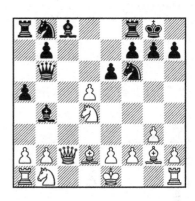

10.e3

This locks in his dark-squared bishop and exposes his light squares. However, this is immaterial in a maneuvering battle. Compared with the continuation 10.♘f3 exd5, it's probably important that white's knight remains in the center.

10...♘xd5

Previously, the Hungarian grandmaster playing white fought against a structure with a backward pawn – 10...exd5 11.0-0 ♘c6 12.♘xc6 bxc6. The games Farago – Voiska (Porto San Georgio 2008) and Farago – Miezis (Triesen 2011) featured white putting on the pressure, but both ended in draws. Tratar didn't want to play this known depressing line, hoping for counter chances to appear.

11.0-0 ♗c5

Let's look at how Peruvian grandmaster Bachmann – a specialist in this variation – continued here: 11... ♗d7 12.♘c3 ♘f6 13.a3 ♗e7 14.♕b3 ♕xb3 (black evaded exchanges, but was unable to preserve queens) 15.♘xb3 a4 (15...♗c6!?) 16.♘d4 e5 (Cori – Bachmann, Medellin 2017). Now the strong 17.♘db5 ♖a5 18.♘c7 ♗d6 19.♘3d5 ♘xd5 20.♘xd5 ♖b5 21.♗c3 guarantees white a small advantage with no counterplay for black.

12.♘b3 ♗e7 13.♘c3 ♘b4

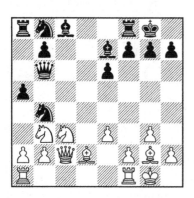

14.♘a4

If 14.♕b1 a4 15.♘d4 ♘8c6 black has hopes of gaining the initiative, and Farago hence plays interim moves.

14...♕b5 15.♕c7 ♘8c6 16.♘c3

An objectively stronger continuation was probably 16.♗xb4!? ♗d8!? (16...♕xb4 17.♖fd1 ♕xa4 18.♗xc6 ♕xc6 19.♕xe7 obviously favors white) 17.♗xc6 bxc6 18.♕d6

axb4 19.♘ac5 e5, though white will still have to watch out for his king's safety.

16...♕e5?!

Tratar chose the wrong time for simplifications. After 16...♕a6! 17.♖fd1 ♗d8 18.♕d6 ♗e7 a draw is the logical conclusion.

17.♕xe5 ♘xe5 18.♘a4 ♘c4?!

Black wastes tempi in order to exchange a locked-in bishop. The continuation 18...♘d5 19.♗xd5 exd5 20.♘b6 ♗h3 21.♘xa8 ♘f3+ 22.♔h1 ♘xd2 23.♘xd2 ♗xf1 24.♖xf1 ♖xa8 leaves black with chances of defending a strategically difficult endgame.

19.♖fc1 ♘xd2 20.♘xd2 ♘d3 21.♖c3 ♖d8 22.♘b6 ♖b8 23.♘dc4 ♗f6

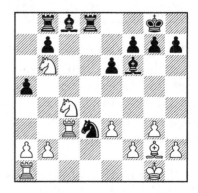

24.♖d1! ♗xc3

24...♘xb2 25.♘xb2 ♖xd1+ 26.♘xd1 ♗xc3 27.♘xc3 wouldn't have influenced the outcome of the game.

25.bxc3 e5 26.♗e4 ♗g4 27.♖xd3 ♗e2 28.♖xd8+ ♖xd8 29.♘xe5 f6 30.♘ed7

Black resigned.

The line 6.♕c2 ♘c6 7.♗g2 dxc4 8.♕xc4 ♕d5 is now considered old-fashioned and grants white only a minimal advantage in an uninteresting game. The continuation 6...c5!? clearly appears more exciting. However, black should remember that white can confidently transpose to a Catalan Gambit earlier without playing ♕d1-c2.

Chapter 15

4...a5 5.g3 b6 variation

No. 83 V. Dobrov – O. Nikolenko
Moscow 2002

1.♘f3 ♘f6 2.c4 e6 3.d4 ♗b4+
4.♗d2 a5 5.g3 b6

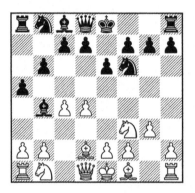

Since a lot of the games played in this line begin with the Queen's Indian Defense, my book on that opening is a useful additional reference point. The variations are logically divided between that book and the current one, but many of the ideas are similar.

6.♗g2 ♗a6

Although the development of the bishop to b7 is statistically far more popular, this idea of Romanishin's is far from eccentric. It has obvious similarities with the Nimzowitsch variation of the Queen's Indian Defense (3...b6 4.g3 ♗a6), while the rook's pawn has kindly freed up room for his rook.

After 6...0-0 7.♘e5 ♖a7 8.0-0 ♗xd2 9.♕xd2 d6 10.♘d3 the continuation ♗c8-a6 is possible, but 10...♗b7 is more logical. After

11.♘c3 ♗xg2 12.♔xg2 c5 13.d5 exd5 14.cxd5 a4 15.b4 (V. Mikhalevski – Fedorchuk, Trieste 2009) white had better prospects. Neither the exchange of the white king's defender, nor his opponent's pawn majority on the queenside, play a material role.

7.♘e5

> **TRANSPOSITION ALERT.** If 7.b3, then it is best to be guided by the variation 7...d5 8.a3 ♗e7 9.cxd5 exd5 10.♘c3 0-0 11.0-0 ♗b7. The usual QID move order would be 3... b6 4.g3 ♗a6 5.b3 ♗b7 6.♗g2 ♗b4+ 7.♗d2 a5 8.0-0 0-0 9.a3 ♗e7 10.♘c3 d5 11.cxd5 exd5 with equality thanks to the pressure on a3.

It's useful to meet the move 7.♕c2 by activity in the center: 7...0-0 8.0-0 d5 9.♘e5 c6 10.♖d1 ♘fd7 11.♘d3 ♗xc4 12.♘xb4 axb4 13.♗xb4 c5 14.♗a3 ♘c6 15.e3 ♕f6 (Bindrich – Schlosser, Austria 2014). Thanks to the pressure on d4 black is no worse.

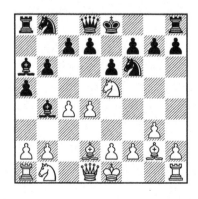

7...♖a7

Romanishin's initial idea was 7...c6, but the barrier on the path of the g2 bishop in the form of d7-d5 is out of place here. White breaks black's pawn structure by exchanging on b4, while if black first exchanges on d2, then white continues e2-e4.

8.0-0 0-0 9.♕b3

An example of how black should act if white exchanges on b4 can be found in the fragment Narayanan – Kamsky (Moscow 2017): 9.♗xb4 axb4 10.♘d2 d6 11.♘d3 c5 12.a3 bxa3 13.♖xa3 ♖d7 (the rook has successfully moved to the center) 14.b4 cxd4 15.♕a1 ♗b7 16.♕xd4 ♗xg2 17.♔xg2 ♘c6 18.♕b2 h5 19.♖fa1 ♕b8 20.♔g1 ♖c8 with a solid yet flexible position.

9.♕c2 is probably the most accurate line, and if black continues like in the actual game, white's queen doesn't get attacked and controls e4. After 9...♗xd2 10.♘xd2 c5 11.dxc5 bxc5 12.♘e4 ♘xe4 13.♗xe4 white's position is preferable.

9...♗xd2 10.♘xd2 c5 11.dxc5 bxc5 12.♖ad1 ♕c7 13.♕c3 ♗b7 14.♗xb7 ♖xb7 15.♘d3 d6

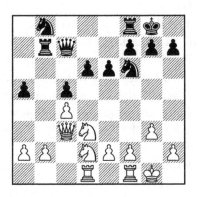

This is a typical structure of the Queen's Indian Defense, where white doesn't pressurize the backward d6 pawn and doesn't have much of a plan. The game is unlikely to end in a win for anybody.

16.e3 ♘c6 17.b3 ♘b4 18.♘c1 ♖a8 19.a3 ♘c6 20.♘d3 ♖ab8 21.♖b1

White is consistently preventing a5-a4 (as he would reply b3-b4). A little later, his knight will get to a4 and he will gain the chance to build a battery on the d-file.

21...♖b6 22.♕c2 h6 23.♘b2 ♖6b7 24.♘a4 ♕e7 25.♖fd1 ♘e5 26.♕c3 ♕c7 27.f4

This is a somewhat committal way to build the battery – at some point he may have to contend with the breaks e6-e5 and g7-g5.

27...♘c6 28.♕d3 ♘e7 29.♖bc1 ♕c6 30.♖c3 ♘f5 31.♕e2 ♘e4 32.♘xe4 ♕xe4 33.♕d3 ♕c6 34.♔f2 h5 35.♕c2 ♖d7

The computer favors 35...f6!?, and then g7-g5. Instead black sent his rook's pawn further down, making do with perpetual check.

36.♖cd3 ♖bd8 37.♕d2 h4 38.g4 h3 39.gxf5 ♕g2+

Draw agreed.

No. 84 H. Teske – P. Gmeiner
Germany 1997

1.d4 ♘f6 2.c4 e6 3.♘f3 ♗b4+ 4.♗d2 a5 5.g3 b6 6.♗g2 ♗b7

At this point the number of moves in the database grows substantially due to the QID move order 1.d4 ♘f6 2.c4 e6 3.♘f3 b6 4.g3 ♗b7 5.♗g2 ♗b4+ 6.♗d2 a5.

7.0-0

White wants to move his bishop from d2, free up the a5-e1 diagonal and highlight the vulnerability of the bishop on b4. On the other hand, the move 7.♘c3 would further clutter the diagonal and is played rarely (it appears in this position more often when it has reached c3 earlier via a different move order). However, the knight's development to c3 on move 8 is growing in popularity after black castles on move 7 (as in game 85).

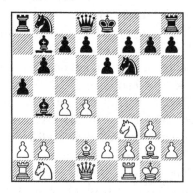

7...♝xd2

Examples of black castling without this bishop exchange are studied in games 85-87.

8.♕xd2

In reply to 8.♘bxd2 black should avoid 8...♘e4?! due to 9.♘e5. Therefore, each player prepares to advance their own e-pawn, and the knight would be out of place on d2. In the game Turov – Vaibhav (Mumbai 2019) the grandmaster playing white mobilized his knight a second time – 8...d6 9.♕c2 ♘bd7 10.e4 e5 11.♖fe1 0-0 12.♖ad1 ♖e8 13.♘b1 exd4 14.♘xd4 ♘c5 15.♘c3.

Still, this standard position favors white.

8...0-0 9.♘c3

9.♕f4!? is an interesting move, intending to prepare e2-e4 without accompanying simplifications. After 9...♘h5 10.♕e3 d6 11.♘c3 ♘d7 12.♖fe1 ♘hf6 13.b3 ♕b8 14.♕d3 c5 15.e4 cxd4 16.♘xd4 ♖d8 17.♖ad1 ♘c5 18.♕e2 ♘e8 19.♖d2 ♕c7 20.♖ed1 (Sakaev – Pelletier, France 2006) the Swiss grandmaster, an adherent of this line for black, was in a difficult position.

9...♘e4 10.♘xe4 ♝xe4

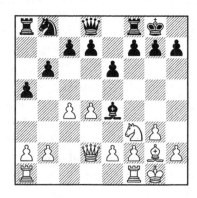

11.♖ac1

The move 11.♕f4!? is most often met by the Dutch setup 11...f5, after which white places his rooks on c1 and d1.

11...d6 12.♖fd1 ♕e7 13.♕e3 ♝b7 14.c5 ♝d5?!

Black doesn't respond to his opponent's key idea in the best way. 14...bxc5 15.dxc5 ♘a6 was stronger, without worrying about the queen's invasion with 16.cxd6 cxd6 17.♕b6 ♝d5.

15.cxb6 cxb6

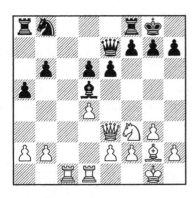

16.♘g5!

> **KEY TIP.** The assessment of the exchange of light-squared bishops depends on whose light squares will be more painfully exposed. Here white doesn't need to worry about his king, whereas the invasion of white's rook on c6 (after black develops his b8 knight, which he needs to do) becomes a realistic prospect.

16...♗xg2 17.♔xg2 ♘a6 18.d5 e5?!

After 18...♘c5 19.dxe6 fxe6 black's pawns may look ugly, but that's still the lesser evil.

19.♖c6 ♘b4

Seeing as after 19...♘c5 20.♖xb6 ♖fb8 21.♖xb8+ ♖xb8 22.b3 a4 black has counterplay, white should reply 20.♘e4.

20.♖xb6 ♘xa2 21.♘e4 ♖fd8 22.♘xd6! ♖xd6 23.♕a3 ♘b4 24.♖xb4 ♕d8 25.♖b5 f5 26.♕c3 e4 27.♖a1 a4 28.♕d4 ♕d7 29.♖xa4 ♖xa4 30.♕xa4

Black resigned. Great play by white, but his opponent's level was much lower (they were rated 2515 and 2199, respectively).

No. 85 I. Naumkin – S. Fedorchuk
Cesenatico 2011

1.d4 ♘f6 2.c4 e6 3.♘f3 ♗b4+ 4.♗d2 a5 5.g3 b6 6.♗g2 ♗b7 7.0-0 0-0 8.♘c3

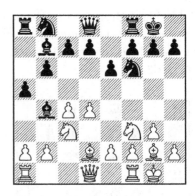

8...d6

It's interesting to compare this position with the fragment Krejci – Bartel (Prague 2019): 8...♗xc3 9.♗xc3 ♗e4 10.e3 d6 11.♕e2 ♘bd7 12.♖fd1 ♕b8 13.♗f1 ♕b7 (the standard plan of occupying the long diagonal will fail with a bang) 14.♘e1 d5 15.f3 ♗g6 16.♖ac1 c6 17.g4 ♘e8 18.♗g2 ♘d6 19.cxd5 exd5 20.♗e1 ♖fd8 21.♗g3 ♘f8 22.♘f4 h6 23.e4 dxe4 24.♘xg6 ♘xg6 25.fxe4 with the bishop pair and a great position. White played magnificently!

The best way to challenge for e4 is to follow Igor Lysyj's receipt: 8...♘e4 9.♘xe4 ♗xe4 10.♗f4 ♗e7, and if 11.d5 then black should switch diagonals with 11...♗f6. After 9.♖c1 or 9.♕c2 the plan with d7-d6 and ♘b8-d7 gains in strength after the exchange of minor pieces.

9.♕c2

8.♘c3 makes 9.d5 logical. However, black achieves a reasonable position via 9...♗xc3 10.♗xc3 exd5 11.♗xf6 ♕xf6 12.♘d4 ♘a6 13.cxd5 ♘c5.

9...♘bd7 10.♖fe1 ♗xc3 11.♗xc3 ♗e4

This highlights the drawback of the move 9.♕c2. The same idea could have been played one move earlier.

12.♕d2

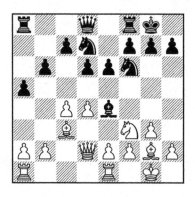

12...♕b8

Fedorchuk isn't planning to organize a battery along the long diagonal (as Bartel did in the above note), but to send his b-pawn into battle. He could also have played 12...c6 with the same idea.

13.♖ad1 b5 14.cxb5 ♕xb5 15.♗f1 ♗b7

It was probably more accurate to play 15...♕b7!? 16.♗xa5 ♕d5 17.b4 (17.♗xc7? ♖fc8) 17...♘b6, and black has no problems.

16.♘h4

There is a curious computer line 16.e4 ♕h5 17.♕f4 h6 18.h4 c5!? 19.dxc5 e5 20.♕e3 ♘xc5 21.♘xe5 ♘fxe4 22.♗e2 ♕f5 23.♗g4 ♕xf2+ 24.♕xf2 ♘xf2 25.♔xf2 dxe5

26.♗xe5 with a small advantage for white. Obviously, that is hard to calculate even for grandmasters. That said, it's easy to select the retreat 16...♕h5, as the hanging knight looks like he's asking for trouble.

16...♘e4 17.♕c2 f5 18.f3

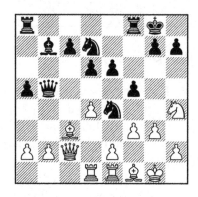

18...♘xc3 19.♕xc3

A series of errors will soon leave Naumkin in a critical position. After 19.bxc3 ♕c6 20.e4 fxe4 21.♕xe4 ♕xe4 22.fxe4 chances are equal, and white has nothing more.

19...♕b6 20.♘g2 ♘f6 21.♘e3 ♘d5 22.♘xd5 ♗xd5 23.b3 e5 24.♗g2?!

He could have defended successfully with 24.e4 fxe4 25.fxe4 ♗e6 26.♗c4 ♗xc4 27.♕xc4+ ♔h8 28.♖f1 ♖xf1+ 29.♔xf1.

24...a4 25.e4 fxe4 26.fxe4 ♗e6 27.♕e3 axb3 28.axb3 exd4 29.♕xd4 ♕xb3 30.♖a1?

Despite the loss of a pawn, white would not have lost after 30.e5 ♖a2 31.♗e4. Thanks to white's powerful centralization, black's achievements down the files are not material.

30...♖xa1 31.♖xa1 ♕b5 32.♕c3

♕b6+ 33.♔h1 h6 34.♖c1 ♖f2 35.♕xc7??

Fedorchuk had missed the strongest continuation 34...c5 35.e5 c4, and now 35.e5 would have preserved some chances. But it looks like white had already given up on this game.

35...♕b2 36.♖g1 ♖xg2 37.♖xg2 ♕b1+

White resigned.

No. 86 M. Chetverik – V. Meijers
Reutlingen 2009

1.d4 e6 2.c4 b6 3.♘f3 ♗b7 4.g3 ♘f6 5.♗g2 ♗b4+ 6.♗d2 a5 7.0-0 0-0 8.♗g5

8...♗e7

After 8...h6 9.♗xf6 ♕xf6 10.a3 ♗e7 11.♘c3 d6 12.e4 black's position lacks harmony. In particular, the queen has left herself vulnerable to e4-e5.

9.♘c3

Given the exchanges that occur after this, it was worth considering voluntarily exchanging the dark-squared bishop. The game could continue 9.♗xf6 ♗xf6 10.♘c3 d6

11.♕c2 g6 12.♖fd1 ♘d7 13.♘b5 ♗g7 14.♘e1 ♕b8 15.d5 ♘c5 16.e4, and at least one of black's bishops is locked away for some time (Karpov – Larsen, Monaco 1992, rapid).

If 9.♕c2 ♗e4 10.♕d2 the standard break e2-e4 is still on the agenda: 10...h6 11.♗xf6 ♗xf6 12.♘c3 d5 13.♖fd1 ♘c6 14.e3 ♗h7 15.♕e2 ♖c8 16.♖ac1 ♘e7 17.e4 dxe4 18.♘xe4 ♗xe4 19.♕xe4 ♕d6 20.c5. That said, two games, Benjamin – Speelman (Hastings 1988) and Parligras – Al. Donchenko (Medias 2015), have demonstrated the fleeting nature of white's advantage.

9...h6

Meijers doesn't want to simplify the position against a weaker opponent (his Elo was about 130 higher than mine). However, it was long known that 9...♘e4 was safer. For example, 10.♗xe7 ♕xe7 11.♖c1 d6 12.♕d3 ♘xc3 13.♖xc3 f5 14.c5 (the conditions are absent to support a decent charge with the white b-pawn) 14...bxc5 15.dxc5 ♘a6 16.c6 ♗c8 17.♖a3 ♘b4 18.♕d2 e5 with good prospects for black (Oll – Xu Jun, Biel 1993).

10.♗xf6 ♗xf6

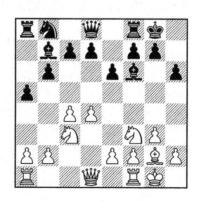

11.♖c1

11.e4 d6 12.e5!? dxe5 13.dxe5 ♗e7 14.♕e2 ♕c8 15.♖fd1 a4 16.♘d4 ♗xg2 17.♔xg2 ♕b7+ 18.♕e4 ♕xe4+ 19.♘xe4 ♖d8 20.f4 favors white (A. Muzychuk – Hou Yifan, Monaco 2015), but I wasn't yet ready to cross the border.

11...g6 12.♕d2 ♗g7 13.♖fe1 d6 14.e4 ♘d7 15.♕e3 ♖c8 16.♘b5 ♔h7 17.♖cd1 ♕e7 18.b3 c6 19.♘c3 ♗a6

After 19...c5 20.d5 or 20.♘b5 white has a more pleasant position, but now he counts on gaining a decent advantage.

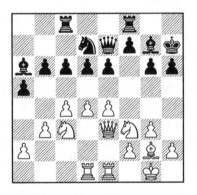

20.d5!?

With hindsight, 20.e5 d5 21.♗f1 looks preferable.

20...cxd5 21.exd5 e5 22.♘d4! ♖ce8??

A fatal oversight. The recommendation of Frank Zeller 22...♘c5 23.f4 f5 24.fxe5 dxe5 25.d6 looks questionable from move 24 onwards in view of 25...♕f6 26.♘db5 ♗xb5 27.♘xb5 e4, and white is best not to exchange on e5 at all (24.♘e6!?). The complicated position that arises is the one that Meijers was aiming for.

23.♘c6 ♕g5 24.♕xg5 hxg5 25.♘e4 g4 26.♘xd6 ♖a8 27.h3 gxh3 28.♗xh3 f5 29.f4 exf4 30.gxf4 ♘f6 31.♖e7 ♘h5 32.♖f1

Due to time trouble, I had drawn out the process of converting my advantage into a point. 32.♔f2! ♘xf4 33.♖h1 would have done the job immediately.

32...a4 33.♘e5 axb3 34.axb3 ♗c8 35.♘df7

Here 35.♘e8 ♔g8 36.♘xg7 ♘xg7 37.d6 was more convincing.

35...♔g8 36.d6 ♘f6 37.♗g2 ♖a3 38.♘g5 ♖d8 39.♖d1

I had roughly calculated a variation that extended well beyond move 40 but as there was no time increment per move I had no time to find 39.♖c7!

39...♗f8 40.♘xg6 ♗xe7 41.♘xe7+ ♔f8 42.♘xc8 ♖xc8 43.d7 ♖d8 44.♘e6+ ♔e7 45.♘xd8 ♔xd8 46.♗h3 ♘g4

After 46...♖xb3 47.♗xf5 ♖g3+ 48.♔f2 ♖g7 49.♔f3 black cannot save the pawn ending.

47.♗xg4 fxg4 48.♖d3 ♖a2 49.f5 ♖e2 50.♖d6 ♖e5 51.f6 b5 52.f7 ♖f5 53.c5 ♖xf7 54.c6 ♖f8 55.♖e6 ♖g8 56.♔g2 g3 57.b4

Black resigned.

No. 87 D. Jakovenko – R. Rapport
Shenzhen 2019

1.d4 ♘f6 2.c4 e6 3.g3 ♗b4+ 4.♗d2 a5 5.♗g2 0-0 6.♘f3 b6 7.0-0 ♗b7 8.♗f4

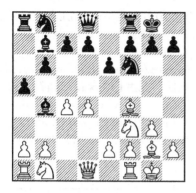

This is the main continuation. Unlike with 8.♗g5 white will only agree to exchange dark-colored bishops if it is to his advantage...

8...♗e7

...for example, with 8...♗d6 9.♗xd6 cxd6 10.♘c3 ♘e4 11.♘b5. The knight has rejected exchange and occupied a strong square; white has a lasting advantage.

9.♘c3

The well-known "Catalan" traveling bishop 9.♕c2 ♗e4 10.♕c1 ♗b7 failed to justify itself in the game Vitiugov – Fawzy (Khanty-Mansiysk 2017) – 11.♘c3 ♘e4 12.♘b5 ♘a6 13.♘g5 (there's the advantage of having the queen on c1!) 13...d5 14.♘xe4 dxe4 15.♖d1 f5 16.d5 (16.f3!? exf3 17.exf3) 16...exd5 17.cxd5 ♗d6 18.♘xd6 cxd6 19.♕e3, and white soon increased his advantage. Obviously, black should have preferred 9...c5, taking advantage of the queen's exit from the d-file.

9...♘e4

9...♘a6 is well met with 10.♘e5 (10.d5 ♗b4 is harmless for black) 10...♗xg2 11.♔xg2, and switching to a Dutch setup doesn't grant

black equality: 11...♘h5 12.♗d2 f6 13.♘f3 f5 (Wang Yue – Zhou Weiqi, Jiangmen 2014) 14.e4 fxe4 15.♘xe4.

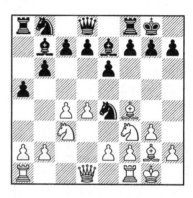

10.♘b5

Jakovenko steps on uncharted territory, and the game turns sharp one move later. In the position after 10.♕c2 ♘xc3 both sides can claim a number of big-name devotees. Capturing with the pawn maintains control over e4 and promises a small advantage – 11.bxc3 ♕c8 12.e4 d6 13.♖fe1 ♘d7 14.♖ab1 ♖e8 15.♘d2 e5 16.♗e3 ♗c6 17.♗h3 ♕d8 18.f3 ♗f6 19.♘f1 ♘f8 20.♗f2 ♗d7 21.♗xd7 ♕xd7 22.♖bd1 ♕c6 23.♕d3 g6 24.♘e3 ♗g7 25.♘d5 (Rodshtein – Kelires, Skopje 2019).

10...c6

To avoid nasty surprises, it's more careful to play 10...♘a6 and only then c7-c6. But not the blunder 10...d6? in view of 11.♘d2 f5 12.♘xe4 fxe4 13.♕c2 winning a pawn (Wojtaszek – Wang Yue, China 2016). In defense of the strong Chinese grandmaster, I would point out that this incident happened during a game of Basque chess (when the players play against each other simultaneously as white and black).

11.♘c7!?

I once played against the fire-proof setup arising after 11.♘c3 ♘xc3 12.bxc3 d6. White's game is of course more pleasant, but he will not find it easy to destroy black's bastions without his opponent's help.

11...♖a7 12.♕b3

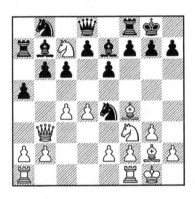

12...d6

There is an alternative way to break the link between white's pieces: 12...g5!? 13.♘xg5 ♗xg5 14.♗xg5 ♘xg5 15.♕xb6 ♘a6 16.♕xa7 ♕xc7 17.c5 f5. After the exchange of queens on b6 chances are about equal.

13.c5

The variation 13.♕xb6 ♘d7 14.♕xa7 ♕xc7 15.d5 cxd5 16.cxd5 ♘dc5 17.♘d2 ♖a8 18.♕xa8+ ♗xa8 19.♘xe4 ♗xd5 20.♘xc5 ♗xg2 21.♔xg2 ♕xc5 leads to a two rooks versus queen position where white has slightly better prospects.

13...♕xc7 14.cxb6 a4!

This intermezzo equalizes chances. Now 15.♕b4?? is very bad due to 15...♘a6.

15.bxc7 axb3 16.cxb8=♕ ♖xb8 17.axb3 ♖ba8 18.♖xa7 ♖xa7 19.♖c1

It's unclear why Jakovenko didn't place his rook on b1 immediately.

19...♖a2 20.♘e1 d5 21.♖b1 g5 22.♗c1

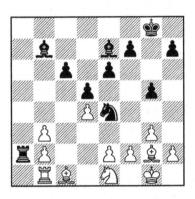

22...♗a6

Rapport could have immediately played the cramping move 22...g4, as now 23.f3 would have chased the knight away with some advantage.

23.♗xe4 dxe4 24.♔f1 ♖a5 25.♘c2 g4 26.♘e3 h5 27.♘c4 ♖a2 28.♗e3 ♗b4 29.♔g2 ♔g7 30.h3 ♗b5 31.♖c1 ♗e7 32.hxg4 hxg4 33.♖c2 ♖a1 34.f3 exf3+ 35.exf3 gxf3+ 36.♔xf3 f6 37.♖c1

Draw agreed.

In QID setups, the move a7-a5 grants the queen's rook some space but doesn't fit well with black's plans. White can count on better prospects thanks to play in the center.

Chapter 16

Various after 4...♕e7

No. 88 M. Rocius – A. Gipslis
Pardubice 1994

1.d4 ♘f6 2.c4 e6 3.♘f3 ♗b4+ 4.♗d2 ♕e7

This is the most common move, and allows white a large number of options. After 5.♗xb4?! ♕xb4+ 6.♕d2 ♕xc4 7.e3 ♕c6 8.♘c3 white does have a little bit of compensation for the pawn, but this is not a solid line and not in keeping with the spirit of the Bogo-Indian Defense.

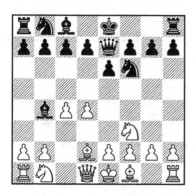

5.♕c2

The queen takes control of e4, and in reply to 5...b6 or 5...0-0 white definitely wants to play 6.e4. Most often, black plans d7-d6 and e6-e5, and to do so he first wants to exchange bishops. White's other options are: 5.e3 – game 89, 5.♘c3 – games 90-92, and 5.a3 – games 93 and 94.

5...♗xd2+ 6.♘bxd2 d6 7.e3

With black's queen on e7 there is no obvious gain from playing 7.e4.

After 7...e5 8.♗e2 0-0 9.0-0 ♗g4 10.♖fe1 ♗xf3 11.♘xf3 exd4 12.♘xd4 ♕e5!? 13.♖ad1 ♘bd7 black intends to capture the pawn, and any form of protecting it causes white other difficulties.

7...e5

Black occasionally makes different use of the pawn on d6. After 7...c5 8.dxc5 dxc5 9.♗d3 ♘c6 10.a3 b6 11.0-0 white has a more pleasant game (due to control over e4), but nothing more.

8.♗d3

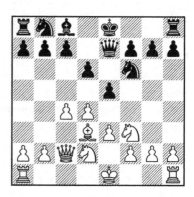

8...0-0

8...♗g4!? is interesting, in order to break up white's pawn chain by capturing on f3. If 9.♗f5 ♗xf5 10.♕xf5 white has no more than a symbolic advantage.

9.♗f5

Here the exchange is imprecise, as it helps the black army to complete mobilization. After 9.0-0 ♗g4 the non-standard exchange of knights 10.♘g5 h6 11.♘h7 is interesting with slightly better prospects for white after 11...♘xh7 12.♝xh7+ ♚h8 13.♝e4 c6 14.h3 ♝c8 (Gislason – Vantola, Ohrid 2009) 15.♛c3 ♘d7 16.♝c2. If 9...♖e8 the sortie 10.♘g5 is also fine, but in reply to 10...h6 the knight will head to e4.

9...♘c6 10.♝xc8 ♖axc8

11.d5

A seemingly "textbook" move – the pawn occupies a light square after the exchange of light-squared bishops. However, black's better development allows him to open up play to his advantage, and so it was better for white to maintain the tension by castling short.

11...♘b4 12.♛c3 ♘a6 13.0-0 c6 14.dxc6 ♖xc6

The choice of captures here was a matter of taste.

15.b4 ♘c7 16.♛b2 ♘e6 17.c5

It was more careful to place the rooks on c1 and d1 with deeply defensive aims.

17...e4 18.cxd6 ♖xd6 19.♘e5 ♖fd8 20.♘dc4 ♖d5

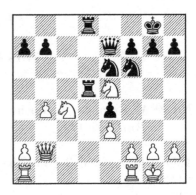

Black has an excellent position. He controls the entire file, while the e4 pawn causes white so much pain that he attacks it.

21.a4 h5 22.f3 exf3 23.♖xf3?

He should have captured the pawn with his knight, as now the maneuver of the enemy knight decides the outcome of the game.

23...♘g5 24.♖f5 ♘ge4 25.♖af1 ♛e6 26.♖5f4 ♘d2

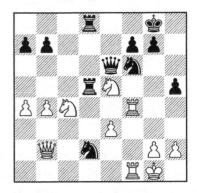

27.♘xd2

The variation 27.♖e1 g5 28.♖f2 ♘fe4 illustrates white's predicament – the pair of black horses dominate their opposite numbers.

27...♖xd2 28.♛c3 ♛a2 29.♘f3 ♖xg2+ 30.♚h1 ♘g4 31.♖xg4 hxg4 32.♛c7 ♖f8 33.♘h4 ♖f2 34.♖d1

♕e2 35.♖g1 ♖f1 36.♕xb7 ♖xg1+
37.♔xg1 ♖d8

White resigned.

No. 89 B. Jobava – J. Van Overdam
Vlissingen 2015

1.d4 ♘f6 2.♘f3 e6 3.c4 ♗b4+
4.♗d2 ♕e7 5.e3

White aims to complete his kingside
development as quickly as possible.

5...♘c6

We shouldn't be surprised at the
popularity of the somewhat meatless
variation 5...b6 6.♗xb4 ♕xb4+
7.♕d2 ♕xd2+ 8.♘bxd2. It's often
used to formalize short draws. If white
wants more, then he should continue
6.♗d3 (black, as usual, plans to swap
bishops and carry out e6-e5) or, more
often, he should avoid 5.e3.

6.♗e2

Jobava is playing this opening
without ambition. After 6.♗d3 0-0
7.0-0 ♗xd2 8.♕xd2 d6 9.♘c3 e5
10.♗c2 white achieves a little more.
The knight on c6 is too inflexible.

6...♗xd2+ 7.♘bxd2

Burmakin preferred here
7.♘fxd2!?, in order to develop his

second knight to c3. The captures are
of equal strength.

7...d6 8.0-0 0-0 9.♘e1 e5 10.d5
♘b8 11.e4 a5 12.g3 ♘a6 13.♘g2

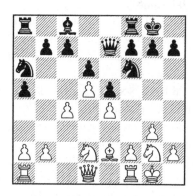

The knight's maneuver is unusual
(instead of the standard ♘e1-d3).
Judging by the following moves, Baadur
considered following up with f2-f4.

13...♘c5 14.♕c2 ♗d7 15.♖ae1
c6 16.♕b1 b5

An objectively reasonable
move, but after this the Georgian
grandmaster playing white is in his
element – open battle. If black just
marks time (with the possible push a5-
a4), then white has no obvious plan.

17.dxc6 ♗xc6 18.cxb5 ♗xe4
19.♘xe4 ♘cxe4 20.♖d1 d5 21.♘e3
d4 22.♘c4

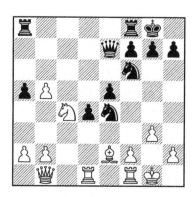

22...♘c5

22...♘d6 23.♘xd6 ♕xd6 is a safer continuation.

23.♖fe1 ♖fd8 24.♘xa5 ♖xa5 25.b4 ♖aa8?!

The Dutch master failed to withstand the tension. 25...♖a3 was better, as if 26.bxc5 ♕xc5 27.♖c1 he blocks with 27...♖c3

26.bxc5 ♕xc5 27.♖c1 ♕d5 28.♗c4 ♕d6 29.♗d3 ♖e8 30.♖c6 ♕e7?!

30...♕d7 was stronger, preventing the passer from moving up the board. After 31.♖xf6 gxf6 32.♗xh7+ ♔g7 33.♗e4 ♖a5 34.♗c6 ♕e7 35.♗xe8 ♕xe8 white cannot retain his pawn pair, and hence he should have preferred 31.♖a6.

31.b6 ♖ab8 32.a4 ♕a3 33.♕b5 e4

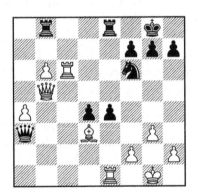

34.♖xf6?!

The continuation 34.♗c4 d3 35.♖d1 ♘g4 36.♗xf7+ ♔xf7 37.♕h5+ ♔g8 38.♕xg4 is better for white, but the battle will continue. Jobava is bluffing.

34...gxf6?

After 34...♕xd3 35.♖f5 g6 36.♖d5 ♕c3 the charge e4-e3 guarantees a draw for black.

35.♖xe4 ♖xe4 36.♗xe4 d3 37.♗xd3 ♖xb6 38.♗xh7+ ♔xh7 39.♕xb6 ♕c3 40.♔g2 ♔g7 41.a5 ♕e5 42.h4

Black resigned.

No. 90 M. Krasenkow – M. Holzhaeuer
Germany 2001

1.d4 ♘f6 2.c4 e6 3.♘f3 ♗b4+ 4.♗d2 ♕e7 5.♘c3

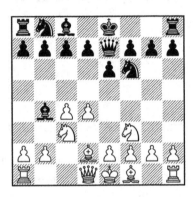

White keeps his plans on how he will mobilize his kingside under wraps for now. After g2-g3 play often transposes to the main 5.g3 system.

5...♗xc3

Specifically, after 5...♘c6 the continuation 6.g3 leads to one of the main Bogo-Indian Defense setups: 5.g3 ♘c6 6.♘c3. Maybe 6.e3 is a better way to exploit the drawbacks of the knight sitting on c6. The game Nikolic – Hausrath (Germany 2014) continued 6...♗xc3 7.♗xc3 ♘e4 8.♖c1 d6 9.♗e2 0-0 10.0-0 ♘xc3 11.♖xc3 e5 12.d5 ♘b8 13.b4 a5 14.♖a3 ♗g4 15.♘d2 ♗xe2 16.♕xe2 with a small advantage. Black has exchanged three pairs of minor pieces in order to defend more easily his slightly cramped position. At the same time, it's also now easier for white to mobilize his army. In game 91 we analyze 5...0-0, and in game 92 we cover 5...b6.

6.♗xc3 ♘e4 7.♕c2

Here 7.♖c1 is played far less often, whereas in the 5.g3 ♘c6 6.♘c3 ♗xc3 7.♗xc3 ♘e4 main line the rook makes this move much more frequently. Partially this is because after 8.♕c2 ♘xc3 9.♕xc3 white has to contend with ♕e7-b4, whereas in our line black cannot force the exchange of queens. After 7...0-0 8.e3 ♘xc3 9.♖xc3 d6 10.♗e2 e5 11.0-0 a5 12.c5 ♘c6 13.cxd6 cxd6 14.d5 ♘b4 15.a3 ♘a6 16.♗xa6 ♖xa6 17.♕b3 ♕d8 18.♖fc1 ♖b6 19.♕c2 ♗d7 (Kraemer – Tregubov, Germany 2013) black is close to equality, all the more so as the aggressive 20.♖c7 ♗c6 21.♘g5 brings the game closer to a draw – 21...g6 22.♖xf7 ♕xg5 23.♖xf8+ ♔xf8 24.dxc6 ♖xc6 25.♕d2 ♖xc1+ 26.♕xc1.

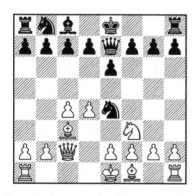

7...♘xc3
The move 7...f5 (continuing, for example, 8.e3 b6 9.♗d3 ♗b7 with

castling on either side) has more meat on it and appears a decent alternative to immediate simplifications.

8.♕xc3 0-0 9.e3
Grabbing space via 9.e4 d6 10.e5 promises very little. After 10...dxe5 11.dxe5 b6 the black bishop is excellently placed on the long diagonal, while the e5 pawn in the long run is most probably a weakness rather than a strong point.

9...d6 10.♗d3
Via a slightly different move order, the game Sanikidze – Asrian (Dresden 2007) illustrates the less than exciting play if the bishops are exchanged – 10.♗e2 ♘d7 11.0-0 b6 12.♘d2 c5 13.♖fd1 ♗b7 14.♗f3 ♘f6 15.♗xb7 ♕xb7 16.dxc5 bxc5 (16...dxc5 takes any remaining life out of the game) 17.♕c2 ♖fb8 18.b3 a5 19.♘b1 a4 20.♘c3 axb3 21.axb3 ♖xa1 22.♖xa1 h5 23.♘b5 d5 24.♖a7 ♖a8 25.♕a2 ♖xa7 26.♕xa7 ♕xa7 27.♘xa7. After having shown each other the weakness of their respective back ranks, the players soon agreed peace.

10...♘d7

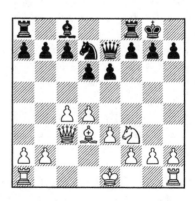

11.0-0-0

Krasenkow decided that his weaker opponent (by nearly 200 Elo points) would be easier to outplay with opposite-sides castling. There are as yet no objective grounds for thinking it was a better move.

11...e5 12.♗c2 ♖e8 13.h3 c6 14.g4 ♕f6

He should have played 14...e4 15.♘d2 d5, shutting the white pieces far from the black king, at least temporarily.

15.♘d2 d5 16.cxd5 cxd5 17.dxe5 ♘xe5?

After 17...♕xf2 18.♕d3 ♘f8 19.♖df1 ♕h4 the German master playing black could have fought almost as an equal, whereas now his position is poor.

18.f4 ♘c4 19.♕xf6 gxf6 20.♘xc4 dxc4 21.♗a4 ♖e7?!

Total confusion. He should have retreated to f8 or taken the pawn straight away.

22.♖d8+ ♔g7 23.♖hd1 ♖xe3 24.♗d7 ♗xd7 25.♖xa8 ♗c6

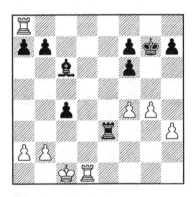

26.♖xa7

26.♖dd8 ♖xh3 27.♖g8+ ♔h6 28.♖ad8 ♖d3 (otherwise 29.♖d6) 29.♖xd3 cxd3 30.♔d2, was of course a more technical path to winning.

26...♖xh3 27.♖a3 ♖h2 28.♖c3 b5 29.a4 ♖e2 30.a5 ♖e7 31.♖d6 ♖c7 32.b3 ♗e4 33.♖b6 ♖c5 34.a6 h5 35.gxh5 ♖xh5 36.bxc4 ♖h1+ 37.♔d2 bxc4 38.♖xc4 f5 39.♖a4 ♖h2+ 40.♔e3 ♖h3+ 41.♔d4 ♖d3+ 42.♔c5 ♖d5+ 43.♔c4

Black resigned.

No. 91 E. Postny – I. Rozum
Yerevan 2014

1.d4 ♘f6 2.c4 e6 3.♘f3 ♗b4+ 4.♗d2 ♕e7 5.♘c3 0-0

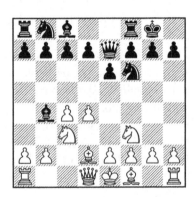

Control over e4 in a somewhat different situation (compared with game 88) – the dark-squared bishops have not been exchanged off.

6.♕c2

The continuation 6.e3 d6 7.♗e2 e5 8.0-0 ♗xc3 9.♗xc3 ♘e4 10.♖c1 ♘xc3 11.♖xc3 via a different move order is identical to the example Kraemer – Tregubov (the note to 7.♕c2 in game 90). However, it's better for white to retain the bishop pair via 10.♗e1 with chances of a small advantage after chasing the knight from e4. In his notes to the game Vidmar – Nimzowitsch (New York 1927) Alekhine assigned a question-mark to the move 6.e3 but an exclam to the move 6.♛c2 (with the idea of e2-e4 and ♛f1-d3). Today's theory sees no difference between these two moves.

6...d6 7.a3

To watch over the e4 square doesn't mean occupying it with white's pawn as soon as possible. If 7.e4 e5 8.d5 ♛g4 9.♛e2 ♘bd7 black has a comfortable position.

7...♛xc3 8.♛xc3

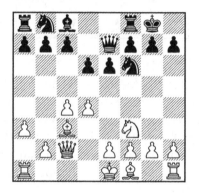

8...♘bd7

TRANSPOSITION ALERT. The continuation 8...♘c6 leads to a line of the Nimzo-Indian Defense 1.d4 ♘f6 2.c4 e6 3.♘c3 ♛b4 4.♛c2 ♘c6 5.♘f3 d6 6.♛d2 0-0 7.a3 ♛xc3 8.♛xc3 ♛e7. If white continues in the main line with 9.e3 e5 10.d5 ♘b8 11.♘d2, then the white army stands in harmony and the drawback of the move 8...♘c6 is clear.

9.e3

After 9.e4 e5 10.d5 ♘c5 11.♘d2 ♛d7 black is ready to exchange his bishop from the unusual square a4. That way he solves the problem of his knight, which in other Bogo-Indian Defense lines after b2-b4 usually ends up out of the action on a6.

9...b6

Usually the choice in such positions is between the fianchetto and developing the bishop along its main diagonal after 9...e5. Logical play by both sides with 10.♛e2 exd4 11.♘xd4 ♘c5 12.0-0 ♘ce4 13.♛e1 (Chernin – Oll, Pamplona 1992) led to black gaining control over e4 without trading white's dark-squared bishop.

> **KEY TIP.** The possibility of retreating ♛c3-e1 in the Bogo-Indian Defense is frequently useful for white, and it should be kept in mind.

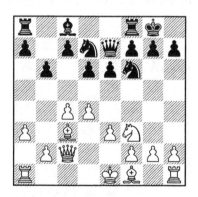

10.♛e2

The position after 10.♛d3 ♛b7 arises from various move orders in the Nimzo-Indian Defense (4.♛c2, 4.e3, 4.♛d2) in those unfortunate cases when white hasn't hurried to castle. Now he can castle on either side, or he can simplify as in the example Burmakin – Ikonnikov, Werfen 1996 – 11.♘g5 h6 12.♘h7 ♘xh7 13.♝xh7+ ♚h8 14.♝e4 ♝xe4 15.♕xe4 ♘f6 16.♕f3 a5. In this lifeless and equal position it doesn't matter anymore where the white king will take refuge.

10...♝b7 11.0-0

11.b4 frees up the b2 square for the bishop and also looks reasonable. The complicated variation 11...♘e4 12.♝b2 f5 13.0-0 ♖f6 14.d5 ♖h6 has been tried several times, in which either side has the chance to develop the initiative.

11...♘e4 12.♝e1

If 12.♘d2, then black either immediately exchanges on c3 (and after ♝e2-f3 a draw is in the offing) or continues to fight on equal terms with 12...f5 13.f3 ♘xc3 14.♕xc3 e5 or c6-c5.

12...f5 13.♖d1 c5 14.♚h1!? ♖f6 15.d5 exd5 16.cxd5 ♖h6 17.♘g1

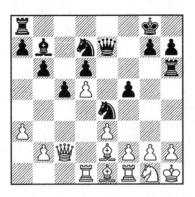

Now we see the reason for the white king's mysterious move to the corner. The knight's career will now impress, although white still doesn't have any advantage.

17...♖f8 18.♘h3 ♚h8 19.♕b3 ♘e5 20.f3 c4 21.♕c2

White can clearly not capture the pawn due to 21...♘c5 and black is winning.

21...♘c5 22.♘f4 b5 23.♕c3 g5 24.♘e6 ♘xe6 25.dxe6 ♖xe6

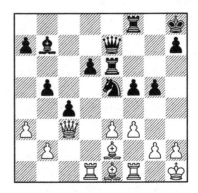

26.♕d4

26.f4?! doesn't win the knight due to 26...gxf4 27.exf4 ♕g7. Instead white carries out a nice idea to build a battery on the long diagonal, but he also had the more dynamic move 26.b3!? at his disposal.

26...♚g8 27.♝c3 f4 28.e4 a6 29.a4 ♖h6 30.axb5 axb5 31.♖a1

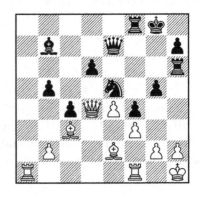

31...♕f7

A very interesting and double-edged position. The rook on the open file will come in very handy for white if 31...g4 32.fxg4 ♕h4 33.h3 ♕g3 34.♖f3 ♕xg4 35.♖a7 ♗c6 36.♕xd6!, and after the exchange of queens chances will be equal.

32.h3 ♗c8 33.♖f2 ♕h5 34.♗f1 g4 35.fxg4 ♗xg4?!

Rozum's idea has a hole in it, and so he should have captured the pawn with the queen.

36.♖a8! f3?! 37.♕d5+ ♕f7

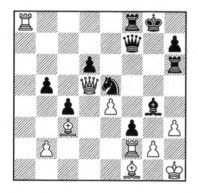

38.♖xf8+?

The low-key move 38.♗d2! would have won. Black's rook's retreat along the sixth rank would have left him without his pin, or moving it along the h-file would have cost him the d6 pawn. The point is that in the event of 38...♕xd5 white first takes with check on f8 and then on h6.

38...♔xf8 39.♗d2 fxg2+ 40.♗xg2 ♕xf2 41.♗xh6+ ♔e8 42.♕xb5+ ♔f7 43.♕b7+ ♗d7 44.♕d5+ ♗e6 45.♕xd6 ♕e1+ 46.♔h2 ♘g4+ 47.hxg4 ♕h4+ 48.♗h3 ♕xh6 49.♕c7+ ♔g6 50.♕d6 ♔f7 51.♕c7+

Draw agreed.

No. 92 E. Solozhenkin – J. Stocek
Pardubice 2016

1.d4 ♘f6 2.c4 e6 3.♘f3 ♗b4+ 4.♗d2 ♕e7 5.♘c3 b6

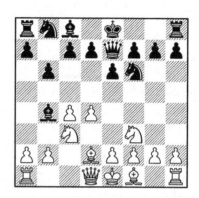

6.e3

The aim is for white to develop the bishop straight away and take control of e4. As we already know, black wants control of the square not so much to prevent the square being occupied by an enemy pawn, but more to support his knight in the center.

6...♗b7 7.♗d3

The actual move order in this game was 3...b6 4.e3 ♗b7 5.♗d3 ♗b4+ 6.♗d2 ♕e7 7.♘c3.

7.♗e2 0-0 8.0-0 d6 via a slightly different move order leads to the game Vidmar – Nimzowitsch (New York 1927). That continued 9.♕c2 ♘bd7 10.♖ad1 ♗xc3 11.♗xc3 ♘e4 (turning the game into a proper Dutch structure) 12.♗e1 f5 13.♕b3 c5 14.♘d2 ♘xd2 15.♖xd2 e5 16.dxe5 dxe5 17.f3 g5. Nimzowitsch and Alekhine prefer black here, but that assessment is only correct if queens remain on the board. After 18.♕d3 ♖ad8 19.♕d6 ♕xd6 20.♖xd6 ♘b8

21.♖xd8 ♖xd8 22.♗c3 the other rook pair will be swapped off and the game should end in a draw.

7...0-0 8.0-0 d6 9.♖e1

The battle for e4 is clearly illustrated in the line 9.♕c2 c5 10.♘g5 h6 11.♘ge4 ♘bd7 12.a3 ♗xc3 13.♗xc3 ♘xe4 14.♗xe4 ♗xe4 15.♕xe4 ♘f6 16.♕d3, which should be a draw but black is slightly better. The players have few resources left to continue playing. In moving his rook, Solozhenkin intends e3-e4.

9...♗xc3 10.♗xc3 ♘e4 11.♗xe4 ♗xe4 12.♘d2 ♗b7

12...♗g6, followed by c7-c6 and d6-d5 is an equally good alternative.

13.e4 e5 14.♘f1 c5

14...exd4 15.♕xd4 f6 neutralizes white's otherwise deadly battery, but isn't enough for equality – the white knight will still get on black's nerves.

15.dxe5

Despite being favored by the computer, 15.d5 promises white very little. He has no prospects on the queenside, while black will meet f2-f4 with f7-f6.

15...dxe5 16.♘e3 ♘c6 17.♘d5 ♕d6 18.♕h5 ♘d4 19.♖ad1 ♖ae8 20.♖d3 ♖e6

21.♕d1

It's also worth noting the following mutually destructive line: 21.f4 f5 22.fxe5 ♖xe5 23.♗xd4 cxd4 24.♖xd4 fxe4 25.♕d1 ♗xd5 26.♖xd5 ♖xd5 27.♕xd5+ ♕xd5 28.cxd5 ♖d8 29.♖xe4 ♖xd5. This type of climax happens when both players have knights in the center and bishops can exchange them. The queen's retreat suggest that 18.♕h5 wasn't the best move.

21...b5 22.b4!

This is the only way for white to maintain some sort of equality.

22...bxc4 23.bxc5 ♕xc5 24.♗xd4 exd4 25.♖xd4 f5 26.♘f4 ♖ee8

26...♖e5!? would require precise play from white – 27.♕a1! c3 (27... fxe4 28.♖xc4) 28.♖d3 ♖c8 29.♘e2 c2 30.♖c3 ♕e7 31.♖xc8+ ♗xc8 32.♖c1 ♖c5 33.♘c3, liquidating the passer.

27.e5 ♗e4 28.e6 c3 29.♖d7 c2

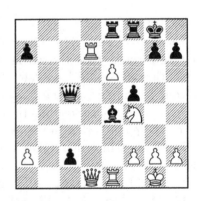

30.♕a1?!

Here the strength of the passer forces white to attack the enemy king as early as possible. But he should have added the knight to the attack – 30.♕d2 ♖b8 31.♘h5 ♔h8

32.♖xg7 ♖b1 33.e7 ♖xe1+ 34.♕xe1 ♖e8 35.♖f7 ♔g8 (the threat of a deadly check from a1 forces a repeat of moves) 36.♖g7+.

30...♖e7 31.♖xe7?

The right continuation was 31.♕b2, whereas Stocek had a way to refute white's placing of his queen on c3.

31...♕xe7 32.♕c3 ♕b7?

It wasn't so easy to find 32...♖d8 33.♕b3 a5! 34.♔f1 ♖d4! with the murderous threat of a5-a4.

33.f3?!

Solozhenkin must surely have seen the draw after 33.e7 ♕xe7 34.♕xc2. It's a mystery why he didn't play it.

33...♖c8 34.e7 ♔f7

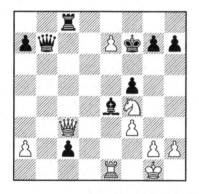

35.♕d2?

After 35.e8=♕+! ♔xe8 36.♕e3 ♕b1 37.♖c1 ♕xc1+ 38.♕xc1 ♖d8 39.♘e2 ♖d1+ 40.♔f2 ♖xc1 41.♘xc1 ♗c6 42.♔e3 white can hold the endgame, whereas now he falls into the abyss.

35...♕xe7 36.♘d3 ♗xd3 37.♖xe7+ ♔xe7 38.♕c1 ♖b8 39.♔f2 ♖b1 40.♕a3+ ♔f7 41.♕xd3 c1=♕ 42.♕xf5+ ♔e7 43.♕e5+

♔d8 44.♕d6+ ♔c8 45.♕e6+ ♔b8 46.♕e8+ ♕c8 47.♕e5+ ♔a8 48.♕e4+ ♖b7 49.♕xh7 ♕b8 50.h4 ♕e5 51.♔g1 g5

White resigned.

No. 93 D. Shinkar – P. Kiriakov
Perm 1998

1.d4 ♘f6 2.♘f3 e6 3.c4 ♗b4+ 4.♗d2 ♕e7 5.a3

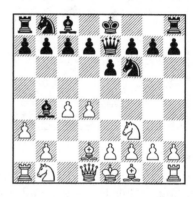

White forces the exchange of dark-squared bishops, believing that the pawn on a3 will come in handy later. This move is even more popular than 5.♘c3, though there are far fewer games at grandmaster level.

5...♗xd2+ 6.♕xd2

Capturing by the knight is reviewed in game 94.

6...d6

6...b6 7.♘c3 ♗b7 is also acceptable. If 8.♕c2 then 8...c5 is logical, given that the queen no longer supports d4-d5. After 8.e3 d6 9.♗e2 ♘bd7 10.0-0 0-0 11.♕c2 c5 12.♖fd1 white plans to push d4-d5, but black preempts this with 12...d5!?

7.♘c3 0-0

If 7...e5 8.dxe5 dxe5 white winning the pawn via a double attack guarantees black a draw – 9.♕g5 ♘c6 10.♕xg7 ♖g8 11.♕h6 e4 12.♘h4 (the best move) 12...♘g4 13.♕xh7 ♘f6. It's better for white to continue 9.e4 with the idea of ♘c3-d5.

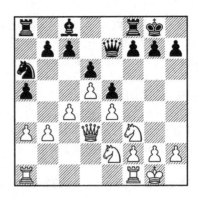

14...f5

White is unable to hold e4 and has to fight for equality.

15.exf5 ♗xf5 16.♕e3 ♘c5 17.♘ed4

17.b4 was stronger, in order to meet 17...♘d3 with an offer to exchange knights from e1, or to meet 17...♘e4 with the same offer, from the c3 square.

17...♗e4! 18.♘e6 ♗xf3 19.♘xf8 ♖xf8 20.gxf3 ♖f4

Kiriakov plays inaccurately, but his opponent fails to punish him. He should have focused on his knight's career (20...a4), and after he missed it white should have continued 21.b4.

21.♖fc1?! a4 22.bxa4 ♕g5+ 23.♔h1 ♕f6 24.♔g2

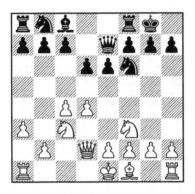

8.e4

If 8.e3 e5 9.d5 a5 10.♕c2 ♘a6 the knight heads to c5, and the bishop via g4 and h5 to g6. Play may merge with the 4...♕e7 or 4... a5 lines, which we will also see later. Obviously, after 5.a3 the move a7-a5 is an apt one.

8...e5 9.d5

If 9.dxe5 dxe5 10.♘d5 it makes sense to reply 10...♕d6 11.c5 ♕d8 – luring the pawn to c5 has deprived the knight of this outpost.

9...a5 10.b3 ♘a6 11.♗d3 ♘h5

It was better to play 11...♗g4. The knight is heading for f4, in order to be immediately exchanged for white's "bad" bishop. Still, black demonstrates concrete arguments to support his idea.

12.0-0 ♘f4 13.♘e2 ♘xd3 14.♕xd3

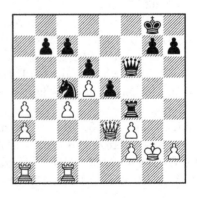

24...h6

This prophylaxis is driven by the need to avoid the line 24...♕g6+ 25.♔h1 ♕h5 26.♖g1 ♖xf3 27.♕g5. Shinkar now misses 25.♖g1, and the game's outcome is decided.

25.a5?   ♕g6+   26.♔h1   ♕h5 27.♔g2 ♖h4 28.h3

Or 28.♖h1 ♕f5 with the same idea of bringing over the knight that is played in the game.

28...♕g6+   29.♔h2   ♕f5   30.f4 ♖xf4   31.♔g2   e4   32.♕g3   ♘d3 33.♖c2 h5 34.♖g1 ♖f3 35.♕h4 ♘f4+ 36.♔f1 e3 37.♖g3 ♖xf2+

White resigned.

No. 94 D. Fernandez – S. Williams
Torquay 2013

1.d4 ♘f6 2.c4 e6 3.♘f3 ♗b4+ 4.♗d2 ♕e7 5.a3 ♗xd2+ 6.♘bxd2

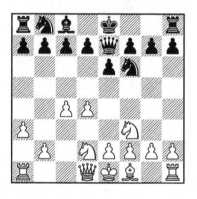

6...d6

If black wants to play a line similar to the Queen's Gambit with 6...d5 then he will still aim for an early e6-e5 – 7.e3 0-0 8.♗d3 ♘bd7 9.0-0 e5 10.♘xe5 ♘xe5 11.dxe5 ♕xe5 12.♕c2. White still has a more pleasant position here, and e6-e5 is

much more often combined with d7-d6.

7.e4

After 7.e3 white often exchanges on e5 and allows e5-e4. The game Hoffmann – Ikonnikov (Untergrombach 1999) continued: 7...e5 8.dxe5 dxe5 9.h3 0-0 10.♕c2 e4 11.♘d4 c5 12.♘b5 b6 13.g3 ♗b7 14.♗g2 ♘bd7 15.♘c3 ♖fe8. The attack on the e-pawn and its protection are balanced, and there is no easy way for white to improve his position.

7...e5 8.d5

White has no reason to preserve tension in the center. In the approximate variation 8.♗d3 0-0 9.0-0 ♗g4 10.♕c2 ♘bd7 11.♖fe1 ♗xf3 12.♘xf3 exd4 13.♘xd4 ♕e5 14.♘f3 ♕f4 black's queen is sitting comfortably on the dark squares and chances are equal.

8...0-0

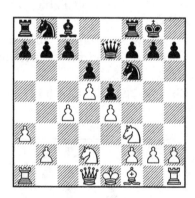

9.g3

White uses the pawn to protect his knight on h4, and never completes a fianchetto. In any case, the white bishop carries out only defensive functions. Another example is 9.♗d3

♘h5 10.g3 g6 11.0-0 ♘g7 12.♖e1 f5 13.c5 f4 14.cxd6 cxd6 15.♖c1 ♗g4 16.♗e2 ♘e8 17.♘c4 ♘d7 18.b4 ♕f6 19.♔g2 g5 20.h3 ♗h5 21.g4 ♗g6 22.♘fd2 ♕g7 23.♘a5 ♘df6 24.f3 ♖f7 with play reaching a dead end and a draw just around the corner. This is not a modern game as it may seem, but from the classics: Nimzowitsch – Tarrasch (Semmering 1926).

9...c6

Grandmaster Williams, in keeping with the English school of eccentric openings, grants the game an unusual character. A more typical game is Erdos – Jakab (Budapest 2005): 9...a5 10.b3 ♘a6 11.♗g2 ♘c5 12.♕e2 c6 (a typical ploy here) 13.dxc6 (a questionable move, as will be seen subsequently) 13...bxc6 14.0-0 ♗g4 15.♖ab1 ♖fb8 16.♖fc1 ♖b6 17.♕e3 ♗xf3 18.♗xf3 ♖ab8 19.♕c3 ♕a7 20.b4 axb4 21.axb4 ♘e6 with the idea of invading on d4 and the advantage.

10.♘h4   b5!?   11.cxb5   cxd5 12.exd5 e4?!

12...g6 was stronger, in order to place the bishop on b7 without allowing ♘h4-f5.

13.♘c4 ♗g4 14.♗e2 ♗h3 15.♗f1 ♗g4

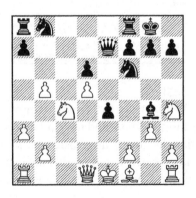

16.♕d4 Fernandez isn't afraid of his titled opponent and continues the fight. 16.♕d2!? was probably an even more ambitious choice.

16...♘bd7 17.h3 ♗f3 18.♘xf3

If 18.♘f5 ♕d8 19.♖g1 ♘c5 chances are equal. Were the queen on d2 white would have continued 20.♕g5.

18...exf3+ 19.♘e3 ♖fe8 20.♗d3 ♘c5 21.♗c2 ♕d7 22.0-0-0

A risky venture. After 22.a4 ♘ce4 white will no longer castle, but with 23.♔f1 he frees up a square for his rook and via ♗c2-d1 is ready to test the health of the f3 pawn.

22...♕xb5 23.♔b1 ♖ab8 24.♘f5

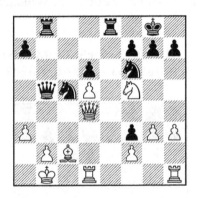

24...♕d7?!

Why did he retreat? The computer points to move repetition via 24...♘ce4 25.♖he1 ♘d2+ 26.♔a2 ♖e2 27.♘xd6 ♕a5 28.♘f5 ♕b5, and the grandmaster was capable of finding it.

25.♖he1   ♖e2   26.♖xe2   fxe2 27.♖e1 ♖e8 28.g4 ♖e5 29.f4 ♖xd5 30.♕c3

After 30.♕e3 black is in a rather poor state, whereas now he gets to improve his position.

30...♘ce4 31.♕b4 ♖b5 32.♕d4 ♕b7?

If 32...♖d5 the only way for white to attempt to win is via 33.♕e3, but then 33...♖d2 holds the defense! Williams overestimates his threat against b2.

33.♖xe2 ♖xb2+ 34.♔c1 ♖xc2+ 35.♖xc2 h6 36.♘xd6 ♘xd6 37.♕xd6 ♕b3

38.♕b4?!

Fernandez is in a hurry to chase black's queen away from the white king, but loses pawns in the process. He would have won quickly with 38.♖c8+ ♔h7 39.♕c5 g6 40.♕e7 ♘g8 41.♕xa7.

38...♕xh3 39.♕b8+?!

He should only have gone hunting the a7 pawn after consolidating (39. ♔b2!).

39...♔h7 40.♕xa7 ♕f1+?

Probably in time trouble, the grandmaster chose the wrong target. After 40...♘xg4 black not only picks up a pawn but is ready to bring his knight to attack white's king. The computer shows the position as all zeros.

41.♔b2 ♕xf4 42.♕xf7 ♕xg4 43.♕c4 ♕f5 44.a4 h5 45.♕c5 ♘d5 46.♖d2 ♕e5+ 47.♖d4 ♕b8+ 48.♔c1 ♘f6 49.♕f5+ ♔g8 50.a5 ♕c7+ 51.♔b2 ♕b7+ 52.♔a3 ♕c6 53.♕d3 ♕c1+ 54.♔a4 ♕a1+ 55.♔b5 ♕b2+ 56.♔c6 ♕g2+ 57.♔c5 h4 58.a6 h3 59.♕b3+ ♔h7 60.♖h4+ ♔g6 61.♖xh3 ♕g5+ 62.♔c6 ♕g2+ 63.♔b6 ♕f2+ 64.♔b7 ♕g2+ 65.♔b8 ♕c6 66.♖g3+ ♔h6 67.♖h3+ ♔g6 68.♕g3+

Black resigned.

We have now analyzed the strong developing move 4...♕e7, where diversions from the main reply, 5.g3, do not promise white anything much. Choices of 5.♕c2, 5.e3, 5.♘c3 or 5.a3 are often made simply to avoid known theory.

Chapter 17

Various after 4...♕e7 5.g3

No. 95 S. Halkias – A. Kelires
Thessaloniki 2017

1.♘f3 ♘f6 2.c4 e6 3.d4 ♗b4+ 4.♗d2 ♕e7 5.g3

The main line, which continues to be popular at both club and GM levels. It's only in this Bogo-Indian Defense system that theory has lines goes well into double figures.

5...♗xd2+

Here the exchange is tied to a specific line that has been widely tried in very recent times. 5...0-0 is analyzed in games 96-99., 5...b6 in chapter 18, and 5...♘c6 in chapters 19 and 20.

6.♕xd2

If 6.♘bxd2 d6 7.♗g2 e5 8.e4 ♗g4 9.♕a4+ ♘bd7 10.0-0 0-0 11.♖fe1 c5!? 12.dxe5 dxe5 13.♘h4 g6 14.h3 ♗e6 15.♕c2 ♘b8 (Chetverik – Van der Stricht, Geraardsbergen 2019) white should justify the position of his knight on d2 with the maneuver

16.♘f1 ♘c6 17.♘e3. The knights will occupy the outposts d5 and d4, where they will probably be exchanged and the players will have equal chances.

6...♘c6 7.♘c3

We will check whether 7.♗g2 is better than its reputation in chapter 19 when we review it through the move order 5...♘c6 6.♗g2 ♗xd2+ 7.♕xd2. After 7.e3 d5 the move 8.♗g2 was seen, in particular, in the game Lysyj – Palchun (Sochi 2017): 8...dxc4 9.0-0 0-0 10.♕c3 e5 11.♘xe5 ♘xe5 12.dxe5 ♘g4 13.f4 ♕c5 14.♖e1 ♖d8 15.♘a3 ♗e6 16.♖ac1 ♕b6 17.♗e4 h5 18.h3 ♘h6 19.♘xc4 ♕a6. Now the prophylaxis 20.♔h2 ensured a significant advantage for white, as 20...♕xa2? is bad due to 21.♘a5.

Black should have carried out the standard break one move earlier – when white was unable to maintain his pawn on e5. In the example Carlsen – Papaioannou (Reykjavik 2015) after 9...e5 10.♘xe5 ♘xe5 11.dxe5 ♕xe5 12.♘a3 0-0 13.♘xc4 ♕e7 14.♖ac1 ♖d8 15.♕a5 c6 the world champion failed to gain any advantage and was unable to outplay his much weaker opponent.

7...d5

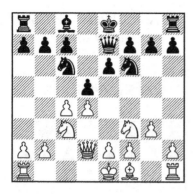

8.♗g2

The line 8.♘e5 dxc4 9.♘xc6 bxc6 10.♗g2 looks similar to a Catalan, but it cannot be arrived at via the Catalan Opening. After 10...0-0 11.♗xc6 ♖b8 12.0-0 ♖d8 13.♖fd1 ♕d6!? (13...e5 14.d5 is slightly more complicated, but also worth playing for black) 14.♗g2 c5 15.d5 exd5 16.♘xd5 ♘xd5 17.♕xd5 ♕xd5 18.♗xd5 ♗e6 19.♗xe6 fxe6 20.♖xd8+ ♖xd8 21.♖c1 ♖d2 22.♖xc4 ♖xb2 23.a4 ♖b4 24.♖xc5 ♖xa4 25.♖c7 white in the game Dreev – Lomasov (Yaroslavl 2018) squeezed water from a stone against the young prodigy.

The exchange 8.cxd5 exd5 grants black's bishop his freedom and doesn't offer white any advantage. In the game Dorfman – Tregubov (Brest 2018) black improved the position of his pawns and easily equalized after 9.♗g2 0-0 10.0-0 ♖e8 11.♕f4 ♘d8 12.♖ad1 c6 13.♕c1 ♘e4 14.♘e5 ♗f5 15.♖fe1 f6 16.♘d3 ♘f7 17.♘xe4 ♗xe4 18.♘c5 ♗xg2 19.♔xg2 ♘g5.

8...dxc4 9.♘e5

If 9.0-0 0-0 10.e4 ♖d8 11.e5 ♘d5 12.♕e2 ♘a5 13.♘d2 b6 white will not win the pawn back and compensation

for it is somewhat lacking. Here, as in the game, play followed the spirit of the Catalan Gambit.

9...♘xe5

In reply to 9...0-0 it's fine to go for a typical Catalan ploy – exchanging the light-squared bishop (while retaining the knight, which is more valuable in such circumstances). In the game Prohaszka – Sagar (Zalakaros 2015) white's strategic advantage grew to quite a solid size: 10.♗xc6!? bxc6 11.0-0 c5 12.♖fd1 ♗b7 13.dxc5 ♕xc5 14.♕d4 ♕xd4 15.♖xd4 ♗d5?! (15...♗a6!?) 16.f3 ♖ab8 17.e4 c5 18.♖d2 ♗b7 19.♖ad1.

10.dxe5 ♘d7

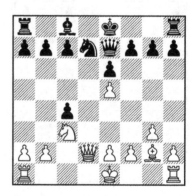

11.♕d4

White should be careful when selecting Kozul's plan 11.f4 0-0 12.0-0-0. He has nicely placed pieces, but his prospects of attacking the enemy king are less clear than black's prospects of doing the same.

11...♕b4!?

An interesting novelty to protect his pawn and at the same time attack one of white's. The exchange of queens after 11...♕c5 12.♕xc5 ♘xc5 13.0-0-0 (as Caruana played in a rapid game) still gives quite some advantage.

If 11...♘b6 12.0-0 0-0 13.♖fd1 ♖b8 14.♖d2 ♗d7 15.♖ad1 white still has the initiative (Michalik – Babula, Mayrhofen 2015).

12.0-0   0-0   13.♖fd1   ♕xb2 14.♖ab1 ♕a3 15.♕xc4 c6

Or 15...♘xe5 16.♕xc7 ♘c6 17.♗xc6 ♕xc3 18.♖bc1 ♕b2 19.♗e4 – it's unpleasant for a human to play this line as black, even if the computer doesn't think there's much in it.

16.f4 ♘b6 17.♕d3 ♕a5 18.♘e4 ♘d5 19.♘g5 g6 20.♘e4 b6

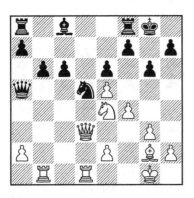

Kelires has skillfully repaired his queenside problems, and white's action around the black king will not catch him unawares.

21.♕f3 ♗a6 22.g4 f5!? 23.exf6 ♘xf6 24.♘xf6+ ♖xf6 25.♕xc6 ♖c8 26.♕e4 ♕xa2 27.♕e5 ♖f7 28.♗f3 ♕c4 29.♖a1 ♗b5 30.♖ac1 ♕xc1 31.♖xc1 ♖xc1+ 32.♔f2 ♗c6

32...♗d7 would have built an impregnable fortress. The exchange of bishops also leads to a draw.

33.♕xe6 ♗xf3 34.♕e8+ ♖f8 35.♕e6+ ♖f7 36.♕e8+ ♖f8 37.♕e6+

Draw agreed.

No. 96 A. Khalifman – P. Golubka
Batumi 2018

1.d4 ♘f6 2.c4 e6 3.♘f3 ♗b4+ 4.♗d2 ♕e7 5.g3 0-0 6.♗g2

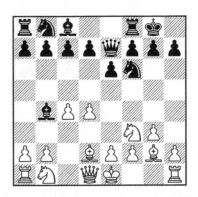

6...d5

The evaluation of the exchange via 6...♘e4 has not changed. All of black's developed pieces leave the board, while it's not easy to develop the remaining ones nicely. For example, 7.0-0 ♗xd2 8.♘bxd2 ♘xd2 9.♕xd2 d6 10.♕c3 (the sides are battling over the move e6-e5) 10...♘d7 11.♖ad1 c6 12.b4 e5 13.dxe5 dxe5 14.c5 ♖e8 (it was better to open a file for the rook via 14...a5) 15.♘d2 ♘f6 16.♘c4 ♗g4 17.♖d2 ♖ed8 18.♘d6 ♘e8 19.h3 ♗c8 20.♖fd1 ♘xd6 21.cxd6 ♕e8 22.♕c5, and victory isn't far off (Bluebaum – Hoemann, Nuremberg 2012).

7.0-0 ♗xd2

If 7...♘bd7 8.♕c2 c6 9.♗xb4 ♕xb4 10.♘bd2 white chases the queen away with a2-a3, and after e2-e4 the position is a Catalan without dark-squared bishops favorable for white.

8.♘bxd2

Currently this is the most popular move, although 8.♕xd2 may be reached via the move order 4...♗xd2+ 5.♕xd2 d5 6.g3 0-0 7.♗g2 ♕e7 8.0-0. This variation, which is similar in ideas to the Catalan, became well known in particular thanks to Kasparov's games: Kasparov – Petrosian (Bugojno 1982), Kasparov – Timman (Belgrade 1989), and Kasparov – Ljubojevic (Tilburg 1989). The evaluation hasn't changed: white can count on an advantage after 8...♖d8 9.♖c1 ♘c6 10.♘a3 dxc4 11.♘xc4 e5 12.♘cxe5 ♘xd4 13.♘xd4 ♕xe5 14.e3 ♕e7?! (14...♕d6!?) 15.♕a5 c6 (15...♗d7 is objectively slightly better) 16.♖xc6! (Vorobiov – Sundararajan, Pontevedra 2016).

8...♖d8

It's probably too early to start a fight in the center with 8...♘bd7. It's not easy for black to neutralize his opponent's advantage, like in the example Postny – Kosic, Dresden 2008: 9.♕c2 c5 10.dxc5 ♕xc5 (10...♘xc5 11.b4 ♘ce4 12.♘xe4 ♘xe4 13.a3 a5 14.b5) 11.♖fc1 ♘b6 12.♘e5 dxc4 13.♘dxc4 ♘xc4 14.♘xc4 ♖b8 15.♘e3 ♕xc2 16.♖xc2 ♗d7 17.♖ac1 ♖fc8 18.♘c4.

9.♕c2

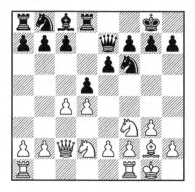

9...♘c6

If 9...c5 10.dxc5 ♕xc5 11.♘b3 ♕xc4 12.♕xc4 dxc4 13.♘a5 c3 14.bxc3 the white pawns are broken up, but he retains his advantage. The difference in the positions of the bishops continues to make itself felt.

10.♖fd1 ♘b4 11.♕c3 a5

After 11...c5 12.dxc5 ♕xc5 13.a3 ♘c6 14.b4 ♕b6 15.e3 ♗d7 16.♖ac1 ♖ac8 17.♕b2 ♘e7 18.c5 ♕a6 19.♘d4 white's strategic success is obvious (Zoler – Rios, La Bordeta 2010). In the analyzed game black prevents b2-b4, but in the key variation the a5 pawn is left hanging...

12.♘e5 c5?!

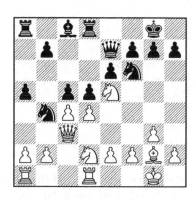

13.♘b3

...and specifically, after 13.dxc5 ♕xc5 14.cxd5 ♕xc3 15.bxc3 ♘bxd5 16.♘dc4 b5 17.♘xa5! In the actual game white's advantage gradually disappears.

13...cxd4 14.♘xd4 ♗d7 15.a3 ♘c6 16.♘xd7 ♕xd7 17.cxd5

It was better to retain the tension with 17.♖ac1.

17...♘xd5 18.♕e1 ♕e8 19.e3 ♘e5 20.♖ac1 g6 21.♕e2 ♖ac8

22.♖xc8 ♖xc8 23.♗xd5 exd5 24.♘f3 ♖c5 25.♘xe5 ♕xe5 26.♖d4 Draw agreed.

No. 97 S. Vidit – J. Cori
Biel 2019

1.d4 ♘f6 2.c4 e6 3.♘f3 ♗b4+ 4.♗d2 ♕e7 5.g3 0-0 6.♗g2 ♗xd2+ 7.♕xd2

We covered the capture with the knight in game 3 of the historical introduction.

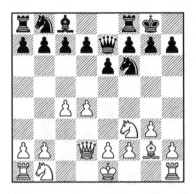

7...d6

After 7...♘e4 8.♕c2 ♕b4+ 9.♘bd2 ♘xd2 10.♘xd2 ♘c6 11.e3 the queen on b4 isn't threatening anything and will have to retreat, losing time. A transposition to a Dutch structure isn't very promising. After 8...f5 9.0-0 d6 10.♘c3 ♘xc3 11.♕xc3 ♘d7 12.b4 ♘f6 (12...e5 13.dxe5 dxe5 14.c5 with the idea of c5-c6) 13.a4 ♗d7 14.b5 a6 15.♘d2 ♖fb8 16.♖fb1 c6 17.bxc6 ♗xc6 18.a5 in the game Dautov – Lisek (Deizisau 2016) black solved the problem of his queen's bishop but remained steadily worse.

8.0-0 e5

In practice, black often waits to move his e-pawn, but has to make this move sooner or later to avoid being cramped to death.

9.♘c3

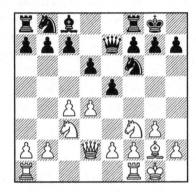

9...♘c6

Attacking d4, black attempts to provoke a crisis in the center. 9...♖e8 will be analyzed in games 98 and 99.

10.♘d5

This highlights the drawback of the queen sitting on e7. After 10.d5 ♘b8 11.e4 a5 12.♘e1 ♘a6 13.♘d3 ♘d7 black is successful in his challenge for c5 and gains counter chances on the queenside. For example, 14.f4 ♘ac5 15.♘f2 ♘b6 16.b3 a4 17.b4 ♘a6 18.a3 ♘xc4 19.♕e2 ♘b6 20.f5 f6 (Kozul – Cekro, Novi Sad 2009) – the black knights are on awkward squares, but he has an extra pawn as compensation.

10...♕d8

Black should avoid 10...♘xd5 11.cxd5 ♘xd4 12.♘xd4 exd4 13.♖ac1 ♗f5 14.♖fe1 ♕e5 15.♖c4 ♖ac8 16.♖xd4 ♖fe8 17.e3 (Epishin – Schulz, Bad Zwischenahn 2010). White has restored the balance and is now ready to attack black's weak queenside pawns.

11.♖fd1

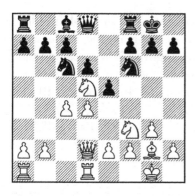

11...♖e8

After 11...♗g4 12.dxe5 dxe5 13.♕e3 ♘d7 14.♖d2 ♖e8 15.♖ad1 ♕c8 16.h3 ♗xf3 17.♕xf3 ♘d4?! 18.♕a3 (Borges Mateos – Quezada, Habana 2001) the centralizing of the knight suddenly goes pear shaped for black – apart from the threat of 19.♘e7+ the move 19.e3 is most unpleasant. Only the white knight is looking good in the center!

12.dxe5 ♘xe5 13.♘xe5 ♖xe5

13...dxe5 is met by the strong 14.♕a5!, and after the forced exchange the d5 pawn looks down on its counterpart on c7.

14.♖ac1 ♗g4 15.♖e1 ♖e8

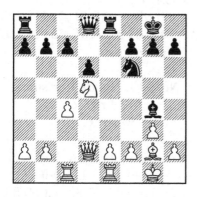

16.♖c3

This move is to double rooks on the e-file after e2-e4. However, it's not easy to find a good move for black after 16.♕f4!

16...♖b8 17.e4 ♘d7 18.f4 ♗e6 19.b3 a5 20.♖ce3 ♖a8 21.♕d4 ♖b8 22.♘c3 f6

Later, this pawn will become a hook for an attack. The Indian grandmaster playing white is doing well, although he could have been more energetic.

23.♘b5 ♖a8 24.♕d2 ♕c8 25.♘d4 ♗f7 26.♕c3 ♕b8 27.h4 ♕a7 28.♗h3 ♖ad8 29.♔h2 ♕c5 30.g4 ♘f8?!

Black is inconsistent. After 30...♕b4 31.♕xb4 axb4 32.♘b5 ♖c8 33.g5 ♗e6 34.♗xe6+ ♖xe6 the useful exchanges give him reason to count on a draw.

31.g5 ♘g6 32.♖f1 ♘xh4?

Clearly he had missed white's 35th move. He should have sought counterplay on the queenside via 32...♕b4 33.♕d3 fxg5 34.hxg5 a4.

33.gxf6 gxf6 34.♖g3+ ♔f8

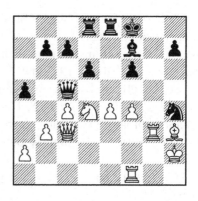

35.♘e6+! ♗xe6 36.♕xf6+ ♗f7 37.♕h6+ ♔e7 38.♕xh4+ ♔f8 39.♕h6+ ♔e7 40.♖g7

Black resigned.

No. 98 P. Prohaszka – V. Kazakovskiy
Fagernes 2017

1.d4 ♘f6 2.c4 e6 3.g3 ♗b4+ 4.♗d2 ♕e7 5.♘f3 ♗xd2+ 6.♕xd2 0-0 7.♗g2 d6 8.♘c3 e5 9.0-0 ♖e8 10.e4

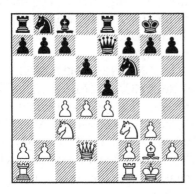

10...c6

The main continuation is 10...♗g4 (game 99). Pushing the pawn can lead to a number of setups, including the unusual "fire-proof" one in this game.

11.♖fe1

It's best to prevent black's bishop from developing on g4, hence 11.h3 is played more often. The game could continue 11...♘bd7 12.♖ad1 ♘f8 13.♖fe1 ♘g6, and then, probably, ♗c8-d7, ♖a8-d8 and ♗d7-c8. Hand to hand combat is postponed, and the starting positions are slightly better for white.

11...♘a6 12.h3 ♘c7 13.♖ad1 b6 14.b4

The Hungarian grandmaster playing white plays very inventively. In the game Bluvshtein – Tu Hoang Thong (Ottava 2007) white played

that move later, making do with the opening of the b-file with the exchange of all the rooks and equality: 14.♘h4 g6 15.♔h2 ♘h5 16.♘f3 ♖b8 17.b4 f6 18.d5 c5 19.a3 ♗d7 20.♖b1 ♕f8 21.♘g1 ♔h8 22.♘ge2 f5 23.bxc5 bxc5 24.exf5 gxf5 25.♖xb8 ♖xb8 26.♖b1 ♖xb1 27.♘xb1.

14...♗b7

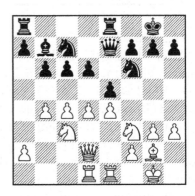

15.c5! exd4 16.♘xd4 dxc5 17.♘f5 ♕f8 18.bxc5 ♕xc5

After 18...♖ed8 19.♘d6 ♖ab8 20.e5 ♘fe8 black's position is difficult, but he has better chances of saving the day than when accepting the sacrifice.

19.e5! ♖ad8

19...♖xe5? loses due to 20.♖xe5 ♕xe5 21.♕g5.

20.♕xd8 ♖xd8 21.♖xd8+ ♘fe8 22.♘e4 ♕b4 23.♖ed1 ♕a4 24.♖1d7 Black resigned.

No. 99 T. Hillarp Persson – A. Eriksson
Vasteras 2016

1.d4 ♘f6 2.c4 e6 3.g3 ♗b4+ 4.♗d2 ♕e7 5.♘f3 0-0 6.♗g2 ♗xd2+ 7.♕xd2 d6 8.♘c3 e5 9.0-0 ♖e8 10.e4 ♗g4

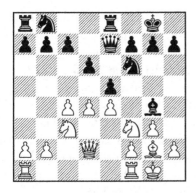

In such closed or semi-closed positions the bishop is no stronger than the knight, and black strives to swap it off. In a cramped position he will be better off without the bishop.

11.♘e1

White avoids the exchange, so that he can rationally use the knight in his base camp. The drawback of the move 11.♘h4 is that after 11...♘c6 it's not easy to protect d4. That said, in the game Sethuraman – Iljin (Leiden 2013) white gained a clear advantage after 12.h3 ♗d7 13.♘b5 ♕d8 14.d5 ♘e7 15.♘c3 ♘g6 16.♘f3 h6 17.b4 ♘h7 18.c5 ♘g5 19.♘xg5 hxg5 20.♖ac1. Counterplay on the queenside via 16...a6 17.b4 ♕c8 18.♔h2 c5 19.dxc6 ♕xc6 partially neutralizes white's advantage.

The short draw Movsziszian – Galego (Can Picafort 2008) is an excellent demonstration of how little white achieves if he goes along with black's plan. After 11.d5 ♗xf3 12.♗xf3 a5 13.♗g2 ♘a6 14.♖fe1 ♘c5 15.h4 c6 16.♕e2 cxd5 17.cxd5 a4 18.♗h3 ♕c7 19.♖ac1 ♕b6 20.♖c2 the players are out of ideas.

11...♘c6

After 11...exd4 12.♕xd4 ♘c6 13.♕d2 white has won all the games in the database. Here he plans to plant his knight on d5 and protect it with his other knight from e3.

12.♘c2

If white first wants to chase the bishop away, then it's best done via h2-h3. After black concedes the center, white attempts to build a pawn chain e4-f4-g3-h3, while 12.f3 would just be a loss of tempo.

12...♘xd4   13.♘xd4   exd4 14.♕xd4

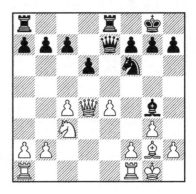

White has more space and reasonable chances of improving his position. It will be quite difficult for black to gain counter chances.

14...c5

Later, Eriksson, as is usual in this line, avoided weakening his pawn chain and continued 14...♕e5 15.♕d2 ♗d7 16.♖fe1 ♗c6 17.♖ac1 ♕a5 18.f3 ♕b6+ 19.♕f2 ♕xf2+ 20.♔xf2 ♔f8 (20...♖ac8 21.♘d5 ♗d7 is somewhat better) 21.♘d5 ♗xd5 22.cxd5 ♖e7 23.♖c4 ♔e8 24.♖ec1 ♔d8 (Moreau – Eriksson, Sweden 2018). He failed to hold this bleak endgame.

15.♕d2 ♖ad8 16.h3 ♗d7 17.♖fe1 ♗c6 18.f4 ♕c7 19.♖ad1 a6 20.g4

20.a4 is more accurate, in order to prevent black's counterplay on the queenside.

20...h6 21.♘d5 ♗xd5 22.cxd5 ♘d7 23.h4 b5 24.g5 hxg5 25.hxg5 c4 26.♗f1 ♘c5

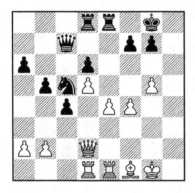

27.♕g2 ♖e7

White has built a threatening pawn chain at the cost of destroying his king's bunker. With this in mind,

it was worth considering 27...♕a7 28.♔h2 g6, threatening to transfer the rook to the h-file.

28.♔h1 ♖de8 29.e5 ♘b7??

A fatal miscalculation. After 29...♕d7 30.e6 fxe6 31.g6 exd5 32.♕h2 ♖xe1 33.♕h7+ ♔f8 34.♕h8+ ♔e7 the rook on e8 is protected by the queen, unlike in the game, and white has nothing better than perpetual check from h4 and h8.

30.e6! fxe6 31.g6 exd5 32.♕h3 ♖e4 33.♖xe4 dxe4 34.♖d5! ♕c6 35.♖f5 e3+ 36.♔g1

Black resigned.

If after the exchange on d2 white can capture with his queen without hindrance (which happens in the 5...0-0 line), then his arguments in the opening will be stronger. The position of the queen on e7 sometimes even harms black due to the possible ♘c3-d5.

Chapter 18

4...♕e7 5.g3 b6 variation

No. 100 I. Enchev – M. Hutois
Sautron 2018

1.d4 ♘f6 2.c4 e6 3.♘f3 ♗b4+ 4.♗d2 ♕e7 5.g3 b6 6.♗g2 ♗b7

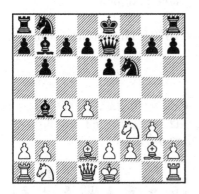

This "QID" variation of the Bogo-Indian Defense is similar in ideas to the 4...a5 system and is played quite a lot. It can be reached via a QID move order 3...b6 4.g3 ♗b7 5.♗g2 ♗b4+ 6.♗d2 ♕e7.

7.0-0

If 7.♘c3 black usually castles and we merge into game 101. Even at this early stage black needs to be on his guard and avoid 7...d6?? 8.♕a4+ ♘c6 9.d5 (there are examples of this!).

7...0-0 8.♗g5

LANDMINE. In reply to 8.♗f4 black must avoid 8...d5? due to 9.c5! Black will lose material, as after 9...bxc5 10.a3 ♗a5 11.dxc5 c6 12.♗d6 the queen is placed disastrously on e7.

Rather, black should play 8...♗d6 9.♗xd6 cxd6. If we compare this with the variation from game 87, then the replacement of a7-a5 with ♕d8-e7 favors black. He has made a useful developing move, while the white knight will not settle on b5.

8...h6

Black has to get rid of the pin one way or another. After 8...d5 9.♘e5 h6 10.♗xf6 ♕xf6 11.cxd5 ♗xd5 12.e4 ♗b7 apart from Avrukh's recommendation 13.♘c4 the more complicated continuation 13.a3 ♗e7 14.♘c3 c5 15.♘d7 ♘xd7 16.e5 ♕f5 17.♗xb7 ♖ad8 18.♗e4 ♕h3 19.f4 is promising.

9.♗xf6 ♕xf6 10.a3 ♗e7 11.♘c3

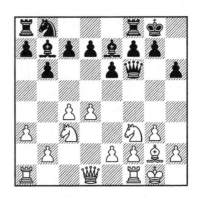

11...d6

Black is in difficulty due to the queen's awkward position. After 11...d5 12.♘e5 c6 13.e4 dxe4 14.♘xe4 she is under attack from the knight, while if 13...dxc4 14.♘xc4 the e-pawn will threaten her.

12.♕c2

White more often plays 12.e4 with a promising position and excellent stats. After 12...g6 13.♖e1 ♕g7 14.♕d2 e5 15.♘d5 ♗d8 16.dxe5 dxe5 17.♖ad1 c6 18.♘e3 ♗c7 19.b4 (Levin – Ulanov, St. Petersburg 2010) the black pieces stand ugly. In the current game, e2-e4 would have helped white.

12...♘d7 13.♖fd1 ♖fd8 14.♖ac1 c5 15.d5 e5 16.h4

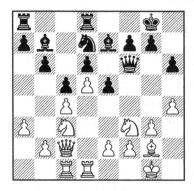

16...g6?!

Now and later, black plays the defense poorly. In the structure that has arisen it's not easy for white to attack, for example g3-g4 is met by ♕f6-f4. The variation 16...♗f8 17.♗h3 ♗c8 18.♘d2 ♕e7 19.♘de4 ♘f6 20.♗xc8 ♖axc8 21.♘xf6+ ♕xf6 eases black's defense thanks to the exchanges.

17.h5 ♕g7

In reply to 17...g5 the standard tactical operation 18.♘h2 ♕g7 19.♘g4 ♘f6 20.♘xe5 dxe5 21.d6 ♗xd6 22.♗xb7 ♖ab8 doesn't destroy black's defenses. So via 19.g4 white should probably strengthen his control over f5, and carry out any ambitious plans on the queenside.

18.hxg6 fxg6 19.♗h3 ♘f8 20.♔g2 ♗c8 21.♖h1 ♘h7 22.♗e6+ ♗xe6 23.dxe6 ♘f8?

He should have strengthened his position via 23...♖e8 24.♘d5 ♖ac8 and only then thought about liquidating the irritating pawn. Although that wouldn't guarantee salvation.

24.♘d5 ♔h7 25.♖xh6+ ♕xh6 26.♖h1

Black resigned.

No. 101 H. Hernandez Carmenates – S. Matsenko
Dallas 2017

1.d4 ♘f6 2.c4 e6 3.♘f3 ♗b4+ 4.♗d2 ♕e7 5.♘c3 b6 6.g3 ♗b7 7.♗g2 0-0 8.0-0

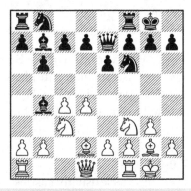

TRANSPOSITION ALERT. Two lines are combined here – 5.♘c3 followed by the fianchetto (as played in the game) and the continuation 5.g3 b6 6.♗g2 ♗b7 7.0-0 0-0 8.♘c3. The latter line is played less frequently, as we have found the great alternative 8.♗g5.

8...d6

This is evidently more precise than the simplifications after 8...

♗xc3 9.♗xc3 ♘e4 10.♖c1 (10.
♗e1!?) 10...♘xc3 11.♖xc3. After the
approximate variation 11...d6 12.♕c2
f5 13.d5 e5 14.e4 f4 15.b4 white lacks
enough resources to attack the black
king, though he will shortly play the
standard c4-c5.

9.d5!?

A relatively rare but still decent
move. If 9.a3 ♗xc3 10.♗xc3 black
has a nice choice between 10...♘e4
(and the extra move a2-a3 may prove
to be wasted) and 10...♘bd7 11.b4 c5
(here if 11...♘e4 the bishop retreats
to b2) 12.e3 a5, forcing white to
commit with his pawn phalanx.

9...c5

Matsenko's choice is easy to
explain. 9...e5?! is poor due to
10.♘h4, while after 9...c6 10.dxe6
fxe6 11.♘d4 d5 12.cxd5 cxd5 13.♖c1
(Damljanovic – Drasko, Petrovac
2015) the centralized knight causes
black a few problems.

10.♘h4

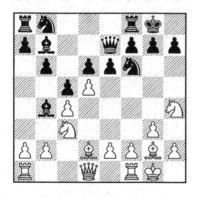

10...♘bd7 11.e4

After 11.dxe6 ♗xg2 12.exf7+
♕xf7 13.♘xg2 ♕xc4 black regains
the pawn. If white now attacks the d6
pawn, then black takes the initiative –

14.♘e3 ♕f7 15.♘b5 ♗xd2 16.♘xd6
♕e6 17.♕xd2 ♘e5 18.♘b5 ♖ad8
19.♕c2 ♘fg4.

**11...♘e5 12.b3 ♘g6 13.♘xg6
hxg6 14.dxe6**

I wonder what the strong
pragmatist Matsenko would
have replied to 14.♖e1. After the
undoubtedly best move 14...e5 it's
not clear how black would outplay
his weaker opponent. As a result of
the exchange, at least the f-file has
partially opened.

**14...fxe6 15.♖e1 e5 16.♕e2
♖f7 17.♖ad1 ♖af8 18.♘b5 ♘e8
19.♗xb4?!**

He should have protected the f2
square with the rook.

**19...♖xf2! 20.♕xf2 ♖xf2
21.♔xf2 cxb4 22.♘xa7 ♕c7**

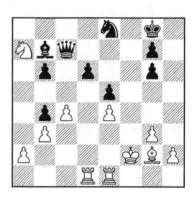

23.♗h3?!

White's rooks look pretty, but
they are ineffective. A stronger
continuation was 23.♘b5 ♕c5+
24.♔f1 ♗c6 25.♘a7 ♗d7 26.♖d5,
cramping the queen.

**23...♕c5+ 24.♔f3 ♕a5 25.♘b5
♕xa2 26.♗e6+ ♔h7 27.c5?!**

He should have protected b3
with one of his rooks on the third

rank. Now it's black and not white who demonstrates excellent piece coordination.

27...dxc5 28.♘d6 ♘c7 29.♗f7 ♗a6 30.♖e3 ♕c2 31.♖a1 ♗e2+! 32.♔f2 ♗g4+ 33.♔f1 ♕d2

White resigned.

No. 102 V. Malakhatko – K. Laustsen
Feffernitz 2012

1.c4 ♘f6 2.♘f3 b6 3.d4 e6 4.g3 ♗b7 5.♗g2 ♗b4+ 6.♗d2 ♕e7 7.0-0

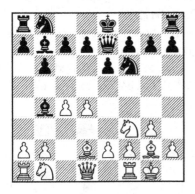

7...♗xd2
After black exchanges his bishop in good time it's harder for white to demonstrate an advantage.

8.♕xd2
Capturing with the knight is almost never seen here in top-level games. Here's an example from the classics: Pirc – Lilienthal (Stubnianske Teplice 1930): 8.♘bxd2 0-0 9.♕c2 d6 10.e4 e5 11.♘h4 (the general-purpose 11.d5 doesn't get white far after the standard a7-a5 and ♘b8-a6(d7)-c5) 11...g6 12.f4 ♘bd7 13.♖ae1 ♖ab8 14.♕c3 exf4 15.♖xf4 ♘h5 16.♖ff1 a5 17.♕e3 with the idea

of transferring his queen to h6 and hope for a small advantage.

8...0-0
Avrukh suggested waiting to castle, with a main line of 8...d6 9.♘c3 ♘e4 10.♘xe4 ♗xe4 11.♕e3 ♗b7 12.d5 e5 13.b4 ♘d7 14.♘d2 a5 15.a3 0-0 16.♘b3, and then gave a line that continued to move thirty. However, I don't think that there is a single correct recipe here. In unforced play each player has several fairly equal alternatives on almost every move.

9.♘c3
With 9.♕c2 white prevents the simplifications of ♘f6-e4 and has a great score, yet this move is played infrequently. Black's best reply is 9...c5, and if 10.dxc5 it makes sense to play 10...♕xc5 given the lack of dark-squared bishops.

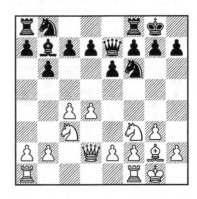

9...d6
The simplifying 9...♘e4 is found in game 103. 9...d5 10.cxd5 exd5 has been played by top players and by Croatian players in particular. This is a solid QID setup that is acceptable for black even without the dark-squared bishops. For

example, 11.♖ac1 ♘a6 12.♘h4 ♘e4 13.♘f5 ♕f6 14.♘xe4 dxe4 15.♘e3 ♖ad8 16.♖fd1 c5 17.d5 ♕g6 with very complicated play (Solomon – Pelletier, Istanbul 2012). It was worth white considering capturing on e4 with the bishop, as his opponent doesn't have the forces to threaten the white king.

10.d5

If 10.♕c2, then 10...c5 is decent, as usual. After 11.e4 ♘c6 12.♖ad1 cxd4 13.♘xd4 ♖fc8 14.b3 a6 15.♕d2 ♖d8 16.♖fe1 ♕c7 (Rubio – Granda, Benasque 2011) the experienced grandmaster playing black was unable to use his hedgehog to overcome his little-known opponent.

TRANSPOSITION ALERT. The continuation 10...♘bd7 leads to a position from game No. 104 of my Queen's Indian Defense book Michalik – Bokros (Slovakia 2016) via the move order 6...♗xd2+ 7.♕xd2 0-0 8.♘c3 d6 9.0-0 ♘bd7 10.♕c2 ♕e7. The border between these two openings is blurred here. Hence I highly advise studying the relevant chapters from both books.

10...e5 11.e4

Now white's queenside attack has slowed a little, and in a later game Malakhatko immediately took the bull by the horns – 11.b4 a5 12.a3 ♘bd7 13.♘b5 ♕d8 14.♘h4 ♖e8 15.e4 ♘f8 16.♖fc1 ♗a6 17.♘f5 (Malakhatko – Suvrajt, Bhubaneshvar 2019). White is more active, but it's questionable whether he can make further progress.

If white only operates on the kingside, then after 11.♘h4 ♗c8 12.e4 ♘h5 13.♘f5 ♗xf5 14.exf5 ♘f6 it's hard to improve the position of the white knight, while his bishop is quite unsuited to aggression. White only has a symbolic advantage.

11...a5 12.b3 ♘bd7 13.♕c2 ♔h8 14.a3 ♖fb8 15.♘d2

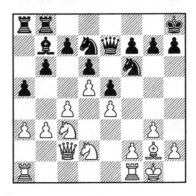

Black can mark time and calmly meet the b3-b4 break, as c4-c5 will be difficult to carry out. Instead, he followed with a suicidal charge on the kingside.

15...g5? 16.b4 axb4 17.axb4 ♕e8 18.♘f3 ♕g8 19.♕d2 g4

The continuation 19...♗a6 20.♕e2 h6 21.h4 g4 22.♘h2 h5 23.♖fd1 won't postpone the white knight's journey to f5 for long (here, via f1 and e3).

20.♘h4 ♗c8 21.♘b5 ♘e8 22.♘f5 ♘df6 23.♘e7 ♕g7 24.♘c6 ♖xa1 25.♖xa1 ♖b7 26.♖a8 ♗d7 27.♘d8

This fighter deserves an equine statue!

27...♗xb5 28.cxb5
Black resigned.

No. 103 I. Farago – C. Kerek
Hungary 2015

1.d4 ♘f6 2.c4 e6 3.♘f3 b6 4.g3
♗b7 5.♗g2 ♗b4+ 6.♗d2 ♕e7 7.0-0
♗xd2 8.♕xd2 0-0 9.♘c3 ♘e4

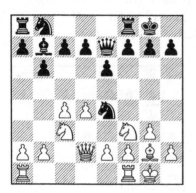

With simplifications in mind, black needs to stay aware of potential changes to the pawn structure that aren't particularly desirable for him.

10.♘xe4

If 10.♕c2 ♘xc3 11.♕xc3 we reach a position very similar to the main line of the Queen's Indian Defense (3...b6 4.g3 ♗b7 5.♗g2 ♗e7 6.0-0 0-0 7.♘c3 ♘e4 8.♕c2 ♘xc3 9.♕xc3). The absence of dark-squared bishops encourages black to plan d7-d6 and e6-e5, but after 11...d6 12.♕c2 the immediate 12...e5? is no good due to 13.♘g5. It's better for black to switch to a Dutch setup via 12...f5, and to leave e6-e5 in reserve.

10...♗xe4 11.♕f4 d5

The double attack on e4 and c7 highlights the drawback of the queen's sortie to e7 combined with the fianchetto. Black has chosen the best reply, as he would be even worse after 11...♗xf3 12.♗xf3 c6 13.♖fd1

d5 14.cxd5 cxd5 15.e4 ♕d7 16.exd5 exd5 17.♕e5 ♖d8 18.♖ac1.

12.cxd5 exd5

The clearly better position of the white army is illustrated by the variation 12...♗xd5 13.♖ac1 ♘a6 14.♘e5 c5 15.dxc5 ♘xc5 16.b4 ♘a6 17.♗xd5 (17.a3!?) 17...exd5 18.♘c6 ♕xe2 19.♖fe1 ♕b2 20.a3 where white will inevitably win back the pawn without worsening his position.

13.♖ac1

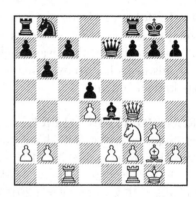

13...♘a6

On several occasions black has tried the transposition to hanging pawns with 13...c5 14.dxc5 bxc5. White has a strong initiative after both 15.♕e5 ♕d8 16.♖fd1 and 15.♕e3 ♕b7 16.♕xc5 ♕xb2 17.♕c3 ♕xa2 18.♘d4.

14.♖c6

It's not easy for white to extend his advantage. After 14.♗h3!? (Avrukh) black strengthens his position via the queen maneuver 14...♕b4 15.♕d2 ♕d6, though he remains somewhat worse after 16.♘e5 c5.

14...♖ac8?!

The right defense was 14...♕b4 15.♕c1 (15.♕d2?? ♗xf3) 15...♕b5 seen in the age-old game Budo – Bondarevsky (Tbilisi 1937). Kerek chooses the wrong way to attack the white pawns.

15.♖fc1 ♕b4 16.b3 ♕b5 17.♗h3 ♘b4??

If 17...♖ce8 18.♗f1 ♕b4 19.♘g5 ♗g6 20.e3 ♕a3 black's position is unappealing but, unlike in the game, white doesn't have a decisive tactic.

18.♖xc7 ♖xc7 19.♖xc7 ♕xe2

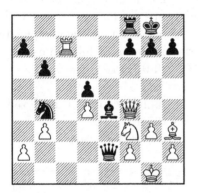

20.♕xf7+!
Black resigned.

The line 5...b6 6.♗g2 ♗b7 7.0-0 0-0 8.♗g5 is clearly better for white. The continuation 7...♗xd2 8.♕xd2 0-0 improves for black and promises him gradual equality. We reach well-known structures from other opening systems but without dark-squared bishops, so it is once again advisable to study the similar variations.

Chapter 19

4...♕e7 5.g3 ♘c6 6.♗g2 variation

No. 104 S. Mamedyarov – R. Rapport
Wijk aan Zee 2019

1.d4 ♘f6 2.♘f3 e6 3.c4 ♗b4+ 4.♗d2 ♕e7 5.g3 ♘c6

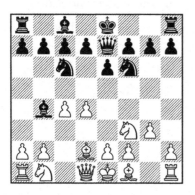

"The drawback of this move is that the knight on c6 will soon be attacked and will lose a tempo. On the other hand, this move contains a concrete tactical idea, creating the threat of 6...♗xd2+ [after white moves his bishop to g2], after which white will have to recapture on d2 with his knight, as after 7.♕xd2? ♘e4 8.♕c2 ♕b4+ he loses a pawn: 9.♘bd2 ♘xd2 10.♕xd2 ♕xc4 or 10.♘xd2 ♘xd4." (Geller).

Back in 1981, when the leading grandmaster and theoretician's view was published, there was still very little theory to the Bogo-Indian Defense. That led to his overstating the importance of the tempo gain d4-d5 and the totally wrong question-mark placed against 7.♕xd2.

6.♗g2 ♗xd2+

The continuation 6...0-0 7.0-0 ♗xd2 8.♕xd2 d6 9.♘c3 e5 leads via a different move order to game 97. We know that here 10.♘d5 favors white, and hence he has no need to play 7.♘c3 and head for the complicated variations from the following chapter (6.♘c3 0-0 7.♗g2).

7.♕xd2

The knight capture is analyzed in games 105-107.

7...♘e4 8.♕c2 ♕b4+

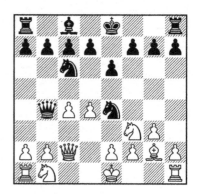

9.♔f1!

A great move that Geller had missed. That said, to cancel the question-mark placed against 7.♕xd2 it's sufficient to analyze the line 9.♘c3 ♘xc3 10.♕xc3 ♕xc3+ 11.bxc3. White has messed up his pawn chain, but is no worse. For example, 11...♘a5 12.♘d2 ♖b8 13.♖b1 b6 14.♖b4 ♗b7 15.♗xb7

♖xb7 16.0-0 ♔e7 17.♖fb1 ♖bb8 18.e3 d6 19.♔f1 (Cheparinov – Bertholee, Wijk aan Zee 2000), and after the white king returned to the center black moderated his ambitions and agreed to a draw.

9...f5

Without queens on the board, the position of the king on f1 is slightly better than if he castles. An interesting example is Ni Hua – Sagar Shah (Doha 2015): 9...d5 10.e3 ♕xc4+ 11.♕xc4 dxc4 12.♘bd2 ♘xd2+ 13.♘xd2 e5 14.♗xc6+ bxc6 15.dxe5 ♗e6 16.♔e2 ♔e7 17.♖hc1 ♖ab8 18.♖ab1 ♖b4 19.a3 ♖a4 20.e4 with a tough Catalan-type ending for black. With queens on the board in a closed position nothing will stop white from freeing up a cozy nest for the king on g2. So it's no surprise that Rapport strives for open play via a Dutch setup.

10.a3 ♕e7 11.b4

A novelty. Previously white would immediately offer an exchange of knights with the possibility of activating in the center. After 11.♘c3 ♘xc3 12.♕xc3 0-0 13.d5 ♘d8 14.♘d4 c6 15.dxe6 dxe6 16.♘f3 ♘f7 17.♘e5 ♕c7 18.f4 ♘xe5 19.fxe5 f4 20.♗f3 (Matlakov – Vlasenko, St. Petersburg 2009) ♔e1-f1 remained unpunished, as 20...♖f5 21.♖d1 ♖xe5 22.♕d4 ♖f5 23.♕d8+ ♕xd8 24.♖xd8+ ♖f8 25.♖xf8+ ♔xf8 26.gxf4 simplifies play with only an insignificant advantage for white.

11...0-0 12.♘c3 ♘xc3 13.♕xc3 d6 14.e3 e5

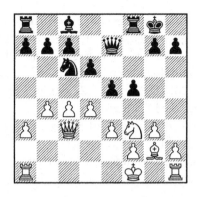

Black can count on grabbing the initiative if the e-file is opened or after the standard 15.d5?! However, the attack against black's knight from the flank leaves white in a better position.

15.b5 exd4 16.♘xd4 ♘e5 17.h3 ♔h8 18.♔g1

The king advances unhurriedly to his bunker and white retains a small advantage, above all thanks to his powerful bishop. Here and further on, Rapport defends brilliantly.

18...♘d7 19.♔h2 ♘c5 20.♖he1 ♗e6 21.a4 a5

He mustn't allow a4-a5.

22.♘b3 ♘e4 23.♕c2 ♕f7 24.♖ac1 ♕g6 25.♘d2

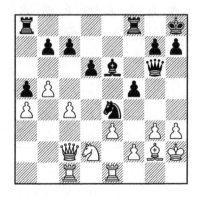

25...♘xf2

Black could have returned his knight to c5, but decided that the non-standard opening of the f-file would do him no harm.

26.♖f1 ♘e4 27.♘xe4 fxe4 28.♗xe4 ♕h6 29.h4

The variation 29.♕g2 c6 30.bxc6 bxc6 31.♗xc6 ♖ac8 32.♖xf8+ ♖xf8 33.♖c2 ♖c8 demonstrates that white has no advantage, due to his weak pawns.

29...♖ab8   30.♗xb7   ♖xf1 31.♖xf1 ♕xe3 32.♗g2 ♗g8 33.♖f4 ♖e8   34.♗c6   ♖e6   35.♖f8   ♖f6 36.♖xf6 gxf6 37.♕f5 ♕e6 38.♕f2 ♕e5 39.♕a7 d5! 40.♗xd5

Draw agreed. A wonderful grandmaster lesson and the complete rehabilitation of 7.♕xd2.

No. 105 F. El Debs – S. Sergienko
Prague 2014

1.♘f3 ♘f6 2.c4 ♘c6 3.d4 e6 4.g3 ♗b4+ 5.♗d2 ♕e7 6.♗g2 ♗xd2+ 7.♘bxd2

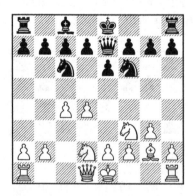

7...a5

This way (just like via the move order 7...d6 8.0-0 a5) black waits to

castle, as on move 11 he throws his other rook's pawn forward.

Black's 7th move somewhat narrows down white's options. After 7...d6 apart from castling the move 8.♘f1!? looks interesting (whereas after 7...a5 or 7...0-0 the maneuver doesn't work due to 8...♕b4+) 8...0-0 9.♘e3 with the aim of improving the knight's position. Geller's recommendation 9...♘e4 (based on the game Trifunovic – Keres, Buenos Aires 1937) still fails to promise an initiative on the kingside due to white's faster central operations – 10.0-0 f5 11.d5 ♘d8 12.♘d4.

Black should not worry that 9... e5 allows white's knight to get to d5. After 10.♘d5 we have a position reached from 5...0-0 6.♗g2 ♗xd2+ 7.♕xd2 d6 8.0-0 e5 9.♘c3 ♘c6 10.♘d5 (game 97) except that white has missed two tempi, as a result of which he cannot count on an advantage, for example if the queen retreats to d8.

8.0-0 d6 9.e4

Improving the knight with 9.♘b1 0-0 10.♘c3 e5 11.♘d5 may merge into the excursion via f1 mentioned above. As played by Kasimdzhanov, instead of 10...e5 black can choose 10...♗d7 and thereby challenge white to prove whether it was worth losing the tempi.

9...e5 10.d5 ♘b8 11.♘e1

Apart from transferring the knight to the center white can consider 11.c5!?, taking advantage via a tactic of black's delay to castling. In the game Beliavsky –

Dueckstein (Vienna 1986) white won spectacularly after 11...dxc5 12.♘c4 ♘bd7 13.d6! ♕e6 14.♖c1 b5 15.♘cxe5! ♘xe5 16.♕xe5 cxd6?! (black could have held the endgame with 16...♕xe5 17.f4 ♕xd6 18.e5 ♕xd1 19.♖fxd1 ♖a6 20.exf6 ♖xf6 21.♖xc5 0-0) 17.♘c6 ♗b7? 18.e5! dxe5 19.♖xc5. After the stronger 11...0-0 12.cxd6 cxd6 13.♘e1 ♘a6 14.♘d3 white's advantage is insignificant.

11...h5

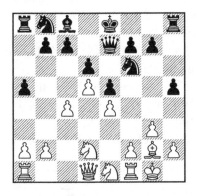

A tempting, but committal continuation, as the black king will never be fully safe.

12.♘ef3

El Debs acknowledged the idea and moves his knight back. Radical prophylaxis with 12.h4 leads after 12...♗g4 13.f3 ♗d7 to the loosening of white's pawn chain and caused her a nasty outcome in the game M. Muzychuk – Nabaty (Gibraltar 2015): 14.♘d3 ♘a6 15.♕e2 b6 16.b3 ♘c5 17.a3 ♘h7 18.♘xc5 bxc5 19.♕e3 0-0 20.♔h2 g6 21.♗h3 ♗xh3 22.♔xh3 f5. It was probably better to play 17.♖ae1, in order to meet 17...♘h7 with 18.f4.

The logical consequence of 12.h3 h4 13.g4 would be the plan 13...♘bd7 14.♘d3 g5 15.b3 ♘f8 16.a3 ♘g6 with the knight invading on f4 at the right time. The game Piket – Shaked (Tilburg 1997) continued 17.♖e1 0-0 18.b4 ♗d7 19.f3 b6 20.♕c2 c5 21.bxc5 bxc5 22.♖eb1 ♖fb8 23.♖b2 ♕d8 – black refuses to cede the open file and maintains equality.

12...♘bd7

The approximate variation with the exchange of the bishop 12...♗g4 13.♕b3 b6 14.♕e3 ♗xf3 15.♘xf3 ♘bd7 16.♘h4 g6 is acceptable for black, but he still needs to keep a watch over the breaks b2(b3)-b4 and f2-f4.

13.♕a4

After 13.b3 ♘c5 14.♕c2 it's interesting to assess the sac 14...h4 15.♘xh4 ♖xh4. I think that black has sufficient positional compensation: 16.gxh4 ♘h5 17.♘f3 ♘f4 18.♔h1 ♕d7 19.♖g1 ♕g4 20.♘e1 ♕xh4.

13...♔f8 14.♕a3 ♖a6

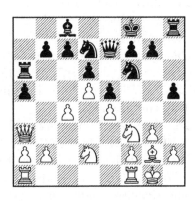

The plan with b2-b4 has been neutralized, and the Brazilian

grandmaster playing white switches his focus to f2-f4. Apart from the moves in the game, he could have prepared that push via 15.h4 and ♘f3-g5.

15.♗h3 g6 16.♘h4 ♔g7 17.f4 exf4 18.♖xf4 ♘e5 19.♗xc8 ♖xc8 20.♖af1 ♘fd7 21.♘df3 ♘xf3+ 22.♘xf3 ♖f8 23.♕b3 ♖aa8 24.♘d4

It's unclear how white can intensify the pressure. g3-g4 will most probably cause problems for his own king.

24...♘c5 25.♕c3 ♔g8 26.♕f3 ♖ae8

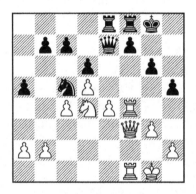

27.♘f5?! ♕e5?!

As the engine shows, white's sac was unsound. If 27...gxf5 28.♕xh5 f6 29.e5! any capture loses (for example, 29...dxe5?? 30.♖h4 ♕g7 31.♖xf5), but 29...♕h7 leaves white clutching at straws in the endgame.

28.♘h6+ ♔g7 29.♘xf7 ♕d4+ 30.♔h1 ♖xe4 31.♖f6 ♕e3?!

It's not obvious to a human that 31...♘d7! 32.♖e6 ♖xe6 33.dxe6 ♘f6 retains equality, while the move in the game does not.

32.♖xg6+! ♔xg6

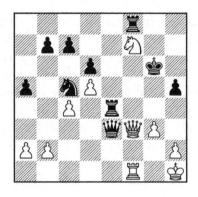

33.♕f6+?!

The study-like pirouette 33.♘h8+! leaves white a pawn up after 33...♔h7 34.♕xf8 ♖e7 35.♕f6 ♕e4+ 36.♖f3.

33...♔h7 34.♕f5+ ♔g7 35.♕f6+ ♔h7 36.♖f4?

This is met by a thunderous refutation. He should have made do with perpetual check.

36...♕c1+ 37.♔g2 ♕c2+ 38.♖f2

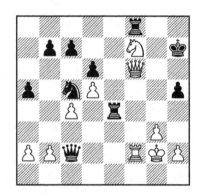

38...♕xf2+!! 39.♔xf2 ♖f4+!!

Knight forks win the day! White has nothing better than a hopeless ending the exchange down.

40.♕xf4 ♘d3+ 41.♔f3 ♘xf4 42.♘g5+ ♔g6 43.gxf4 ♔f5 44.♘e6 ♖f7 45.♘d4+ ♔f6 46.♘e6 a4 47.♔e4 c5 48.f5 b5 49.cxb5 ♖b7 50.♔f4 ♖xb5

51.♘g5 ♖xb2 52.♘e4+ ♔e7 53.f6+ ♔d7 54.♔f5 ♖xa2 55.h4 ♖e2 56.♘g5 White resigned.

No. 106 J. Lautier – U. Adianto
Tallinn/Parnu 1998

1.d4 ♘f6 2.c4 e6 3.♘f3 ♗b4+ 4.♗d2 ♕e7 5.g3 ♘c6 6.♗g2 ♗xd2+ 7.♘bxd2 d6 8.0-0 0-0 9.e4 e5 10.d5 ♘b8

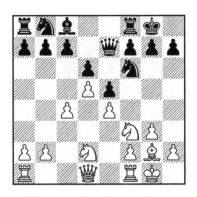

11.b4

An obvious move that has been made by many top players, although 11.♘e1 (game 107) is played much more often.

11...a5

Geller believed that the simplest way to equalize was to exchange the light-squared bishop with 11...♗g4. After 12.♕c2 ♘bd7 13.♘b3 ♗xf3 14.♗xf3 b6 15.c5 bxc5 16.bxc5 a5 17.a4 ♖fb8 18.c6 ♘c5 19.♘xc5 dxc5 20.♖fc1 ♘e8 21.♕xc5 ♕xc5 22.♖xc5 ♘d6 as played in J. Horvath – Loginov (Zalakaros 1994) black has achieved an ideal knight versus bishop imbalance in a blocked position, but has paid for it with a pawn and is fighting for equality, not the initiative.

12.a3 ♘a6 13.♘e1

German grandmaster Hertneck plays this system for both colors. After 13.♕b3 ♗d7 14.♖fc1 ♖fb8 15.♘e1 axb4 16.axb4 c5 17.dxc6 bxc6 18.♘c2 ♘c7 19.♖xa8 ♖xa8 20.♘e3 g6 21.♕d3 ♘e6 22.♘b3 ♖b8 23.♘c2 ♗e8 (Beliavsky – Hertneck, Saint Vincent 2000) thanks to breaking with his c-pawn in time black tied down white's army to protecting the b4 pawn and d4 square, with equal chances.

13...♗g4

It was probably slightly premature to play 13...c6 14.dxc6 bxc6 15.♘d3 ♗g4. After 16.♕e1 white transfers his queen to the excellent e3 square, from where it will control the dark squares.

14.f3 ♗d7 15.♘d3

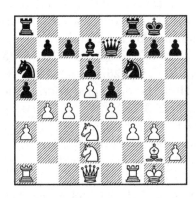

15...♖fc8

Here after 15...c6!? 16.dxc6 bxc6 17.♕c2 d5!? the white queen is on a less appealing square, and if 18.c5 dxe4 19.fxe4 (Rashkovsky – Magerramzade, Ubeda 1999) 19...axb4 20.axb4 ♘g4 21.♖fe1 ♘c7 22.♘c4 f6 23.♘d6 ♘e3! it is exposed to an elegant attack leading to the exchange of his bishop and equality. Adianto's move was weaker, as the rook might also have come in handy on b8.

16.f4 axb4 17.axb4 c5 18.bxc5 ♘xc5 19.♖xa8 ♖xa8 20.♘xc5 dxc5 21.♕b3

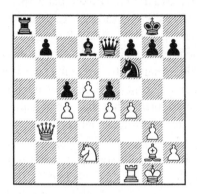

21...b5!? 22.cxb5 c4!?

Adianto sacrifices his pawn pair in order to activate his pieces to the maximum. He wins back one of the pawns immediately, and he will have compensation for the other.

23.♕xc4 ♖c8 24.♕b3 ♕c5+ 25.♔h1 ♝xb5 26.♖b1 ♘g4 27.♝f3

Here the principled continuation was 27.h3!? ♘f2+ 28.♔h2 ♝d3 29.♖b2 exf4 30.gxf4. If 30...♕e3 (with the threat 31...♕xf4+ 32.♔g1 ♘xh3+!) white highlights the weakness of the 8th rank – 31.♕b8! ♖f8 32.f5 ♘d1 33.♖b3 ♕xd2 34.f6! While if 30...g5!? 31.♕b6 ♕xb6 32.♖xb6 he has an advantage in the endgame.

27...♘f2+ 28.♔g2 ♘d3 29.♕xb5 ♕f2+ 30.♔h3 ♕xd2 31.♖b3 ♘f2+ 32.♔g2

A more fun draw would have been reached after 32.♔h4 ♘d3! 33.♖xd3 ♕xh2+ 34.♔g4 h5+ 35.♔f5 ♕xg3 36.♔xe5 f6+ 37.♔f5 ♕h3+ 38.♔g6 ♕g3+.

32...♘d3+ 33.♔h3 ♘f2+ 34.♔g2

♘xe4+ 35.♕e2 exf4 36.gxf4 g6 37.♕xd2 ♘xd2 38.♖d3

Draw agreed.

No. 107 G. Hertneck – F. Roeberg
Austria 2014

1.d4 ♘f6 2.c4 e6 3.g3 ♝b4+ 4.♝d2 ♕e7 5.♝g2 ♘c6 6.♘f3 ♝xd2+ 7.♘bxd2 d6 8.0-0 0-0 9.e4 e5 10.d5 ♘b8 11.♘e1

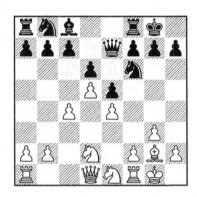

The knight heads for d3, from where it can support the breaks b2-b4 and f2-f4. Black does not usually put up with such an active knight and strives to swap it.

11...a5 12.♘d3 ♘a6

The travelling bishop maneuver 12...♝g4 13.f3 ♝d7 gains black a tempo after 14.f4, but after 14.b3 ♘a6 15.a3 ♘c5 16.♘b2 white can demonstrate the advantage of playing f2-f3. White can also redeploy his queen via 13.♕e1 and 14.♕e3 (tried by Loek van Wely).

13.f4

13.a3 ♝g4 14.f3 ♝d7 15.b4 leads to game 106 via a different move order, while 13...c6 14.dxc6 bxc6 15.b4 ♝g4 16.♕e1 leads to a note from that game. There are no grounds to agree with Geller and prefer the slow 13.b3 instead of 13.a3.

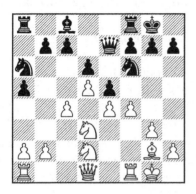

13...exf4

Hertneck had previously faced 13...♘d7 14.f5 f6 15.a3 ♘ac5 16.♘xc5 dxc5 17.a4 ♘b6 18.h4 ♗d7 19.♔h2 ♘c8 20.♖a3 ♘d6 21.g4 (Hertneck – Seul, Germany 2000), but then the hurried 21...g5? collapsed black's own fortress, whose strength up until then was beyond doubt. I expect that Roeberg had carefully prepared for this game and had already decided how he would defend here.

14.gxf4 ♘d7

14...♘g4 is not so reliable due to 15.♖e1 ♘b4 16.♘f3 with the break e4-e5 on the cards.

15.♘b3 a4 16.♘d4 ♘ac5

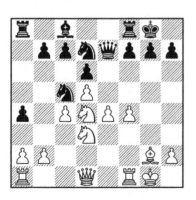

17.♘f2

KEY TIP. It's typical of white to avoid this exchange in such positions, so that black ends up with more cramped pieces. However, in this particular case 17.♘xc5 ♘xc5 18.♕e2 and ♖a1-e1 with the idea of e4-e5 was more promising.

17...♘b6 18.♕c2 ♕f6 19.♘e2 ♖e8 20.♖ad1 ♗d7 21.♖d2 ♘c8

With consistent moves, Roeberg prepares to free his position on the queenside. Maybe white should have played 22.b4 here, as the knight on c8 has interfered with black's communications. That said, this move doesn't fit well with 20.♖ad1.

22.f5 b5 23.♘d4 bxc4

With 23...b4 black isn't risking anything. A couple of careless moves and white again has chances.

24.♕xc4 ♘b6 25.♕c3 ♗c8

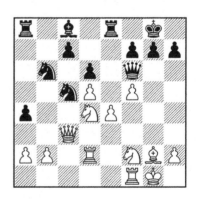

26.b4

Play on the queenside promises white little. The variation 26.e5! ♕g5 27.♘h3 ♕h6 28.e6 should have been easy to spot and leads to a clear advantage.

26...axb3 27.axb3 ♘bd7 28.b4 ♘a6 29.♖a1 ♖b8 30.♘d3 ♘e5 31.♘xe5 ♕xe5 32.♖a4 g6 33.♗f1 ♖b6 34.♗b5?

White underestimates the exchange sac. After 34.fxg6 hxg6 35.♖f2 ♕g5+ 36.♔g2 ♕e5 the players have no reason to reject repeating moves.

34...♖xb5! 35.♘xb5 ♕xe4 36.♘d4?

He should have covered the first rank by retreating his rook from a4.

36...♕e1+ 37.♔g2 ♗b7 38.♖a5 ♘c5

White resigned.

Although the large number of games with 6.♗g2 ♗xd2+ 7.♘bxd2 have not seen black equalize, white has started to play this line less frequently. It's hard for him to vary play, and therefore it is better to choose the revived 7.♕xd2.

Chapter 20

4...♕e7 5.g3 ♘c6 6.♘c3 variation

No. 108 G. Hertneck – J. Timman
Solingen 2019

1.d4 ♘f6 2.♘f3 e6 3.c4 ♗b4+
4.♗d2 ♕e7 5.g3 ♘c6 6.♘c3

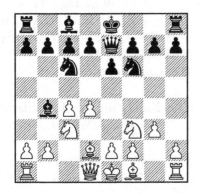

In his book back in 1981 Geller barely mentioned this line, as he didn't have any practical material on it. Since then, theory has advanced considerably on the basis of games played, including by leading grandmasters.

6...d5

6...0-0 is analyzed in game 109, and 6...♗xc3 is covered in games 110-114. The variation played here hit its apex in popularity at the end of the 20th century, but is rarely played today.

7.a3

If 7.♗g2 white needs to contend with the reply 7...dxc4. After 8.0-0 0-0 9.a3 ♗xc3 10.♗xc3 ♘d5 11.♕a4 ♘b6 12.♕c2 white obviously has compensation for the pawn, but black has a solid position.

The drawback of the exchange 7.cxd5 exd5 is that it frees up the c8 bishop. After 8.♗g2 0-0 9.0-0 ♖d8 10.♖c1 h6 11.a3 ♗xc3 12.♗xc3 ♗f5 13.b4 a6 14.♗b2 ♘a7 (this improves the knight and the pawn chain at the same time) 15.♘e5 ♘b5 16.♕b3 c6 17.a4 ♘d6 18.f3 ♘d7 19.e4 ♗e6 20.♘xd7 ♕xd7 21.e5 ♘c4 (Zontakh – Rashkovsky, Bydgoszcz 2001) white's bishop pair are nothing to be proud of.

7...♗xc3 8.♗xc3

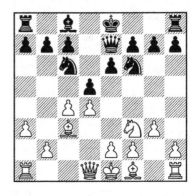

8...♘e4

Avrukh believed that black had to play 8...a5, and there are good reasons for playing it immediately. However, a good response to it is actually found in one of his old games – 9.♗g2 0-0 10.0-0 ♖d8 11.♕c2 ♘e4 12.b3 ♗d7 13.♗b2 ♗e8 14.♖ac1 f6 15.♘h4 g5 16.cxd5 exd5 17.♘f5 ♕e6 18.♗h3 ♔h8 19.f3 ♘d6 20.e4 where the opening up of play favors white (Avrukh – Rashkovsky, Biel 2002).

It's no surprise that Timman diverts from this discredited setup in favor of a Dutch structure.

9.♕c2 f5 10.♗g2 0-0 11.b4 a6

Black has to stop white's b-pawn from advancing further. The knight has to stay on c6, in order to swap for its white counterpart if it moves to e5.

12.♗b2 ♗d7 13.0-0 ♗e8 14.♘e5

White stands better, but maybe he should have played more fundamentally. After 14.e3 ♗g6 15.cxd5 exd5 16.♖fc1 the knight's invasion of e5 gains strength.

14...♘xe5 15.dxe5 dxc4 16.f3 c3! 17.♗c1 ♘d2

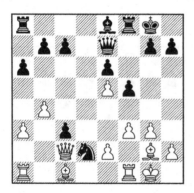

18.♗xd2

If 18.♖e1 ♘c4 19.♕xc3 ♘b6 20.f4 ♘d5 21.♗xd5 exd5 the inexorable knight is liquidated and retains an insignificant advantage.

18...cxd2 19.f4 ♖d8 20.♖fd1 ♕d7

It's unclear why Timman rejected the line 20...♗b5 21.♖xd2 ♗a4 22.♕c3 ♖xd2 23.♕xd2 ♖d8 24.♕e3 c6, which was the simplest and quickest way to achieve equality.

21.♕c3 ♕b5 22.♖xd2 ♖xd2 23.♕xd2 ♖f7 24.♕e3 ♖d7 25.♗c1

♗h5 26.♔f2 c6 27.♖c3 ♔f8 28.♖d3 ♖xd3 29.♕xd3 ♕xd3 30.exd3

The rook maneuver has liquidated black's dominance of the open file and at the same time undoubled white's pawns. However, white is still unable to win this.

30...♔e7 31.a4 ♔d7 32.a5 ♗d1 33.♔e3 ♔c7 34.♔d4 b6 35.♔c3 ♔b7 36.♔d2 ♗b3 37.d4 ♗d5 38.♗f1 b5 39.♗e2 g6 40.g4 fxg4 41.♗xg4 ♔c7 42.♔e3 ♔d7 43.h4 h5 44.♗d1 ♔e7 45.f5 exf5 46.♔f4 ♔f7 47.♔g5 ♔g7 48.♗e2 ♔f7 49.♗d1

Draw agreed.

No. 109 Kiril Georgiev – L. Yordanov
Skopje 2017

1.d4 ♘f6 2.♘f3 e6 3.c4 ♗b4+ 4.♗d2 ♕e7 5.g3 ♘c6 6.♘c3 0-0 7.♗g2

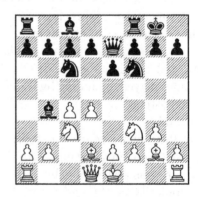

7...♘a5

The knight's move to the edge of the board together with the light-squared bishop fianchetto was introduced to play by the Estonian GM Mikhail Rychagov. The idea was taken up by other grandmasters, although mostly not from the elite.

After 7...d6 8.d5, it's fine to continue 8...♘e5 9.♘xe5 dxe5, as twice played by Grandmaster Ikonnikov. After 10.a3 ♗d6 11.0-0 exd5 12.cxd5 h6 13.♘b5 ♗f5 14.♘xd6 cxd6 (L'Ami – Ikonnikov, Hoogeveen 2010) the advantage of the two bishops is immaterial, as the bishop on g2 is stuck aiming at d5.

8.b3

It was worth considering 8.c5!? The Dutch grandmaster Ernst logically continued 8...b6 9.a3 ♗xc3 10.♗xc3 ♗b7, but now white could have snatched a pawn from him for nothing via 11.♗xa5 bxa5 12.♕a4. In the game Goganov – Slavin (Sochi 2017) the knight incongruously returned to its previous square: 8...♘c6 (8...♘c4 9.♗g5!) 9.a3 ♗xc3 10.♗xc3 ♘e4 11.♕c2 ♘xc3 12.♕xc3 d6 13.♖c1 ♗d7 14.0-0 a5 15.e4 a4 16.d5 ♘a5 17.cxd6 cxd6 18.♘d2 – and white's advantage is obvious.

8...b6 9.0-0 ♗b7

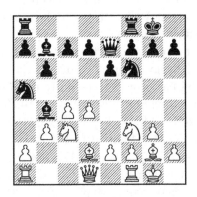

10.♖c1

An earlier game that year Vrolijk – Yordanov (Mamaia 2017) continued 10.♕c2 d5 11.cxd5 exd5 12.♘e5 c5 13.a3 cxd4 14.axb4 dxc3 15.♗xc3

♘c6 16.♘xc6 ♗xc6 17.♗xf6 ♕xf6 18.♖fc1 with a clear advantage for white. After 13...♗xc3 14.♗xc3 cxd4 15.♗xd4 ♘e4 black gains a better version of an isolated queen's pawn structure, and d7-d5 looks like it was a relatively decent idea.

10...d5

If 10...♖ac8, then white should go for 11.♗g5 h6 12.♗xf6 ♕xf6 13.e4 with the interim attack e4-e5 if black exchanges on c3.

11.cxd5 exd5 12.♘e5

After 12.♗g5 h6 13.♗xf6 ♕xf6 14.♘e5 ♖ad8 15.e3 c5 16.♕g4 ♖fe8 17.♘d3 (Arsovic – Kiril Georgiev, Cetinje 2013) black for some reason rejected 17...♗xc3 18.♖xc3 ♘c6 19.♕f4 cxd4 20.♕xf6 gxf6 21.exd4 ♘xd4 – it's only black's broken pawn structure that prevents him from converting his extra pawn into a point. In the current game as white, though, Georgiev immediately centralizes his knight.

12...c5 13.♗g5 ♖ad8

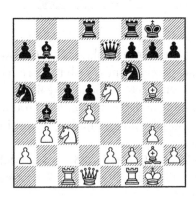

14.♘d3

More promising was 14.♘g4!? ♕e6 15.♘xf6+ gxf6 16.♗h6 ♖fe8 17.♘b5, and if 17...♕d7 the knight isn't forced to retreat, as the move 18.e3! is strong.

14...♗xc3 15.♖xc3 cxd4 16.♖c2

The amusing line 16.♗xf6 ♕xf6 17.♖c7 ♕d6 18.♕c2 ♗c6 19.♖xa7 ♗b7 (where the bishop blocks the rook twice!) 20.♕d2 ♕b8 21.♖xa5 bxa5 22.♕xa5 isn't easy to assess – the connected passers, compensating for the exchange, aren't yet dangerous.

16...♘c6 17.♘f4 ♘b4 18.♖d2 h6 19.♗xf6 ♕xf6 20.a3 ♘c6 21.♘xd5 ♕e5 22.♘f4 ♘a5 23.♗xb7 ♘xb7 24.b4 ♖d6 25.♕c2 ♖fd8 26.♖fd1

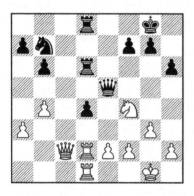

26...g5?!

Up to now the players have shown some decent moves, but here the inexperienced Yordanov weakens his kingside and gets into bigger trouble. He should have adopted a waiting stance.

27.♘d3 ♕f6 28.♘e1 ♖8d7 29.♘f3 ♘d8 30.♕e4 ♖e7 31.♕g4 ♘c6?!

From e6 the knight would have protected not only d4, but also g5.

32.h4 ♘e5 33.♘xe5 ♕xe5 34.hxg5 hxg5 35.♖xd4 ♖xd4

36.♖xd4 f6 37.e3 a5 38.♖d8+ ♖e8 39.♕d7 ♖xd8 40.♕xd8+ ♔g7 41.♕xb6 axb4 42.♕b7+

Black resigned.

No. 110 V. Potkin – A. Jankovic
Plovdiv 2012

1.d4 ♘f6 2.c4 e6 3.♘f3 ♗b4+ 4.♗d2 ♕e7 5.g3 ♘c6 6.♘c3 ♗xc3 7.♗xc3 ♘e4

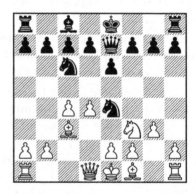

Now white is at a crossroads – to prevent the doubling of pawns he can either capture with his queen (as in this game) or with his rook from c1 (games 111-114).

8.♕c2 ♘xc3 9.♕xc3 0-0

The exchange of queens via 9...♕b4 has proved to be quite reliable, but unambitious. After 10.♖c1 ♕xc3+ 11.♖xc3 d6 12.♗g2 ♔e7 13.d5 ♘b8 14.dxe6 fxe6 15.c5 ♘c6 16.e3 ♗d7 (16...d5 17.♘d4 ♗d7 18.f4 is too passive) 17.♘d4 ♖ab8 18.♗xc6 bxc6 19.b3 ♖hc8 20.f4 (Sargissian – Vitiugov, Khanty-Mansiysk 2010) black was only thinking about the draw that he later achieved.

10.♗g2 d6

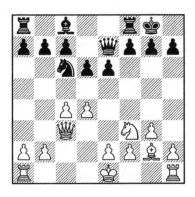

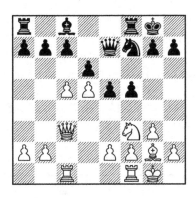

11.0-0

11.d5 leads to separate variations if white exchanges on e6 after the knight retreats. After 11...♘b8 12.dxe6 fxe6 13.0-0 ♘c6 14.b4 ♕f6 15.♕d2 ♗d7 16.b5 ♘e7 17.a4 h6 18.♘d4 ♖ab8 19.e3 e5 20.♘b3 ♗e6 21.♕c3 (Rustemov – Murdzia, Germany 2014) the long-range bishop ensures an advantage for white. The continuation 11...♘d8 12.dxe6 ♘xe6 13.0-0 ♗d7 (and then ♗d7-c6) provides black with better chances of equalizing.

11...e5 12.d5 ♘d8

The continuation 12...♘b8 13.c5 ♘a6 14.cxd6 cxd6 15.♖ac1 ♗d7 promises black equal opportunities. White's minor pieces aren't particularly active, and his queen on the open file stands awkwardly in front of her rook.

13.c5

As two of Aronian's games have shown, black's defenses after 13.e4 c5 14.♘e1 ♗d7 15.a4 a5 16.f4 f6 17.♘d3 b6 18.b3 ♘f7 are impregnable. Levon did lose this position to Dautov, but only because of a tactical oversight.

13...f5 14.♖ac1 ♘f7

15.a4

The invasion 15.cxd6 cxd6 16.♕c7 doesn't promise any real advantage. After 16...♕f6 17.e3 f4 18.exf4 exf4 19.♖c4 g5 20.h4 h6 21.hxg5 hxg5 22.gxf4 gxf4 23.♖e1 ♗g4 (Eljanov – Gasanov, St. Petersburg 2002) white had to exchange queens with 24.♕e7 in order to maintain equality. The inactivity of his knight on f3 and bishop on g2 is striking.

15...♗d7 16.♕b4 ♖fb8 17.cxd6 cxd6 18.♖c7 a5 19.♕b6 ♕d8 20.♖fc1 ♗xa4

If black wants to capture the pawn via 20...♖a6 21.♕e3 ♗xa4, then he faces the unexpected 22.♘d4! exd4 23.♕e6 ♕f8 24.♖c8.

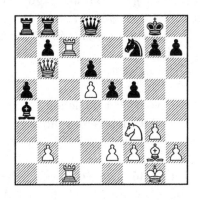

21.e4 ♗d7

The computer recommends 21...fxe4 22.♘d2 e3 23.♕xe3 ♗d7 24.♘e4 b5, and white's activity is not worth more than the sacrificed pawn.

22.♗h3 ♖c8 23.♗xf5 ♗xf5 24.exf5♖xc7 25.♖xc7♖c8 26.♖xb7 ♕xb6 27.♖xb6 ♔f8 28.♖b5 ♖c5

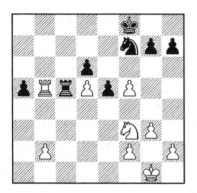

29.♖b8+

White's pawns are too weak to give him real winning chances. Nevertheless, he should have tested the knight endgame after 29.♖xc5 dxc5 30.♘d2.

29...♔e7 30.♖b7+ ♔e8 31.♖b6 ♔e7 32.♖b7+ ♔e8 33.h4 ♖xd5 34.♘g5 ♘xg5 35.hxg5 g6 36.fxg6 hxg6 37.♖g7 ♖b5 38.♖xg6 ♔e7 39.♖g7+ ♔e6 40.♖a7 ♔f5 41.♖a6 ♖d5 42.♖b6 ♔xg5 43.b4 axb4 44.♖xb4

Draw agreed.

**No. 111 A. Delchev –
J. Campos Moreno**
Barcelona 2019

1.d4 ♘f6 2.c4 e6 3.♘f3 ♗b4+ 4.♗d2 ♕e7 5.g3 ♘c6 6.♘c3 0-0 7.♗g2 ♗xc3 8.♗xc3 ♘e4 9.♖c1

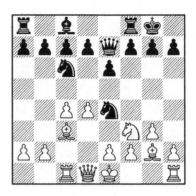

In this and the following games white protects his bishop with his rook (usually on move 8, without the additional moves 6...0-0 7.♗g2). In this example, black rejected ♘e4xc3.

9...d6

If 9...a5 10.0-0 d6 it makes sense to avoid exchanging the bishop via 11.♗e1. Further, the game Postny – Schmitz (Bad Wiessee 2013) continued 11...f5 12.d5 ♘b8 13.dxe6 ♗xe6 14.♘d2 ♘c5 15.♘b3 ♘xb3 16.♕xb3 c6 17.♕e3 ♘d7 18.♗c3 with a tangible advantage thanks to the bishop pair.

10.d5 ♘d8

If black waits to exchange with 10...♘b8 11.dxe6 then he has the option of 11...♗xe6 12.♘d4 ♗d7 (but not 12...♗xc4? 13.♘f5). If 13.0-0 black can count on equality via 13...♖e8 14.♘b5 ♗c6.

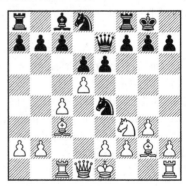

11.0-0

Let's see what happens if white evades the exchange with 11.♗b4. The game Rombaldoni – Caruana (Bratto 2006) continued 11...a5 12.♗a3 e5 13.♘d2 ♘xd2 14.♕xd2 b6 15.0-0 ♘b7 16.b3 ♘c5 (the knight has reached a nice outpost via a slightly unusual route) 17.♗b2 ♗f5 18.h3 ♗g6 19.♔h2 f5. The bishops haven't achieved anything and the game should end in a draw.

The continuation 11.dxe6 ♘xe6 12.♗b4 was introduced by a young Kramnik in 1992, but black soon found strong counter arguments. As an example see the game Chetverik – Loginov (Zalakaros 1994): 12...a5 13.♗a3 f5 14.0-0 ♔h8 15.b3 b6 16.♗b2 ♗b7 17.♘d4 ♘xd4 18.♕xd4 ♖f6 19.♖cd1 ♖e6 20.♖fe1?! (here and earlier the prophylaxis e2-e3 is useful) 20...♖f8 21.♗f3 (21.e3 c5! 22.♕d3 ♘g5) 21...f4 with an initiative for black.

11...e5 12.c5 f5 13.cxd6 cxd6 14.♘d2

Let's try 14.♗b4 in the changed structure: 14...♘f7 15.a4 b6 16.a5 ♘c5 17.♗a3 ♗d7 18.♘d2 ♖fc8 19.b4 ♗a4 20.♕e1 ♘d7 21.♘b1 ♘f6 22.♕d2 ♗b5 23.♗b2 bxa5 24.bxa5 ♖ab8 25.♘a3 ♗a6 26.♖xc8+ ♖xc8 27.♘c2, and a draw (Korchnoi – Loginov, Moscow 1994). Grandmaster Loginov, a known expert in this variation, extinguished his opponent's ambitions on the queenside in exemplary fashion.

14...♘xd2 15.♗xd2

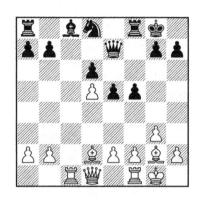

15...f4

If 15...b6 16.♖c3 ♗b7 17.♕b3 e4 18.f3 the vulnerability of the d5 pawn cannot be exploited. Any black activity on the kingside promises nothing either.

16.gxf4 exf4 17.♖c4 ♕g5 18.♔h1?!

He should have taken control of the third rank via 18.♕b3 thanks to the nice tactic 18...♗g4 19.♖xf4! ♖xf4 20.♕g3. Now it's black who has a tactical opportunity.

18...♗h3! 19.♗xh3 ♕xd5+ 20.♗g2 f3

This is to capture the rook after 21.♗xf3 (lengthening the operating reach along the file of the f8 rook). The variation 20...♕xc4 21.♗c3 ♖f5 22.♕xd6 f3 23.exf3 ♕f4 leads to unclear consequences.

21.♖g4!? fxg2+ 22.♖xg2 ♘e6 23.♗b4 ♕xa2 24.♕xd6 ♖f7 25.♗c3 ♖d8 26.♕b4 ♕d5 27.f3 ♖dd7 28.♖g4 b6 29.♖fg1 h6 30.♖e4 ♘f8

Instead of the knight's unjustified retreat 30...♖f5 was better, in order to neutralize the dangerous rook on g1 from the g5 square.

31.♖e5 ♕d6 32.♕c4 ♖c7??

It's not easy for white to extend his advantage once black moves out of the pin with 32...♔h7. This big blunder was likely due to time trouble.

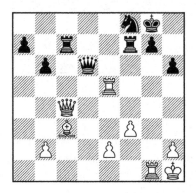

33.♖xg7+! ♔xg7 34.♖e7+ Black resigned.

No. 112 R. Markus – E. Toth
Hungary 2014

1.d4 ♘f6 2.c4 e6 3.♘f3 ♗b4+ 4.♗d2 ♕e7 5.g3 ♘c6 6.♘c3 0-0 7.♗g2 ♗xc3 8.♗xc3 ♘e4 9.♖c1 ♘xc3

Black occasionally continues 9...a5, which supports the sortie ♘c6-b4. However, the knight gets chased from b4 to a6, and in the game Prohaszka – Tratar (Sarajevo 2010) it was stuck there until the end: 10.0-0 ♘xc3 11.♖xc3 d6 12.d5 ♘b4 13.a3 ♘a6 14.dxe6 fxe6 15.♘d4 c6 16.♖e3 ♗d7 17.f4 ♖ae8 18.♘f3 ♗c8 19.♕c2 ♕c7 (if 19...♕d8 the variation from this game wouldn't have worked due to the hanging knight on g5) 20.♘g5 g6 21.♕c3 e5 22.fxe5 ♖xf1+ 23.♗xf1 ♖xe5 24.♖xe5 dxe5 25.c5 ♔g7? 26.♘e4

b6? 27.♘d6. Black of course played weakly, but the reputation of the maneuver ♘c6-b4-a6 is generally pretty poor.

10.♖xc3 d6

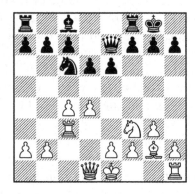

11.d5

Here we view the plan to capture d5xe6.

11...♘b8

After 11...♘d8 12.dxe6 fxe6 13.0-0 e5 14.c5 black's camp lacks coordination, whereas 12...♘xe6 looks solid. Even a worse endgame after 13.0-0 ♗d7 (13...♕f6!? not allowing white's knight to get to the center) 14.♘d4 ♘xd4 15.♕xd4 ♕xe2 (not forced and 15...♗c6 was solid) 16.♖e3 ♕g4 17.♕xg4 ♗xg4 18.♖e7 ♖ab8 19.♖xc7 ♖fc8 20.♖xc8+ ♖xc8 21.b3 b6 and black defends easily (Arkell – Vlassov, Marianske Lazne 2016).

12.dxe6 fxe6 13.♘d4

This prevents 13...♘d7 in view of 14.♘xe6! In the later game Markus – S. Popov (Kragujevac 2016) white allowed the enemy knight to travel to f6 and he retained a small advantage after 13.0-0 ♘d7 14.♘d4 ♘f6 15.♕d2 e5 16.♘c2 ♗e6 17.♘e3

♖ab8 18.b4 a6 19.♞d5 ♛d7 20.♖d1. That said, he failed to win the game.

13...e5 14.♞c2

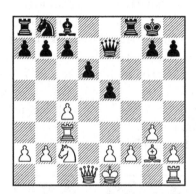

14...c6

If black wants to prevent the advance of white's b-pawn via 14...♞c6 15.0-0 a5, then the game should continue 16.c5 dxc5 17.♛d5+.

> **KEY TIP.** Here and further we see that the standard break c4-c5 involves a pawn sac, but in most cases not a real one. If white is unable to win the pawn back, then his piece activity promises compensation.

15.0-0 ♝e6 16.e4

Avrukh recommended 16.b4, in response to which it's useful for black to strengthen his defense using his knight – 16...♞d7 17.b5 cxb5 18.cxb5 ♞c5. It will be hard for white to increase his tiny advantage.

16...♞d7 17.♞e3 ♖ad8 18.♛d2 a5 19.♖c2 ♞c5?!

If 19...b6 black has only one weakness, on d6, and it will be hard for white to force another weakness to appear. The exchange of pawns on the a-file is to white's advantage.

20.♛xa5 ♖a8 21.♛d2 ♖xa2 22.b4 ♖xc2 23.♛xc2 ♞d7 24.♖a1 c5 25.♖a7 ♖b8 26.b5 ♞b6 27.♝f3 ♛f7 28.♝e2 g6 29.h4 ♖a8

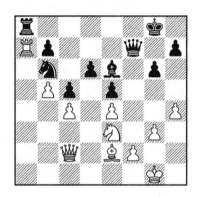

As a result of the exchange, black has reduced the pressure on the c4 pawn, and white exchanges bishops. However, with precise defense black will still hold this.

30.♖xa8+ ♞xa8 31.♝g4 ♞c7 32.b6 ♞e8 33.♛a4 ♚g7?

Now the queen's invasion proves decisive, whereas after 33...♝xg4 34.♞xg4 ♚g7 35.♛a8 ♞f6 the knights disappear and with them white's remaining chances of winning.

34.♝xe6 ♛xe6 35.♛a8 ♛d7 36.♛b8 ♚h6 37.♞d5 ♛f7 38.♛d8 ♚g7 39.♞c7 ♞f6 40.♛xd6 ♛xc4 41.♞e6+

Black resigned.

No. 113 P. Eljanov – G. Jones
Reykjavik 2013

1.d4 ♞f6 2.c4 e6 3.♞f3 ♝b4+ 4.♝d2 ♛e7 5.g3 ♞c6 6.♞c3 ♝xc3 7.♝xc3 ♞e4 8.♖c1 0-0 9.♝g2 d6 10.d5 ♞xc3 11.♖xc3

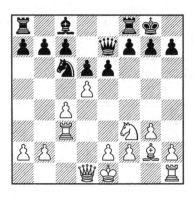

11...♘d8

The continuation 11...♘b8 12.0-0 e5 is considered in the next, final game.

12.0-0

White doesn't have to rush with castling, in order to try and gain a tempo to invade along the c-file. See the example Khenkin – Winants (Belgium 2004): 12.♘d2 e5 13.c5 f5 (13...dxc5 14.♘b3) 14.cxd6 cxd6 15.♕c2 ♘f7 16.♖c7 ♗d7 17.♖xb7 ♖fc8 18.♕d1 ♖ab8 19.♖xb8 ♖xb8 20.♘c4, and black's compensation for the pawn is unlikely to be enough. At the same time, black is not forced to rush with e6-e5 and may first play 12...a5 or 12...f5.

12...e5

In the game Beliavsky – Macieja (Portoroz 2001) black hoped for counter chances on the queenside, but he failed to achieve his aim – 12...♗d7 13.♘d2 a5 14.f4!? ♖b8 15.♕c1! (undermining the plan b7-b5) 15...b6 16.♗e3 (with the threat 17.f5 e5 18.f6!) 16...e5 17.c5 f6 (17...bxc5 18.fxe5 dxe5 19.♘c4 f6 20.♘xa5) 18.c6 ♗e8 19.♘f3 ♗f7 20.♘d4 g6 21.♘b5 ♔g7 22.fxe5 fxe5 23.♖ef3 ♖e8 24.e4 – and the outcome of the game has been settled.

13.c5

Avrukh criticized this move, but the latest practice requires that his assessment be updated. At the same time, in the main line 13.♘d2 f5 14.c5 ♘f7 15.♕b3 b6 16.cxd6 cxd6 17.♕a3 black should try 17...♗d7 18.♖fc1 ♖fc8 19.♕a6 ♕e8, which has never been played.

13...dxc5

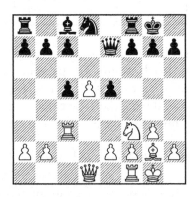

14.♕c2 e4

If 14...b6 15.♖e3 f6 16.♘xe5! fxe5 17.d6 white wins the exchange. Had white played 14.♕c1?! black would have 15...e4 to counter ♖c3-e3.

The following fragment is most interesting: 14...c6 15.♖xc5 ♗f5 16.♕c3 ♖e8 17.♖d1 cxd5 18.♖dxd5 f6 19.♖c7 ♕f8 20.♘h4 ♗e6 (B. Socko – T.R. Hansen, Stockholm 2014) 21.♕c2! ♗xd5? 22.♗xd5+ ♔h8 23.♕f5 with the murderous idea 24.♘g6+! The strong Norwegian master Hansen had previously played 14...e4 (recommended by Avrukh) and suddenly found himself on unsteady ground!

15.♘e1!?

This is an interesting idea belonging to the Romanian player Nanu. The point is that the knight stands better here than on d2 given that white plans to undermine the black e4-f5 pawn chain via f2-f3. After 15.♘d2 f5 16.♖xc5 (16.f3 e3!? 17.♘c4 f4) 16... c6 (liked by Avrukh) 17.♖d1 cxd5 18.♖c7 ♗d7 (S. Savchenko – Hulak, Baile Herculane 1994) it's time for white to repeat moves – 19.♘c4 ♘e6 20.♖xb7 ♘c5 21.♖c7 ♘e6.

15...f5 16.f3 exf3

If 16...e3?, then 17.f4 , separating the e-pawn from its neighbor and condemning it to a certain death.

17.♗xf3 c6

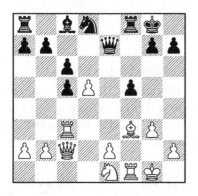

18.♘d3

After 18.♖xc5 ♗d7 19.♘d3 cxd5 20.♗xd5+ ♔h8 21.♘f4 ♘c6 22.♕c3 ♖ae8 23.♖d1 ♖f6 24.♗f3 ♖d6 25.♖xd6 ♕xd6 26.♖d5 ♕e7 27.h4 white is significantly more active (Nanu – Markos, Austria 2010). Eljanov plays differently, but I'm not convinced that this is an improvement.

18...b6

After 18...cxd5 19.♗xd5+ ♗e6 20.♘f4 ♗xd5 21.♘xd5 ♕d6 22.♖d1

♔h8 black should extinguish his opponent's initiative at the cost of his extra pawn.

19.dxc6   ♘e6   20.♘f4   ♘d4 21.♕a4

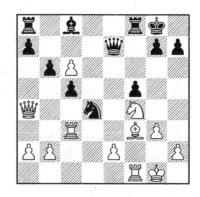

21...♔h8?!

This was too inert for such a sharp position. After 21...g5 22.♘d5 ♕e5 23.♖d1 ♘xe2+?! 24.♗xe2 ♕xe2 25.♕b3 black has problems, but via 23...f4 he can create counterplay on the kingside.

22.♗g2 ♘xe2+ 23.♘xe2 ♕xe2 24.c7 ♗a6 25.♖fc1 ♗d3?!

If 25...♖ac8 26.♗f1 ♕xb2 27.♕xa6 ♖xc7 then unlike in the game black picks up a third pawn for the bishop. Then he would have better chances of resisting.

26.♕d1 ♖ac8 27.♖xd3 ♕e5 28.♕d2 ♖xc7 29.♖e1 ♕f6 30.♖d6 ♕f7 31.♕d5 g6 32.b3 ♕xd5 33.♗xd5 ♔g7 34.♔f2 ♖b8 35.a4 ♔h6 36.♗c4 ♖bb7 37.h4 ♖d7 38.♖ee6 ♖xd6 39.♖xd6 ♖e7 40.♔f3 ♔g7 41.a5 bxa5 42.♖a6 a4 43.♖xa4 ♔f6 44.♖a5 ♖c7 45.♔f4 h6 46.♖a6+ ♔g7 47.♔e5 ♖d7 48.♔e6 ♖f7 49.♖d6 ♖f6+ 50.♔e7 ♖f8 51.♖d7 g5 52.h5 f4 53.g4

f3 54.♔e6+ ♔g8 55.♔e5+ ♔h8
56.♖f7 ♖e8+ 57.♗e6

Black resigned.

No. 114 M. Lagarde – S. Schneider
Rhodes 2013

1.d4 e6 2.♘f3 ♘f6 3.c4 ♗b4+
4.♗d2 ♕e7 5.g3 ♘c6 6.♘c3 ♗xc3
7.♗xc3 ♘e4 8.♖c1 0-0 9.♗g2 d6
10.0-0 ♘xc3 11.♖xc3 e5 12.d5 ♘b8

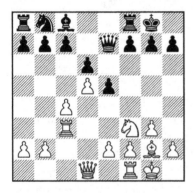

13.b4

White aims to break with c4-c5
supported by his b-pawn, as after
13.c5 ♘a6 14.cxd6 cxd6 15.♘d2
♗d7 the c-file is opened too early,
and black will not concede it. The
same has happened in practice after
13.♕c2 a5 14.c5 ♘a6 15.cxd6 cxd6
16.♘d2 b5 17.♖c1 ♗d7.

The more flexible continuation
13.♘d2 after 13...a5 offers white the
opportunity to play 14.f4!?, while if
14.c5 ♘a6 15.cxd6 cxd6 it's useful
to bring the knight into play, instead
of building a harmless battery with
major pieces. After the complicated
continuation 16.♘c4 ♕d8 17.♕b3 ♘c5
18.♕b6 ♘a4 19.♕xd6 ♘xc3 20.bxc3
♕xd6 21.♘xd6 f6 22.c4 (Gupta –

Amin, Dubai 2012) 22...♖d8 23.c5 b6
the initiative gained at the cost of the
exchange is only sufficient to draw.

13...♗g4

If 13...a5 then the pin 14.♖a3!?
has proved a good answer. In
the game Chetverik – Passchyn
(Geraardsbergen 2019) after 14...
b6 15.♘d2 ♘a6?! 16.bxa5 ♘c5
17.♘b3 ♘xb3 18.axb3 bxa5 19.♕d2
white won a pawn without any clear
compensation for black. After the
better 15...♘d7 white still retains
some initiative on the queenside.

14.♕c2

The standard break c4-c5 has
been carried out several times with
support from a knight via 14.♘d2
♘d7 15.♘b3 b6. After 16.c5 a5
17.♖c4 ♘f6 18.h3 ♗h5 19.cxd6 cxd6
20.b5 ♘d7 (Fridman – Timoshenko,
Eforie Nord 2009) the rook's invasion
is harmless, and the players soon
exhausted their fighting resources.

**14...a5 15.a3 axb4 16.axb4 ♗xf3
17.♗xf3**

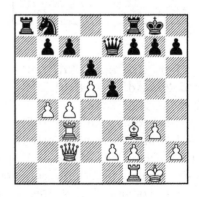

17...♕d7

An unexpected and rather
questionable decision by black. If
17...b6 18.e4 c5 19.b5 ♕a7 white's

spatial advantage didn't promise him anything real.

18.♖b1 ♕a4 19.♕c1

The principled continuation was 19.c5 ♕xc2 20.♖xc2 f5. Black has freed the f7 square for his rook in the event the c-file is immediately opened, but white can gradually improve his position with 21.e3 ♖a3 22.♗e2.

19...♘d7 20.e4 ♘f6 21.g4 ♕d7 22.h3 h6 23.c5 ♕d8

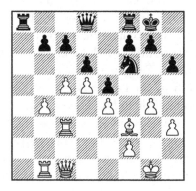

24.g5

The young French grandmaster playing white tries to outplay his weaker opponent in a sharp struggle, given that quiet continuations (such as 24.♖a3) promise nothing more than equality.

24...hxg5   25.♕xg5   ♕d7 26.♗g2 ♘h7 27.♕d2 ♕d8 28.♖g3 ♕f6 29.♖bb3 ♖a1+ 30.♔h2 ♕f4 31.♕xf4 exf4 32.♖gf3

32.♖gc3 ♖a2 33.b5 dxc5 34.♖xc5 ♖xf2 35.♖xc7 ♖a8 leads to a draw, and Lagarde attempts a rook adventure from the edge of the board.

32...g5 33.♖a3 ♖e1 34.♖a7 ♘f6 35.♖xb7?

White has crossed a bridge too far. The right continuation was 35.♖fa3,

in order to exchange one rook pair and thereby neutralize his opponent's counterplay on the kingside.

35...♔g7 36.♗h1 ♖h8

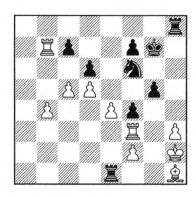

37.♔g2

Now compared with the variation 37.♖xc7 ♘g4+ 38.♔g2 ♘e5 the knight alters its victory march.

KEY TIP. The knight's triumph over the fianchettoed bishop is notable, and this is frequently found in the Bogo-Indian Defense. White should weigh up carefully whether he wants to create a strong pawn chain with d5-e4, only to suffer for his efforts with his bishop.

37...♘xe4 38.♖xc7 ♘d2 39.♖d3 f3+ 40.♔g3 ♖xh1 41.♖xd2 ♖1xh3+ White resigned.

This final chapter contained what is considered to be the main line of the Bogo-Indian Defense. On the whole, white's position is preferable, but the variety of possible structures and plans that arise promises further deepening of the 6.♘c3 system and, hence, potential changes to evaluations.

Conclusions

Historically, the Bogo-Indian Defense has been a bit unlucky. On the one hand its borders have been distinctly set by the moves 1.d4 ♘f6 2.c4 e6 3.♘f3 ♗b4+, but then it constantly trespasses onto the territory of the Queen's Indian Defense, Catalan Opening, Nimzo-Indian Defense, and sometimes other openings. These powerful opening systems have somewhat overshadowed their "poor relative", though in actual fact she is anything but poor. All fans of closed openings who after 1.d4 ♘f6 2.c4 e6 go for 3.♘f3 need to figure out how they are going to fight for an advantage after the bishop checks in reply.

The Bogo-Indian Defense has a reputation as a most solid of openings. Sharp variations (such as the 3...♗b4+ 4.♘bd2 0-0 5.a3 ♗e7 6.e4 d5 line from chapter 5) are rare, and tactics play very much a subordinate role to strategy. The key focus is pawn structures, with most pawns remaining on the board in generally closed positions. Of the original structures, the best known is the Vitolins Defense 1.d4 ♘f6 2.c4 e6 3.♘f3 ♗b4+ 4.♗d2 c5 5.♗xb4 cxb4. While the main standard structure, i.e. the standoff in the center between the c4-d5-e4 and c7-d6-e5 pawn chains, is also found in other closed openings.

World champions have set the fashion in the Bogo-Indian Defense, but players of all levels, from grandmasters to club players, have followed suit. Many players are attracted by the possibility to avoid a competition to see who has the best memory, and who prefer to prepare for middlegame battle with a decent strategic foundation. Therefore, our opening is destined to enjoy a long and productive life.

Players' index
(the number refers to the game number; games in white are highlighted in bold)

Made in the USA
Middletown, DE
23 January 2020